Chiefs in South Africa

Law, Power & Culture in the Post-Apartheid Era

BARBARA OOMEN
Assistant Professor of Law & Development
University of Amsterdam

James Currey
OXFORD

University of KwaZulu-Natal Press
PIETERMARITZBURG

palgrave
NEW YORK

James Currey Ltd
73 Botley Road
Oxford OX2 0BS
www.jamescurrey.co.uk

University of KwaZulu-Natal Press
Private Bag X01
Scottsville, 3209
South Africa
www.ukznpress.co.za

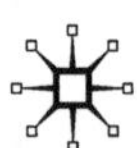

First published in the United States by
PALGRAVE, 175 Fifth Avenue, New York, NY 10010
Companies and representatives throughout the world, PALGRAVE is the new global imprint of St. Martin's Press, LLC Scholarly and Reference Division and Palgrave Publishers Ltd (formerly Macmillan Press Ltd)

First published 2005

1 2 3 4 5 09 08 07 06 05

ISBN 10: 0-85255-881-3 (James Currey cloth)
ISBN 13: 978-085255-881-2 (James Currey cloth)
ISBN 10: 0-85255-880-5 (James Currey paper)
ISBN 13: 978-085255-880-5 (James Currey paper)
ISBN 1-86914-067-2 (University of KwaZulu-Natal Press paper)
ISBN 1-4039-7085-8 (Palgrave cloth)

British Library Cataloguing in Publication Data
Oomen, Barbara
Chiefs in South Africa
1. Tribal government - South Africa 2. South Africa - Politics and government - 1994
I. Title
321.1'0968

Library of Congress Cataloging-in-Publication Data available on request

Typeset in 10/11 pt Photina
by Long House, Cumbria
Printed and bound in Malaysia

CONTENTS

List of Acronyms

ANC	African National Congress
CODESA	Convention for a Democratic South Africa
Contralesa	Congress of Traditional Leaders of South Africa
CP	Constitutional Principle (as in Act 200/1993)
CP	Conservative Party
CPA	Communal Property Association
DC	District Council
DFA	Development Facilitation Act (67/1995)
DLA	Department of Land Affairs
DNA	Department of Native Affairs
ECOWAS	Economic Community of West African States
EU	European Union
GNMT	Greater Ngwaritsi Makhudu/Thamaga
IDP	Integrated Development Plan
IFP	Inkatha Freedom Party
ILO	International Labour Organisation
IMF	International Monetary Fund
IPACC	Indigenous Peoples of South Africa Co-ordinating Committee
LGTA	Local Government Transition Act (209/1993)
MEC	Member of the Executive Committee
MINMEC	Minister and Members of the Executive Committee
MP	Member of Parliament
MPNP	Multi-Party Negotiation Process
NG	Nederlands Gereformeerd (church)
NGO	Non-governmental organisation
NLC	National Land Committee
NP	National Party
PAC	Pan Africanist Congress
RDP	Reconstruction and Development Programme
SACP	South African Communist Party
SADEC	Southern African Development Community
SADF	South African Defence Force
SALGA	South African Local Government Association
SANCO	South African National Civics Organisation
TLC	Transitional Local Council
TUSAA	Trade Union of South African Authorities
TMC	Transitional Metropolitan Council
TRC	Transitional Representative Council
UDF	United Democratic Front
UDM	United Democratic Movement
UN	United Nations
WGIA	Working Group of Indigenous Minorities in Southern Africa

Acknowledgements

'A chief is like the moon; if it shines it is because of the sun and stars that surround it,' a Sotho saying goes. If there is any merit in this work, which deals with the reappraisal of chiefs and custom in contemporary South Africa, it is because of all the people who have enlightened me on the subject over the past years. Without the wonderful literature already published, the protracted e-mail conversations with colleagues, the brief chats and the long interviews in South African offices and homesteads, in conference hallways or in the Van Vollenhoven Institute over coffee, this book would simply not exist. And even if there is no way of illuminating the whole constellation that facilitated the research, I would like to start by expressing my deepest gratitude to at least part of it – without, of course, placing responsibility on anyone but myself for possible errors in this final product.

Firstly, there are all those people in Sekhukhune who so generously opened their courts, palaces and houses to a – at times overtly – curious stranger. That they were prepared to do so was mostly thanks to my cheerful research companion Patson Phala, who spoke the language of kings and commoners, men and women, pensioners and youngsters alike, and was always prepared to throw in a joke or a good story if our interviews threatened to become too tedious. The fact that the farewell party we threw after the field research was attended by so many people was not only because of the two giant cooking pots full of *nama* and *bogobe*, but also because there were simply so many people to thank. Within this group, Tsepo Pasha, Welsh Ratau, the royal families of Kgoloko, Masha, Nkosi, Sekhukhune and Sekwati, the Nkosi family, the brothers Kgalema, Dankie Lesaba, Elias Sepodumo, Teshell Shikwambane, Toko Suteka, Philip Vilakazi and Jacob Zulu exemplify the hospitality and friendship I encountered in Bopedi. It is my sincere hope that this study and its recommendations will somehow, in the long run, not only benefit the academic community but also all those Bapedi whose resourcefulness and patience I have come to admire so much.

Part of my field research was conducted high up in the Leolo mountains, while a cottage kindly loaned to me by the Sekhukhune Educare Project in the bustling township of Jane Furse formed another base. Here, in the evenings, my laptop linked me to a wide community of ever-supportive colleagues – some of whom I have never met personally, but who commented on wild thoughts and early drafts, and generally gave me the impression that I was on to something worthwhile. There is no way of expressing, for instance, my gratitude to John Comaroff for taking an interest in the research, reading research memos and – finally – meticulously and perspicaciously commenting on the draft manuscript. Similarly, I have learnt a great deal from and appreciated the interest shown by Pat McAllister, Tom Bennett, Erhard Blankenburg, Martin Chanock, Peter Delius, Marnix de Bruyne, Martin Doornbos, Willemien du Plessis, Axel Harnett-Sievers, Manfred Hinz, André Hoekema, Deborah James, Freddy Khunu, Ian Liebenberg, Mahmood Mamdani, Patrick Mtshaulane, Kennedy Mojela, Annika Mökvist,

Christina Murray, Thandabantu Nhlapo, Carl Niehaus, Seth Nthai, Lungisile Ntsebeza, Nic Olivier, Roel Pieterman, Steven Robins, Albie Sachs, Theo Scheepers, Eltjo Schrage, Peter Skalnik, Robert Thornton, Kees Van der Waal, Franz and Keebet Von Benda-Beckmann, Olufemi Vaughan, Louis Vorster and Mike Williams.

Back at Leiden University, I once again felt that a student of African law could not wish for a better academic home. The vibrant African Studies Centre, under the direction of (lawyer) Gerti Hesseling, not only has a great library collection and staff, but also provided me with a platform where I could share and discuss ideas. I am particularly obliged to Ineke van Kessel, Robert Ross and Emile van Rouveroy van Nieuwaal for their genuine and continuous interest in my work. In addition, the anthropologists in Peter Geschiere's Africanist PhD seminar welcomed me to their ranks, never making me – as a lawyer and a political scientist – feel like the odd one out. Other research networks proved to be equally stimulating: the 'South Africa PhDs' with Erik Bähre, Julia Hornberger and Wiebe Nauta; the 'Law and Culture' group with Kristin Henrard and Saskia Tempelman as close comrades; the Centre for Non-Western Studies with its colleagues like Laila Al-Zwaini and Ellen-Rose Kambel, and the research networks of the Meijers Institute on both social cohesion and global governance. Outside Leiden, I highly appreciated the continuous flow of information provided by Kairos staff members Hans Hartman and Erik van den Bergh, as well as the intellectual support and friendship of colleagues like Gerhard Anders, Arne Musch and Joris van der Sandt.

Also, I could not have wished for a warmer and more friendly base than the Van Vollenhoven Institute for Law, Governance and Development. If the VVI emulated McDonalds in choosing an 'employee of the month', Adriaan Bedner would be a long-time title-holder, both for his interest in the work of others as well as for the astuteness of his comments on it. Maaike de Langen, on the other hand, would be a close runner-up, not least because of her good-natured acceptance of my neglect of other obligations while I was wrapping up this thesis. Julia Arnscheidt, Albert Dekker, Nel de Jong, Sylvia Holverda, Carola Klamer, John McCarthy, Harold Munneke, David Nickolson, Nicole Niessen, Sebastiaan Pompe, Benjamin van Rooij and Janine Ubink all read drafts, gave literature tips and generally made it a great pleasure to work at the Institute. Marianne Moria and Kari van Weeren worked very hard to provide practical support, while Amin Kassam is to be complimented on his speedy and thorough editing.

Of all the strange customs I encountered in Sekhukhune, few could beat the tradition at Leiden University of not thanking one's supervisors at the end of a PhD trajectory. This preface to the book that came out of that PhD would not be complete without an expression of sincere gratitude to Jan-Michiel Otto for the wisdom and understanding with which he guided me through the various phases of the research. Co-supervisor Stephen Ellis brought great insight into both African affairs and human relations, and the discussions the three of us had on the manuscript played no small role in ensuring that I enjoyed the research until the very end.

Now that this work has been completed (even if my interest in the subject has only increased) I would have loved to have showed it to Drü Sutton, who played such an important role in my life and with whom I hitchhiked around South Africa in the year after Mandela walked free. Sadly, he did not live to see the result of my first infatuation with his country, and the book is dedicated to him. There are many others close to me to thank, for a variety of reasons, but I would like to single out my parents Janus and Tonny Oomen, and my friends Margreet Korsten and Roeland Ris for their interest, not only in the author of this research, but also in the work itself. Finally, for all the small and large stars that guided me in conducting this research, there can only be one sun: Herman Lelieveldt's support went far beyond what is usual for even the best of partners. After having played an important role in the research design, he specialised in (and published on) 'how to write your PhD'. And when it was time to wrap the whole thing up, he helped by creating the best of natural deadlines and remedies against post-dissertation depression: our radiant son Tom. For all this, I am immensely grateful.

1. The coronation of Chief Ramabulana in Venda, at which President Nelson Mandela was also present (all photographs © Barbara Oomen)

2. The Kgôrô; the re-instated customary court in Mamone (see p.141)

3. Kgosi Billy Sekwati Mampuru in leopard skin purchased by migrants upon his coronation, during a 'heritage day' for schoolchildren

4. Retraditionalisation in Mamone: Kgosi Billy Sekwati Mampuru III and his wife during his coronation (see p.123)

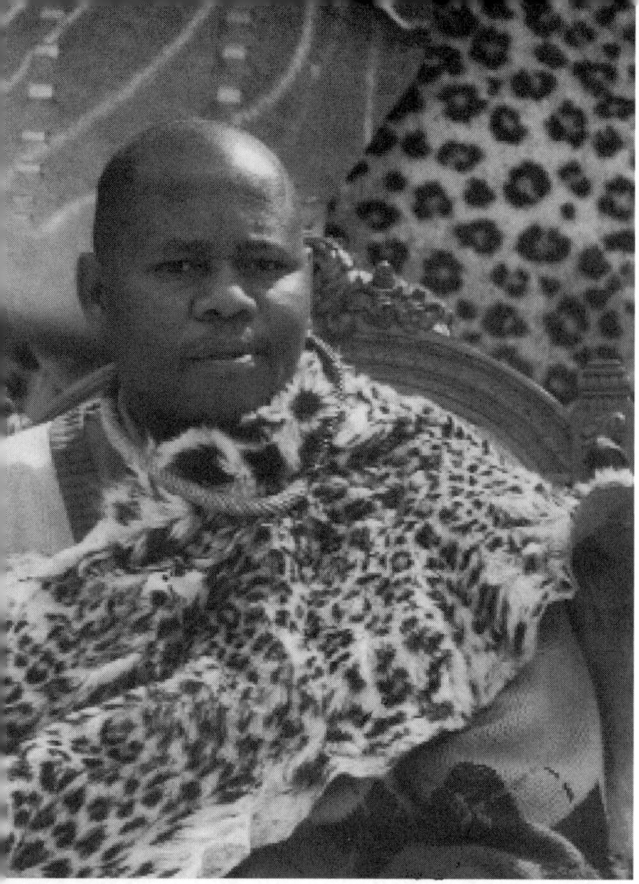

5 & 6. Kgosi Billy Sekwati Mampuru in front of a villa built in his honour, during a meeting with schoolchildren (see p.195)

7. One of the many people present during president Mandela's visit to Sekhukhuneland (see p.142)

8. Member of the vigilante organisation Mapogo a Mathamaga ('If you are a leopard, I'll be a tiger', see p.149)

1. Introduction
Reawakenings

1. The dawning of the dawn

Sekhukhune, 19 December 1998 – 'The time has come to go back to our history', declares Mr Manala as he helps himself to another chunk of maize porridge. We are guests at a 'VIP dinner' celebrating the coronation of Mamone traditional leader Billy Sekwati Mampuru III. Outside the party tent the pounding of cowhide drums and shrieking of children echo the excitement of the day. In front of us, the young chief – in pink suit, leopard pelt – sits on display behind a long table decorated with a crocheted table-cloth and silk flowers. He is surrounded by dignitaries: government officials, politicians and the traditional leader who earlier in the day greeted me 'in the name of the African Renaissance'. With a depreciative look at my salmon and white wine – the dinner has been sponsored and flown in by helicopter by the mining company where many Bapedi work – my table companion continues, 'We have to reinstall our traditional customs, re-erect the customary court. For a long time, our lives were mixed up and we were like pieces of paper flying in the wind. Watch us, this young kgoši will make us get together again...'

This call for retraditionalisation, uttered far from the public eye in an often forgotten dusty corner of South Africa, seemed to foreshadow the words spoken by another leader at his inauguration, six months later. In contrast to Sekwati's coronation, Thabo Mbeki's ascent to the presidency was world news, with press, presidents and royalty gathered to see how the newcomer would take over from his already historic predecessor, Nelson Mandela. While Air Force jets drew the red, yellow, blue and green of South Africa's flag in the clear blue sky above Pretoria's Union Buildings, once symbols of apartheid, thousands listened breathlessly to the new President's understanding of the challenges facing South Africa.

> Our country is in that period of time which the seTswana-speaking people of Southern Africa graphically describe as '*mahube a naka tsa kgomo*' – the dawning of the dawn, when only the tips of the horns of the cattle can be seen etched against the morning sky.... We have to keep pace with the rising sun, progressing from despair to hope... As Africans, we are the children of the abyss, who have sustained a backward march for half a millennium... As South Africans, whatever the difficulties, we are moving forward in the effort to combine ourselves into one nation of many colours, many cultures and divers origins. No longer capable of being falsely defined as a European outpost in Africa, we are an African nation in the complex process simultaneously of formation and renewal.[1]

For this, the new President assured his captive audience, South Africa needed to

[1] Speech of President Thabo Mbeki at his Inauguration as President of the Republic of South Africa: Union Buildings, Pretoria, 16 June 1999.

rediscover and claim the African heritage. 'Being certain that not always were we the children of the abyss, we will do what we have to do to achieve our own Renaissance.' When he concluded with '*Pula! Nala!*' (may the rains fall) a wave of applause washed through the audience, into television sets throughout the country and the world.

This book is about the surprising resurgence of traditional authority and customary law in post-apartheid South Africa. It grapples with three questions: what was the relation between the changing legal and socio-political positions of traditional authority and customary law in the new South Africa, why was this so and what does this teach us about the interrelation between laws, politics and culture in the post-modern world?

The lavish coronation of one of South Africa's 787 traditional leaders and Thabo Mbeki's emphasis on returning to the roots were hardly aberrations, spasms of a dying order as democracy dawned. Rather, they captured the mood of the times, marked by vicious political fights over the return of a Bushman skeleton; the enthusiastic introduction of 'heritage studies' in the official school curriculum; televised debates on 'Who is an African?' and a fashion bringing ethnic shirts, Zulu beadwork and tribal art to Johannesburg's shopping malls. Identities long dormant were dusted off as the Griqua moved to the political centre stage, clamouring for museums, minerals and land, and as South Africa adopted a coat of arms in a dying language: *Ike e:/xarra//ke* – Khoisan for 'Unity in Diversity'.[2] The notion of *E Pluribus Unum* also informed the call to participate in writing South Africa's new Constitution: '20 million women, 18 million men, 8 religions, 25 churches, 31 cultures, 14 languages, 9 ethnic groups, one country; please feel free to help us write some rules that will make this work.'[3] Those rules, collected in one of the most modern constitutions in the world, would be written in eleven languages and would call for the protection of culture and the recognition of the 'status, institution and role of traditional leadership'.[4] The Constitution would not only allow for the recognition of 'customary marriages' – polygamy and bridewealth included – but also make room for a National Council of Traditional Leaders, a Khoisan Forum, a Zulu Kingdom and an Afrikaner Volksstaat. If South Africa was grappling for a post-apartheid identity, it seemed to have found two central elements in tradition and cultural diversity.

This enthusiastic embracing of diversity and emphasis on tradition were, in the light of South Africa's past, somewhat surprising. For was not South Africa the country in which legal recognition of cultural diversity had led to the terrible injustices of apartheid? Where racial contradictions had been turned into ethnic ones with the introduction of ten homelands to actualise apartheid's central ideology: that each race and nation had a unique, divinely ordained destiny and cultural contribution to make to the world and that they should be kept apart so that each could develop along its own inherent lines?[5] Where the triad of 'culture, tribe and chiefdom' had been used to deny Africans access to

[2] Cf. Sapa. 'Address by Deputy President Jacob Zuma to the Opening Ceremony of the National Khoisan Consultative Conference.' ANC news briefing email service: ANC, 2001.

[3] This is my own translation from Afrikaans flyers handed out in 1995.

[4] Ss 31 and 211, *The Constitution of the Republic of South Africa*. Act 108 of 1996.

[5] Mahmood Mamdani. 'A Response to the Comments,' *African Sociological Review* 1, no. 2 (1997), p.146. See also Omer-Cooper, 1996, p.7.

democracy (Bennett, 1997:7): 'They,' after all, 'already had their own system of governance.' Was it not Thabo Mbeki's own father, Govan, who had written in the 1960s: 'If Africans have had chiefs, it was because all human societies have had them at one stage or another. But when a people have developed to a stage which discards chieftainship...then to force it on them is not liberation but enslavement' (Mbeki, 1964:47)? The struggle against apartheid had been mainly against this imposition of cultural diversity, which had caused even the even-tempered Bishop Tutu to fulminate, in the 1980s: 'We blacks – most of us – execrate ethnicity with all our being.'[6] If the whole fight had been about attaining a nation in which all citizens would be equal, with 'one man, one vote', why were chiefs, customs and cultural diversity once again so important, once democracy had dawned?[7]

There seems to be a contradiction between the abuse of such notions as 'chief, culture and custom' in South Africa's not-too-distant past and their enthusiastic embracing within the new, democratic order. The starkness of this contradiction makes South Africa an extremely interesting case for studying the relations between law, politics and culture in a changing world. It is a central contention of this book that the events in South Africa cannot be understood without looking at global developments: the fragmentation of the nation-state, the embracing of culture, the applauding of group rights. When even South Africa, just stepping out of a nightmare scenario as regards the abuse of culture, chose to make diversity a founding stone of its new order, what does this teach us about this world and what questions does it pose to students of law, politics and culture? What does the resurgence of traditional leadership and customary law in South Africa, of all places, teach us about the relations between nations and chiefdoms, the global, the national and the local?

This Introduction serves to outline the changing world in which South Africa's democracy dawned; the questions it poses to those concerned with the relations between law, politics and culture; and the relevance of ethnic identities in the modern world. It thus seeks to sketch some of the general debates in which this study is located and from which it draws its inspiration. First, in section 2, we need to look at the general features of the world at the end of the twentieth century, when South Africa finally became democratic. This world, which (for want of a better or at least less worn-out term) I shall call post-modern, had undergone drastic changes since the 1960s, both in fact and in the way in which it was understood. For one, the nation-state, still in the 1960s the shiny vehicle in which to embark on the path to progress, had fallen out of favour, its powers contested by a variety of sub- and supranational polities. One way in which this scramble for legitimacy in an increasingly interconnected, globalising world was played out was through the culture card: reviving traditional systems of governance, emphasising autochthony in politics, granting 'group rights' to

[6] Quoted in Arend Lijphart. 'Self-Determination Versus Pre-Determination of Ethnic Minorities in Power-Sharing Systems.' in *The Rights of Minority Cultures*, ed. Will Kymlicka, pp.275–87. Oxford: Oxford University Press, 1995, p.280.

[7] In the course of this work I shall, for the sake of variation, use 'traditional leader', 'chief', the Zulu term *nkosi (amakhosi)* and the Sepedi word *kgosi (magosi)* as synonyms. Even if some traditional leaders prefer not to be called chiefs but opt for the equivalent in the local language, or 'kings', the term 'chiefs', for all its colonial connotations, is still widely used in South Africa. Note that my copying of such terminology does not connote my approval of it.

indigenous peoples or 'first nations'. The legal recognition of cultural diversity was the distinguishing feature of politics worldwide in the 1990s.

Suddenly, a new world order had emerged in which tribes were trendy, culture was cool, and of which chiefs could be central constituents. Nevertheless, this celebration of cultural diversity, enthusiastically embraced in the new South Africa, was at times oddly reminiscent of what had been considered a nightmare not too long before. It is therefore worthwhile to consider, in section 3, seemingly forgotten lessons of 'customary law studies'. These concern the malleability of culture and the dangers inherent in fixing it in 'the austerity of tabulated legalism' (D'Engelbronner-Kolff, 2001:71). They stipulate how customary law was, above all, a historic formation created for certain reasons within a particular socio-political context that set it at 'the cutting edge of colonialism' (Chanock, 1985:4). Traditional leaders played a central role as bureaucratised representatives of forcibly created tribes, enjoying more legitimacy within the state than with the people they claimed to represent.

It is at the juncture of these two sets of givens – the enthusiastic embracing of chiefs, custom and culture in a new world and the lessons customary law studies hold about their artificial origins – that a set of key theoretical challenges arise. These are discussed in section 4. First, now that states derive part of their legitimacy from associations with traditional leaders and other polities – chiefdoms, first nations – and rely on 'cultural difference' to attain independence from that same state, there is a need to rethink the relation between law, power and culture. What *is* law in these situations, what does it reflect? A second question concerns the constitutive effects of cultural rights legislation: what does state recognition of chiefs and customs *do* locally? Finally, and related to all this, there is a challenge in rethinking the connections between state recognition of traditional leadership and its resurgence which, as we shall see, took place all over Africa, not only in constitutions and parliaments but also in villages like Mamone, far from the wider world. What legitimacy do these chiefs have? Is their revival merely the local adoption of a bureaucratic myth, the embracing of an imposed reality, as deconstructivists would have us believe, or does it go further than that?

This study is therefore an explicit attempt to link the local to the national and even the global, and to focus on the interaction between these polities. Although a large part of it is concerned with describing the position of chiefs and customary law in one place, Sekhukhune in South Africa's Northern Province, its concern is with the complex dialogue between this locality and the wider world. This calls for a specific methodology that combines extensive and in-depth 'field-work' with a more multi-sited ethnographic approach. Section 5 looks briefly at the choice of methods used and the theoretical assumptions on which they rest. Thus, this introductory chapter not only outlines the theoretical concerns which shaped this study on chieftaincy and custom in the new South Africa, but also presents some of the tools used to approach its central questions.

2. A new world

Sekhukhune, 10 September 1999: A meeting at the Hlatulanang (Let's Help Each Other) Community Centre about the return of a mineral-rich plot of land to the Masha community. Beneath the faded posters in the hall – Be Wise: Condomise;

> *There's No Milk like Mother's Milk; Let's Build our Nation – sit the 'stakeholders': the Land and Mineral Affairs officials and their lawyers in jeans, sleeves rolled up for this 'field trip', three chiefs and their delegations in worn-out suits, the community representatives in ANC T-shirts. A braided NGO representative gives the chiefs a flyer on 'Aboriginal Community and Mining Company Relations', which she received during training by Canadians a few weeks ago. 'This aboriginal thing is interesting', ponders Kgoši Masha as he gives me a lift after the meeting. Would I know more? I promise to check on the Internet...*

If one single event symbolises the birth of the new South Africa, it is Nelson Mandela's release from prison – eyes squinting in the February sun, fist clenched in exultant victory. There, in front of the roaring masses, he repeated the words spoken at his last public appearance, his trial twenty-six years earlier:

> I have fought against white domination and I have fought against black domination. I have cherished the ideal of a democratic and free society in which all persons live together in harmony and with equal opportunities. It is an ideal which I hope to live for and to achieve. But if needs be, it is an ideal for which I am prepared to die.[8]

However true those words were for Nelson Mandela, the concept of the unitary nation-state as a central building block of the world order had undergone a watershed transformation during the three decades he had spent in prison. In the 1960s, the countries around South Africa throwing off the shackles of colonialism had adopted the nation-state with all its symbols – flags, anthems, constitutions – as the ideal vehicle in which to undertake the great and unstoppable journey towards progress and modernisation. By the early 1990s, however, their dreams had worn rather thin and had been replaced by new ones – modernisation through authenticity and development through ownership – as the state came to be considered as just another actor in an increasingly complex and interwoven global order. It is precisely because of these changes that it seems fit to start our investigation with a sketch – however elementary – of the world in which the 'new South Africa' saw the light of day.

Renegotiating the nation-state

With the benefit of hindsight, the fall of the Berlin Wall can be seen as an epilogue to the Cold War of the previous decades, while the subsequent implosion of the Soviet Union into a multitude of ethnic polities was a premonition of the times to come. W.B. Yeats' prophetic words, 'Things fall apart; the centre cannot hold', were dusted off by journalists to describe a plethora of ethnic conflicts, from Indonesia to the Balkans, from Rwanda to countries in Latin America. The attack on the nation-state came from many sides and took many forms: international organisations taking over its central functions; citizens challenging its capacity to deliver; academics singing its swan-song.[9] More than 350 years after the Treaty of Westphalia and 200 years after the French Revolution, the nation-state and

[8] Nelson Mandela. 'Speech on his Release from Prison.' Cape Town: African National Congress, 1990.

[9] A vast literature has appeared on this subject since the late 1980s. *Loci classici* on the central claims of the nation-state are Anderson (1983), Gellner, (1983), Hobsbawm and Ranger (1983). The failure to make good on these claims and the central characteristics of a 'post-nationalist' world order have been excellently described by Appadurai (1996), Mbembe (2001), Migdal (1988), Scott (1998), Young (1993b).

the central assumptions on which it had come to rest – territorial integrity, monopoly of violence, political independence, domestic jurisdiction, non-intervention, unity – were under the most severe attack ever. Of course, the transformation took place in different ways. Some nations relinquished central powers freely, at conferences on an International Criminal Court or monetary unions, or in decentralisation and liberalisation programmes negotiated with alternative local actors. Others, like the Congo and Somalia, just imploded, their government buildings taken over by squatters, their postal services paralysed, their resources plundered by warlords and multinationals, and their public services, if they existed, provided by churches and other non-governmental organisations.

Although it was a worldwide phenomenon, the fragmentation of the nation-state was particularly apparent in sub-Saharan Africa. After all, this continent abounded in artificial boundaries resulting from colonisers' nineteenth-century attempts to cut up 'this magnificent African cake' as Leopold II put it. Even if most colonies did preserve the 'steel grid of colonial partition' after decolonisation, this was more because of the 'commanding force of circumstance' than for any other reason (Young, 1993a). By the 1990s, many African states had become a liability, at best irrelevant to those who lived in them, at worst a threat to their existence.[10] And everywhere this caused citizens to disengage and reorganise themselves in other ways, their nations at times no more than mere 'geographic expressions' as power was marshalled along other lines (Baker, 1997; Bierschenk and Olivier de Sardan, 1997).

The crisis of the African state was often conceptualised as a crisis of modernisation itself. As Crawford Young wrote on the 'high tide' of the nation-state in the 1950s and 1960s:

> A confluence of circumstances, whose particularity emerges only in retrospect, yielded a historic moment when this form of polity appeared astonishingly ascendant. With the idea of progress still robust, those polities which were perceived as leading humanity's march to a better future had singular power as authoritative models. Analytical vocabulary was saturated with such imagery: 'modernity' versus 'traditionality'; 'developed' versus 'underdeveloped' (or developing); 'advanced' versus 'backwards. (Young, 1993a:7)

This vocabulary itself came under the critical scrutiny of African people, academics and policy-makers alike. As 'Structural Adjustment Programmes' and ambitious development projects designed on European and American drawing boards unceremoniously failed, there was increased protest against these 'neo-colonialist' interventions. In turn, academics emphasised the essentially political agenda behind apparently neutral terms such as 'development' and 'progress' and openly questioned why Africa had to be measured along a schematic-evolutionary line with the Western individualist and capitalist state at its apex (Ellis, 2001; Ferguson, 1994; Leftwich, 1996; Leys, 1996; Sachs, 1992). Instead of clinging to these imported solutions, this colonial heritage which had brought so little of worth, some African philosophers and policy-makers started to argue in favour of indigenous solutions to the problems of the continent (Ayittey, 1991).

[10] Cf. Davidson (1992), who argues that the imposed nation-state is the main impediment towards democracy in Africa. Also: Bayart (1989), Chazan (1988), Ellis (1996), Englebert (2000), Herbst, (2000), Mbaku (1999); Werbner (1996), Yusuf (1994).

New polities

Intimately related to the transformation of the nation-state was the rise of a multifarious mix of alternative polities – some vintage, others virgin – eager to take over some of its practical and symbolic functions. As Appadurai wrote with foresight (1996:23):

> It may well be that the emergent postnational order proves not to be a system of homogeneous units (as with the current system of nation-states) but a system based on relations between heterogeneous units (some social movements, some interest groups, some professional bodies, some nongovernmental organisations, some armed constabularies, some judicial bodies).

Instead of the orderly system of territorial units, the new world was characterised by heterogeneous, network-like polities, operating locally, transnationally and internationally (Castells, 1996; Chatterjee, 1993; Friedman, 1999; Meyer and Geschiere, 1999; Silbey, 1997; Wilmer, 1993; Young, 1999). Globalisation – the increased flow of goods, information and people around the world and the ensuing interconnectedness between people and polities – gave these units new platforms on which to make their claims and new media through which to publicise them (Appadurai, 1996; Wilson, 1997:23).

For one, there was the rise of international organisations, all implicated in one way or another in 'global governance'. The Bretton Woods institutions like the IMF and the World Bank, for instance, by the 1990s no longer contented themselves with economic assistance to developing countries, but firmly tied this assistance to demands for 'good governance': democratisation, decentralisation and the scaling down of the state (Abrahamsen, 2000; IMPD,1998; Otto, 1997). Even though international organisations like the United Nations, SADC, ECOWAS or the European Union remained stifled by bureaucratic problems, their impact was large, and the 1990s' acceptance of an International Criminal Court was indicative of the degree to which (some) states were prepared to surrender sovereignty to a higher body. Their interventions in many African countries were accompanied by those of powerful international NGOs, many of which were far more influential in health care, education and disaster relief than the governments of the countries concerned. And although their purpose was different, they wielded as much power as those many multinational corporations whose budgets far exceeded the GNP of some of the countries in which they operated.

The 'information age' also enabled a strengthening and politicisation of transnational polities. Of course, there had for long been religious communities with missions from Mauritania to Madagascar, Filipino housemaids working in the West, Muslims connected through their pilgrimage to Mecca, Lebanese shopkeepers in every dusty African outpost. But Yahoo e-mail accounts, satellite television, charter flights, Internet sites and fast cash transfers made possible an unprecedented degree of contact within these imagined communities, allowing for a strengthening of their identity and their political mobilisation. Never was this clearer than on 11 September 2001, when a terrorist network, trained in Germany and Saudi Arabia, America and Afghanistan, attacked the twin symbols of capitalism, causing commentators to conclude that the new warfare was not about states but about nebulous networks bound together by communal values, e-mail exchanges and bank transfers.

Some of the most vicious attacks on the nation-state, however, came from the inside. On the basis of research into nearly 300 ethnopolitical communities worldwide, Gurr concluded that nearly every kind of ethnic conflict was exacerbated from the 1950s to the 1990s (Gurr, 1994). Serbs, Basques, Irian Jayans expressed, often by violent means, their feelings of no longer being represented by the nation-states under which they fell. Even the seemingly benign processes of democratisation and decentralisation in sub-Saharan Africa – often a result of strong outside pressure – unleashed forces of ethnicity, autochthony and exclusion along ethnic lines (Bierschenk and Olivier de Sardan, 1997; Gould, 1997). The discrediting of the state also led to a call for informal justice, and to the rise of vigilante organisations which, from South Africa to Nigeria, committed themselves to maintaining law and order because 'the police can no longer protect us' (Abrahams, 1996:23; Cotterell, 1992; Wilmer, 1993; Young, 1999:14).

One common thread linking these diverse polities in a fragmented world was the fact that many of them formed alternative 'imagined communities', and provided other scripts of belonging than that of citizenship in a nation-state. But another similarity was the essentially *normative* character of the claims many of them made on the nation-state (Appadurai, 1996; La Prairie, 1996; Oomen, 1999a:14). Might, it seemed, no longer made right. Now that the legitimacy of the state was no longer a given, the floor was open to all sorts of contestation to the justification of its rule, many of them couched in the language of human rights. Others put the state to the test by playing 'the culture card', whether combined with human rights discourse or not.

The culture card

> *Mamone, 25 August 1999: The customary court has been revamped, with freshly cut branches surrounding the withered thorn-tree. Today, the old men of the village have gathered to welcome a group of girls from the Guardian Angels Boarding School: city kids in Tommy Hilfiger clothes and expensive sneakers, undoubtedly sent to the 'rural areas' by their wealthy parents to shield them from drugs and clubbing. They've been reading O.K. Matsepe's* 'Kgôrong ya Mošate' *(The Customary Court) and the assembled old men act out a case for them. Afterwards, they gaze at the chief, sitting on an ornate chair in front of his palace, surrounded by faded pictures, tortoise-shells, grain-baskets and divining bones. After their bus has driven off in a cloud of dust, the chief's brother evaluates the benefits of, and pleads for, a permanent museum. 'I saw a Ndebele woman decorating a BMW in tribal patterns on television the other day. Do you think she does that for nothing? I am telling you, old men, there is money in these traditional things these days...'*

Arguably, one of the great surprises of the late twentieth century was the strengthening of the relationship between 'culture' and wider political and economic processes. Long considered 'backward', 'tribalist' and 'an obstacle to modernisation', culture became one of the prime ways in which to engage with a fast-changing world (Hunter, 1991; Meyer and Geschiere, 1995; Wilmsen and McAllister, 1996; Young, 1993a). 'Around the world,' as Sahlins (1999:ii) was to write, 'the peoples give the lie to received theoretical oppositions between tradition and change, indigenous culture and modernity, townsmen and tribesmen, and other clichés of the received anthropological wisdom'. Peruvian pan-pipe players in European shopping malls, French Camembert makers joining the anti-globalisation movement, Masaï reviving traditional dances to please tourists, indigenous Internet sites all over the Web – all showed how culture had become a means by which to assert 'authenticity' in a fast-changing world, to localise modernity and expropriate some of its central forces. As such, culture itself seemed to have become commodified, subject to market forces. As Chanock remarked (2000:17): 'Cultures, like brands, must essentialise, and successful and sustainable cultures are those which brand best.'

Not only was the revival of culture related to wider economic processes, it was also often essentially political. From the Basques to the Brazilian Indians, from New Zealand aboriginals to Zanzibar secessionists, all stated their demands for greater autonomy in cultural terms, thus adding legitimacy to what were essentially political claims. To describe the political ends to which culture was put to use, Appadurai (1996:30) coined the term 'culturalism': the conscious mobilisation of cultural differences in the service of a larger national or transnational politics. Two closely related manifestations of this culturalism and the way in which culture, politics and law became entwined in the 1990s are of interest to our study: the rise of 'group rights' and the resurgence of traditional leadership.

The rise of 'rights to roots'

It was not without reason that the 1990s became the UN 'International Decade of the World's Indigenous People' (1995–2004). Not only did an increasing number of sub- and trans-national polities make political demands couched in cultural terms, there was also a growing consensus that these demands were just, and that they should be honoured.[11] In the course of the 1990s, many countries adopted legislation on cultural rights, ranging from the far-reaching right to secede which the Ethiopian Constitution granted to its ethnic groups, to various minor guarantees such as language rights, affirmative action or the right to representation of minority groups in governmental bodies, given in nearly every other country in the world.[12] Even in strong and homogenising states like the United States, Canada, Australia and New Zealand, ethnic communities were suddenly redubbed 'first nations', a powerful expression of the type of claim they were making on the nation-states that incorporated them (Depew, 1994; Wilmer, 1993). But far more than in national legislation, it was through international law that the position of 'indigenous people' was strengthened, for instance in the 1989 ILO Convention on Indigenous and Tribal Peoples in Independent Countries and in the 1994 United Nations Draft Universal Declaration on Indigenous Rights.[13] The latter document recognised 'the urgent need to respect and promote

[11] There is a wide range of legal and political science literature on the rise of 'group rights', 'collective rights' and 'cultural rights' and their justification. Good introductions can be found in: Anaya (1996), Assies et al. (2000), Donders et al. (1999), Gabor (1998), Galenkamp (1993), Henrard (2000), Kymlicka (1995), Preece (1997), Segasvary (1995), Seleoan (1997), Taylor (1992), Wilmer. (1993).

[12] Abbink (1997), Henrard and Smis (2000). A very useful classification of cultural rights can be found in: Levy (1997). Cf. Oomen (1998a).

[13] *ILO Convention 169, revising the ILO Convention on Living and Working Conditions of Indigenous Populations* and *UN Doc. E/CN.4/SUB.2/1994/2/Add.1 (1994)*, prepared by the Working Group on Indigenous Populations of the Economic and Social Council of the United Nations. See the overview in Marquardt (1995).

the inherent rights and characteristics of indigenous peoples, especially their rights to their lands, territories and resources, which derive from their political, economic and social structures and from their cultures, spiritual traditions, histories and philosophies'.[14]

The fact that cultural communities were increasingly stating their essentially political claims in the language of the law had to do with another key feature of politics in the 1990s: the rights revolution. In the course of the decade, many a commentator remarked, often with regret, how political discourse had been reduced to 'rights talk', and how social movements chose to adopt strategies based on law rather than other forms of politics (Glendon, 1991; McCann, 1998; Sarat and Kearns, 1997). Political differences seemed to be fought out more efficiently in courts than in parliaments or through warfare. A striking illustration of this development was the appearance of a group of (white) Afrikaner farmers, complete with khaki outfits and feathered hats, at the 1994 session of the UN's Working Group on Indigenous Populations, to voice their demand for recognition as an 'indigenous people'.[15] Clearly they reckoned that, with the violent repression typical of apartheid having failed, and having lost out at the negotiating table, their last chance lay in obtaining recognition of their group rights.

But the novelty of the 1990s did not lie only in the fact that rights in general became more important, but also in a change in the type of rights that were recognised and the moral justification for them. There was widespread debate on why and how 'rights to roots'[16] should be recognised in addition to 'rights to options', with the general argument seeming to run as follows. (i) Cultural diversity is a central feature of present-day society; states incorporate many cultures. (ii) This is a good thing, worthy of legal reflection and protection for two reasons: a) there is an intrinsic value in cultural diversity, especially when it concerns cultures like those of indigenous peoples who have been marginalised and discriminated against in the past, and b) legal recognition of cultural diversity adds to the classical rights repertory because it acknowledges the degree to which 'human identity is dialogically created and constituted' and thus adds to individual well-being as well as group protection.[17] The increase in legal recognition of cultural diversity was thus based on both empirical and normative assumptions: the idea that cultural diversity *was* a feature of current society and that it *should* be so. These assumptions, as we shall see, also formed the foundation for a related phenomenon: the resurgence of traditional authority.

[14] UN Doc. E/CN.4/SUB.2/1994/2/Add.1 (1994), S6.

[15] Commission on Human Rights – Sub-Commission on Prevention of Discrimination and Protection of Minorities, 'Discrimination against Indigenous Peoples: Report of the Working Group on Indigenous Populations at Its Twelfth Session.' Geneva: United Nations, 1994.

[16] These terms were coined by B. de Sousa Santos, 'State, Law and Community in the World System: An Introduction', *Social & Legal Studies* 1 (1992), p.136. A more classic distinction is between first-, second- and third-generation rights: the first-generation rights are classic human rights such as those of liberty, equality and bodily integrity; the second-generation includes socio-economic rights; and the third generation includes both 'cultural' and 'group' rights such as rights to a clean environment.

[17] This is the general spirit of many national laws on cultural diversity as well as the international debate. Cf: Anaya (1996); Donders et al. (1999); Marquardt (1995). Nevertheless, there is a great variety of political positions on the subject, well set out in: Ivison et al. (2000). The emphasis on the intrinsic value of culture can be found, for instance, in Johnston (1995), Musschenga (1998), while the argument of individual well-being was famously put forward by Kymlicka (1995) and Taylor (1992:7).

The resurgence of the traditional leaders

The core features of the 1990s global order – the changing role of the nation-state, the related space for the rise of alternative polities, the rise of culture as a means through which to engage with modernity, the recognition of group rights – also facilitated a surprise re-entry: that of traditional leaders.[18] While in the 1950s and 1960s many newly independent African states had attempted to crush chieftaincies on the path to a common nationhood, they were back with a vengeance. And even though they continued to derive a large part of their legitimacy from their relationship with the past, the conditions for their return and the way in which it took place were decidedly those of the post-modern world order.

Roughly, two scenarios seemed to govern the revival of traditional leadership in sub-Saharan Africa. The first was that of weak, or even collapsed, states like Angola, Somalia and the Congo, in which government institutions had ceased to function and (neo)traditional authorities – as if by default – had taken their place. In the second scenario, relatively strong states, reacting to the global and local forces described above, sought to attain extra legitimacy by recognising traditional structures of rule. Zimbabwe, for instance, re-welcomed traditional leaders to Parliament and reinstalled the customary courts; Zambia established a House of Chiefs; Uganda officially revived the Buganda kingdom; and traditional leaders received strengthened recognition in Nigeria and Ghana.[19] As we shall see, this state revival of traditional authority often turned out to be a Pandora's box; once unleashed, the forces of ethnicity proved difficult to contain and developed into a much larger threat to the nation-state than they had been before their recognition.

Thus, the resurgence of traditional leadership took different forms, depending on the character of the nation-state concerned. The states that switched to an (increased) official recognition of traditional leaders, their structures of governance and their representative bodies were often former British colonies with a tradition of indirect rule. But the resurrection also took place outside the Anglophone sphere, with an increase in the involvement of chiefs in governmental structures from Togo to Niger, from Mozambique to Namibia.[20] However, just as often the resurgence of traditional authority was unintended; in Angola, for instance, traditional leaders claimed they could run the country much better than the formal government. And for many countries a link between decentralisation, democratisation, donor policies and retraditionalisation was reported; the strengthening of the local sphere and the emphasis on grass-roots politics often led to a surprise revival of traditional authority.[21]

[18] Good general works that acknowledge and – in part – explain the resurgence of traditional authority in the 1990s are Englebert (2000); Harding (1998); Hofmeister and Scholz (1997); Konrad Adenauer Stiftung (1997), Van Rouveroy van Nieuwaal and Van Dijk (1999), Van Rouveroy and Ray (1996); Van Rouveroy van Nieuwaal and Zips (1998).

[19] Traditional Authorities Research Group. Vol. V: 'Theoretical Framework and Comparative Perspective on Traditional Leaders in Africa.' 1996 (unpublished). Cf. Doornbos (2000); Englebert (2000); Geschiere (1993); Gould (1997); Hammer (1998), Harneit-Sievers (1998); Maxwell (1999); Rathbone (2000); Vaughan (2000).

[20] 'Chefferie Traditionnelle et Politique.' *Regard: Mensuel Burkinabe d'Information* 179, 29 July–25 August (1996); Hinz (1999); Van Rouveroy van Nieuwaal (1996); Van Rouveroy van Nieuwaal and Zips (1998).

[21] Bierschenk and Olivier de Sardan (1997); Englebert (2001); Claude Fay. 'La Décentralisation dans un Cercle (Tenenkou, Mali)' *Autrepart* 14 (2000):121–42; Jeremy Gould. 'Resurrecting Makumba:

In sum, the reasons for which states chose to (re-)recognise traditional authority seemed to be threefold and, again, both normative and empirical: first, there was the belief that indigenous institutions were worthy of recognition; second, the fact that they could add extra legitimacy to the ailing nation-states; and third, that they could not be wished away anyway. Many authors joined Van Rouveroy van Nieuwaal and Ray (1996:1) in stating that an important explanation of state failure in Africa lies in the 'overlooked relationship between the contemporary African state and traditional authority'. Indigenous African institutions and values deserved to be recognised within the official state and would contribute to it (Ayittey, 1991; Skalnik, 1996). For one thing, states could derive additional legitimacy from their association with 'that other traditional, moral and political order' which would enable them to get 'around their own administrative weaknesses and the physical and emotional distance from their populations'.[22] Other authors underlined the need for African states to be realistic: traditional authorities had shown a 'remarkable resilience' and were an undeniable part of the African socio-political landscape and, as such, hard to ignore (Herbst, 2000; Hofmeister and Scholz, 1997; Mawhood, 1982).

In the course of this book we shall see how post-apartheid developments in South Africa reflected this global mood, and how alternative polities were successful in relying on cultural difference to challenge the unitary nation-state that had once been the dream in the struggle against oppression. This development, for instance, caused the mineral-rich 'Royal Bafokeng Nation' to clamour for complete independence from South Africa before 2005, a claim which was published in national newspapers and glossy folders with investment opportunities, and promoted by ambassadors like 'honorary tribesman' American pop singer Michael Jackson. It also led to the new South African government enthusiastically embracing a 'Khoisan consultative conference', with the Deputy President stating:

> This consultative conference stands as testament to the fact that we, as a nation, are successfully moving away from the darkness of the past into the brightness of the future. It is a future that seeks to achieve a living African Renaissance, where the dignity of all our citizens is respected, and where all communities are free to explore, explain, reflect and rejoice in that which makes them unique.

The official encouragement to South African communities to 'explore, explain, reflect and rejoice' in their cultural differences appeared to be based on the same empirical and normative assumptions as those fuelling the recognition of group rights and the revival of traditional authorities in other countries. There seemed to be an idea not only that society consisted of a tapestry of distinct cultures, but also that the ascertainable, normative and governmental systems of these cultures were worthy of official legal recognition. While these images and notions were presented as novel postulates of post-modern times, they nonetheless often bore a startling resemblance to the paradigms of a not-too-distant past, when they had formed the building blocks of indirect rule and apartheid policies. It is

21 (cont.) Chiefly Powers and the Local State in Zambia's Third Republic.' Paper presented at the 14th International Congress of Anthropological and Ethnological Sciences, Williamsburg, VA 1998; Hofmeister and Scholz (1997); Mawhood (1982).

22 Herbst (2000); T. Quinlan. 'The State and National Identity in Lesotho.' *Journal of Legal Pluralism and Unofficial Law* Vol. 37–8, Special double issue on The New Relevance of Traditional Authorities to Africa's Future (1996):377–405; Van Rouveroy van Nieuwaal (1996:54).

for this reason that we shall now turn to some of the long-forgotten lessons that those times, inside and outside South Africa, taught us about the malleability of culture, the creation of customary law and the character of bureaucratic chieftaincy.

3. Past nightmares

One of the founding legal texts of apartheid's homeland policies started with the words: 'Whereas the Bantu peoples of the Union of South Africa do not constitute a homogeneous people, but form separate national units on the basis of language and culture....'[23] Apartheid was not unique in assuming the existence of separate homogeneous cultural units with their own systems of law and governance, in need and capable of official recognition. On the contrary, it built on and refined the British policies of indirect rule, which took comparable notions of culture, community, customary law and chieftaincy as their point of departure (Beinart and Dubow, 1995; Costa, 1999a; Evans, 1997; Mamdani, 1996; Worden, 1994). By the end of the twentieth century, these notions and their usage as part of the colonial project were subject to severe debunking by both anthropologists and colonial historians, scholars interested in South Africa as well as other former British colonies. Instead, they offered some alternative interpretations of the relations between law, power and culture in colonialism and apartheid, which we shall briefly examine in the following sub-sections.

Culture and colonialism

In chapters on 'cultural diversity' and 'black political organisation', the 1990 *Yearbook* of the South African Bureau of Information offered an idyllic description of South Africa's population: 'a rich mosaic of distinctive minorities without any common cultural rallying point' which reflect 'the full global spectrum – from the Stone Age lifestyle of the Bushmen through the subsistence socio-economic organisation of traditional black communities to the modern urban industrial society' (p.171). The ten ethnic black homelands, in which one could find Zulus with beehive-shaped huts and bone and ivory ornaments; Swazi who sculpted their hair with aloe leaves; Ndebele girls wearing up to 25 kilograms of copper, leather and beads; South Sotho with cone-shaped hats and brightly coloured blankets; all, according to this book, knew a political system in which 'public opposition from outside the traditional system of government is foreign and frowned upon. Therefore, political parties and factions in the Western sense are unknown.' In any event, democracy would not have worked for South Africa because

> there was no such thing as a homogeneous 'Black majority'. In fact, there were no fewer than nine major distinctive ethnic groups, all minorities, each with its own cultural identity, including language, and a territorial base reasonably clearly defined by history and gradually being expanded and consolidated. (ibid., p.174)

This neat classification, reproduced in tourist folders and state-sponsored anthropology text-books alike, not only legitimated minority rule and completely bypassed the degree of force that had gone into the creation of this 'rich mosaic',

[23] Preamble, *Promotion of Bantu Self-Government Act 46/1959.*

such as the forced removal of 3.5 million people. It was also based on the anthropological assumptions of a long-gone era, when Maine and Malinowski described 'tribes' as bounded, homogeneous entities, isolated both from change and from contact with other communities, with cultures that could be known, recorded and explained.[24]

By the time the 1990 *Yearbook* appeared, these insights had long been pulverised in academic discourse and replaced by new ones. Culture had come to be considered a process instead of an entity, a verb instead of a noun (Boonzaaier and Sharp, 1985; Wilson, 1997:9). In a widely influential definition, Geertz linked the notion to the way in which people give meaning to their lives and stated that culture can be considered a 'historically transmitted pattern of meaning, embodied in symbols, a system of inherited conceptions expressed in symbolic forms by means of which men communicate, perpetuate, and develop their knowledge about and attitudes toward life' (Ferguson and Gupta, 1997; Geertz, 1973). As these meanings could differ from individual to individual, from context to context, over time and space, some authors preferred to use the term 'cultural orientations' (Van Binsbergen, 1999). These were not given but created dialectically, and subject to permanent contestation and negotiation within the power relations in a community (cf. Ivison et al., 2000; Mbaku, 1997; Schipper, 1993; Sewell, 1999).[58] 'Tradition' could be invoked (often after first having been invented), not so much as an inheritance from the past but rather to legitimise certain values and actions in the present (Hatt, 1996; Hobsbawm and Ranger, 1983; Vail, 1989; Vansina, 1992). This processual, negotiated and contextual view of culture also influenced thinking about the related concept of community: – rather than a homogeneous entity bound by a pre-existing culture, this was now considered to be the loosely defined and fluctuating site within which some of these contestations take place (Gellner, 1995).

For others, some of these contestations take place not within but across the boundaries of communities. Here, the term ethnicity is often used, as in the famous 1960s work of Barth, who was the first to argue explicitly that cultural or ethnic identity could be considered not as a given, preceding cross-cultural contact, but rather as an outcome of such contact (Barth, 1969; Vermeulen and Gorens, 1994). Even though this position soon became paradigmatic, his successors remained divided over the essence of ethnicity: purely instrumental, a resource in social and political competition, or also partly primordial, or a way in which individuals give meaning to their social existence (cf. Young, 1993a). Recently, successful attempts have been made to synergise both viewpoints and to underline that both the substance and the usage of ethnicity are important and feed on each other, and that there is a 'dual logic that encompasses identity (re)construction as well as instrumental and strategic activity'.[25]

The understanding of ethnicity, or culture, as a thoroughly relational concept

[24] The most famous works of these two authors are: Maine (1861) and Bronislaw Malinowski. *Argonauts of the West-Pacific*. Prospect Heights: Waveland, 1984. There is no space here for an overview of the development in anthropological thought from Maine to present-day thinkers. Good introductions are Eriksen (2001), Falk Moore (1993); Geertz (1973), Strathern (1995).

[25] Assies (2000); Cohen (2000); Cora Govers and Hans Vermeulen, 'From Political Mobilization to the Politics of Ethnic Consciousness.' in *The Politics of Ethnic Consciousness*, ed. Cora Govers and Hans Vermeulen, Basingstoke: Macmillan, 1997; Nederveen Pieterse (1997); Brian S. Turner (ed.) *The Blackwell Companion to Social Theory*. London: Blackwell, 1996; Edwin N. Wilmsen, 'Premises of Power in Ethnic Politics', in Wilmsen and McAllister (1996:1–23).

created in a dialogue within or between 'communities' does not mean that such dialogue takes place on equal terms. Instead, it is often an encounter between the powerful and the powerless, the dominators and the dominated, in which the former are able to set the rules of the game and in which the dice are heavily loaded, to quote Mamdani (1996:22; cf. Comaroff, 1996; Wilmsen, 1996). One of the classic examples is, of course, that of the dialogue between colonisers and colonised, in which, according to some, 'the Europeans first built their own cognitive view of rural African society' – strongly based on tribes, culture and chieftaincy – 'and then imposed it on daily life'.[26]

Nevertheless, even colonialism was hardly a one-sided affair, a mere imposition of ethnic categories on a submissive African population. For one thing, recent authors have emphasised how in creating an 'Other' – primitive, native, tribal – the European colonisers also formed a new identity as an enlightened, individualist 'Self' (Comaroff and Comaroff, 1997; Mudimbe, 1988; Said, 1978). Furthermore, Africans were mere not passive recipients of the ethnic categories imposed upon them, whether as subjects of indirect rule policies or of apartheid, Instead they actively engaged with them, appropriating and transforming parts of the package while rejecting others (Vail, 1989). Pedi migrant workers, for instance, would stress tribal or home allegiances but 'this emphasis was neither an anachronistic hangover from their rural origins, nor a quiescent acceptance of ethnic identities engineered by the apartheid state, but a newly constituted way of interacting with other people within the world of work and city'.[27] And in Qwaqwa, ethnic entrepreneurs started painting idyllic rural scenes and clan totems on the walls of shops named 'Basotho, let's love each other', thus adopting parts of an identity which had not existed a few decades before the homeland system.[28] The most powerful South African example, of course, remains the appropriation of the Zulu identity and its use as a weapon of resistance (De Haas and Zulu, 1994; Golan, 1994).

Both colonialism and apartheid can thus be considered as dialogues on culture that took place in many ways, ranging from day-to-day encounters to grand narratives. Even though they occurred within clearly unequal relations of power, multiple voices could be heard in these dialogues and were involved in the production of certain understandings of culture. What has only recently come to be fully appreciated, however, is the importance of one of the languages in which the dialogues took place: the law.

The creation of customary law

Madibaneng Tribal Office, 9 December 1998: A ramshackle school doubles as the community hall in which four male and two female officially recognised 'Tribal Councillors' spend the whole of Wednesday adjudicating cases. Chickens and goats scuffle by and children peek in through the broken door as a lengthy case on land

[26] Terence Ranger, 'The Invention of Tradition Revisited: The Case of Colonial Africa', in *Legitimacy and the State in Twentieth Century Africa: Essays in the Honour of A.H.M. Kirk-Greene*, ed. Terence Ranger and O. Vaughan. Basingstoke: Macmillan, 1993, p.77.

[27] Ashforth (1997); Beinart and Dubow (1995); Iliffe (1983); James (1999: 70); Mare (1993); Ross (1993); J. Segar, *Fruits of Apartheid – Experiencing 'Independence' in a Transkei Village*. Belville: Anthropus, 1989.

[28] L. Bank, 'Of Livestock and Deadstock: Entrepreneurship and Tradition on the South African Highveld', in *Farewell to Farms: De-Agrarianisation and Employment in Africa*, D.F. Bryceson and V. Jamal eds., Aldershot: Ashgate: African Studies Centre Research Series, 1997, pp.196–7.

ownership is discussed. One of the parties has not shown up, even though he received a hand-written letter from the 'Tribal Clerk'. Around sunset, we evaluate the day and I get a chance to ask some questions. No, not much has changed since 1994, although the 'Tribal Police and the Tribal Drivers' have difficulties in receiving their salaries. As I try to discuss the councillors' ideas on customary law, one of them, an old man in a patched suit, says apologetically 'Actually, we're just settling cases here according to our own insights. If you want to find out about customary law, you'd better go to the Magistrate or the Traditional Affairs Official. They have all the books...'

Apartheid was largely legitimised and implemented through the language of the law, albeit with force lurching closely behind (Abel, 1995; Comaroff and Comaroff, 1997; Evans, 1997; Klug, 1996; Mamdani, 1996). After the National Party had narrowly won the 1948 elections it slowly started working out a system of 'administering the natives' that was built not only on 'multi-nationalism' – the idea 'that each group must have its own sphere where it can enjoy and exercise in full the privileges of a free society' – but also on all these groups having their own, distinct systems of law and governance which deserved recognition within the wider state context.[29] In recognising 'tribal governance' and 'native laws and customs' the governments of Verwoerd and his successors built on and refined the British policy of 'native administration', described by Lugard in 1918 as: 'a single Government in which Native Chiefs have well-defined duties and an acknowledged status equally with British officials'.[30] The system of 'indirect rule' he proposed put law 'at the cutting edge of colonialism' and made it 'an area in which Africans and Europeans engaged one another – a battleground as it were in which they contested access to resources and labour, relationships of power and authority, and interpretations of morality and culture'.[31] As a perceptive Tswana remarked at the end of the nineteenth century: 'Some say this is the English mode of warfare – by 'papers' and agents and courts'.[32]

In South Africa, the legal recognition of 'culture, tribe and chiefdom' was achieved through hundreds of laws, regulations and bye-laws dealing with all aspects of life: governance, property ownership and interpersonal relations. Even though the Zulu, Xhosa, Tswana, Sotho Customary Law that was codified and perpetuated in laws, text-books and judicial decisions claimed to reflect reality, it was as retrogressive as it was normative and instrumentalist. It was retrogressive because, by the time the government started to install state-appointed chiefs, to demarcate tribes, to 'move people back to their homelands' and to codify and implement tribal laws and customs, capitalism and individualisation had long corroded communal life, which, in any case, had never corresponded to the picture painted by the architects of apartheid (Chanock, 1985; Costa, 1999; Hobsbawm and Ranger, 1983: 247; Klug, 1995; Mamdani, 1996). It was also normative, because the government explicitly tried to shield Africans from the

[29] B. Coetzee, Deputy Minister of Bantu Administration and Development, quoted in Posel (1991: 232).

[30] Sir Frederick Lugard, speaking of Nigeria, quoted in: Mann and Roberts (1991:20).

[31] Ibid., p.3.

[32] John Mackenzie, *Austral Africa: Losing It or Ruling It*. Vol. 1. London: Sampson Low, 1887, p.80, quoted in Comaroff and Comaroff (1997:370).

'onslaught of modernisation' through the codification of custom. As the then Minister of Bantu Administration and Development said: 'Whatever the world may say, the Bantu city dweller is someone who still yearns for his homeland, and that yearning must be stimulated.'[33] Also, those aspects of customary law deemed unwanted, such as polygamy, were barred from recognition through a 'repugnancy proviso'. Apart from a paternalistic attempt to freeze parts of an idealised past, the administration of Africans through customary law was, of course, 'hugely convenient' for the governments of the day: The setting aside of a separate sphere in which Africans were 'containerised', barred from purchasing or individually owning property and relegated to separate homelands, where they were administered according to their 'own' laws and customs and thus not in need of individual rights or democracy, was central to a political economy that not only enabled but also justified wealth accumulation in white South Africa.[34]

The codification of customary law was thus all about the creation, for political purposes, of a uniforming and bureaucratic fallacy and its codification and implementation through courts and native administrators. The question was, of course, in what way this 'official customary law' related to what I, following Ehrlich, shall call 'living law' in this book: law as lived in day-to-day life and the norms and values it draws on.[35] In the course of the twentieth century, academic thinking on this question went through a number of distinct phases, both ontologically and epistemologically.

Early legal anthropologists, who often doubled as colonial administrators, shared most of the central premises of the colonial and apartheid projects: the idea of bounded tribes, with fixed systems of law and governance which could be ascertained through conversations with village elders and should be catalogued before being washed away by modernisation. Schapera's famous 1938 *Handbook of Tswana Law and Custom* was an example of this approach, as was Anthony Allot's ambitious project of restating African Customary Law (Allott, 1970). In the 1960s, authors like Max Gluckman began to emphasise that customary law could only be ascertained by looking at actual processes of adjudication rather than abstract statements by village elders, and by keeping a watchful eye on the social context in which this adjudication took place (Gluckman, 1955, 1965; Gulliver, 1963; Nader, 1969; Nader et al., 1966). This planting of law within the societal context was worked out in the course of the 1980s, for instance by Holleman who emphasised the need to look not only at troublesome but also at trouble-free cases, and in the celebrated *Rules and Processes* (Comaroff and Roberts, 1981; Holleman, 1986; Falk Moore, 1986). In this latter work, Comaroff and Roberts synergised a rule-centred and processual approach, describing the Tswana concept of the world as 'rule-governed yet highly negotiable, normatively regulated yet pragmatically individualistic' (Comaroff and Roberts, 1981:215). In later years, attention increasingly turned to the dynamic role of law in society: as reflective and constitutive of power relations, as a discursive forum for the

[33] Minister Botha, quoted in Posel (1991:233).

[34] Beinart (1994); Beinart and Dubow (1995); Chanock (1991); Comaroff (1997); Klug (1995); Mamdani (1996); Worden (1994).

[35] Ehrlich (1936:493). For other distinctions between codified customary law and local norms, see Bennett (1995); D'Engelbronner-Kolff (2001); Roberts (1984, 1979). One main objection to Ehrlich has been that his definition of law was too broad, and could include any social norm. This can be remedied by adopting Tamanaha's non-essentialist definition of law: 'law is whatever people recognize and treat as law through their social practices'. Tamanaha (2000:319).

creation of meaning (Collier, 1976; De Gaay Fortman and Mihyo, 1993; Merry, 1992; Von Benda-Beckmann, 1989; Wilson, 2000). For, as academics came to realise: 'presenting the "traditional" categories of legal discussion without the context of discourse offers statements without speakers, ideas without their occasions, concepts outside history' (Falk Moore, quoted in Just, 1992:382).

The more it became clear that there was no such thing – and never had been – as a fixed body of customary law ready to be ascertained, but that living law was a fluid, relational and negotiable system intimately tied to fluctuating social and political relations, the more the claims of 'official customary law' became untenable. Not surprisingly, many (legal) historians in the 1980s and 1990s turned their attention to descriptions of 'the invention of tradition' and to debunking the 'myth of customary law' (Chanock, 1985; Costa, 1998, 1999; Vail, 1989; Hobsbawm and Ranger, 1983). In a number of excellent works, customary law came to be understood as 'a dynamic historical formation which at once shapes and is shaped by economic, political and social processes' (Mann and Roberts, 1991; cf. Comaroff and Comaroff, 1997). Law, it was now held, was an eminent and hitherto underestimated way of understanding wider social and political processes, a prism for looking into a society's power relations, but one which could never be distinguished from them.

As the 'creation of customary law' within the wider socio-political setting itself became an object of study, academics were quick to realise that this – just like the implementation of cultural difference – had not been a top-down, one-way endeavour in which apartheid administrators merely planted their vision of customary society on a passive African population.[36] Here, too, there had been a dialogue, even if it was within skewed power relations. For one, the African population concerned had also appropriated parts of the categories imposed on them and used them as a means of resistance, litigating over chieftaincy disputes, against expropriation, for additional recognition (Abel, 1995; Comaroff, 1997). Also, there was the realisation that, of the African voices which had had some input into the types of ideas that were frozen within the 'austerity of tabulated legalism', one voice was privileged: namely, that of the traditional leaders. As one observer put it: 'In a context in which there were multiple institutions with a customary claim – such as gender institutions, age groups, clan assemblies, hereditary ("customary") alongside bureaucratic (state-appointed) chiefs – colonial powers privileged a single institution, the bureaucratic chief, as the "customary" authority whose version of custom would henceforth be enforced as law' (Mamdani, 1999:98). Let us therefore now turn to this institution.

The character of bureaucratic chieftaincy

If the customary law officially recognised under apartheid could be considered as created in dialogue, an outcome of negotiation, two parties occupied the front seats at the negotiating table: the Department of Native Affairs (DNA) and the traditional leaders. While South Africa's ten homelands were considered to be separate political spheres, progressively working towards independence – as was attained by the Transkei, Boputhatswana, Venda and the Ciskei – the DNA was responsible for their running (Ashforth, 1997; Evans, 1997). The hundreds of laws, regulations and bye-laws that it produced to this end were – albeit loosely

[36] The *locus classicus* here is Chanock (1985).

– based on ethnographic data derived from encounters between native administrators-cum-state anthropologists and traditional leaders and village elders (Hammond-Tooke, 1997). Text-books like *The Pedi* (Mönnig, 1967), *Laws and Customs of the Bapedi and Cognate Tribes* (Harries, 1929), *Bafokeng Family Law and Law of Succession* (Coertze, 1990) and the much-used *Preliminary Survey of the Bantu Tribes of South Africa* (Van Warmelo, 1935) listed, like the ten commandments, the private, public and criminal laws of the tribes concerned. Pictures of their authors show how these data were collected: the native administrators on field visits in folding chairs, surrounded by village elders who undoubtedly responded to questions such as 'Who owns this land?' and 'What punishments can a chief inflict?' by giving those versions of customary law that suited them best.[37]

It was this information, with its inevitable bias in favour of traditional leaders and against the more marginal voices in the rural communities – women, young people – that formed the raw material for policies on 'native administration'. As had been the case with indirect rule, these policies placed traditional leaders centre stage, thus strengthening the assumption which formed their points of departure: that of traditional leaders as representatives of their communities and guardians of their laws and customs. They also essentially transformed the institution into a bureaucratised and uniform entity, strongly enmeshed in the state apparatus. Laws such as the 1927 Black Administration Act, the 1951 Black Authorities Act and the 1957 Regulations Prescribing the Duties, Powers, Privileges and Conditions of Service of Chiefs and Headmen placed a uniform grid over the multifarious existing structures of governance.[38] They introduced tribal, territorial and regional authorities, firmly linked communal land tenure to chiefly authority and gave chiefs an array of – often unpopular – bureaucratic functions. As the 1959 Bantu Self-Government Bill explained:

> Tribal authorities assist and guide the chief in the administration of the affairs of the tribe and in the performance of his other functions, which are to maintain law and order, disperse unlawful assemblies, and ensure the enforcement of regulations such as those relating to public health, the collection of taxes, registration of births and deaths, the prevention of animal diseases, occupation and use of land, control of workseekers, and prevention and punishment of crime.[39]

Not surprisingly, traditional leaders who were reluctant to cooperate were replaced by more cooperative brothers or sent to re-education camps.

Though the bureaucratised nature of chieftaincy and its centrality to apartheid rule had long been the staple of studies on South Africa's rural conditions, it was Mahmood Mamdani's much acclaimed *Citizen and Subject* that offered unprecedented insight into how chieftaincy was crucially hooked up to the mode of domination in the apartheid state (Mamdani, 1996; cf. Beinart and Dubow, 1995; Bundy, 1979; Hammond-Tooke, 1975; Mbeki, 1964). Considering South Africa as a generic form of a colonial state, Mamdani described how this state

[37] Chanock (1985). Cf. the dialogue between Cetshwayo and the Cape Native Laws and Customs Commission quoted in Mamdani (1996:44–5).

[38] *Regulations Prescribing the Duties, Powers, Privileges and Conditions of Service of Chiefs and Headmen (as Amended for Northern Province).* Proclamation 110/1969, *Black Administration Act.* 38/1927, *Black Authorities Act,* 68/1951.

[39] South African Institute of Race Relations. *Annual Report 1956–1957*. Johannesburg: South African Institute of Race Relations, 1957, p.55.

was 'bifurcated', with an institutional structure that created ethnic subjects inside, and citizens outside, the homelands, and how this form of power also determined the type of resistance to it: 'whereas civil society was racialised, Native Authority was tribalised' (Mamdani,1996:19). In this structure, chiefs stood central, and functioned as 'decentralised despots':

> Not only did the chief have the right to pass rules (bylaws) governing persons under his domain, he also executed all laws and was the administrator in 'his' area, in which he settled all disputes. The authority of the chief thus fused in a single person all moments of power: judicial, legislative, executive and administrative. This authority was like a clenched fist, because the chief stood at the intersection of the market economy and the nonmarket one.

Inside the homelands, under the authority of traditional leaders, Africans were turned into subjects, their rights and privileges tied to the acceptance of chiefly authority in formerly unprecedented ways. Whether it was about attaining a plot of land, getting a work permit or an old-age pension, or obtaining access to justice, the chief had by legislation been made into the sole portal to government.

The fact that traditional leadership was now bureaucratised and chiefs propped up by state power did not, of course, mean that they could completely disregard the opinions of 'their subjects' – an issue neglected by Mamdani.[40] If traditional leaders did not want to be murdered, stoned, burnt in their palaces or driven out, as happened in many instances, they had to maintain some form of local legitimacy. For instance, the father of Billy Sekwati Mampuru (whose coronation was described at the beginning of this chapter) stimulated publication of a book explaining the necessity and the mode of his cooperation with the administrators of the day:

> *Kgoši* Sekwati Mampuru never jumped to join the Native Authorities, but it was only after he realised that they were about development that he decided to take part... He negotiated with the administrators and was not scared to tell the Native Commissioner to move away if he was unhappy about something, and even refused some of the duties assigned to him ... As such, he governed together with all those big elephants (*ditonaditlou*) from different governments, doing his own thing while they came and went, fighting with each other because in white governments people do not rule for life. (Nkadimeng, 1973)

In general, there was a wide variance in local arrangements, all of them dependent on the interplay between traditional authorities, alternative institutions, other government representatives and the population. Whatever the debates on chiefly authority within communities, it was nevertheless clear that both apartheid and colonialism had singled out one voice – that of the chiefs – for privileged attention within the state system, recognition in legislation and, ultimately, perpetuation and strengthening of the assumptions on which it rested.

4. Theoretical challenges

Let us now return from our brief excursion into the past and the scholarly lessons of relations between law and colonialism, back to the surprises of the late

[40] Englebert (1997); Mamdani (1999); Oomen (1998b); 'Review Symposium: Mahmood Mamdani and the Analysis of African Society,' *African Sociological Review* 1, no. 2 (1997):96–144.

twentieth century. As we have observed, it was an era which saw the new global system described as 'a Culture of cultures', in which culture – cast in rights discourse – became the prime language in which a multifarious mix of sub- and trans-national polities took on the nation-state and saw its demands for 'group rights' and 'cultural rights' met by it (Sahlins, 1999:x; cf. Oomen. 1998a).

Even though the situation had changed from one in which, as the joke went, every anthropologist had his own tribe to one in which every tribe had its own anthropologist, much of the rhetoric used was disturbingly familiar. The websites of first nations enthusiastically quoted nineteenth-century ethnographic works; ardently appropriated what was once considered discriminatory discourse; presented images of bounded, atemporal cultures; put forward traditional leaders adorned in antiquated outfits; and above all underlined their difference. This reversal of roles, combined with the familiarity of the play enacted, generates questions concerning the relevance of the lessons of customary law studies to the present situation. As we have seen, these lessons came to understand culture not as a state but as a process, all about the discursive creation of meaning within and beyond the border of polities; customary law as essentially a creation central to the colonial project of institutionalising difference; and its contents as determined in a dialogue between chiefs and administrators and both reflective and constitutive of the power relations of the times. With subnational polities – tribes, first nations, chiefdoms – starting to assert claims to sovereignty in the language of culture, custom and chieftainship and *democratic* nations everywhere responding to them, how could the relations between these polities, the way in which law, power and culture are woven into them, be reconceptualised?

It is a question which, I believe, socio-legal studies in general and legal anthropology in particular still has to tackle. For the past two decades, the paradigmatic position in legal anthropology has been that of legal pluralism (Fuller, 1994; Griffiths, 1986; Merry, 1992, 1998; Petersen and Zahle, 1995; Tamanaha, 2000; Von Benda-Beckmann, 1996; Wilson, 2000).[41] In what was as much a political as an analytical project, 'legal pluralists' set out to demonstrate convincingly the existence of a plurality of normative orders outside those of the centralist state, orders that issued norms as deserving of the predicate 'law' as the norms issued by the state. The state, in this reading, was considered 'monolithic', a statist Moloch for which, even if it did recognise cultural diversity as a hangover from colonisation, 'unification remained the goal' (Griffiths, 1986:18; Von Benda-Beckmann, 1996). For all its sensitising value, this approach seems to have been overtaken by events (or its own success, depending on your reading): many national states are no longer sites of uniformisation, but rather of 'organisation of diversity' in which the recognition of the plurality of normative systems within their borders plays a central role.[42] As De Sousa Santos has pointed out, this calls for bringing the state back into socio-legal analysis, but in an entirely different way:

> Under current conditions the centrality of the state lies in the way the state organises its own decentering ... the distinction between state and non-state is called into question, and consequently the socio-legal topics that have been based upon it, such

[41] Cf. the *Journal of Legal Pluralism and Unofficial Law* dedicated to this subject.

[42] Ulf Hannerz, 'Cosmopolitans and Locals in World Culture', in *Global Culture*, ed. M. Featherstone, London: Sage Publications, 1990, p.327.

> as community justice and legal pluralism, have become increasingly problematic. (De Sousa Santos, 1992:133)

The analytical challenges posed by the new order all revolve around the dialogues between the nation-state and other polities, which are cast in culture and rights discourse and related to wider socio-political forces, and their mutually constitutive character (cf. Darian-Smith and Fitzpatrick, 1999; Merry, 1992). Three groups of issues seem pressing. (i) If we indeed accept that culture, by its very nature, can never be adequately reflected in law, which versions of customary law and governance make it to 'the austerity of tabulated legalism' and why is this so? (ii) In a given polity, what are the constitutive effects of the legal recognition of cultural diversity? (iii) How, in this context, is the local resurgence of traditional authority to be understood? Although these questions form the backbone of this book and can only be answered in full in its concluding chapter, the following sections will uncover some of the groundwork that has shaped the enquiry.

Law, power, culture

'The myth of the mirror', one could say, still dominates as much of present political and academic thinking on the legal recognition of cultural diversity as it did in the past. This is the idea that state law can, and should, reflect cultural diversity – the existence of alternative systems of law and governance, defined in terms of cultural difference – within its borders.

Any alternative reading, as in the case of many scholars, should start by drawing attention to the fact that law cannot be understood outside of social and political relations, which it both shapes and reflects.[43] This is as true of the nation-state as it is of the subnational polities now demanding official recognition of their 'customary' systems of law and governance. The laws – or normative systems, as some would prefer to put it – of these tribes, chiefdoms or first nations are not a given, distinguishable from socio-political reality, but both reflect and reinforce it.[44] Multiple voices, the old, the young, the conservative, the radical, the male, the female, within a given polity will have different ideas on what local, living law is and should be, and their ideas depend on power relations, which versions and visions get perpetuated, accepted and institutionalised (Gulliver, 1969, 1979). Here, too, Foucauldian insights apply: power emanates in many places, and it is in discourse that power and knowledge are joined together to create – in this case legal – subjects, categories, divisions (Foucault, 1993, 1994). As such, law not only mirrors and creates power relations but also makes for meanings and understandings of identity (Cheater, 1999; Goheen, 1992).

If law is created discursively *within* polities – those porous social fields with a specific political make-up recognised internally and externally – this is also the case *between* them. For all their self-regulatory capacity, the (fluid and shifting) 'cultural communities' are not bounded entities but are engaged in a

[43] Cf. Comaroff and Roberts (1981); Du Toit (1998); Falk Moore (1978); Fleming (1996); Garth and Sarat (1998); Griffiths (1997); Just (1992); Merry (1992, 1988); Starr and Collier (1989).

[44] In the next section, I will take a non-essentialist approach to law and consider it as that which is considered as law by the people concerned. The notion that 'legal thought is constitutive of social realities rather than merely reflective of them' is well worked out in: Berry (1989); Geertz (1983); Griffiths (1997); Merry (1988).

permanent and mutually constitutive dialogue with other polities. This can be with other 'cultural communities' or with the international community or donor organisations but in one important case, also with the nation-state (Abel, 1995b:3; De Sousa Santos, 1992; Sugarman, 1983; Wilson, 2000). One increasingly successful way of getting claims to autonomy and access to resources recognised is through playing the 'culture card': underlining difference. There are ample indications that in these dialogues certain voices get recognition in preference to others, that certain versions of culture are accepted more readily, and that certain visions are more apt than others to be chiselled into the granite of the law.

Scholars working on the recognition of group rights, for instance, have noted with concern how atemporal and homogenising notions of cultural difference often inform the policy process and determine which rights do, or do not, get recognised. As Manuhuia Barcham writes on New Zealand (2000:15):

> academic and policy-oriented definitions of Maori tend to be derived from notions of indigeneity contingent upon the possession of 'authentic' cultural norms and traditions. The result is that a socially and politically constructed notion of indigenous authenticity is then used to judge between relative degrees of indigeneity as a means of determining which groups are more deserving of 'indigenous rights' than others.

Bern and Dodds (2000:163) make a similar observation in stating that 'recognition of Aboriginal self-determination of self-government within Australia is significantly shaped by legislative and other institutional forces that frame aboriginal claims'. It is especially the focus on cultural difference that forms the rationale for state recognition of group rights, and which 'risks locking in unrealistic and paternalistic views of indigenous cultures' (Ivison et al., 2000:10).

The problem here is threefold. First, there is the general difficulty of 'representing culture', voiced over and over by anthropologists in recent years: if one accepts that culture is permanently debated and negotiated, conceptualised differently by different members of 'communities', then a logical consequence is that, by definition, there cannot be one reading of The Culture, The Customs or The Structure of Governance of a Community (Eriksen, 2001; Geschiere, 1989; Levett et al., 1997; Schipper, 1993; Strathern, 1995). Another problem lies in the rationale for recognition: it is *because of* their cultural difference, the existence of a distinct legal and governmental system, that polities demand state support, so it is this cultural difference that they will have to underline.[45] But a third, additional set of problems is posed by the character of bureaucratic state law itself, with its demand for clear definitions, legal certainty, simplifications, ascertainability and readability (Abel, 1995b; Cotterell, 1983; Douglas, 1986; Scott, 1998; Weber, 1978).

A brilliant and often quoted example of the predetermined mismatch between the fluidity of culture and the rigidity of the law is given by James Clifford in his recounting of the court case whereby New England Mashpee Indians tried to

[45] For instance, the introduction to the research project on customary law embarked on by the South African Law Commission, which states that 'any authentic system of customary law rests squarely on the existing and generally accepted social practices of a community.' South African Law Commission. 'Project 90: Customary Law.' Pretoria, 2000, p. 24. Cf. Van Binsbergen (1999:2); (writing in Dutch) that the public pose of authenticity and integrity is a prerequisite for the success of any identity claim.

claim a piece of land. 'In the conflict of interpretations,' Clifford writes, 'concepts such as "tribe", "culture", "identity", "assimilation", "ethnicity", "politics" and "community" were themselves on trial... Modern Indians, who spoke in New England-accented English about the Great Spirit, had to convince a white Boston jury of their authenticity' (1988:8). In the process, anthropologists called in as experts were forced to speak out in much more essentialist and deterministic terms than they would ever have used in academic discourse: the law posed certain demands of homogeneity and cultural continuity that simply did not correspond with reality.

The exigencies of the law thus leave little room for alternative voices and discord within communities. For instance, in one of the few critical analyses of the legal recognition of cultural diversity in South Africa to date, Robins demonstrates how in a ≠khomani San land claim 'strategic narratives of community solidarity, social cohesion and cultural continuity were produced by the claimants and their lawyers during this process' but how in 'the post-settlement period ... social fragmentation and intra-community conflict became increasingly evident' (2001:833). Which voices do get heard depends not only on the power relations within the polity seeking state recognition, but also on who best fills the images of culture, custom and chieftaincy that those representing 'the law' wish to see (Tempelman, 1997). Just as in New Zealand, the traditional institutions of the Iwi (tribe) are, for all their marginality, the only representative institutions recognised by the state, so, for instance, the state recognition of chiefdoms is bound to favour the voices of chiefs (Barcham, 2000). The importance of these mediating institutions in defining culture and determining which aspects of identity should and should not be recognised has often been pointed out, as has their interest in stressing cultural differences: 'perfect communication will mean that the middleman is out of a job' (Bailey, 1969 quoted in Collier, 1976; Shipton and Goheen, 1992).

We thus leave this brief tour of present insights into the relations between law, power and culture with the understanding that law, by its very nature, cannot mirror cultural diversity. Instead, it will privilege and freeze certain voices, versions and visions of culture, often those that best emphasise the difference that forms the rationale for state recognition.

The constitutive effects of cultural rights legislation

Mamone, 30 June 1999: The sun sets and the village flares up orange as the kgôrô disperses. The warm wind brings not only whiffs of woodfires but also snippets of heated conversations on the case discussed all afternoon: that of a man who had started to allocate plots of land without the chief's permission, and as a punishment had – a few days earlier – been beaten up severely and tied to the thorn-tree, his bleeding wounds smeared with vaseline to make them doubly attractive to the red ants. Two men stand leaning against a tree. 'How can they do this? We are not a separate nation here, where the laws of the land don't apply,' says one as he draws a circle in his wrinkled hand to underscore his point. The other shakes his head quizzically: 'Of course we are. Why else would we have a chief?'

In the previous section we considered what cultural rights legislation *is* and concluded that, for all its claims to represent cultural diversity, it will always amount to an imperfect mirroring of fluid local realities, the strengthening of some voices and the exclusion of others. Immediately, a related but even more neglected question comes up: What does cultural rights legislation *do?* In other words, what are the local constitutive effects of the legal recognition of cultural diversity? For example, Clifford's description of the Mashpee case referred to above did not stop with a description of how suburban New Englanders were forced to produce a narrative of continuous and bounded tribalism to have their claims recognised. He also showed how, in the course of the trial, the Mashpee Indians increasingly started to live the story the law forced them to tell, complete with forming new tribal structures, holding pow-wows and wearing beads, in a way that went far beyond the merely performative (Clifford, 1988). These and other cases raise the question: does state recognition of certain aspects of custom, culture and chieftaincy, of certain narratives of communalism and difference, lead to a strengthening of these forces and visions within the local political arena? And if so, in what way?

It has long been recognised that this issue, 'the dialectic, mutually constitutive relation between state law and other normative orders', should be the central concern of contemporary socio-legal studies (Falk Moore, 1973; Fuller, 1994; Merry 1988; F. Von Benda-Beckmann, 1984; Wilson, 2000). To quote Sally Engle Merry (1992:358):

> A focus on the dialectic, mutually constitutive relations between state law and other normative orders emphasises the interconnectedness of social orders and the vulnerability of local places to structures of domination far outside their immediate worlds. This theoretical position considers how state law penetrates and restructures other normative orders and how non-state normative orders resist and circumvent penetration or how they even capture and appropriate state law.

Again, customary law studies have laid some of the foundation. There is, for instance, Sally Falk Moore's famous analysis of the Chagga in Tanzania as a semi-autonomous social field, which has the capacity to make rules and ensure compliance but is simultaneously firmly placed within the 'wider social matrix' of the state (Falk Moore, 1973; 1978, 1986). This interpretation caused her to write, long before her colleagues would, that 'the place of state-enforceable law in ongoing social affairs, and its relation to other effective rules, needs much more scholarly attention' (1973:81). Similarly, there is work such as Mamdani's, which stresses how the form of colonial power also shaped the resistance to it, with people partially appropriating the ethnic categories imposed upon them and using them (the Zulu nation, Pedi dances, chieftaincy structures) as instruments for emancipation (Kossler, 1998; Mamdani, 1996; Ranger, 1993, 1982; Vail, 1989). His analysis has recently been complemented with a growing body of subtle analysis of how chiefship 'was made acceptable, given meaning and imbued with respect and awe' (Spear, 2003:10). Vaughan's work on Nigerian chiefs and Berry's and Rathbone's analysis of the discursive relations between chiefs and the Ghanaian state, and the role of customary law in this discourse, offer some prime examples (Vaughan, 2000; Berry, 2000; Rathbone, 2000). But these works, with their focus on colonialism, fail to address the essential novelty of the present situation, with democracies legally recognising cultural pluralism within a globalising world order.

In the enquiry into the 'constitutive relation' between state law and other polities some of the more general conceptual tools of socio-legal studies can also be of use, for instance those devised to understand the relations between law and social change. Here, two approaches have emerged in the course of the twentieth century: the instrumentalist and the constitutive (Garth and Sarat, 1998:2). The instrumentalists, who set out to examine 'what social results can be attributed to law or legal reforms', ended up disappointed and concluded that 'the effects of law are highly unpredictable (ibid.)[46] Of late, however, the constitutive approach has reconceptualised law more as 'a pervasive influence in structuring society than as a variable whose occasional impact can be measured. Law is seen as a way of organising the world into categories and concepts which, while providing spaces and opportunities, also constrain behaviour and serve to legitimate authority' (ibid.). The emphasis is thus on the culturally productive capacity of law, the way in which people 'conceive, create and sustain definitions of situations'.[47] The constitutive approach once again firmly places law in the social and political domain: 'While against instrumentalism, it reaffirms both the importance of social science to law and the importance of law to social science' (ibid.:4).

The challenge is thus to apply such a constitutive approach to the specific topic of cultural rights: what does state recognition of customary law and chiefly authority mean locally? Despite its theoretical importance being widely recognised, this topic has suffered a surprising neglect in legal anthropology, which has long tended to (and often still does) concentrate on an isolated description of the legal process in a given community.[48] In one of the few exceptions, an excellent study on marriage law amongst the Bakwena in Botswana, Anne Griffiths notes with surprise how even the paradigmatic *Rules and Processes* pays no attention to the influence of Western or European law on local debates on Tswana laws and customs, and relates this to apartheid conditions: 'legal pluralism was not viewed in positive terms and local people strenuously sought to insulate local dispute processes from the broader domain of the state' (Griffiths, 1987:28). This, was no longer possible in the 1990s, when she found that 'an ethnographic approach to the study of law ... undermines any theoretical distinction that is drawn between Western and customary law' (ibid.:2).

Some of the literature on group rights outside Africa underlines the importance of looking at the constitutive effects of cultural rights legislation. Wendy Espeland, for instance, described how a bureaucratically implemented law created a forum and framework for reinterpreting the collective identity of a Native American community involved in a dispute over the location of a dam in central Arizona (1994: 1150). She remarked how, in representing the interests of a group, the law may simultaneously construct the subject holding those interests: 'law, whether enacted by bureaucrats, lawyers, or litigants, creates categories that become imposed on and practised in the world' (ibid.:1176).

[46] J.M. Otto, 'Law and Administration in Developing Countries,' in 'Introduction – Seminar 'Traditional Authorities in a New South Africa'. Leiden: unpublished, 1996. p.7. Cf. Allott, (1980); Griffiths (1996); John Griffiths, 'De Effectiviteit Van Het Recht: Is 'Rechtspluralisme Een Deel Van Het Probleem of Is Het Een Deel Van De Oplossing?' in *De Onvermijdelijkheid Van Rechtspluralisme*, ed. G. Anders, S. Bloemink and N.F. Van Manen, 23–30. Amsterdam: Ars Aequi Libri, 1998.

[47] Foucault (1993); Sally Engle Merry, '1994 Presidential Address Law and Society Association'. *Law & Society Review* 29, no. 1 (1995): 11–26; Snyder (1981).

[48] A few South African examples are: Bekker (1989); Coertze (1990); Olivier et al. (1995); Prinsloo (1983). Exceptions to this general observation are, notably, the work of Sally Falk Moore quoted earlier and the excellent Collier (1976).

Similarly, Willem Assies considered the 'ethnogenesis' that took place in many South American countries in the 1990s, a dialectic between voluntary identification and forced ascription, and underlined how the chances offered by the law also affected relations of power and processes of stratification in indigenous society (2000:6).

> Indigenous mobilisation can be viewed as involving processes of identity (re-)formation through the interaction between ascription and identification. It shows how, whatever their roots in tradition, qualities such as a special non-materialist and spiritual relation to the land, consensual decision-making and communitarianism are emphasised and given new meaning in an ongoing confrontation or dialogue with other social actors (ibid.)[49]

This also resounds with fears voiced by those legal scholars who are posed against the recognition of communal rights and who emphasise that 'groups are not homogeneous but dynamic, heterogeneous historical associations of individuals...To treat them otherwise is to risk empowering elites within groups and creating problems for "internal minorities"' (Ivison et al., 2000:6)

A focus on what cultural rights legislation *does* locally is also important because it allows us to move beyond a mere debunking of the myth of customary law to questions of substance (Assies, 1997:16) Now that it is clear that traditions might often be invented and communal identities, myths and customs created, it is time to move on and look at the substance and meaning of the surprising reappropriation of parts of these imposed identities by 'traditional communities'. One such appropriation is the resurgence of chieftaincy. If we accept that official customary law not only comprises an imperfect mirroring of local reality but *also* possibly beams back at this reality, affecting social and political formations, constituting identities, strengthening certain positions and suppressing others, the question arises as to how this relates to the revival of traditional authority.

The resurgence of traditional leadership

The time has come to extend these hypotheses to the resurgence of traditional leadership all over Africa. Starting from the assumption that cultural rights legislation not only mirrors but also constitutes locally lived realities, creates categories and shapes identities, the following question arises: Could it be that the fact that nation-states all over Africa strengthened the formal position of traditional leaders at the end of the twentieth century, was not only reflective but also constitutive of chiefly powers? Is there a much more complex relation between the local resurrection of traditional authority and its reflection in national legislation than is commonly assumed? If cultural rights legislation could lead to the 'Iwi-isation of New Zealand's Maoris, the communalisation of South America's *pueblos indigenas*, and the reviving of pow-wows amongst the Mashpee, could it not form part of the causes of the resurgence of traditional authority instead of a mere consequence? It is this idea that will be explored further in the course of this study, guided by observations such as that of Englebert, who noted that the surprising resurgence of traditional authority seems to take place especially in *strong* states – Uganda, Ghana, South Africa – alongside their (default) revival in collapsed or failed states (Englebert, 2000).

[49] Cf. Abbink (1997); Robins (1997, 2001).

Such an approach would amount to quite a radical departure from the views commonly held on the position of traditional leaders locally. Here, there are two positions, both striking in their simplicity. The first amounts to a variation on 'debunking the myth of customary law'. It points out how state-recognised chieftaincies were colonial inventions, 'tinpot autocrats' rigged up with a host of non-traditional functions, bureaucratic fallacies put in place merely to bolster the state's legitimacy (Costa, 1999b; Hammond-Tooke, 1975; Herbst, 2000; Jordan, 1997; Mamdani, 1996). By implication, the argument goes on, the traditional leaders have been distanced from their followers, who would prefer to have them replaced with democratic structures, even if false consciousness might stop them from realising this themselves (Mamdani, 1996; Ntsebeza, 1999; Ntsebeza and Hendriks, 2000; Zuma, 1990). A second approach swings the other way but is equally straightforward. It underlines how traditional leadership yields a legitimacy that is rooted in culture and tradition, in a completely different rationale from that of the state.[50] 'They operate from cosmological views that are totally different from other groups within society' and 'are the representatives of that other traditional, moral and political order' (Van Rouvenoy van Nieuwaal, 1996:48,54). As South African Minister Valli Moosa said on the introduction of the Council of Traditional Leaders Bill to Parliament: 'As long as the people who live in faraway valleys, majestic green hills, on widely stretched out plains and mountainsides honour and support traditional leaders, the Government of the day will support and respect traditional leaders, as they are the custodians of people's culture and we are a people's government.'[51]

How can these fairly unsophisticated positions continue to resound in spite of evidence of people embracing and reviving the 'bureaucratic fallacies' imposed on them by national governments, on the one hand, and, on the other, chiefs seeking alliances with the state and becoming state agents rather than representatives of a completely different moral order? A main reason, as we shall see, is the lack of empirical research delving into *people's opinions* on traditional leadership and their motivations for such views.

As stated above, the growing and often excellent scientific literature on chieftaincy is mostly concerned with interactions between traditional leaders and the national (often colonial) state. A review of this literature by Thomas Spear shows how its emphasis shifted from the notion of a top-down 'invention of tradition', as central in Ranger's *locus classicus*, to a more nuanced analysis of the discursive relation between states and chiefs, and the reciprocal processes of legitimation (Ranger, 1993). Olufemi Vaughan, for instance, in a comprehensive discussion of a century of interactions between the state and chiefs in Nigeria, describes 'the creative response of indigenous political structures to the problems of modernization and governance that have engulfed the African continent during the past century' (2000:1). Two recent works on Ghana, Berry's *Chiefs Know Their Boundaries* and Rathbone's *Nkrumah and the Chiefs* also specifically focus on this level of interaction.

Thus, the ideas of chiefly subjects on the legitimacy of those who rule them is a relatively neglected topic (cf. Mamdani, 1996; Van Rouveroy van Nieuwaal and Van Dijk, 1999; Vaughan, 2000). In addition, the ethnographic studies that

[50] Herbst (2000); Konrad Adenauer Stiftung (1997); Kossler (1998); Van Rouveroy van Nieuwaal (1999); Van Rouveroy van Nieuwaal and Ray (1996); Von Trotha (1996).

[51] RSA House of Assembly Debates, 14 November 1994, cl 4237, quoted in Myers (1999:52).

do look at the position of traditional leaders locally tend to omit the state, either for political reasons or because it had not encroached too far on community life when they were written (Comaroff, 1974, 1978; Hammond-Tooke, 1974; Kuper, 1970; Prinsloo, 1983). Thus, the 'competing forms of authority within government systems at the "base" of society' remain 'grossly under-researched and undertheorised.'[52] It is in this field that this book also seeks to make a contribution.

5. An approach to the study

Even if this study is essentially about chiefs and customs in one area – Sekhukhune in the Northern Province of South Africa – it arises out of an interest in the complex ties that link this locality and its chieftaincy politics to the national and even the global level, making these interactions its central focus. This theme, the complex links between official legal recognition and socio-political change, calls for a specific approach that provides a detailed ethnographic account of local dynamics concerning chieftaincy and customary law while also keeping a firm eye on the 'wider social matrix' in which they are positioned. In the following pages I shall give a brief outline of this approach – that of multi-sited ethnographic research – and some of the issues of definition and research methods that it raises.

'The locality'

> *The Leolo mountains, October 1998: Beehive-shaped straw huts, banana trees, boys drinking milk straight from the cows they are herding, children peeking in amazement at the first white face they have seen – the villages that we come across while looking for a field site in the mountains, all unreachable by car, are storybook Africa, and live up to any field-work fantasy I might have had. Even if I decide not to do the research in this part of the mountains, I shall always cherish memories of the uniqueness and remoteness of the world we briefly peek into. However, a few months later my memories have to be slightly adjusted: I sit in the provincial capital, eating pizza with university students. 'Were you up in the Leolo mountains?' they squeak. 'Don't you know that they have the best dagga in the world there, even better than the stuff you have in Holland? Why didn't you bring us some....' Suddenly I realise that the remoteness of the villages we visited might well be by choice, and instead of being an indication of their detachment from the outside world may be precisely the opposite: a sign of their interlinkage with the global economy and dope smokers worldwide...*

Since Malinowski's work, anthropology has essentially been about doing 'field research' in remote places that 'one could fly, paddle or trek to in order to record all of the material practices, ecological adaptation, marriage patterns, religious beliefs, and legal habits of a spatially-contained people (Drummond, 2000:49). However, now that 'traditional societies' are 'negotiating their own multifaceted, globally connected modernities, having long left behind legal anthropology's

[52] Jeremy Gould. 'Resurrecting Makumba: Chiefly Powers and the Local State in Zambia's Third Republic' (1998: 3). Cf. Falk Moore (1975:744); Gould (1997); Khadija Magardie, 'Customary Law Undermines Constitutional Rights.' *Mail & Guardian*, 15 June 2000; Ray and Van Rouveroy van Nieuwaal (1996:3).

conventional pieties about holistic legal systems', such a bounded approach becomes increasingly untenable. A researcher interested in Peruvian Indians cannot merely travel to a remote village with a field diary under his or her arm, but should also show up at the UN General Assembly, in BBC studios, at national protest marches and in the virtual community of first nations linked through the Internet. Of late, anthropologists have begun to recognise this need, to speak of a 'process geography' and 'travelling cultures' and to emphasise how localities are 'primarily relational and contextual rather than scalar or spatial' (Appadurai, 1996:13; Hughes, 1999; Piot 1999).

Of course there is a paradox here. On the one hand, the official strengthening of a multitude of subnational polities as a result of the dismantling of the nation-state (whether voluntary or not) forces all social scientists, not merely anthropologists, to focus increased attention on them. They have, after all, gained in importance in the (inter)national order. But, on the other hand, the Constitutions and internal political dynamics of these polities cannot be understood without taking into account their encounters with other polities, the state, donor organisations, the international community. The only way to grapple with these 'dialectics of flow and closure' seems to be through what Sally Engle Merry (2001) has called a 'multi-sited' ethnographic approach (see also Meyer and Geschiere, 1999). The interactions between polities, their 'mutually constitutive character', should be central in such an enquiry, in which the researcher moves between points of gravity in changing political formations. 'Too often,' Ferguson writes, 'anthropological approaches to the relation between "the local" and something that lies beyond it (regional, national, international, global) have taken the local as a given, without asking how perceptions of locality and community are discursively and historically constructed' (1994:6).

The dialogue that is central to this book is between two loosely defined sets of polities: the South African national state and the chiefdom of Sekhukhune, in the Northern Province. There are, of course, many other polities involved in the creation of meaning concerning chiefly powers and customary laws that will have a place in the narrative: from old-time classics such as the municipalities, the provinces and the international community to powerful donors, churches and vigilante organisations. One consequence of this approach is that it serves to relativise the role of the nation-state while simultaneously acknowledging the uniqueness of the tasks it has officially reserved for itself. Considering the nation-state as not simply yet another player in a wider and fluid playing field of sub- and supra-national polities demands that it, too, be approached ethnographically, so that its social and political forces can be unearthed, its discourses critically examined and its laws considered in context. As such, the state in itself comes to be considered as a locality, in a way not very different from the ethnographic approach taken in Sekhukhune.

In its approach to the locality and its interlinkages with the outside world this study can draw on the way in which many (legal) anthropologists have conceptualised local 'social fields' or 'political arenas'.[53] For all their differences, they emphasise how these fields are characterised by some form of political authority, their ability to produce rules and to ensure their compliance. It is

[53] Bierschenk and Olivier de Sardan (1998, 1997); Bierschenk and Le Meur (1999); Bourdieu (1990, 1977); Crehan (1997), Falk Moore (1973); Kuper (1970); Otto (1987); Sahlins (1999); Scott (1985).

because of this political dimension that I prefer to use the term 'polity' or 'political arena'. The more sophisticated work on 'localities' has also pointed to their porousness and the way in which, for instance, they filter state laws, deconstructing them and taking over what is of use while ignoring the rest (Collier, 1976; Falk Moore, 1973). The work of development anthropologists like Bierschenk and Olivier de Sardan is particularly useful in this context. In examining how local political arenas deal with the three Ds of the 1990s – democratisation, decentralisation and development – they came up with a theoretical framework, based on that of the Manchester school, which distinguishes actors, resources and '*logiques d'action*' (strategies) (Bierschenk and Olivier de Sardan, 1998; cf. Gulliver, 1979). Such an approach, as we shall see, can also be applied successfully when analysing local law-making and the legitimation of chiefly rule.

Traditional leaders, living law

The multi-sited research approach that I have chosen and the focus on the skewed dialogue on chiefly authority and customary law within and between polities inevitably throw up some issues of definition. If we accept that meanings are created dialogically, and both reflect and constitute social and power relations, then it becomes practically impossible to divorce these meanings from the context in which they are created. For example: the South African state might well have on its payroll as a 'traditional leader' someone who lives in Johannesburg and has no contact with his supposed subjects. Conversely, people in Sekhukhune might follow a *kgoši* (traditional leader) who hands out land, settles disputes, is widely respected but has no contact whatsoever with the state. The same goes for 'customary law': there are rules codified as such that lead no 'social life' whatsoever, since people have hardly heard of them. Simultaneously, local, living law, 'the outcome of the interplay between international law, state law and local norms that takes place through human interaction in different historical, social and legal contexts', might contain rules that are widely known and followed and easily enforced, but to which the national state turns a blind eye (Hellum, 1999:62).

How then can we define the notions that are central to this study: traditional leadership and customary law? The only way would seem to be through taking a non-essentialist approach and planting definitions and meanings firmly in the contexts in which they are generated, instead of seeking to sever them from their contents. The lessons offered by customary law studies are, again, pertinent: culture cannot be understood outside of its context of social interactions and power relations, and the best that researchers can do is to map out this whole fluctuating landscape. A similar approach seems to have gained common ground in contemporary socio-legal studies. Long after legal anthropologists had declared the rule-centred paradigm in law to be moribund, socio-legal scholars such as Brian Tamanaha also came to acknowledge law as a 'thoroughly cultural construct' (2000:312; see also Comaroff and Roberts, 1981; Just, 1992). In his influential 2000 article, he argued that the litmus test for any definition of law should be whether it 'enhances our ability to describe, understand, study, analyse and evaluate legal phenomena' (2000:300). This can only be done by taking a non-essentialist approach and stating that 'law is whatever people identify and treat through their social practices as law' (ibid.:313). A similar definitional approach could be taken to traditional leadership in considering as a traditional leader someone who, in a given set of circumstances, is recognised as such. Just as the 'spatial and temporal validity' of law needs mapping out, so does the spatial and temporal authority of traditional leadership (Hellum, 1999:62).

This contextualist, non-essentialist approach does not mean that issues of substance are irrelevant. Law, whether considered as such by the people of Sekhukhune or by the South African state, will always be about rules, and the institutions involved in issuing them, perpetuating them and punishing their violation. Likewise, traditional authority will always refer to a structure of governance that derives part of its legitimation from an association with the past. It also does not mean that definitions are insignificant, mere labels without consequences. Quite the contrary: a traditional leader officially recognised as such by the South African state is entitled to a state salary, a host of official functions, the support of a bureaucratic apparatus. Whether a South African court recognises a marriage as sealed according to 'customary law' can make the difference between obtaining or being refused a deceased husband's pension benefits. Similarly, being recognised as a *kgoši* in Sekhukhune opens the door to many privileges, just as the question of whether or not a norm is *molao*, can mean the difference between winning or losing a case or a plot of land, or being chased from the village. My point is merely that these definitions cannot, and should not, be understood outside of the context in which they are generated. The vital point is not how 'law' and 'traditional leadership' are defined, but who has the power to issue definitions, or, as Tamanaha puts it, 'who identifies what as "customary law", why, and under what circumstances' and how definitions generated in different polities intersect and help to constitute one another (2000:318)

The locality of study

The 'locality' in this study, the paramount chieftaincy of Sekhukhune, in South Africa's Northern Province, is characterised by red sands, agaves and cacti, ant hills, with its crowded betterment settlements with shining corrugated iron shacks scattered around bottlestores and jam-packed taxi ranks, advertisements for Sunlight soap and Omo towering above them, as well as extensive settlements, with cows grazing peacefully next to the maize fields. To some, locals and migrants alike, Sekhukhune, or Bopedi, is home, the heartland of Pedi identity, cradle of its customs and bearer of a proud history. To the majority of South Africans, however, who will not find Sekhukhune on any map, it is a dustbowl, an unattractive rural backdrop, one of the country's poorest areas in one of its poorest provinces. If the name sounds vaguely familiar, it is because of the Sekhukhune youth revolt against the bantustans in the 1980s, or the rampant witchcraft killings in the 1990s, that made sensational headlines. In Mandela's frequent references to the courageous Sekhukhune, it is not clear whether he meant Sekhukhune I, who stood up to the Boers at the end of the nineteenth century, or Sekhukhune II, who led the 1950s revolt against the bantustan policies. Their resistance was the main reason that the paramountcy was divided into 56 chieftaincies and the name Sekhukhune was wiped off the official map, only to resurface again in 2000 when a new municipality was dubbed 'Greater Sekhukhune'.

The estimated 200,000 people who live on its approximately 1100 square kilometres are mostly Bapedi, speakers of the Northern Sotho language Sepedi.[54] Although the larger settlements house an increasing number of not only other South Africans but also immigrants, these are often frowned upon: 'Since Mandela married Graca Machel all those Mozambicans think that they are welcome here.' If any label sticks to the Bapedi, it is that of a proud and resilient people. 'Die Bapedi is korrelkoppe en hul stamme almal deurmekaar' (The Bapedi are hotheads and their tribes completely mixed up), commented the government anthropologist who tried to talk me into selecting a 'neater tribe'. It is true that Sekhukhune history is largely one of revolt: against the Swazi and the Boers in the 1880s, against the imposition of the Lebowa bantustan in the 1950s, and against oppressive chieftaincy structures in the 1980s. Also, their 'splendid isolation', if it ever existed, has for more than a century been replaced by an intensive engagement with the outside world, with Bapedi working in mines on the Reef, in homes in Johannesburg and wherever else money can be made.

This combination of factors was one of the reasons to choose it as a research site. A second was the relative emphasis in South African studies on questions of Zulu and Xhosa identity formation and engagement with the wider state (cf. De Haas and Zulu, 1994; Switser, 1993). A third, equally important, reason was the availability of some excellent historical work on Sekhukhune: Delius' *The Land Belongs to Us* and *A Lion amongst the Cattle,* both largely based on oral testimonies, allow for a retracing of chieftaincy politics into the beginning of the nineteenth century, while Van Kessel's '*Beyond our Wildest Dreams*' gives an equally detailed account of the Sekhukhune youth uprising of the 1980s (see also Delius, 1990). And while the (legal) anthropological research done in Sekhukhune is no match for the size and sophistication of the work done for instance, on the Tswana-speaking people, the work of Deborah James on kinship and ethnicity in bordering areas provides a very useful point of reference.[55]

Even if Sekhukhune can, according to the people who live there, be considered a separate polity, bounded by history, linguistic ties and the paramountcy, it is also a large area which accommodates 56 officially recognised chiefdoms. This study has concentrated on three of them, which have been selected as paradigm cases and provide diverging scenarios of the engagements between the locality and the state, and between chiefs, their subjects and the wider world. The chiefdom of Ga-Masha was clearly a product of apartheid social engineering and *kgoši* Masha spent most of his time in the magistrate's office at the Provincial Department of Traditional Affairs or with the Land Claims Commission, seeking, like a true ethnic broker state support for his claims to authority. The way in which Mamone, our second case-study, engaged with the state was quite the

[54] These figures can only be but rough estimates: as we shall see in Chapter 4, the boundaries of Sekhukhune are disputed and there is very little recent reliable demographic information available. The population and size quoted are those of the Greater Ngwaritsi Makhudu-Thamaga Transitional Local Council, which roughly – but far from completely – corresponded with the borders of what many people consider Sekhukhune to have been in the 1995–2000 period: A. McIntosh, 'Situational Analysis: Status Quo Report for the Setting of Land Development Objectives for Ngwaritsi TLC.' 219, Undated, pp. 100–1.

[55] The (legal) ethnographic works on the Bapedi are all very much old-school, with clear links to apartheid policies. Cf. Harries (1929); Mönnig (1978, 1983); Prinsloo (1970). An exception is the unpublished PhD research of Sansom (1970) who withdrew the manuscript for fear of fuelling apartheid notions on difference. The excellent works of James on the Ndundza Ndebele and issues of ethnicity are good points of reference: James (1990, 1999, 1985).

opposite: even though the area developed rapidly, with electricity and telephone lines being installed every day, the Mamone traditional authority seemed to disengage from involvement with the state and to position itself against it. Hoepakranz, a tiny village in the mountains, provided a third scenario: that of a virtually absent state and quasi self-reliant community. Although none of these cases can be considered as 'representative' (nor could any three others have been), I hope that delving into the debates on chieftaincy and customary law in three such different polities and placing these in the context of Sekhukhune chieftaincy politics does allow for broader analysis of the dynamics at work in the 'mutually constitutive' relations between chiefdoms and the state in present-day South Africa.

Methodology

Even though I had visited South Africa earlier, my first encounter with its traditional leaders came in 1995, when I was recruited as a student-assistant to the Traditional Authorities Research Group. Funded by the Dutch Ministry of Foreign Affairs, this South African–Dutch research collaboration had a year to look into the present position of traditional leadership and come up with policy recommendations. For all the excitement and merits of the project – working with a cross-cultural team in a fast-changing South Africa in which everything still seemed possible – the year went much too fast. At the end, after we had presented a ten-volume report to the Minister, containing the 1500-odd laws on traditional leadership still applicable, an overview of the literature, a few interviews and a discussion of the policy options, many of us felt that we had only scratched the surface (Traditional Authorities Research Group, 1996). There had been too little time to examine the changing local dynamics, and people's perceptions on traditional leadership. The group dispersed and went back to every-day academic work, but I had the freedom of doctoral funding and was able to devise a project that would concentrate on what was changing in the countryside and how the watershed national events affected South Africa's rural areas.

During visits to South Africa in 1995–6 (two months), 1997 (three months) and at the beginning of 1998 (three months) I concentrated mostly on the national policy process.[56] Even after I shifted focus to the 'locality' in October 1998, I kept in contact with national actors and followed the major discussions. As a result, the primary data woven into the following narrative roughly cover the 1995–2001 period and allow for a relatively longitudinal analysis.

After having struggled with Sepedi to the level where I could communicate independently and follow normal conversations, I set off in 1998 for twelve months field-work. The first priority was to find a research assistant. After a series of interviews with Bapedi law students, I was lucky enough to run into Patson Phala, a local newsreader widely known and liked but not attached to any political or chiefly faction, who proved to be an indispensable companion. While he communicated just as easily with kings and vagabonds, tribal elders and female activists, he schooled me in the mores of traditional society. After a tour of about fifteen traditional authority areas, we settled on the three divergent chieftaincies identified above, spending about four months in each of them.

The research in each chiefdom followed a familiar pattern. In the first weeks,

[56] My MA thesis in political science reflects part of this work: Oomen (1996).

we would very much be the official guests, asked to explain our mission and given a front seat at meetings. Interviews would be *'en groupe'*, with people providing staccato answers which nearly always were much more an indication of what they thought we wanted to hear than a real reflection of local affairs. Gradually, however, the novelty of our presence wore off and we were able to take a more 'fly on the wall' approach, observing meetings and court cases, chatting with villagers, mapping out the institutional landscape and getting into the dynamics of local politics.

My initial fear, as a white woman, of not having access to chiefs and court cases proved unfounded. On the contrary, many men appeared flattered by the research project and keen to demonstrate and discuss the value of the traditional way of conducting politics and settling cases, even if it did take some time before they were comfortable enough to inflict corporal punishment in our presence (a phenomenon I personally never managed to come to terms with). What proved more difficult was the chance to speak to the subaltern voices, the marginalised, the strangers, the people outside the heat of village politics. The decision to do quantitative research with questionnaire interviews in addition to the qualitative ethnographic research proved useful here; 607 people responded, about 120 in each chiefdom plus another 240 in wider Sekhukhune as a control group.[57] The Probability Proportionate to Size method we used also enabled access to homesteads we would never have visited otherwise. Nevertheless, at the end of each case study we would be struck by the feeling that we were only just 'getting behind things', only in part remedied by later return visits and correspondence long after I had returned to the Netherlands at the end of 1999.[58]

It is on the basis of these conversations – under the peach trees with an old lady in Hoepakranz, driving Constitutional Court Judge Albie Sachs around Johannesburg with a tape recorder on my lap, over a luxury lunch with *kgoši* Sekwati Mampuru – as well as a host of observations and archival, primary and secondary sources, that the following narrative has been written. Each of these conversations, in a way, is a snapshot of a country undergoing massive changes, both nationally and locally, at a time when there was unprecedented belief in the ability to forge change, to bring about 'a better life for all'. It is hoped that stringing these snapshots together and holding them against the light of other evidence will enable a more longitudinal and dynamic analysis of the forces at work in a country with a people in the midst of 'the complex process simultaneously of formation and renewal', of identity search and reinvention.

[57] N = 607, of which 52% female; 5% aged under 20, 28% 20–30, 22% 30–40, 19% 40–50, 14% 50–60 and 12% 60 +; 20% no education, 21% up to standard 6, 42% standard 6–10, 7% matric, 7% technicon, 3% university; only 27% formally employed; This is more or less representative of the Sekhukhune *adult* population as a whole (cf: CSS, Development Bank of South Africa. 'Statistical Macroeconomic Review Northern Province.' Midrand: Development Bank of South Africa, 1995). and based on Probability Proportionate to Size samples in the three fieldwork areas (N=367) and other Sekhukhune traditional authority areas (N=240) (see on PPS-sampling Russel Bernard (1995)). The interviews were conducted by Tsepo Phasha, Patson Phala and myself or by two of us, usually in Sepedi, in personal, face-to-face interviews based on a Sepedi questionnaire with 45 closed and open questions, which would typically take 1–2 hours and have been translated into English by the interviewers.

[58] In devising a field research strategy, I have been greatly assisted by the works of Glaser and Strauss (1967) and their emphasis on grounded theory, as well as the general work by Russell Bernard (1995) and Strauss and Corbin (1990).

6. Outline of the study

Reflecting its interest in the linkages between two polities – the national and the local – this book is divided into two parts. Its opening chapters deal with the national debates that erupted in post-apartheid South Africa on the future of traditional leadership and customary law. Chapter 2 seeks to establish what has been assumed up to now: that, far from disappearing with the new order, chieftaincy and customary law were strengthened in vital areas like land tenure and local government, Chapter 3 investigates *why* this was the case. It argues that a specific set of circumstances, both inside and outside South Africa, enabled traditional leaders themselves to take centre stage in debates about their future. As a result, the policy options formulated and the laws passed were largely based on the assumptions they presented: about rural-urban difference, the character of rural communities, the coherence of customary law and the centrality of traditional leadership in rural governance.

It is with these assumptions in mind that we then turn to the locality of Sekhukhune and consider how they compare with the local realities of chieftaincy and custom. Chapter 4 serves as an introduction to the local political arena and its history, introducing its main actors and the revival of traditional authority among them. Chapter 5 deals explicitly with the 'under-researched and under-theorised' question of the present-day legitimacy of traditional leadership, revolving around three sets of questions: who supports traditional leaders, in what way do they do so, and what does this mean for the legitimacy of the institution? Surprisingly, traditional leaders derive legitimacy not only from tradition, religion or their own performance, but also explicitly from the government support they receive. Chapter 6 focuses on the local perspectives towards the second research topic, customary law. What is the local living law pertaining to traditional leadership? This living law is essentially negotiated within the local social and political field, in numerous areas of debate, where state law, whether 'official customary law' or the Constitution, can also be called in as a resource.

Thus, the linkages between the local and the national, the dynamics of their 'mutually constitutive relation', are woven throughout the narrative. Their theoretical implications are set out in Chapter 7, the concluding chapter. I begin by summarising the answers provided to the first two research questions; what were the relations between the changing legal and socio-political position of traditional authority and customary law in the new South Africa and how did they arise? Third, what does this teach us about the interrelation between laws, politics and culture in the post-modern world? By focusing on both the process in which cultural rights legislation is formulated and its local constitutive effects, I hope to contribute to theory formulation in this increasingly important field of study.

2. The Patchwork Democracy

Boundary Politics after 1994

What happens to a dream deferred?
...
Maybe it just sags
like a heavy load.
Or does it explode?[1]

1. Introduction

Athough the South African Department of Native Affairs was renamed Traditional Affairs after the transition to democracy, many things stayed the same. For instance, the maps depicting the borders of homeland and chieftaincy areas like a colourful patchwork continued to adorn the department's corridors long after the country had officially been reunified. Apartheid, as has often been remarked, was essentially a spatial endeavour, an exercise of mapping, creating separate territorial spaces each with its own political, administrative and legal rationalities.[2] The political geography set out in atlases produced before the transition in 1994 is one which, apart from presenting 'white', 'coloured' and 'Indian' areas, is flecked with the four independent homelands – Transkei, Boputhatswana, Venda and Ciskei – and the six self-governing territories, many of them scattered in ragged tatters in the vast surrounding area.[3]

It is not surprising that it was remapping, just like rewriting history, that was one of the new regime's first priorities. The prospect of a unitary, democratic South Africa in which artificial boundaries like those of the homelands and created chieftaincies would be erased once and for all to make way for equality in spatial planning loomed large. At first glance, the new government was

[1] The African-American poet Langston Hughes, quoted in Thabo Mbeki's famous 'Two Nations' speech in 1998: 'The African Renaissance, South Africa and the Rest of the World', Address at the United Nations University, Tokyo: Unpublished, 1998, p. 76. The complete poem is:
What happens to a dream deferred?
Does it dry up
Like a raisin in the sun?
Or fester like a sore–
And then run?
Does it stink like rotten meat?
Or crust and sugar over–
like a syrupy sweet?
Maybe it just sags
like a heavy load.
Or does it explode?

[2] Cf. Hughes. (1999:3) speaking of the 'territorialization of power' and the transformation of 'rule by enslavement to rule by land-holding.'

[3] The self-governing territorites were KwaZulu, Kangwane, Qwaqwa, Gazankulu, Kwandebele and Lebowa.

successful. Atlases published after the transition proudly show one country, with nine new provinces and no mention of areas like Qwaqwa, Kangwane and Lebowa. In the more detailed versions, regional and municipal boundaries replaced those of chieftaincies. But the overhaul was largely superficial, and it was not without reason that the Traditional Affairs officials stuck to their old maps. Six years after the first democratic elections in 1994, almost all the institutional arrangements that singled out the former homelands as separate spheres of rule, largely under chiefly jurisdiction, were still in place. The social reality largely remained a reflection of the geographical inequality created and implemented under apartheid, and driving into a former homeland automatically meant potholed roads, barefoot children and overcrowded corrugated iron shacks. What is more striking is that the whole web of administrative and legislative arrangements that partly gave rise to these conditions also remained in place. For instance, even when new legislation on local government and land tenure was passed, the old arrangements based on the Black Administration Act and the Black Authorities Act continued to apply simultaneously.

The chapter will take a closer look at the way the South African legal and institutional map was redrawn after 1994. In doing so, it attempts to address the question of the extent to which the new government managed to efface the country's patchy and unequal institutional legacy, and argues that this was hardly the case. In particular with regard to the position of traditional authorities in, for instance, local government, land use and the administration of justice, the changes were far fewer than most observers would have expected in 1990. Not only, for instance, did the more than 1500 pieces of legislation conferring powers on traditional leaders continue to apply into the twenty-first century, they were also confirmed and supplemented with new privileges.[4]

As mentioned in Chapter 1, the paradigmatic position from which to understand the institutional legacy of apartheid has become that of the Ugandan professor Mahmood Mamdani, who refined earlier thinking on the character and structure of power in the post-colonial state.[5] In his *Citizen and Subject*, he describes the 'bifurcated' legacy of the colonial state, with its different modes of rule for 'citizens' in the urban areas and 'subjects' in the rural parts of the country. In the latter, traditional leaders wield power as 'decentralized despots' over a forcibly created customary world in which Africans are 'containerized' as tribespeople and custom is the outcome of a struggle skewed heavily in favour of the state (Ntsebeza, 1999:2–5). As Thabo Mbeki would put it in 1998: 'The reality of two nations, underwritten by the perpetuation of the racial, gender and spatial disparities born of a very long period of colonial and apartheid white minority domination, constitutes the material base which reinforces the notion that, indeed, we are not one nation, but two nations.'[6]

[4] Sapa. 'SA Has Moved Beyond Its Devide Past: Mbeki'; ANC news briefing email service: ANC, 2000, in which President Mbeki states that the government will start reviewing the 1500 pieces of legislation pertaining to traditional leaders after the elections. Officials involved in drawing up the Status Quo Report on Traditional Leadership even speak of 10,000 pieces of legislation: Prof. N.J.J. Olivier, project leader Policy Formulation Process on Traditional Leadership 1997–2000, Bremen, 19 April 2002.

[5] Mamdani (1996). To say that a work is paradigmatic does not of course mean that it has not been criticised, cf. Mamdani (1999); Oomen (1998b).

[6] Mbeki. 'The African Renaissance, South Africa and the Rest of the World', p. 72.

What Mamdani's dualistic analysis fails to recognise is the wide variety of local power configurations, structures of rule and degrees of democratisation that occurred as a result of segregationist policies (cf. Oomen, 1998b). In the South African case, the many different laws and regulations passed in individual homelands, regional authorities, and by traditional authorities led to, and comprised proof of, different governance scenarios, but, what is more important, the contours of local rule were essentially created in a dialogue between administrators and traditional authorities, both with wide discretionary powers. It was precisely the combination of the formal autonomy granted to the 'decentralized despots' to govern their areas as 'clenched fists', combining judicial, executive and legislative functions, and the simultaneous presence of other government representatives, that resulted in widely dissimilar outcomes in terms of democratisation and the position of chiefly subjects. While traditional leaders were given large powers on paper, these, in practice, had to be exercised within the confines drawn by the bureaucracy. This created differences in the degree of popular political participation in traditional authority areas, and thus in the degree to which people were citizens or subjects. In that sense, it would seem more appropriate to imagine apartheid's institutional legacy not as bifurcated, but as a *patchwork* of institutionally drawn boundaries within which the degree of public participation was left largely to the discretion of the traditional authority.

Even if the degrees of power that chiefs could wield in their areas differed, it was their formal sovereignty that was essentially at stake, time and again, in the discussions concerning South Africa's future that erupted after De Klerk yielded to the winds of change in 1990. The plea for sovereignty, the ability to control those people living within traditional authority areas and the resources available combined with a lack of outside interference in 'local' affairs, came in different guises. The attempt to have 'the right to culture' exempted from the Bill of Rights was one, as were the efforts to maintain sole jurisdiction within the traditional authority areas, to retain land tenure legislation and to make traditional leaders the 'primary layer' of local government in the rural areas.

How successful this 'boundary politics' was will become clear as we investigate the – scant – changes made to the official position of traditional leaders in the period ranging from 1990, through the transition to democracy in 1994 to roughly the turn of the century. We first take a closer look at the patchy institutional map that formed apartheid's legacy. Subsequently, the way in which South Africa's institutional future was imagined during the constitutional negotiations and in the interim and definitive Constitution will be discussed. The provisions negotiated here, as will be shown, were very general and required working out in subsequent legislation. Until new laws were passed, the old legislation such as the Black Authorities Act and the Black Administration Act would remain in place. After discussing the difficulties encountered in formulating a general Traditional Authorities Act in section 4, we look at the three fields which together determine a great deal of the chiefly sovereignty, and thus the patchwork character of the institutional map: local government, land and customary law (sections 5–7). In all these fields, former privileges were retained, if not consolidated, and the yellowing apartheid maps continued to reflect the institutional and power relations much more adequately than their shiny new replacements. The possible reasons for this form the subject matter of the next chapter.

2. The legacy

'Waiting, waiting for the pain that splits us apart to end, waiting for the birth of our nation,' Lindiwe Mabuza wrote in 1978. Above all, the new rulers inherited a compartamentalised country, an institutional and political patchwork out of which they somehow had to create a unified nation. The homelands, for instance, created as part of the widespread ideology of segregation formulated by Verwoerd and his successors, had become not only political but also demographically distinct entities. Although by 1990 the fiction that *all* black people were to live in the ten homelands had long been abandoned, 44 per cent of the population (nearly 17 million people) still lived in these areas, which comprised a mere 14 per cent of the South African territory.[7] These 'rural slums' – with their high population density and appalling living conditions – were intimately linked to the national economy by means of migrant labour, and literally functioned as 'reserves': for the elderly, the handicapped and the young, at little cost to the mainstream economy.[8]

Ideologically, the pillars of the apartheid government's philosophy were ethnicity, communalism and an emphasis on rural-urban difference (Mamdani, 1999:99).[11] Segregationist, and later apartheid, ideology combined citizenship, political authority, territory and ethnicity into one potent mix (Ashforth, 1997: 109). In an archetypal example of divide-and-rule politics the bantustans were each destined for one ethnic group – Lebowa for the Northern Sotho, Gazankulu for the Shangaan, Venda for the BaVenda and so forth – and thus managed to turn a racial contradiction into an ethnic one.[9] Communalism was a second cornerstone. Under the adage of 'rather Bantu communalism than Bantu communism', Africans were containerised in a world defined by chiefs, customs and communal ideology (Jordan, 1997; Bennett, 1991). The rural/urban dichotomy was a third legitimising principle forcefully implemented in the second half of the twentieth century: even when the rural was often more densely populated than the urban, the two would be presented as vastly different worlds. By the early 1990s, these ideologies, which either drew on remnants of precolonial social structures or had been implemented with such vengeance that they had transformed paper constructions into aspects of local reality, were appropriated and lived as much by local people as by traditional leaders and apartheid policy-makers.[10]

[7] The notion that all Africans were destined to be citizens of one of the homelands had been discarded by 1980 and by 1990 over 12 million black people lived in that part of South Africa designated as 'white.': South African Institute of Race Relations. *Race Relations Survey 1991/1992*. Johannesburg: SAIRR, 1991.

[8] Cf. Beinart and Dubow (1995); Murray (1987); Worden (1994). Although the ten homelands were deemed 'independent', or on their way to being so, South Africa did pump large sums of 'development cooperation' funds into them.

[9] The Transkei and Ciskei were considered Xhosa, Kwazulu Zulu, Qwaqwa Southern Sotho, KwaNdebele (created later) for the Ndebele population and Boputhatswana for the Tswana people. The forced removals took 3.5 million people, many of whom hardly identified with the ethnic category under which they were labelled', back' to these homelands. Cf. Marks and Trapido (1987); Vail (1989); Wilmsen and McAllister (1996).

[10] The fact that 'paper creations' often did become locally lived realities, with parts of the myths presented to them appropriated and internalised by the people concerned, was only recognised in the literature from the 1980s onwards, in works such as Hobsbawm and Ranger (1983), and Vail (1989).

Chieftaincy could be considered the cornerstone of rule in these 'bantustans'. Africans who were ruled in accordance with their own traditional systems (so the official thinking went) would not aspire to anything as threatening for the government as democracy. Traditional leaders formed the majority in all the 'national parliaments', and sat in the gargantuan buildings that – like national flags, stamps and other emblems – served to legitimise the existence of polities that only the South African state would recognise. The 800-odd traditional authorities appointed and paid by the government were also given all the necessary legal, administrative, financial and military support to act as autocrats within their own jurisdictions, though within the confines of the state bureaucracy, on the one hand, and of what was acceptable to their subjects, on the other.[11]

Their formal centrality had only really been developed after the National Party won the 1948 parliamentary elections and started replacing segregationist politics with the more comprehensive ideology of apartheid. Segregationist politics had, of course, been a part of South African life since the arrival of the settlers in the seventeenth century. Worked out by Shepstone – who was inspired by British indirect rule – for KwaZulu/Natal in the 1850s, it was copied for the whole country with the introduction of the 1913 and 1936 Land Acts.[12] Nevertheless, all these laws were mostly about territorial segregation, and not about the creation of separate political spheres. This changed with the implementation of the 1927 Black Administration Act, which provided that the Governor-general, as 'Supreme Chief of all the Blacks' in the country, could recognise and depose chiefs, define the boundaries of any tribal area and could, for instance, 'divide any existing tribe into two or more parts ... or constitute a new tribe ... as necessity or the good government of the Natives may in his opinion require' (Black Administration Act 38/1927, ss 1–3).

Nevertheless, it was only after the narrow NP victory in 1948 that the contours of the policy linking the political, territorial and ethnic within the notion of 'separate development' became visible. 'What was envisaged,' as the South African Bureau of Information would write in its 1990 *Yearbook* (p.4), 'was a number of nation states based in the historical territories of the various Black peoples. Regardless of where they lived, all Blacks associated culturally or otherwise with a particular emergent state would satisfy their political aspirations in that state.' For this, legislation like the Black Authorities Act of 1951 was passed. Implementing this vision was, by any standard, an unsurpassed exercise in social engineering. Not only did 3.5 million deportations to 'ethnic homelands' take place between 1960 and 1979, but these homelands were also parcelled up and subjected to large-scale bureaucratic agricultural projects directed at achieving the impossible: actually creating the pastoral, rural self-subsistence idyll that figured so prominently in government propaganda (Robertson, 1990:128). Expanding the territory of the homelands was not an option, as Verwoerd would explain; 'because they are not good farmers, they should not be

[11] Department of Constitutional Development. *Traditional Leaders*, Pretoria: Department of Constitutional Development, 1994, p. 191. Cf. Maloka (1996), who speaks of 17 kings, paramount chiefs and queens, 787 chiefs, and 2210 headmen.

[12] Cf. Beinart and Dubow (1995); Vail (1989); Worden (1994). The Natives Land Act 27/1913 reserved 7% of the South African territory for native occupation (and limited land ownership rights outside these territories), and this was expanded to 13% in the Native Trust and Land Act 18/1936.

given more land.'[13] There was thus a striking tension between the highly modernist and authoritarian governmental agenda and its central claim: that its policy was all about preserving, or sometimes restoring, 'the native way of life' (cf. Scott, 1998; Thornton, 1996). The form of government created reflected this tension: over existing political structures was laid a neat grid of territorial, regional and tribal authorities, which sought to reflect 'native traditions', on the one hand, but provide for modernist government and uniformity on the other. Uncooperative chiefs would be replaced, demoted to headmen or sent to special re-education camps, albeit always with reference to often highly manipulated genealogical lineages (Robertson, 1990).

Apart from force, the law was a main instrument by which to attain the drawing-board world envisaged by Verwoerd and his colleagues. According to the official ideology, apartheid was about perpetuating 'by *statute* the spontaneous "segregation" which had always been part of the South African way of life' (emphasis added).[14] Both the ideology of segregation and the nitty-gritty of its daily implementation were phrased in legal terms and laid down in hundreds of laws, bye-laws and regulations, the 1927 Black Administration Act (38/1927) and the 1951 Black Authorities Act (68/1951). The former not only turned the Governor-general (and later the President) into Supreme Chief of all the blacks but also contained regulations on land tenure, the application of 'black law' to blacks and chiefly jurisdiction.[15] The Black Authorities Act went further by establishing tribal, regional and territorial authorities and allocating them a wide range of local government functions, together with the right to pass bye-laws and demand levies.[16] Together, these twin legislative pillars of apartheid spawned over 1500 regulations and subregulations, dealing with topics as varied as administrative functions, the creation of tribal authorities, and the duty of chiefs to 'maintain law and order' in their tribes.[17]

Most of these laws were concerned with enforcing the position of traditional leaders, now part of Tribal Authorities, as the first tier of local government, with functions pertaining to areas as varied as public health, taxation, registration of births and deaths, census-taking, preservation of fences, the 'prevention, detection and punishment of crime', the 'efficient use of labour resources', the 'unauthorised influx of Blacks into urban areas' and the protection of public property. In addition, the Tribal Authorities were given a host of agricultural

[13] H.F. Verwoerd, 'Speech in the House of Assembly on January 23rd, 1962 (on the Granting of Self Government to the Transkei)', in *Readings in South African Society*, ed. Henry Lever, Johannesburg: Jonathan Ball Publishers, 1978, p. 218.

[14] Bureau of Information. *Official Yearbook of the Republic of South Africa*, p. 49.

[15] The nationalist ideology was worked out further in the Promotion of Self-Government Act in 1959 (46/1959), which abolished indirect representation in the central government and created eight distinct African national units: North Sotho, South Sotho, Swazi, Tsongo, Tswana, Venda, Zulu and Xhosa. Later, the Xhosa were divided into Transkei and Ciskei, and a Ndebele homeland was created. In pursuit of the goal of 'no more black South Africans' the Bantu Homeland Citizenship Act was passed (26/1970). In 1971, the National States Constitution Act gave the President the power to grant differing degrees of self-government to these indigenous authorities. In 1990 there were four independent homelands Transkei, Bophutatswana, Venda and Ciskei and six self-governing territories. Tanya Woker and Sue Clarke. 'Human Rights in the Homelands', in *South African Human Rights and Labour Law*, p. 153.

[16] Cf. Ss 1, 4, 5 of *Black Authorities Act 68/1951*. Bye-laws could be made by regional authorities.

[17] *Regulations Prescribing the Duties, Powers, Privileges and Conditions of Service of Chiefs and Headmen (as Amended, for Northern Province)*, s.4.

functions such as those covering land allocation, the use of commonages, the eradication of weeds, the preservation of flora and fauna, the rehabilitation of land and cattle culling.[18] A headman's diary of 1965, quoted by Hammond-Tooke (1975:229–30), shows how by the early 1970s traditional leaders had become 'native administrators', bureaucrats on their own parcels of land. A week's work could, for instance, entail arranging business licences, registering the death of a child, giving permission to transfer a beast, meeting a hospital committee, giving permission for the digging of holes for fence posts and holding court.

Central to the chiefs' political authority was their authority to allocate land. This fierce enforced communalism took different forms: most of the land was part of the Native Trust held by the government, but there was also land owned by the tribes in various ways. In all cases, however, access to land had been made dependent on accepting the political authority of the traditional leader, with an inevitable insecurity of title as a result. Again, this can hardly be considered a continuation of practices existing at the beginning of the twentieth century. Not only had individual tenure already begun to be the dominant pattern before the implementation of the 1913 Natives Land Act, which forbade individual ownership (Van Onselen, 1996:7), but the chiefs' position was also buttressed by an army of administrators with a strongly cadastral mentality which followed government directives on the division between residential, agricultural and grazing sites and aided in the allocation.

The legal position of traditional leaders was also reinforced by their being granted explicit jurisdiction over people, if necessary by force. A 1957 law, for instance, provided that the chief was entitled to the 'loyalty, respect and obedience of all the Blacks resident in his area' and that he could 'in accordance with the laws and customs mainly obtaining in his tribe or community, take such steps as may be necessary to secure from them such loyalty, respect and obedience'.[19] Customary law, like local government regulations and land tenure arrangements, underwent a metamorphosis on the state drawing board and in dialogue with traditional leaders to become a unified, implementable and homogenised sub-system of South African law, codified in legislation such as the Black Administration Act, and verified in state courts and developed into a coherent system, a subsystem of South African law.

Nevertheless, detailed though the laws backing up the political geography in the homelands were, they did leave discretion to both administrators and traditional leaders. The Department of Native Affairs, responsible for running the homelands, had considerable freedom, as the so-called 'Native Question' was 'largely quarantined from "politics" within the national state.... From the political and administrative standpoint of the national state, the governance of Africans was the business of a "state within a state" within which legislative, executive and judicial powers were fused' (Ashforth, 1987). The administrators, often Afrikaner ethnographers, had great, albeit paternalistic, sympathy for their 'chiefs' and developed close relations with them. Their administration, as Costa has aptly pointed out (1997:42), was directed not so much towards accordance

[18] Ibid., s.9.

[19] *Regulations Prescribing the Duties, Powers, Privileges and Conditions of Service of Chiefs and Headmen (as Amended, for Northern Province)*, s. 6.

with custom as towards maintaining peace in the communities concerned. Simultaneously, their presence curbed the powers formally granted to the traditional leaders, and comprised the local representation of the apartheid state.

Thus, the bureaucratised relationship between chiefs and administrators was largely based on a trade-off in which traditional leaders were granted a great deal of autonomy as long as they followed official regulations. More often than not, the reality did not follow these neat administrative schemes. Rather, it should be seen as a compromise on both sides, as Ritchken (1995:i) put it: 'Through Tribal Authorities the state attempted to transform the chieftainship into an agent of administrative and political control. The chieftainship, on the other hand, was trying to use its position within the state to bolster its own powers, and establish its independence from the state.' As already noted, how this was actually played out differed by traditional leader and by area. While some leaders did their utmost to keep 'the state' out and maintained covert relations with the Struggle, others called in the state army to protect them against their citizens. So many chiefs, so many kingdoms.

What also differed was the extent to which traditional leaders became specifically involved in homeland politics. Peires (1992:384) remarked that it was often not the senior rulers, but the junior chiefs – Kaiser Matanzima, Lucas Mangope, Gatsha Buthelezi – who actively engaged in bantustan rule and derived their status from these political careers. These leaders would spend most of their time in the homeland parliaments, alienated from 'their' people through distance and the substance of what they were doing. Added to this were numerous accounts of corruption and bribery as well as the violence and repression, that became increasingly common in the homelands during the 1980s (Robertson, 1990:157). As Boputhatswana leader Lucas Mangope once told his subjects: 'I have heard that you do not want to see my police force in this place. Know that I actually love them. I love them for carrying out my instructions... I am going to order them to come to this place. They will see that there is order in this place.'[20]

It is not surprising that the new role assumed, enthusiastically or hesitantly, by traditional leaders hardly led to an increase in popularity with their subjects. In many parts of 'rural' South Africa, revolts were aimed directly at the chiefs. *'Pansi magoši pansi,'* 'Down with the chiefs' chanted the Sekhukhune youth, the Transkei protesters, the KwaNdebele revolutionaries. And when the ANC in exile began talks with the Congress of Traditional Leaders of South Africa (Contralesa), this caused a severe crisis of confidence among their rural supporters who saw in the chiefs their main day-to-day oppressors.[21] The general expectation, therefore, was that the role of traditional leaders as 'puppets of the regime', 'little kings in their areas', 'native administrators' or the 'homeland bourgeoisie' would fade away once the democratic, unified South Africa had dawned.[22]

[20] *Weekly Mail & Guardian*, 7 July 1989, quoted in Robertson, 1990.

[21] Relations between Contralesa and the ANC are discussed extensively in Chapter 4.

[22] Cf. an article in the official ANC bulletin, stating that 'there can be no compromise with our perspective of a unitary, democratic South Africa where there shall be no bantustans'. ANC, 'The Bantustan Question: A New Approach?' *Sechaba* 24, no. 4 (1990):13–14.

3. Imagining the future: constitutional negotiations

It was a bright sunny day when Nelson Mandela walked free and addressed the masses assembled to welcome their leader back after 27 years of imprisonment. Those who listened attentively to that first speech on 11 February 1990 could already have seen an indication that this ANC member, for one, had no intention of relegating South Africa's traditional leaders to the dustbin of history. Even before he thanked the young lions, 'whose endless heroism energised the struggle', the country's designated leader exclaimed: 'I salute the traditional leaders of our country – many of you continue to walk in the footsteps of great heroes like Hintsa en Sekhukhune.' He showed a similar commitment once the process of designing a new South Africa had got under way, by inviting the country's highest-ranking traditional leaders as observers to the first 'talks about talks'. 'Just as such leaders were present at the formation of the ANC, they should be present at the watershed events that herald the dawn of a new, democratic South Africa,' he argued.[23] Nevertheless, even Mandela could probably not have predicted how, in the course of the constitutional negotiations, the traditional leaders would manage to move from the back benches reserved for observers to centre stage, making increasingly strong demands, threatening to boycott elections and managing, in more than one way, to retain past privileges.

Just as apartheid's main language had been that of the law, so the law was the form in which South Africa's future was imagined (cf. Abel, 1995a). Thus, the parties who got together in various fora for the 'gruelling, frustrating and yet thrilling trajectory' of discussing South Africa's future did not work towards a memorandum of understanding or a contract, but a fully fledged Constitution.[24] Although the outcome of the negotiations would be rightfully heralded as the 'South African miracle' and one of the most modern constitutions in the world, it was also very much the product of a negotiated revolution, a 'vicious struggle for political power' that demanded concessions on all sides.[25] In order to investigate what these concessions meant to the traditional leadership, it is instructive to look at the three subsequent phases of the negotiation process: (i) the 'talks about talks' in CODESA I and II, in 1991–2 which ended in deadlock; (ii) the Multi-party Negotiating Process in 1993, which drew up an interim Constitution and prepared the way for the first general elections in 1994; and (iii) the Constitutional Assembly, the body chosen during these elections that drew up South Africa's first democratic Constitution, adopted in May 1996.

1991–2: Talks about talks

It would take two years of bilateral talks in an unstable and violent climate before the first formal negotiations on South Africa's institutional future, the Convention for a Democratic South Africa (CODESA), could get started. The parties meeting in the World Trade Centre in Kempton Park in November 1991 repre-

[23] Nelson Mandela, 'Participation of Traditional Leaders at Codesa.' http://www.anc.org.za/ancdocs/pr/1991/pr1217.html: ANC, 1991.

[24] Chairperson of the Constitutional Assembly Cyril Ramaphosa, quoted in Ebrahim (1998: xvii).

[25] Cf. Corder (1994). The fascinating process of negotiating South Africa's Constitution, which I can only discuss briefly, is the subject of a number of excellent studies. See, for instance: Corder (1996); Summer (1996); De Villiers, (1996); Nicol (1997), Sachs (1997); Waldmeier (1997); Van Wijk et al. (1995).

sented two blocks: the opposition parties, like the ANC, the South African Communist Party (SACP) and the Pan Africanist Congress (PAC), and the 'regime block', including the South African government and the National Party but also representatives from the ten homelands. Although traditional leaders were not officially represented, many of them – even the more progressive ones – made up part of the homeland delegations: Contralesa leaders Holomisa and Nonkonyana, for instance, joined the Transkei delegation in their capacity as a lawyer and a representative of the Transkei football organisation respectively.[26] The talks would become deadlocked in June 1992 over issues such as the procedure for adopting the Constitution, regional powers and the protection of minorities, but they did set the stage for later negotiations.[27] For instance, the parties signed a declaration of intent committing them to draw up a Constitution to ensure 'that South Africa will be a united, democratic, non-racial and non-sexist state in which sovereign authority is exercised over the whole of its territory' and to acknowledge 'the diversity of languages, cultures and religions of the people of South Africa'.[28]

The CODESA I and II talks also provided an indication of later stumbling blocks. One was the role of Inkatha leader Buthelezi, who withdrew from CODESA I once it became clear that the Zulu king would not be allowed a separate delegation from those of the Inkatha Freedom Party and the KwaZulu government. It became increasingly obvious that Buthelezi, who had been strongly opposed to independence for the KwaZulu bantustan in the 1980s, was now seeking to attain whatever sovereignty was possible for the 'Zulu nation' and the king and traditional leaders ruling it (Oomen, 1996). A strongly federalist agenda was one way to achieve this, as was an emphasis on sovereignty for King Zwelithini and strong powers for traditional leaders as local governors, especially concerning control over land. With the provocative adoption of a draft constitution by the KwaZulu legislature in December 1992, for instance, Buthelezi effectively threatened secession (Ebrahim, 1998:142).

But the main bone of contention was the extent to which the contours of the new South Africa could already be outlined by the negotiating forum, or would only be decided once the first democratically elected Parliament was in place. Understandably, the ANC wanted to keep its hands as free as possible until it had officially received the overwhelming popular support forecast by the polls. The NP, on the other hand, sought to make use of the fact that it was still officially in power to consolidate as many privileges as possible for its – white – constituency, notably through regional powers and minority rights.[29] It was the SACP chairman Joe Slovo who signalled the way out of the deadlock. In a 1992 article entitled 'Negotiations: What Room for Compromise', he argued that it might be necessary, for a limited transitional period, to include 'sunset clauses' in the Constitution which guaranteed regional interests and the position of

[26] Interview P. Holomisa, Amsterdam, 22 September 2000.

[27] The concrete reason for the ANC's decision to break off negotiations and call for mass action instead was the Boipatong massacre, in which 40 people were killed and government involvement was suspected.

[28] CODESA I Declaration of Intent, signed 21 December 1991 and quoted in Du Plessis and Corder (1994:5).

[29] Cf. the extensive discussion in Henrard (2000) and Kristin Henrard, 'The Interrelation between Individual Human Rights, Minority Rights and the Right to Self-Determination for an Adequate Minority Protection.' Katholieke Universiteit Leuven, 1999.

members of the security forces and the civil service (Corder, 1994:500). This insight would eventually contribute to the ANC's acceptance of the notion of a Government of National Unity for the first five-year period after the elections and of negotiated 'constitutional principles' that would bind the future legislators.

1993: Formulating the interim Constitution

After the 1992 breakdown, multilateral negotiations got under way again in the form of the Multi-Party Negotiating Process (MPNP). It was this body that would somehow manage to overcome the seemingly insurmountable differences between parties and, before the end of 1993, come up with an interim Constitution outlining South Africa's new order. Not only did this document establish 'a sovereign and democratic constitutional state in which there is equality between men and women and people of all races' and contain a fully fledged Bill of Rights, it also included 33 Constitutional Principles with which a future definitive Constitution would have to comply. The contents of these principles covered everything from the most central features of the future state – common citizenship, a three-tiered democratic system of government, a Bill of Rights, constitutional supremacy and an independent judiciary – to seemingly banal remarks such as 'government shall be structured at national, provincial and local levels'.[30] The weight of this negotiated settlement was captured by the *Sunday Times*, which commented on 21 November 1993: 'We, the people of South Africa, have wrought a miracle. We have accomplished what few people anywhere in the world thought we could do: we have freed ourselves, and made a democracy, and we have done so without war or revolution' (quoted in Ebrahim 1998:171).

One feature of the negotiations leading to the interim Constitution was the much larger role played by traditional leaders. In order to allay Buthelezi's demands for the inclusion of the Zulu king and general protests from the Congress of Traditional Leaders, a committee of eight members had been established under CODESA II to look into the participation of leaders in the negotiating process. Its recommendation to include four delegations of traditional leaders, one from each province, each with twelve members and five advisers, was followed, ostensibly because the ANC hoped that the three other provincial delegations would provide some counterweight to that from KwaZulu.[31] Contralesa, the burgeoning Congress of Traditional Leaders of South Africa, had lobbied vehemently for separate inclusion but was not admitted, as this would make space for other interest groups such as business and labour. Still, 48 traditional leaders had been added to those already present through the homeland delegations, and this would soon have an effect on the negotiations.

Their first clash with other, mostly female, delegates, occurred in July 1993

[30] Schedule 4 of the *Interim Constitution*, in particular, CP XVI.

[31] A majority of traditional leaders was in favour of participation. Among the few dissident voices was the Qwaqwa administration, which wrote, ' Let us respect the status of Kings and Traditional Leaders. Let them remain at home and we, their subjects, will report to them accordingly. Their political participation in the past has done more harm than good.' It is interesting to note that the seat for the KwaZulu traditional leaders was not taken by the king after all but by the KwaZulu government. Other new players in the MPNP were the CP, the PAC and the Afrikaner Volksunie. The suspicion that the three other delegations were included to provide a counterweight to the KwaZulu faction comes from an interview with P. Holomisa, Amsterdam, 22 September 2000. Cf. Waldmeier (1997: 172).

over the relation between customary law and the equality clause, and can be considered a prelude to their later positions and negotiating tactics. From the outset of the negotiations, the traditional leaders had demanded that culture be exempted from the Bill of Rights, in particular the equality clause.[32] 'The essence of the chiefs' proposal was that customary law and general South African law should be parallel legal systems, neither empowered to interfere with the other.'[33] The notion of the equality of women, as M. Nonkonyana would state, 'is foreign to us': 'We are in Africa and we remain in Africa. We are not prepared to sacrifice our Africanism' (Albertyn, 1994:57).[34]

To break the deadlock a panel of experts was established, and instructed informally to come up with something 'to give to the chiefs', such as exclusion of chiefly succession from the equality clause (ibid.:58). A compromise clause was drawn up, giving people the right to opt in or out of customary law by voluntary association with a community which observed such law or freely choosing to have customary law apply to one's personal relationships.[35] Though the traditional leaders initially appeared to accept this clause, while the women had difficulties with it, they withdrew their support within hours of the acceptance of the whole constitutional package by the MPNP, and returned to their original position of demanding – once again – blanket protection of 'cultural rights' from the Bill of Rights (Albertyn, 1994; Du Plessis, 1994:98–9).

As a result, no specific provision on customary law was included and the issue would be dealt with on the basis of s 181(1) of the interim Constitution, which entitled a 'traditional authority observing a system of indigenous law and recognised by law immediately before the commencement of this Constitution' to 'continue to function as such and to exercise and perform the powers and functions vested in it in accordance with the applicable laws and customs, subject to any amendments or repeals of such laws and customs.' This, as Du Plessis remarked, was not good news for the women's lobby, as it 'implies that traditional leaders can of their own accord exercise whatever authority they have pursuant to indigenous law without leaving individuals under their authority a free choice of whether they want to have indigenous law applied or not' (Du Plessis, 1994: 99; Oomen, 1999).[36]

[32] Cape, OFS, and Transvaal traditional leaders, 'Submission to Constitutional Committee, Tec Committee and Negotiating Council: Joint Position Paper Concerning Role of Traditional Leaders', 1993, Cf. Henrard. 'The Interrelation between Individual Human Rights etc.'

[33] Iain Currie, 'Indigenous Law', in *Constitutional Law*, ed. Matthew et.al.. Kenwyn: Juta & Co, 1998.

[34] See also E. Maloka, 'Traditional Leaders and the Current Transition.' *African communist*, no. 141 (1995), p. 184.

[35] http://www.constitution.org.za

[36] S 35(3) of the interim Constitution does urge *courts* to interpret and develop the common law and customary law, having due regard to the spirit, purport and objects of the Bill of Rights. Also, Constitutional Principle XIII would make indigenous law subject to the fundamental rights contained in the Constitution. This, however, concerned the officially codified customary law, and not living law. The issue was also discussed in terms of the horizontal application of the Bill of Rights: would it be directly enforceable against the state and its organs only, or also against private persons and institutions? Eventually, it was decided that the chapter should operate vertically only, but that 'provision be made for a seepage into horizontal relationships'. As a result, indigenous law was in large measure kept beyond direct reach of the chapter because of its vertical application. Cf. Currie. 'Indigenous Law'; Henrard. 'The Interrelation between Individual Human Rights'. These issues are discussed more extensively in the debate on customary law later in this chapter.

A comparable issue – chiefly sovereignty versus equality and individual choice, and thus the future of apartheid's patchwork – came up in the debates on the future of local government. This, again, was a highly contentious issue, with the traditional leaders demanding continuation of their position as the local government in their areas, while the ANC sought to establish democratically elected government all over South Africa. It was also highly sensitive, and was postponed until the very end of the negotiations. On the eve of the adoption of the interim Constitution, the ANC agreed to a two-phase approach, in which democratically elected municipalities would be installed only in 2000. It was agreed that a traditional leader 'of a community observing a system of indigenous law and residing on land within the area of jurisdiction of an elected local government ... shall *ex officio* be entitled to be a member of that local government, and shall be eligible to be elected to any office of such local government'.[37] This provision thus left the specifics of the relation between elected and traditional authority to be worked out in subsequent legislation.

Nevertheless, the ubiquitous traditional leaders at the MPNP managed to enshrine a host of other guarantees in the interim Constitution. There would be Provincial Houses and a National Congress of Traditional Leaders, entitled to 'advise and make proposals' on 'matters relating to traditional authorities, indigenous law or the traditions and customs of traditional communities'.[38] Now that the homelands were to be reincorporated into the 'new' South Africa, many of the traditional leaders who had been part of the homeland parliamentary structures would get a place, and a salary, in these representative bodies. For the rest, there was a provision stating that all the existing legislation, including the 1927 Black Administration Act and the 1951 Black Authorities Act, would continue to exist, though subject to the Constitution.[39]

The most important achievement of the royal negotiators, however, could be found in the tail of the interim Constitution: the Constitutional Principles. These provisions would bind the democratically elected Constitutional Assembly when drawing up the final Constitution and thus enshrined the power wielded by the traditional leaders during the MPNP for years to come. Thus, Constitutional Principle XIII held that:

> 1. The institution, status and role of traditional leadership, according to indigenous law, shall be recognised and protected in the Constitution. Indigenous law, like common law, shall be recognised and applied by the courts, subject to the fundamental rights contained in the Constitution and to legislation dealing specifically herewith.
>
> 2. Provisions in a provincial constitution relating to the institution, role, authority and status of a traditional monarch shall be recognised and protected in the Constitution.

Section 2 of this Principle was inserted six days before the 1994 general elections, in a desperate last-minute attempt by the ANC to get Buthelezi and the IFP on board.[40] Together with the transfer of extensive state land in the name of the Zulu king, this did indeed ensure Inkatha's participation in the elections, though the party's name had to be stickered onto the ballot papers.[41] The

[37] s 182 Act 200/1993.
[38] Ss 183–184 Act 200/1993.
[39] s 229 Act 200/1993.
[40] By means of s 2 of Act 3/1994.
[41] Also, the ANC and NP promised that international mediators would look into Inkatha's federalist claims Ebrahim (1998). This mediation never materialised, which is officially why Inkatha

Afrikaner right wing had already been placated a month before, when the ANC and NP had partly given in to its demands for a 'volksstaat' by enshrining the right to 'self-determination by any community sharing a common cultural and language heritage' in the Constitutional Principles.[42] Clearly, the traditional leaders were not alone in calculating that what was effectively a continuation of segregationist policies would now be in their best interests.

1994–6: drafting the final Constitution

The interim Constitution was still, in the words of Albie Sachs, an 'unconstitutional Constitution', and the final version had to be drawn up by the Constitutional Assembly elected in the historic elections of 27 April 1994 (Nicol, 1997; Sachs, 1997). The process of writing up the final Constitution was at least as miraculous. During an enormous campaign including everything from rural workshops to television shows, millions of South Africans were invited to 'make your contribution to the new Constitution'. For, though the broad boundaries had been drawn up by the Constitutional Principles, the frantic 1993 negotiations had left many issues for further deliberation – among them the position of traditional leaders.

While their final constitutional position was discussed in working groups, workshops and numerous conferences in the 1994–6 period, a number of events demonstrated how traditional leaders had undergone a metamorphosis from outdated puppets of the apartheid regime to authentic representatives of a large part of the South African population, and thus a political force to be reckoned with. The first was the discussion concerning their remuneration. In what was effectively an ANC attempt to gain control over them, particularly in KwaZulu/Natal, the central government passed a Remuneration of Traditional Leaders Act (29/1995) in July 1995.[43] Though the interim Constitution clearly ruled that 'traditional authorities' fell under exclusive provincial legislative competence, it was held that the national government would now pay the traditional leaders.[44] In retaliation, the IFP-dominated KwaZulu/Natal provincial government brought in legislation prohibiting traditional leaders from receiving payment from the central ANC government.[45] In the end, the Constitutional Court ruled that paying traditional leaders was indeed a provincial competence, but the case did demonstrate how the ANC had suddenly come to realise the political potential of the traditional leaders.[46] In the final Constitution, 'traditional leaders' was made

41 (cont.) pulled out of the negotiations on the final Constitution. The state land was transferred by means of the highly contentious KwaZulu Ingonyama Trust Act 3/1994 which put 93% of the KwaZulu land under trusteeship of the king. The Minister of Land Affairs after the elections, Derek Hanekom, would try to amend this by means of the KwaZulu Ingonyama Trust Amendment Act 9/1997.

42 CP XXXIV sub 3, as inserted by sec 13(b) of Act 2/1994.

43 Cf. Ann Eveleth, 'Luring Chiefs to Democracy', *Daily Mail & Guardian* electronic archive, 23 June 1995; Mvelase, Mehlo, 'Chiefs May Still Profess Money or the Boss.' http://web.sn.apc.org/wmail/issues/950707/wm950707-12.html: *Daily Mail & Guardian* electronic archive, 1995.

44 S 5 Act 20/1998.

45 The KwaZulu-Natal Amakhosi and Iziphakanyiswa Amendment Bill of 1995 and the Payment of Salaries, Allowances and Other Privileges to the Ingonyama Bill of 1995. For details, see Currie. 'Indigenous Law.'

46 *In Re: Kwazulu-Natal Amakhosi and Izipahkanyiswa Amendment Bill of 1995; in Re: Payment of Salaries, Allowances and Other Privileges to the Ingonyama Bill of 1995*, 7 903 (1995).

a concurrent provincial and national legislative competence.[47]

This political clout was also demonstrated in the run-up to the country's first local government elections. Ever since the adoption of the interim Constitution the traditional leaders had grumbled over its s 182, which granted them an *ex officio* role in local government, and the way in which this had been worked out in the Local Government Transition Act, which allowed traditional leaders to make up a maximum of 10 per cent of rural council members.[48] Arguing that 'two people cannot drive the same vehicle at the same time', they demanded to be recognised as the primary tier of local government.[49] The ANC's reluctance to accept this, combined with dissatisfaction over the slow establishment of the provincial Houses of traditional leaders, caused chiefs – particularly in the Eastern Cape and KwaZulu/Natal – initially to boycott the local government elections.[50] This was one of the main factors in delaying the elections for seven months, until November 1995.[51]

It was against this backdrop that discussions on the future constitutional position of traditional leaders took place. Again, they showed how they had gained in lobbying power. The special Hearing on Traditional Authorities, for instance, attracted more people than any other Constitutional Assembly hearing.[52] In all the talks, Contralesa was highly vocal, arguing, for instance, that 'the Constitution should ... be a mirror of the soul of the nation – it must include all aspirations, beliefs and values. The Constitution will not be successful if it only relies on foreign concepts and institutions.'[53] Effectively, this meant a lobby for the exemption of culture from the Bill of Rights, and for strong local government powers.

As a result, discussions on the future of traditional leadership became a 'hot potato shoved forwards' (Maloka, 1996:186). Even though the responsible Commission on Provincial Government had been quick to conclude that it would be 'politically and administratively prudent' to involve traditional leaders in government, there was little consensus on how this should be done.[54] It was

[47] Schedule IV part A Act 108/1996.

[48] Cf Act 209/1993, in particular section 9a of the Act as amended by *Local Government Transition Act Second Amendment Act*. 89/1995. One reason for the chiefly discontent was the unclarity over whether 'ex officio' membership meant that traditional leaders had full voting rights or not Oomen (1996:94).

[49] Terence Fife. 'Improving the Participation Rate in Rural Elections: A Report of the November 1995 Rural Local Government Elections.' Stellenbosch: Centre for Rural Legal Studies, 1996, p.5.

[50] Justin Pearce. 'A Little Tlc Will Help Local Government.' http://web.sn.apc.org/wmail/issues/941202/wm941202-1.html: *Daily Mail & Guardian* electronic archive, 1994; Sapa. 'Impossible for Prisoners to Vote: Mchunu.' ANC news briefing email service: ANC, 2000, C. Smith, 'Barrier of Spears: Political Tensions', *Finance Week* 64, no. 5 (1995): 9.

[51] There were other factors – mostly logistical, but also white right-wing opposition – slowing down the process. Still, articles like Herb Payne, 'Anc Considers Appeal.' *Financial Mail*, 7 March 1997, 44. attribute the delay wholly to the traditional leaders.

[52] Ebrahim states (1998:356) that 220 people and eight structures attended the hearings on traditional authorities in Parliament on 12–13 May 1995. Second and third most popular were the hearings on women (170 people) and on youth (160 people). The submissions to the hearings are available via www.constitution.org.za (visited 14 January 2002). Cf. 'Constitutional Assembly Public Hearing on Traditional Leaders.' Cape Town: Constitutional Assembly, 1995; 'Traditional Democracy.' *Constitutional Talk* 7 (1996): 3.

[53] 'Constitutional Assembly Public Hearing on Traditional Leaders.'

[54] Commission on Provincial Government. 'Preliminary Submissions on Provincial Government Systems.' 1995, p. 3.1.

decided at an early stage that the contentious *ex officio* clause should be deleted. But the rest, as one of the drafters said, was left open till the very last moment, 'because of the contentious nature of the subject; it was considered easier to deal with the more simple questions first.'[55] Two weeks before the adoption of the final Constitution, in May 1996, heated meetings were still being held between the government and Contralesa – by then promoted to a full negotiating partner – on the exemption of customary law from the Bill of Rights, chiefly representation at all levels of government, the demand that traditional leaders be the primary structures of local government and the establishment of a special ministry for traditional affairs (Ebrahim, 1998:198).

Again, the only way to resolve the deadlock seemed to be to delay the issue. The final Constitution was indeed adopted on 8 May 1996, within the deadlines set by the government. And President Mandela was undoubtedly also referring to the traditional leaders when he stated in his adoption address that 'today we affirm in no uncertain terms that we are mature enough to derive strength, trust and unity from the tapestry of language, religious and cultural attributes that make up our nation'.[56] But all commentators focusing on the provisions on traditional leaders remarked on their vagueness and how all the real decisions still had to be made.[57]

What *did* the 1996 Constitution provide concerning traditional leaders? Firstly, culture was made part of the Bill of Rights, by means of Ss 30 and 31, which stated that:

> 30. Everyone has the right to use the language and to participate in the cultural life of their choice, but no one exercising these rights may do so in a manner inconsistent with any provision of the Bill of Rights.
>
> S 31. 1) Persons belonging to a cultural, religious or linguistic community may not be denied the right, with other members of that community – to enjoy their culture, practise their religion and use their language; and to form, join and maintain cultural, religious and linguistic associations and other organs of civil society;
>
> 2) The rights in subsection (1) may not be exercised in a manner inconsistent with any provision of the Bill of Rights.[58]

On the question of whether the Bill of Rights would also apply horizontally, or only bind organs of state, the new Constitution held that 'A provision of the Bill of Rights binds a natural or juristic person if, and to the extent that, it is applicable, taking into account the nature of the right and the nature of any duty imposed by the right' – thus to a large extent leaving decisions on the subject to future legislative and judicial deliberation.[59]

[55] Interview Prof. J. Kruger, 14 November 1995.

[56] Speech to the Constitutional Assembly, 8 May 1996, http://www.polity.org.za/govdocs/speeches/1996/sp0508.html

[57] Bank and Southall (1996) Currie. 'Indigenous Law.', 36–4; Van Kessel, and Oomen. (1999); Chris Tapscott, 'The Institutionalization of Rural Local Government in Post-Apartheid South Africa', in Hofmeister and Scholz (1997), p. 302.

[58] For extensive discussion of the meaning of this provision, see Henrard. 'The Interrelation', *passim* and Currie. 'Indigenous Law.'

[59] s 8 Act 108/1996. This was in fact a codification of the ruling of the Constitutional Court in *The Gauteng Provincial Legislature in Re: Dispute Concerning the Constitutionality of Certain Provisions of the School Education Bill of* 1995. Cf. Henrard. 'The Interrelation', p. 521.

Traditional leaders themselves are the subject of Chapter 12 of the Constitution, which in its totality reads:

> S 211. 1) The institution, status and role of traditional leadership, according to customary law, are recognised, subject to the Constitution.
>
> 2) A traditional authority that observes a system of customary law may function subject to any applicable legislation and customs, which includes amendments to, or repeal of, that legislation or those customs.
>
> 3) The courts must apply customary law when that law is applicable, subject to the Constitution and any legislation that specifically deals with customary law.
>
> S 212. 1) National legislation may provide for a role for traditional leadership as an institution at local level on matters affecting local communities.
>
> 2) To deal with matters relating to traditional leadership, the role of traditional leaders, customary law and the customs of communities observing a system of customary law – national or provincial legislation may provide for the establishment of provincial Houses of traditional leaders; and national legislation may establish a national House of traditional leaders.

Until these general provisions had been worked out in more specific legislation, the existing laws – like the Black Administration Act and the Black Authorities Act – would continue to apply.[60]

It was the frequent use of the word 'may' – in, for instance, S 211(2) and the whole of S 212 – that infuriated the traditional leaders and caused them to argue that 'the majority of voters in South Africa have been cheated. When they voted for the present Parliament they were led to believe that the institution of traditional leadership was going to be respected, given that this is an African state, the majority of whose people are African' (Holomisa, 1996: 126). The current arrangements, they felt, were much more vague than the guarantees contained in CP XIII of the interim Constitution. The Constitutional Court, however, which had to certify that the final text complied with the Constitutional Principles, did not agree. In its certification ruling it stated that:

> The Constitutional Assembly cannot be constitutionally faulted for leaving the complicated, varied and ever-developing specifics of how such leadership should function in the wider democratic society, and how customary law should develop and be interpreted, to future social evolution, legislative deliberation and judicial interpretation.[61]

Admittedly, the guarantees in the new Constitution were much vaguer and more open-ended than those in its predecessor. But they did constitute a bid for time: the real decisions concerning the replacement of apartheid's general legislative framework on traditional authorities as well as their specific future role in local government, land allocation and the settlement of disputes, and thus the future of South Africa's institutional patchwork, still had to be taken. It is on these specific developments that the following sections will concentrate.

[60] s 2 *Transitional Arrangements Act* 108/1996.

[61] *Ex Parte Chairperson of the Constitutional Assembly: In Re Certification of the Constitution of South Africa*, 1996, SA, CC. para 197 834 F/H. Cf Schmidt-Jortzig (1998), pp. 61–5.

4. Towards a Traditional Authorities Act

How were the provisions in the 1996 Constitution worked out in the years that followed? Much of the discussion, as we shall see, concentrated on specific functional areas like local government, land and dispute resolution. But there were also general questions as to how the recognition of the 'status, institution and role' of traditional leadership would materialise and what legislation would replace the Black Administration Act and the Black Authorities Act in this regard. It was for this reason that the government decided in 1996 to produce a White Paper which in turn would lead to a fully-fledged Traditional Authorities Act.[62] At the time, the plan was to pass such an Act in 1998. In the event, it would take until 2000 before the government adopted a discussion document tentatively entitled 'Towards a White Paper on Traditional Leadership and Institutions' setting out the main questions to be answered. By the end of 2001 President Mbeki could be heard saying that it was important 'that we *begin* a national dialogue that will involve all sections of our society in defining the role of this institution,' causing Buthelezi to sigh in despair: 'Nothing was done. Still, nothing is being done.'[63] He would have to wait until 2003, when a White Paper on Traditional Leadership and Governance, and legislation on the subject were finally adopted.

Though Buthelezi's laments highlighted the excruciating slowness of the process, it did not do full justice to the government's attempts to arrive at a comprehensive policy on traditional leadership. In 1996, for instance, many officials of the Department of Traditional Affairs, who consider it their mission 'to give support to the institution of traditional leadership', felt that they needed to hurry up and complete the policy process before 'traditionalist' Mandela handed over the presidency to his 'modernist' successor in 1998.[64] After compiling a report containing academic opinions on the subject, they set out an ambitious policy plan that was endorsed by the MINMEC (meeting of provincial ministers) on Traditional Affairs, the main political organ responsible, and should have led to a draft White Paper by the end of 1997.[65] According to this plan, the White Paper process would start with an audit of all South Africa's traditional leaders,

[62] Interviews with officials of the Department of Constitutional Development, Pretoria, July 1996. A White Paper process is the generic policy process in South Africa and consists of the adoption of a (draft) Green Paper to be commented upon by the public and a subsequent White Paper which is adopted by Parliament as official government policy and can be worked out in legislation.

[63] Sapa. 'Address by Pres. Mbeki to the House of Traditional Leaders.' ANC news briefing email service: ANC, 2001, ———. 'Buthelezi Slams Government over Recognition of Amakhosi.' ANC news briefing email service: ANC, 2001.

[64] Interview, official, Department of Traditional Affairs, November 1997. South African Embassy. *Yearbook 1999*. http://usaembassy.southafrica.net/ YearBook1999/Government/govsys.htm: South African Embassy, 1999. The differences in position between Mandela and Mbeki will be discussed in Chapter 4.

[65] Department of Constitutional Development, 'Guideline Document: The Handling of Traditional Institutions and Their Leaders by the Department of Constitutional Development.' Pretoria: Department of Constitutional Development, 1995; Minister for Provincial Affairs and Constitutional Development, 'Budget Speech in the National Assembly by Mr Mohammed Valli Moosa, Minister for Provincial Affairs and Constitutional Development.' 1997: interviews with officials, Department of Traditional Affairs (called Chief Directorate Traditional Affairs after 1997) in 1996 and 1997. MINMEC stands for Minister and Members of the Executive Committee, and thus the provincial and national ministers concerned with a certain subject.

their financial and legal situation, and then look at more substantive questions such as the structure of traditional leadership, its relations with other areas of government, its representation through national and provincial Houses and 'community values' regarding the subject.[66] In the original plan, all stakeholders – from traditional leaders to rural women – were to be involved in providing inputs to the process.

The first phase, the national audit, did indeed take place in 1998. However, instead of involving a wide variety of stakeholders and constituting an open process, it was – mainly because of budgetary constraints – largely carried out by provincial and national officials. In another departure from the original plans, there was little time and money for field and other empirical research. Instead, the provincial officials answered the long questionnaires provided to them – 'what are the functions of traditional leaders?' – with reference to the piles of legislation that still applied in their provinces.[67] The resulting 10-volume report was, again despite earlier promises, never released to the public. The information on the 1500-odd pieces of legislation applicable, the total number of chiefs and headmen on the state payroll, the disparities in their incomes and the overview of traditional leaders deposed under apartheid was deemed so sensitive that the government preferred to release a drastically abbreviated and much less factual document.[68]

This 'discussion document', released in 2000, a year and a half after the White Paper should have been produced, mainly contained questions rather than answers and marked 'the beginning of a process aimed at engaging South Africans in a dialogue regarding the institution of traditional leadership.'[69] Nevertheless, it did give an insight into the Department's vision on the matter as well as the most contentious issues at stake. The main challenge in this vision, for instance, is 'restoring the traditional nature and respectability of the institution of traditional leadership,' which is considered 'a monument to our past and a true icon of our identity as Africans'.[70] Future policy should provide for an institution which, above all, 'responds and adapts to change'; 'is in harmony with the Constitution and the Bill of Rights'; 'strives to enhance tradition, culture and cultural values'; 'respects the spirit of communality'; 'strives to achieve unity and peace amongst people' and 'facilitates a strong relationship between the institution and the different spheres of government – in particular, the local government sphere'.[71] Some of the challenges set out are: the appointment, disqualification and retirement of traditional leaders; the role of women and youth; party political affiliation; the remuneration of traditional leaders; the relation with other spheres of government; the role of statutory bodies representing traditional leaders and traditional communities with transprovincial and transnational boundaries.

Because this first phase of the White Paper process took so long to materialise,

[66] Department of Constitutional Development, 'Phased Reports: Terms of Reference for a Status Quo Report on Traditional Leadership and Institutions.' Pretoria: Department of Constitutional Development, 1998, N.J.J. Olivier, 'Presentation on Behalf of the Minister of Constitutional Development and Provincial Affairs.' Paper presented at the SASCA Conference 'Rural Governance in the new Millennium', Port Elizabeth, 23 June 1999.

[67] Own observations, Northern Province and Mpumalanga, 1998 and interviews with Traditional Affairs officials in this period. Cf. Department of Constitutional Development. 2000, p. 71.

[68] Ibid., p. 5; interviews with departmental officials in 1998.

[69] Ibid., p. 3.

[70] Ibid., p. 3, 6.

[71] Ibid., p. 6.

some of the issues raised– such as remuneration, the existence of statutory bodies representing traditional leaders, party-political affiliation and the disqualification of traditional leaders – had already been partly addressed in policy and legislation by the time it finally came out. Concerning remuneration, the Independent Commission for the Remuneration of Public Office Bearers had recommended in 1998 that South Africa's 11 kings and paramount chiefs should receive R300,000 annually, while the traditional leaders were given R72.000 a year.[72] They were, much to their discontent, excluded from medical aid schemes and pension benefits.[73] Nevertheless, it was estimated in 1999 that merely paying the salaries of traditional leaders (excluding the headmen and representatives in the national and provincial Houses) cost the South African government R577 million a year, of which R18 million went to the Zulu king alone.[74] Although these salaries far surpassed those paid to elected rural councillors, they remained a focus of discontent, and in 2000 Contralesa called on the government to match all traditional leaders' salaries to those of members of parliament.[75] These demands, combined with the traditional leaders' effective status as public servants, launched a discussion on whether the chiefs should sign performance contracts, a proposal immediately condemned as being 'too westernised'.[76]

Another issue on which some progress had been made was the representation of chiefs at provincial and national levels. In the 1994–7 period, provincial Houses of traditional leaders had, often with great political difficulty, been established in the six provinces with officially recognised traditional leaders: the North West, Mpumalanga, the Northern Province, the Free State, KwaZulu/Natal and the Eastern Cape.[77] Although both composition and functions differed from province to province, the provincial Houses were mostly given an advisory role on topics concerning traditional leadership, customary law and issues affecting their communities, causing some traditional leaders to grumble that they were just 'toothless talking shops.'[78] In any case, much of the talk that took place in these Houses concerned budgetary issues, and particularly the salaries and perks of the traditional leaders represented in them, causing Eastern Cape premier Stofile to consider the local House more of a 'trade union' than anything else.[79]

[72] Dustin Chick, 'Body to Look into Traditional Leaders' Pay.' *Business Day*, 19 May 1998, p. 2, 'Equal Pay for Traditional Leaders.' *Business Day*, 26 June 1998 1998, p. 2; *Remuneration of Public Office Bearers Act*. 20/1998, s 5.

[73] Ibid., s 8 sub 6 and s 9 sub 5.

[74] 'Traditional Leaders: Amount Paid out Each Month in Allowances/ Disbursements', in *Hansard*, 1478, 1999.

[75] 'Traditional Leaders Request Same Benefits as MPs.' http://www.bday.co.za/bday/content/direct/0,3523,642002-6078-0,00.html: *Business Day* online, 2000.

[76] Farouk Chothia, 'Traditional Leaders' Roles Examined.' http://www.bday.co.za/bday/content/direct/0,3523,597872-6078-0,00.html: *Business Day* online, 2000.

[77] Cf. Van Kessel and Oomen (1999:166). The types of difficulties differed: in the Northern Province, for instance, establishment of the House was hampered by discussions over its ethnic composition and the division of seats between the three former homelands; in Mpumalanga, factions of Ndebele people would have preferred to have a separate House in the province of Gauteng; in the Free State there was a great deal of friction between the premier and the House; in KwaZulu/Natal the House was established quickly but hardly ever convened, while in the Eastern Cape discussion was over the number of chiefs in the House: the traditional leaders wanted 72 seats, while there was financial room for only 20. Here, a compromise was finally reached on 42 seats.

[78] For instance, during the meeting Mandela held with the Sekhukhune traditional leaders on 27 May 1999.

[79] Interviews, departmental officials 1997–8 (apart from in Mpumalanga, where the House falls

As soon as the six provincial Houses were in place, they were each able to delegate six representatives to the National Council of Traditional Leaders. The inauguration of this National Council, in April 1997, was a triumph for traditionalism, with the South African Parliament filled with hundreds of chiefs and their councillors, praise-singers and *sangomas* with their healing powers, sporting leopard pelts, knobkerries and traditional totems.[80] Cowhide drums throbbed as President Mandela declared that, finally, 'The country is in the hands of the people, dear friends.' The President went on to say:

> I feel truly humbled to officially open the National Council of Traditional Leaders; to stand before my leaders, at last to acknowledge their status and role as full participants in national affairs; as part of the corps of leaders in the reconstruction and development of our country.
>
> When the new Constitution was drafted there were concerns that we did not define in sufficient detail the status and role of traditional leaders...but we argued as the majority party and the government that we would be true to our word, true to our South Africanness, true to the traditions that form part of our rainbow nation.[81]

Although the vision of the Council (renamed House after 1998) was to 'become an autonomous, dynamic, non-sexist, and progressive institution unifying the Traditional Leaders of South Africa, towards the restoration of dignity and pride in the institution of Traditional Leadership and its role in promoting the welfare of the people in a new world of democracy,' its activities – again – consisted mostly of demanding a 'bigger slice of the cake', both in political and budgetary terms.[82]

The discussions concerning the foundation of the National House had highlighted another recurrent issue in the debate on the future of traditional leadership: that of their political affiliation. In the run-up to the 1994 elections, as earlier during the homeland regimes, quite a few traditional leaders had joined political parties. Contralesa leading members Holomisa and Nonkonyana, for instance, also became ANC members of parliament. And when the ANC did not move as quickly on the 'traditional authorities issue' as hoped, many chiefs, particularly in the Eastern Cape, joined competing parties like the UDM.[83] With regard to the National Council, the specific fear within the ANC was that it would provide (self-proclaimed) traditional leaders like Buthelezi with an alternative

[79 (cont.)] under the legislature, provincial Houses fall under the relevant provincial department), own observations and the minutes of the Northern Province House of Traditional Leaders for the 1997–8 period; Stofile, 'Opening Address to the House of Traditional Leaders Eastern Cape.' http://www.ecprov.gov.za/speeches/premier/2000/traditionalhouse.htm: Eastern Cape Provincial Government, 2000.

[80] 'Council of Traditional Leaders Inaugurated.' http://www.mg.co.za/mg/za1/18apr-news.html#trad: *Daily Mail & Guardian* electronic archive, 1997; A. Sotomi, 'Assegais, Ancestors and Cellphones.' *Drum*, no. 243 (1997): 14–15.

[81] Nelson Mandela, 'Speech at the Inauguration of the National Council of Traditional Leaders.' http://www.anc.org.za/ancdocs/history/mandela/1997/sp970418.html: African National Congress,, 1997.

[82] Cf. Parliamentary Monitoring Group. 'Tabling the Annual Report on Behalf of the National House of Traditional Leaders.' http://www.pmg.org.za/minutes/000317appendix2.htm: Parliamentary Monitoring Group, 2000.

[83] Chiara Carter, 'Chiefs Welcome UDM in E Cape.' http://www.sn.apc.org/wmail/ issues/990226/ NEWS36.html: *Daily Mail & Guardian* electronic archive, 1999; Wally Mbhele, 'New Force Rising.' http://web.sn.apc.org/wmail/issues/971001/NEWS25.html: *Daily Mail & Guardian* electronic archive, 1999.

road to power. To prevent this, a section popularly dubbed the 'anti-Buthelezi clause' was included in the Council of Traditional Leaders Act prohibiting joint membership of the Council and the national or provincial legislature.[84] Nevertheless, general discussion on the topic continued, with traditional leaders claiming that although, ideally, they should not be involved in party politics it was only 'by being MPs that they could influence government'. In 2001, the National House of Traditional Leaders even threatened to stand for the next elections as a political party.[85]

An equally thorny issue remained the legitimacy of those traditional leaders on the government payroll. As Provincial and Local Government Minister Sydney Mufamadi said: 'The integrity of traditional leadership cannot be adequately restored without dealing with those cases of traditional leaders who were allegedly imposed on people, or those who were illegitimately deposed for their opposition to the old order,' and the ensuing succession disputes.[86] Some provinces had already contemplated an 'audit of genuine traditional leaders', but the Northern Province was the only one to actually establish a commission to look into the legitimacy of its traditional leaders.[87] Although this highly controversial Ralushai Commission, that started its work in 1996, never published its findings for fear that they would lead to too much unrest in the province, the national government frequently proclaimed that it would be a good idea to extend the initiative to other provinces.[88]

The main issue thrown up by the discussion document, however, was the one that would – all too quickly – cause the White Paper process to grind to a halt: the relation between traditional and elected local government, or the existence of 'two bulls in a kraal'. This had been hotly debated ever since the beginning of the 1990s and led to another crisis in the run-up to the December 2000 local government elections. One result was that the traditional leaders refused to participate in a conference on the discussion document, arguing 'each time we are being asked to explain what our role is, as though we are a new institution in this country. We are tired of having to explain ourselves to people who know our role very well.'[89] Since the debate on a future Traditional Authorities Act and the issue of local government became so entangled, we look first at the general discussion on local government in the run-up to the 2000 crisis before turning

[84] s 6 Act 10/1997; Various authors, 'Correspondence between Various Parties on the Council of Traditional Leaders Bill,' 1996.

[85] Chothia, 'Traditional Leaders' Roles Examined.'; Holomisa (1996), Sapa. 'Amakhosi Consider Entering Politics.' ANC news briefing email service, 11 October 2001. Although remarkable, the move was not new: during the 1995 local government elections, Contralesa had stood for elections as a political party in a few municipalities in the Eastern Cape.

[86] Sapa. 'Traditional Leaders Bill This Year: Mufamadi.' ANC news briefing email service: ANC, 2001.

[87] The Eastern Cape also contemplated establishment of such a commission, while in the Free State the Provincial House of Traditional Leaders had a specific in-house commission to look into the matter.

[88] 'Body to Study Role of Kings, Chiefs.' http://www.dispatch.co.za/1998/10/06/southafrica/LEADERS.HTM: Dispatch Online, 1998; Kathu Mamaila, 'Traditional Leaders Divided on Report.' *Sowetan*, 17 March 2000; Sapa. 'Address by Pres. Mbeki to the House of Traditional Leaders.', ———. 'Investigation into Appointment of Northern Province Chiefs Could Be Extended.' ANC news briefing email service: ANC, 2000.

[89] Kathu Mamaila, 'Traditional Leaders Take Dim View of New Talk.' http://www.iol.co.za/html/frame_news.php?click_id=&art_id=ct20000817212505918K521768: *Independent* online, 2000.

to its consequences for general policy on traditional leadership and the 2003 legislative proposals.

5. 'Two bulls in a kraal?': the local government discussion

Nowhere was apartheid's patchwork legacy more visible than in local government. What would euphemistically come to be known as the 'rural areas', those areas in former homelands under traditional authority rule, still had a population density of 199 people per km^2 by 2000, as opposed to 19 elsewhere. The employment rate was 42 per cent, as opposed to 66 per cent in the rest of South Africa, and 34 instead of 246 out of every 1000 people had access to a telephone.[90] Institutionally, traditional authorities had been the only form of local government in these areas up to 1994, with the Black Administration and the Black Authorities Acts granting them functions ranging from taxation to weed eradication. Behind these authorities and curbing their powers, in the homeland era, stood an ever-expanding army of technocrats and civil servants directed from the central government. Their point of departure was that elective local government was only for urban areas, while the 'rural areas' merely had to be administered, technocratically and without reference to politics,[91] as illustrated by the Regional Services Councils set up in the 1980s as umbrella bodies responsible for the bulk delivery of services in fields such as health and agriculture.[92]

Paradoxically, though it was in these areas that democratisation and deracialisation of governance were most needed, it was also here that this would prove most difficult. While, from the onset of the 1990–94 negotiations, the ANC's aim had been the installation of universal (wall-to-wall was the local phrase), democratically elected local government and the introduction of viable municipalities, this turned out to be politically unattainable. Vested interests, among both the traditional leaders and white-ruled municipalities, were simply too powerful, and in the end the negotiators settled for a three-stage process of local government transition.[93] In a pre-interim phase, Local Government Negotiating Forums would be established all over South Africa to debate the future form of local government. An interim phase, governed by the interim Constitution and ensuing legislation and still largely on the basis of old privileges and borders, would start after the 1995 local government elections. Only then would the final democratic local government system be discussed, which would lead to a concluding phase to be implemented after the 2000 local government elections.

[90] Parliamentary Monitoring Group. 'Provincial and Local Government Portfolio Committee: Traditional Leadership and Institutions Discussion Document: Hearings.' http://www.pmg.org.za/minutes/000606pclocalpm.htm: Parliamentary Monitoring Group, 2000.

[91] D.A. Kotze, 'Rural Field Administration: From Apartheid to a New South Africa.' *Africanus* 24, no. 2 (1994): 31–39, Alastair McIntosh, 'Rural Folk in Limbo/Traditional Leaders' Role', in *Governing at Local Level: A Resource for Community Leaders*, ed. Paul Graham, Cape Town: Idasa, 1995, p.76. For good overviews of the local government legacy of apartheid cf. Ismael (1999); Alastair McIntosh, 'Rethinking Chieftaincy and the Future of Rural Local Government: A Preliminary Investigation', *Transformation* 13 (1990); Tapscott, 'Institutionalisation of Rural Local Government'.

[92] 'RSCs: Control Is the Name of the Game', *The New Nation*, 2–8 April 1987: 6–7.

[93] Cf. Ismael (1999); Christopher Pycroft, 'Restructuring Non-Metropolitan Local Government in South Africa,' *Public Administration and Development* 19 (1999): 179–92; Tapscott. 'Institutionalisation of Rural Local Goverment'.

Needless to say, the traditional leaders were vehemently opposed to what they perceived as a system of 'two bulls in a kraal'. From the beginning it was clear that the newly elected councils would be expected to perform many of the same functions as had been allocated to them in the past. The interim Constitution, for instance, stated that a local government would make provision for access 'by all persons residing within its area of jurisdiction to water, sanitation, transportation facilities, electricity, primary health services, education, housing and security'.[94] In the following sub-section we trace the traditional leaders' increasingly successful opposition to the democratisation and deracialisation of local government in 'their' areas.

The Local Government Transition Act

South Africa's first local government elections were held by the end of 1995. They had been delayed, especially by traditional leaders' protests against the introduction of universal local government in KwaZulu/Natal and the Eastern Cape, and by violent clashes between traditional leaders and the civics (grassroots organisations) in the Eastern Cape.[95] In the end, however, they did take place quite peacefully and with a relatively high voter turn-out.[96] The system that was put in place was based on the interim Constitution and the Local Government Transition Act (209/1993), and reflected the negotiated settlement they contained: it still largely followed the old boundaries, the divisions between white and black areas and the privileges attached to them.[97]

In general, five different types of councils were introduced, each with varying jurisdictions. The urban areas were to be ruled by Transitional Metropolitan Councils or Transitional Local Councils. In the rural areas, provinces had a choice between (elected) Transitional Rural Councils, (partially appointed) Transitional Representative Councils and (appointed) District Councils, the latter functioning either as first-tier local government or as umbrella organisations charged with the delivery of bulk services in an area with various TRCs or TLCs.[98] The actual arrangements differed from province to province: the Northern Province, for instance, installed elected Transitional Local Councils in all its rural areas, combined with District Councils as umbrella organisations. Provinces like the North-West and KwaZulu/Natal, on the other hand, opted for a system with only 'first-tier' District Councils in their rural areas.[99]

[94] S 175 (3) Act 200/1993.

[95] Marion Edmunds, 'Chiefs Want More Power in Local Government.' http://web.sn.apc.org/wmail/issues/950818/wm950818-8.html: *Daily Mail & Guardian* electronic archive, 1995, ———. 'Tension in ANC over Traditional Leaders' *Daily Mail & Guardian* electronic archive, 1 December 1995; 'Elections: Too Many Chiefs.' *Finance Week* 65, no. 2 (1995): 16; Graeme Gotz *The Process and the Product: The November Local Elections and the Future of Local Government*. Johannesburg: Centre for Policy Studies, 1996, Eric Naki, 'Delay Angers Eastern Cape Chiefs.' http://web.sn.apc.org/wmail/issues/941202/wm941202-11.html: *Daily Mail & Guardian* electronic archive, 1994; Payne, 'ANC Considers Appeal', Pearce. 'A Little Tlc Will Help Local Government.'

[96] Terence Fife. 'Improving the Participation Rate in Rural Elections: A Report of the November 1995 Rural Local Government Elections.', 'Local Government Elections 1 November 1995: Summary Statistics 4 October 1995.' Pretoria: Government Printers, 1995.

[97] For good discussions of the interim arrangements cf. Cloete (1994); Düsing, (1996); Ntsebeza (1998).

[98] Cf. Act 209/1993, in particular section 9a as amended by *Amendment Act 89/1995*.

[99] The Eastern Cape, like the Northern Province, opted for elected TRCs, while the other provinces opted for Transitional Representative Councils combined with District Councils in the rural areas.

The role legally destined for traditional leaders in the different councils depended on whether they were elected or not. For elected councils, as we have seen, the interim Constitution provided that 'the traditional leader of a community observing a system of indigenous law and residing on land within the area of jurisdiction of an elected local government ... shall *ex officio* be entitled to be a member of that local government, and shall be eligible to be elected to any office of such local government'.[100] For those councils in rural areas that were not, totally, elected, a special amendment was made to the Local Government Transition Act in 1995, making traditional leaders one of the possible stakeholder groups that could make up a maximum of 10 per cent of the councillors in both District Councils and Transitional Representative Councils.[101]

The provisions also caused an enormous amount of confusion. In KwaZulu/Natal, for instance, the combination of the fact that all traditional leaders had to be represented, but at the same time could make up only a maximum of 10 per cent of non-elected councils, led to an 'arcane' system with District Councils of 200–300 members in areas with a lot of traditional leaders.[102] The ANC tried to put an end to this by demanding that the Constitutional Court declare that traditional leaders did not have to be represented on District Councils but lost its case, with the Court arguing that it was precisely the intention of the interim arrangements that traditional leaders would be represented on the local councils without having to stand for election.[103] But even in the case of elected councils, where the '10% rule' did not apply, the *ex officio* representation of chiefs caused problems in those areas where, for instance, there were 25 chiefs and only 10 elected councillors.[104] Once the government realised this, it sought to remedy the situation by amending s 182 of the interim Constitution to state that only those traditional leaders identified as such could become *ex officio* council members.[105] The guidelines for such identification were only published weeks after the elections, and made the provincial premiers responsible for identifying the *ex officio* traditional leaders. These premiers would first have to consult the House of Traditional Leaders (if there was one) to find out which leader held 'the supreme office of authority' among all the leaders of the tribes concerned, and only then identify the relevant chiefs.[106]

In addition, there was confusion about what *ex officio* membership meant: full voting rights or mere observer status? Although any correct legal interpretation would be that of full voting rights (*ex officio*, after all, implying that traditional leaders were members of the elected councils because of the office they held), the national and provincial governments were quick to state that the phrase meant

[100] s 182 Act 200/1995.

[101] S 9 Act 209/1993 as amended by *Amendment Act 89/1995*. Other stakeholder groups were (a) farmers, landowners or levy payers; (b) farm labourers and (c) women.

[102] Electoral Institute of South Africa, 'Revisiting the Rural Model of Local Government in South Africa.' Johannesburg, 23 January 1997, Munro and Barnes (1997); Interview, S. Naidoo, Executive Officer SALGA, 20 February 1998.

[103] *ANC v MEC for Local Government and Housing, Kwazulu-Natal and Others*, unreported (1997), at para 19.

[104] Interviews with officials at the responsible departments in the North-West, Northern Province and Mpumalanga, 1996.

[105] *Constitution of the Republic of South Africa Second Amendment Act*. 44/1995, s 8.

[106] *Proclamation: Manner and Guidelines for the Identification of Traditional Leaders Who Shall Be Ex Officio Members of Elected Local Government*. R 109.

that traditional leaders would merely be observers.[107] Thus, by 1995, traditional leaders all over the country could be heard grumbling along the lines of: 'why should we only be *ex officio*?'[108] Also, even if the traditional leaders were to be allowed to vote, they foresaw problems. One was the possibility of being outvoted by their 'subjects', many of them the ANC supporters who had revolted against them in the 1980s. Another was the potential problem of having to decide issues outside their territorial jurisdiction, such as whether to build a swimming pool in a neighbouring town. Finally, there was uncertainty over the question of whether traditional leaders – used to operating 'in council' – could be represented by proxies or would have to attend council meetings in person.

Except in the KwaZulu case, these questions would remain theoretical. The *ex officio* clause was hardly implemented in any of the other provinces, and both elected councillors and traditional leaders kept to their own business.[109] Although a variety of relations were forged at the local level – varying from chiefs being elected mayor to violent clashes between chiefs and councillors – this mostly meant that there was very little contact between the two structures.[110] This lack of penetration by elected local government also had everything to do with the striking undercapacity of the rural councils. As Chief Nonkonyana would remark: 'the ancestors came to our rescue, they made it so that the TRCs didn't deliver.'[111] Rural councils were indeed the 'orphans' of South African local government, with only an estimated 10 per cent of government revenue directed towards the estimated 52 per cent of the population living there.[112] Not only did the newly elected councillors lack experience, they were often hardly given the material and technical support needed to carry out the host of functions bestowed upon them.[113] It was estimated, for instance, that 85 per cent of the income of these 'councils born on crutches' went directly towards the payment of salaries, which in themselves were hardly extravagant.[114] All this seemed particularly iniquitous in the light of the attention paid by the government to the chiefs: 'the support that is given to traditional authorities by the

[107] The 'wide interpretation' of the *ex officio* provision can be found in McIntosh. 'Rural Folk in Limbo/Traditional Leaders' Role'; Payne. 'ANC Considers Appeal', implicitly in *ANC v MEC for Local Government and Housing, Kwazulu-Natal and Others*, and was held by constitutional experts such as Prof. J. Kruger (interviewed 14 November 1995). A more narrow interpretation – observer status only – was propagated in the widely dispersed 'Local Government – Focus on Rural Local Government, Edited by S. Nthai: Book Review', *Local Government Digest* 16, no. 1 (1996): 2, and encountered in practically all interviews on the implementation of the clause, with the Director of Traditional Affairs in the Northern Province indicating that this confusion was created deliberately by the elected local councillors (Interview, 6 March 1998).

[108] For instance, at a Masakhane meeting in Lebowakgomo, 9 November 1995.

[109] Interviews with, for instance, S. Naidoo, Executive Officer SALGA, 20 February 1998 and Rev. Kekana, Director Traditional Affairs in the Northern Province, 6 March 1998.

[110] Xolani Xundu. 'This Is No Ordinary Chief Running for the Job of Mayor.' *Business Day*, 4 December 2000, 4. Cf. Williams (2000).

[111] Nkosi M. Nonkonyana, Paper presented at the Good Governance at the Local Level: Traditional Leaders and Rural Local Councillors Conference, East London, 10–11 March 1998.

[112] Department of Constitutional Development, 'Rural Local Government – an Unpublished Internal Discussion Document.' 1995, p.3.

[113] Cf. Northern Transvaal MEC for Land and Housing, 'The Status of Transitional Local Councils in the Rural Areas of the Northern Province.' Pietersburg, 1997; Ntsebeza (1999: 58–61).

[114] William Mervin Gumede, 'Councils Born on Crutches: Another Bailout by Taxpayers.' *Financial Mail*, 19 January 2001, p. 35.

government contrasts sharply with the minimal support that rural elected councillors get.'[115]

In the cases where councils did attempt to start up local development by implementing the government's ambitious Reconstruction and Development Programme, this often led to immediate tensions with the traditional leaders. 'These people are living on our land and still they want to rule us. They even want to draw up laws in our own homes,' as one traditional leader voiced the frustration of many colleagues.[116] More often than not, the disputes were about land use. The Local Government Transition Act, for instance, required councils to make an Integrated Development Plan (IDP) containing Land Development Objectives (LDOs).[117] Setting such objectives also meant making plans for land over which, according to the Black Administration Act and other applicable laws, traditional leaders still had jurisdiction. The ensuing tussle over land ownership would often lead to development projects being paralysed and cause those involved to cite the old African proverb: 'where two bulls fight, it is the grass that suffers'.

The White Paper and new municipal legislation

While the interim arrangements were arduously implemented on the ground, discussions continued over the final form of South Africa's local government. The 1996 Constitution had set out a general framework by introducing the notion of 'co-operative government', in which national, provincial and local government would form three 'distinctive, interdependent and interrelated *spheres* of government' (emphasis added).[118] As one such sphere, the objectives of local government included: providing democratic and accountable government for local communities, ensuring the sustainable provision of services, promoting social and economic development and a safe and healthy environment and encouraging the involvement of communities.[119] Its functions could range from markets and municipal roads to health services, trading regulations, water supply and sanitation.[120] In addition, the Constitution determined that there would be three types of municipalities: category A, with exclusive executive and legislative authority (for instance in the large towns), and category B, which shared this authority with larger 'umbrella-type' category C municipalities.[121] As to traditional leaders, as we have seen, all that had been decided was that 'national legislation *may* provide for a role for traditional leadership as an institution at local level on matters affecting local communities' (emphasis added).[122]

[115] Lungisile Ntsebeza, 'Chapter 5: Attempts to Extend Democracy to Rural Areas.' Unpublished, 2000, p. 27.

[116] This Reconstruction and Development Programme was replaced by the Growth, Employment and Redistribution Strategy (GEAR) in 1998. Cf. Lucas Styles Ledwaba, 'Chief Is at Odds with Change', *Sunday World*, 25 April 1999, p.9.

[117] Stephen Berrisford, 'A New Approach to Planning and Development: The Development Facilitation Act', *Land Info* 4, no. 3 (1997): 11–12; Department of Constitutional Development, 'Integrated Development Planning for Local Authorities: A User-Friendly Guide.' Pretoria: Department of Constitutional Development. on the basis of Act 209/1993 and *Development Facilitation Act*. 67/1995.

[118] S 40 Act 108/1996.

[119] S 152 (1) Act 108/1996.

[120] The B-parts of Schedules 4 and 5 to Act 108/1996.

[121] S 155 Act 108/1996.

[122] S 212 (1) Act 108/1996.

Nevertheless, this general framework still had to be spelled out in a White Paper, and subsequently elaborated in specific legislation. In the White Paper discussion, the relation between traditional leaders and elective local government once again proved to be one of the most onerous issues. Dozens of workshops and conferences were held, both by government and by NGOs, in which possible scenarios were discussed: two bulls in a kraal? A democratic bull and a traditional ox? A traditional bull and a democratic ox? The slaughtering of the traditional bull? Or the democratic one? A democratic bull and a traditional sheep?[123] While traditional leaders' representatives generally clung to their demand to be recognised as the primary layer of local government, other proposals included making chiefs the executive heads of rural local government or creating councils with 50-50 representation.[124]

The text of the 1998 White Paper, however, again failed to come up with any clear decisions on the matter. It referred to the – supposedly – upcoming White Paper on Traditional Authorities and indicated that traditional leaders' role would 'include attending and participating in meetings of the Councils and advising Councils on the needs and interests of their communities (...). Whether traditional leaders should exercise voting rights alongside the councillors ... needs to be determined after further consultation and research into constitutional provisions.'[125] It is instructive to compare these vague and open-ended provisions with the – confidential – final draft of the White Paper, which foresaw a much more explicitly restricted role for the traditional leaders: as ceremonial heads of the municipal councils without voting rights.[126] Apparently, the late-night meetings between traditional leaders and the responsible Minister, Valli Moosa, which in themselves had delayed publication of the document, had also led to a severe revision of the section on traditional authorities, once again postponing progress on real decision-making.[127]

The three main laws formulated on the basis of the White Paper did not bring much extra clarity either. The first, the Municipal Demarcation Act (27/1998), addressed the challenge of redrawing apartheid's institutional boundaries to create viable municipalities. Among the criteria the newly established Municipal Demarcation Board had to take into account were not only the 'interdependence of people, communities and economies', 'the need for cohesive, integrated and unfragmented areas' and 'the financial viability and administrative capacity' but also the 'areas of traditional rural communities'.[128] The crucial Municipal Structures Act imitated the openness of earlier arrangements:

> S 81 (1) Traditional authorities that traditionally observe a system of customary law in the area of a municipality, may participate through their leaders, identified in terms of

[123] Kyra Naudascher, *Between Traditional Conservatism and Modern Democratic – Is There a Role for Traditional Leadership in African Democratic Systems?* Johannesburg: Friedrich Ebert Stiftung, 1997. gives these scenarios.

[124] Holomisa (1996); Ngoako Ramathlodi, 'Traditional Leaders "Have Role"', *Sowetan*, 10 December 1997, p.12.

[125] Ministry for Provincial Affairs and Constitutional Development, *The White Paper on Local Government*, Pretoria, 1998, pp. 77–8.

[126] 'The White Paper on Local Government – Final Confidential Draft.' 1998, p. 63.

[127] This was confirmed in interviews with officials of the Department of Provincial Affairs and Constitutional Development and SALGA executive members in March 1998: 'that one, that's the most sensitive issue,' one of them said.

[128] S 25 sub a,b,c and f, Act 27/1998.

subsection 2, in the proceedings of the council of that municipality, and those traditional leaders must be allowed to attend and participate in any meeting of the council.[129]

The responsible MEC (provincial minister), the law stated, would identify those traditional leaders to sit on the council on the basis of their residence and 'holding the supreme office of authority' among all the chiefs concerned.[130] In all, the traditional leaders were not allowed to make up more than 10 per cent of the council. The extent of their participation – full voting rights or not? – was left open, as the law ruled that 'the MEC *may* regulate the participation of traditional leaders in the proceedings of a municipal council' and 'prescribe a role for traditional leaders in the affairs of a municipality'.[131] Although the role was not clear, the Municipal Systems Act, passed to regulate the relationship between citizen and government and to enshrine values such as accountability, transparency, efficiency and consultation, did make those traditional leaders who were members of councils subject to a Code of Conduct, and gave MECs the right to suspend their participation in case of misbehaviour.[132]

The 2000 implementation crisis

As has so often proved the case, it was not so much the legislative discussion as the actual implementation of local government policies, and especially the physical redrawing of boundaries, that led to vehement clashes between the government and the traditional leaders.[133] The Municipal Demarcation Board had, in particular, vowed to create financially viable municipalities and this, as it soon turned out, meant at times amalgamating existing traditional authority areas into wider municipalities, or even cutting through their borders.[134] Once this became clear, the chiefs' reactions were fast and furious. At an *imbizo* in Umlazi in January 2000, thousands of traditional leaders brandishing spears, shields, fighting sticks and battle axes lashed out at the government's plans.[135] Violence erupted all over KwaZulu/Natal and the Eastern Cape, with life-and-death battles over boundaries such as that in Flagstaff, which, as surprised observers would remark, had been created artificially with the introduction of the Transkei bantustan 40 years earlier.[136] By the end of January, six people had died

[129] *Municipal Structures Act*. 117/1998, s 81 (1).

[130] Schedule 6, S Act 117/1998.

[131] S 81 (4) Act 117/1998.

[132] *Local Government Municipal Systems Act* 32/2000, s. 15.

[133] Cf. Thomas Bierschenk, and Jean-Pierre Olivier de Sardan, 'Call for Papers: Decentralisation, Democratisation and Good Local Government: What Lessons from Anthropology?' Paper presented at the 14th International Congress of Anthropological and Ethnological Sciences, Williamsburg, VA, 1998.

[134] Chris Heymans, 'SA's New Municipalities Will Face a Host of Challenges', *Business Day*, 28 November 2000, p. 11; Jubie Matlou, 'Chiefs Face Mbeki over Traditional Land.' http://www.mg.co.za/mg/news/2000feb1/3feb-boundary.html: *Daily Mail & Guardian* electronic archive, 2000; Pycroft, 'Restructuring Non-Metropolitan Local Government in South Africa'; Michael Sutcliffe, 'Demarcation a Part of Broader Transformation.' *Business Day*, 4 December 2000, p. 11.

[135] Bronwen Roberts, 'Angry Zulu King Protests at Pretoria's Land Plans', http://www.mg.co.za/mg/za/archive/2000jan/15jan-news.html#zulu: *Daily Mail & Guardian* electronic archive, 2000, 'Traditional Rule, Power and Greed', http://www.bday.co.za/bday/content/direct/0,3523,550257-6078-0,00.html: *Business Day* online, 2000.

[136] Paul Kirk and Jubie Matlou, 'Boundary Clashes Leave Six Dead.' http://www.mg.co.za/mg/news/2000jan2/24jan-kwazulu.html: *Daily Mail & Guardian* electronic archive, 2000; Bronwen Roberts, 'Warnings over Municipal Boundaries.' http://www.mg.co.za/mg/za/archive/2000jan/28janpm-news.html: *Daily Mail & Guardian* electronic archive, 2000.

and 30 had been injured in what astonished newspapers called 'tribal violence over borders'.[137]

Multiple grievances were voiced by traditional leaders and their followers during these protests. Some were purely demagogic, like the statement by National House of Traditional Leaders chairman Mzimela that the new municipalities would never allow people to own more than 200 cattle, would prevent Zulus from performing traditional ceremonies like slaughtering cows, and would generally destroy traditional customs, law and culture.[138] Or of a colleague saying that 'it's like telling the people of Israel to go back to Egypt'.[139] But others did contain elements of truth. There was, for instance, the idea that the redrawing of boundaries would diminish the control traditional leaders wielded over land.[140] In addition, chiefly subjects, who in the apartheid era had become used to their basic needs being subsidised by the South African government, would now have to start paying for services such as roads, electricity, water, and waste collection and disposal.[141] Nevertheless, the main fear concerned the potential loss of political authority. For, as one observer remarked: 'Ultimately this threatens the chiefs' interests. If councils do their job properly and promote development it will speed up urbanisation and strengthen the electoral principle.'[142] For this reason, the traditional leaders continued to demand recognition as the primary layer of local government, linked only through 'umbrella' regional councils to urban municipalities, even though this, according to opponents, was nothing but a perpetuation of 'separate development'.[143]

With the very real threat of local government elections planned for the end of 2000 being disrupted by traditional authority boycotts, the government did its best to placate the chiefs. As the latter considered the Minister for Provincial Affairs and Local Government Sydney Mufamadi to be biased against them, most meetings took place with President Mbeki himself.[144] By June, the President conceded that it might be necessary to amend the Constitution to come up with

[137] 'Solving Tribal Conflicts Should Be High on the Agenda.' http://www.bday.co.za/bday/content/direct/0,3523,541701-6078-0,00.html: *Business Day* online, 2000.

[138] 'Traditional Leaders Reject Municipalities.' *Business Day*, 21 January 2000, http://www.bday.co.za/bday/content/direct/0,3523,546824-6078-0,00.html.

[139] Bobby Jordan, 'Let My People Go, Says Chief.' *Sunday Times*, 20 January 2000, 2.

[140] Marianne Merten. 'Not Enough Information.' http://www.mg.co.za/mg/news/2000apr1/6apr-igoli3.html: *Daily Mail & Guardian* electronic archive, 2000; 'A Storm to Be Ridden.' http://www.bday.co.za/bday/content/direct/0,3523,544549-6078-0,00.html: *Business Day* online, 2000.

[141] 'Big Changes for Property Law on Cards.' http://www.bday.co.za/bday/content/direct/0,3523,553007-6078-0,00.html: *Business Day* online, 2000, 'Demarcation Upsets Chiefs.' http://www.bday.co.za/bday/content/direct/0,3523,687326-6078-0,00.html: *Business Day* online, 2000; Pycroft. 'Restructuring Non-Metropolitan Local Government in South Africa.'

[142] 'A Storm to Be Ridden'.

[143] There were differences of opinion between the traditional leaders: Contralesa, for instance, was not opposed to universal elected local government but did feel that traditional authorities should then form the primary tier. Many KwaZulu leaders, on the other hand, did not want any elected local government in their areas (interview P. Holomisa, Amsterdam, 22 September 2000). Cf. Jordan. 'Let My People Go, Says Chief.'

[144] 'Chiefs Refuse to Participate in Talks.' http://www.bday.co.za/bday/content/direct/0,3523,680624-6078-0,00.html: Business Day online, 2000; 'Meetings with Traditional Leaders', in *Hansard*, 4952, 2000; Lungisile, 'Whither South Africa's Democracy? The Case of Rural Local Government in the Former Bantustans', p. 14; 'Traditional Leaders Are Sailing against the Wind', *Business Day* online, 17 August 2000.

'a dual system (providing) for the retention of traditional leadership, while at the same time allowing local communities to elect public representatives'.[145] And when, in August, it became clear that traditional leaders were hampering voter registration in many areas, the President offered them another 'olive branch': the Municipal Structures Act would be amended so as to allow a 20 per cent, instead of a 10 per cent, chiefly representation in the municipal councils.[146]

Nevertheless, this did not prove enough for the traditional leaders who demanded that their functions be specifically addressed. The government therefore hurriedly introduced an amendment to the Municipal Structures Act, stating that the functions of traditional leaders included 'to collect and administer all fees and charges which are, according to custom, payable to the traditional authority'; 'to perform such functions as may be delegated to [them] by a municipal council'; 'to be the custodians of culture and customs' and to 'convene meetings of community members'.[147] The fact that this proposal left the traditional leaders no real power infuriated them. It was particularly the whole list of functions such as 'to facilitate the gathering of firewood', 'to co-ordinate first fruit ceremonies', 'to co-ordinate rain-making ceremonies' and 'to attend to matters relating to witchcraft and divination' that they tagged as 'an insult to their intelligence, decorum and good faith'.[148] Postponement of the elections seemed inevitable.

In a desperate attempt to still hold them in 2000, the government set up a Joint Technical Committee, consisting of Traditional Affairs Department officials and traditional leaders, to determine if the power of the latter had indeed been diminished by the new municipal legislation, and if so, to recommend steps to remedy the situation.[149] In addition, the government – clearly in response to more of the familiar late-night meetings with the chiefs – practically completely rewrote the amendment.[150] When Parliament was recalled at the end of November to fast-track the Bill in order to enable elections in early December, the long list of 'exotic functions' and hollow promises had been deleted and replaced by what looked like a solid retention and even expansion of existing powers:

> Despite anything contained in any other law, a traditional authority observing a system of customary law continues to exist and to exercise functions conferred upon it in terms of indigenous law, customs and statutory law, which powers and functions include:

[145] John Seiler, 'Trappings of Power in Local Govt Not Enough for Traditional Chiefs.' http://www.bday.co.za/bday/content/direct/0,3523,703006-6078-0,00.html: *Business Day* online, 2000.

[146] 'Govt Gives Traditional Leaders More Say' *Business Day* online, 31 August 2000; Sapa. 'Impossible for Prisoners to Vote: Mchunu.', ———. 'Registration Weekend Off to a Slow Start.' ANC news briefing email service: ANC, 2000.

[147] *Local Government: Municipal Structures Second Amendment Bill.* B – 2000.

[148] The whole amendment proposed to s 81 of Act 117/1998 by the Bill includes 24 functions. Cf. 'Bill Is an Insult, Say Traditional Leaders.' http://www.bday.co.za/bday/content/direct/1,3523,735109-6078-0,00.html: *Business Day* online, 2000.

[149] Joint Technical Committee on traditional leadership issues. 'Statement by the Joint Technical Committee on Traditional Leadership Issues.' Pretoria: GCIS, 2000.

[150] 'Chiefs' Pressure Delays Poll Date Again', http://www.dispatch.co.za/2000/10/10/southafrica/ADATE.HTM: Dispatch Online, 2000; 'Chiefs Seek to Keep Power after Local Poll.' http://www.dispatch.co.za/2000/10/17/southafrica/CHIEFS.HTM: Dispatch Online, 2000; 'Contralesa Gearing up for Court Battle.' http://www.bday.co.za/bday/content/direct/0,3523,716579-6078-0,00.html: *Business Day* online, 2000.

> the right to administer communal land (...)
>
> 81a) Traditional authorities and municipal councils must exercise their powers and perform their functions in a manner that respects the functional and institutional interests of one another.[151]

It soon became apparent that passing this completely reworked version, which had not been gazetted for comments, would be unconstitutional, but the traditional leaders were promised that it would be handled first thing in the new year.[152]

Thus, from an institutional point of view, very little had happened by the time the local government elections took place on 5 December. Nevertheless, the traditional leaders had gained more than they had lost. It was not without reason that commentators grumbled about the democratic government being held 'to ransom' by chiefs, and how 'isolated pockets where the normal rules of voting and accountability are suspended cannot be sustained in the long term': the traditional leaders had managed to retain a great deal of their sovereignty and had been promised legislative reaffirmation of it. Just before the elections the government released a Statement of Intent that meekly spelled out the traditional leaders' demands, 'in order to ensure that the powers and functions of traditional leaders in local government are not eroded'. For this purpose, 'relevant sections of Chapters 7 and 12 of the Constitution will be amended to provide for the powers and functions of traditional authorities in local government. In dealing with these matters, government and traditional leaders will be guided by the principle of respect for, and recognition of, the critical role of traditional leaders in the system of governance in our country, particularly among the rural communities.'[153]

The government started to drag its feet as soon as the elections were over and managed to postpone passage of the promised amendments as well as action in the direction of a White Paper on Traditional Authorities throughout 2001. Nevertheless, the chiefs had won an important battle.[154] The prospect of erasing apartheid's institutional borders to make way for universal democratic government seemed further away than ever. And thus it would remain, even after a White Paper and accompanying draft legislation had finally been adopted in 2003. After a long period of silence, followed by endless rounds of consultation (largely, but far from exclusively with traditional leaders), the Department of Provincial and Local Government finally issued a White Paper on Traditional Leadership in July 2003.

The White Paper, which seemed to be acclaimed by most of the stakeholders

[151] *Local Government: Municipal Structures Second Amendment Bill*. B71 – 2000.

[152] Sapa. 'Withdrawal of Municipal Bill No Crisis: Mufamadi', ANC news briefing email service: ANC, 2000.

[153] Sapa. 'Government and the Coalition of Traditional Leaders – Re the Role of Traditional Authorities in Local Government.' ANC news briefing email service: ANC, 2000.

[154] Ebrahim Harvey, 'Chiefs Make Nonsense of Democracy', *Weekly Mail & Guardian*, 20 October 2000; Sapa. 'Buthelezi Slams Government over Recognition of Amakhosi'; ———. 'Resolve Amakhosi Issue, IFP Urges Mbeki.' ANC news briefing email service: ANC, 2001; ———. 'Traditional Leaders Bill'. During 2001, traditional leaders made all kinds of threats to force the government to carry out its promises: to take it to the Constitutional Court or the public prosecutor, to establish their own political party and to lobby their subjects to vote for parties with a better track-record concerning traditional leaders than the ANC. But though the government frequently asserted that the '*amakhosi* issue' was being looked into, it took very little action.

involved, argued that traditional leadership 'has the potential to transform, to contribute enormously towards the restoration of the moral fibre of our society, and to play a significant role in the reconstruction and development of our country, particularly in the rural areas'. It departed from the notion that traditional leaders should be considered custodians of tradition and culture, and formulated its central policy objectives as: a) defining the place and role of the institution within the new system of democratic governance; b) transforming the institution in accordance with constitutional imperatives; and c) restoring the integrity and legitimacy of the institution in accordance with customary law and practices. These, possibly contradictory, objectives resurfaced in the vision of the institution, which was expected simultaneously to 'promote freedom ... and the achievement of equality and non-sexism' and to strive 'to enhance tradition and culture'. The roles envisaged included promoting socio-economic development, enhancing service delivery and contributing to nation-building. Also, the White Paper suggested that national and provincial departments would provide for traditional councils and their leadership to play a role in such disparate fields as arts and culture, land and agriculture, health and welfare, justice, security and home affairs, economic development, environment and tourism, natural resource management, communication and 'customary functions'.[155]

What these roles should be did not become clear in the accompanying *Traditional Leadership and Governance Framework Bill*, later to be adopted as an Act, either.[156] The Bill did, on the one hand, resolve some of the issues that had been debated so vehemently since the early 1990s. For one, it defined traditional leadership as 'the customary institutions or structures, or customary systems or procedures of governance, recognised, utilised or practised by traditional communities'. In addition, it recognised both traditional communities and traditional councils, giving the latter wide-ranging but largely unspecified functions in the field of development and 'administering the affairs of the traditional community in accordance with custom and tradition', It also set out the three leadership positions to be recognised: kingship, principal traditional leadership and headmanship. Furthermore, it provided for national and district houses of traditional leaders and – as a novelty – a separate Commission on Traditional Leadership Disputes and Claims. The memorandum explained that these changes, ranging from the formal recognition of headmen to the installation of the Commission, would cost the South African state an additional R100 million a year. Finally, the Bill explicitly provided for female traditional leaders, and demanded that one-third of the members of traditional councils be women.[157]

What the Bill, and the Act that followed it, did not do, however, was address the three key questions at hand: the exact relation between traditional leadership and elected local government, the role of traditional leaders in land allocation, and the jurisdiction of customary courts. Once again, it merely put off decisions on this subject, stating that 'A traditional leader performs the functions provided for in terms of customary law and practices of the traditional community concerned, and in applicable legislation.' This vagueness was reiterated in a section stating that national or provincial government *may* make provision for a

[155] Department of Provincial and Local Government, *The White Paper on Traditional Leadership and Government*, pp 8, 71, 11, 25–6, 32, 36–7.

[156] *B 58 – 2003 and Act 41/2003.*

[157] Ibid. The sections quoted are respectively 1(1) and 4f.

role for traditional leaders or councils in the functional areas quoted above, ranging from arts and culture to land administration and the administration of justice. On the relationship with municipal councils the Bill merely stated that partnerships between municipalities and traditional councils, based on principles of mutual respect and the status and role of the respective parties, must be promoted.[158] Whether traditional leadership was to be considered a separate sphere of government remained an open question, as did other key issues in the debate on the sovereignty of traditional leaders: their role in land allocation and in dispute resolution. In order to understand why this was so, let us now turn to the debates on these two topics before 2003.

6. Keeping control over land

If local government reform in the former homelands turned out to be exasperatingly dilatory, the treatment of apartheid's land distribution legacy was even more so. As we have seen, the linkage between access to land and acceptance of chiefly authority had become a central element in the bantustan policies. Since the way it worked differed by homeland and even by tribal authority, this, once again resulted in a legislative patchwork that would prove very hard to sort out. Nowhere were the clashes between the propagators of individual rights and those in favour of chiefly authority more vehement, and nowhere would they offer, in the years after the elections, more surprises to those who had expected chieftaincy to 'melt like ice in the sun'.

What did this part of the institutional inheritance look like? Most of the estimated 1700 laws, regulations and bye-laws pertaining to land in the 'rural areas' were based on the 1927 Black Administration Act and the 1913 and 1936 Land Acts.[159] These pillars of segregation restricted black land ownership to the 'native reserves', later the homelands, gave traditional authorities the right to allocate land and, in all cases, prohibited freehold title to land. By the 1990s, most of the land in the homelands was held in trust by the government, while traditional authorities had obtained the right to issue so-called Permissions to Occupy: quit rent titles which, for instance, prohibited selling or mortgaging the land concerned.[160] But there were also other forms of land tenure: some homelands could declare a certain plot of land to be a 'township', while in other areas tribes, as legal entities, had purchased land at the beginning of the century.[161] Also, all the homelands had separate regulations pertaining to issues such as allocation, administration and inheritance.

Developments in the early 1990s only added to this confusion. Some of the first apartheid aberrations to be addressed were the detested restrictions concerning the purchase of land by Africans outside the homelands. The 1991 Abolition of Racially Based Land Measures Act, however, did not change the

[158] Ibid. The sections quoted are respectively 17(1), 18(1) and 5(1).

[159] The number of 1700 land laws was quoted by Constitutional Development officials. Although the names of these laws often changed, the principal ones were Act 38/1927 and the Natives Land Act 27/1913 as well as the Development Trust and Land Act 18/1936

[160] These were normally based on *Land Regulations Proclamation*. R.188/1969.

[161] The 'R293' townships were named after the legislation on the basis of which they were established: *Regulations for the Administration and Control of Townships in Black Areas*. Proclamation 293/1962.

mode of land tenure inside the homelands, and its linkage to chiefly authority.[162] This link, in contrast, was only strengthened by two other laws that were considered by many as last-minute National Party attempts to keep as much land out of the hands of the future government as possible (Cousins, 2000). The first was the 1991 Upgrading of Land Tenure Rights Act (112/1991), which provided for the transfer of tribal land in full ownership to tribes, and the upgrading of Permissions to Occupy to full title deeds. This law was widely abused, for instance in the former Lebowa, where secret deals were brokered between chiefs, the homeland cabinet and the government leading to the eviction of long-time residents and the sale of large plots of land (Cousins, 2001).[163] A second outcome of the pre-election scramble for land was the KwaZulu Ingonyama Trust Act, which reflected a deal closed between President De Klerk and IFP leader Buthelezi on the eve of the elections. It vested large powers in the Zulu king Zwelithini, putting 93 per cent of the former KwaZulu under his trusteeship and ruling that this land could not be alienated or leased without his permission. Even though these laws were largely repealed after the elections, they continued to contribute to the general disarray: many people thought they still applied.[164]

So, by the time the new government was in place and beginning to think about future reforms in homeland tenure, it was confronted with shocking institutional and practical lack of clarity (Adams et al., 1999a; Lahiff, 1999).[165] In 1997, of the approximately 13 million people (32 per cent of the population) living in the former homelands, 64 per cent had a Permission to Occupy, 27 per cent did not have any title and 9 per cent were not sure about the status of their lands.[166] The estimated 1700 laws and regulations applicable were often contradictory, overlapping, lost in the archives or in sharp contrast with what people locally felt to be their rights. In the vacuum created, power-holders, varying from chiefs to development brokers, civic organisations, squatter patrons or warlords, had free-rein, while it was often the women and the very poor whose rights proved most insecure. Systems of administration had, more often than not, completely broken down and the insecurity of tenure stopped investment – both by locals and by outsiders (Adams et al., 1999b).

Hanekom: the socialist years

The Department of Land Affairs, specially established after 1994 to deal with these issues, was eager to 'get the land back to the people'. Newly appointed Minister Derek Hanekom attracted many former activists and human rights lawyers with first-hand knowledge of the issues at stake and a determination to solve them. In the years to come, the Department would be characterised by an atmosphere of wide consultation and a strong desire to remedy what was

[162] 'Contralesa Slates Hanekom', *Business Day* 1997, p. 2, Dudley Moloi, 'Royalty Gathers over an Uncertain Future.' *Land & Rural Digest* 1, no. 6 (1999): 8–9.

[163] Ben Cousins, 'Heath to Investigate Lebowa Land Trust.' *Star*, 15 June 1999, p. 5, J. Scheepers and N.M. Ramodike. 'Joint Press Statement on Land.' http://www.anc.org.za/ancdocs/pr/1992/pr1012b.html, 1992; and various interviews in Ga-Matlala, 14 and 18 December 1998.

[164] Cf. *Kwazulu Ingonyama Trust Amendment Act*. 9/1997, *Upgrading of Land Tenure Rights Amendment Act*. 34/1996.

[165] Thoko Didiza, 'The Importance of a Successful Land Reform Programme, in South African Land.' Paper presented at the National Land Tenure Conference, Durban 2001.

[166] National Land Commission. 'Tenure Reforms.' http://www.nlc.co.za/mdtenref.htm, 2000.

perceived as apartheid's most injurious legacy.[167] One of the first pieces of legislation it passed, the Interim Protection of Informal Land Rights Act (31/1996), sought to secure both customary rights to land as well as those created under apartheid legislation, until definite legislation was adopted.

From the beginning it was clear that the Department's policies for rural areas would be based on a mixture of individualism and communalism, stemming from the belief that 'decisions must be taken by the rights holders in democratic processes so that the interests of a minority cannot lead to the dispossession of the rights of others'.[168] And that there would be very little patience with chiefs, unless they had high popular legitimacy. 'We are,' as one Land Affairs official said, 'a socialist department, committed to the people and not to archaic structures.'[169] Another was more explicit: 'We work for the communities on the basis of their constitutional rights and there is no way in which we will contribute to the perpetuation of apartheid fallacies like Tribal Authorities.'[170] The government was keen to dispose of the land it held in trust, but only to the people and not to undemocratic institutions claiming to represent them.

The first legal instrument of this thinking was the 1996 Communal Property Associations Act (28/1996), destined to enable communities to form juristic persons that could acquire, hold and manage property under the guidance of elected committees. The so-called CPAs had to draw up a constitution which allowed for democratic decision-making, non-discrimination and participatory management.[170] Needless to say, the traditional leaders were far from thrilled with this proposed 'power to the people'.[171] They contended that, as 'the land had been taken from us in the past', any transfer of rights should be to the traditional authorities as legal entities. As chief Mdlethse wrote: 'a community and its land are united by a mystical relationship which ties together past, present and future generations. In our view, traditional leadership remains the final expression and the custodian of this relationship.' Land under traditional authorities, it was felt, 'should be considered already perfectly allocated and should not be part of the land reform programmes.'[172]

[167] There is no space here to discuss anything but the broad lines of South Africa's land reform process. For excellent overviews, Cf. Marj Brown, Justin Erasmus, Rosalie Kingwill, Colin Murray, and Monty Roodt (eds), *Land Restitution in South Africa: A Long Way Home*. Cape Town: Idasa, 1998; D.L. Carey Miller and Ann Pope. 'South African Land Reform.' *Journal of African Law* 44, no. 2 (2000): 167–94; De Villiers and Critchley (1997); Lipton *et al.* (1996); Therea Marcus, Kathy Eales and Adèle Wildschut, *Dowm to Earth: Land Demand in the New South Africa*. Durban: Land and Agriculture Policy Centre, 1996; Mngxitama, 'South Africa's Land Reform 1994–1999: A Critical Review.' Paper presented at the Land Tenure Models for 21st Century Africa, Leiden 1999; Ntsebeza (1999).

[168] Department of Land Affairs. 'White Paper on South African Land Policy.' Pretoria, 1997.

[169] Interview, Land Affairs official, Mpumalanga, 24 March 1998. Interview, Land Affairs official, Northern Province, 18 December 1998. These are but two examples. The widespread belief in the 1994-9 period that the Department of Land Affairs was anti-chief was confirmed in many separate interviews. Cf. Essy Letsaolo, Head of the Provincial Office of the Northern Province Department of Land Affairs, who complained about the DLA's bias against chieftaincy in an interview on 5 March 1998.

[170] S 9 Act 28/1996.

[171] Moloi, 'Royalty Gathers over an Uncertain Future'; Kgosi Morwagaabusi. 'The Impact of Land Restitution on Rural Governance.' Paper presented at the SASCA Conference 'Rural Governance in the new Millennium', Port Elizabeth, 23 June 1999; Charles Phahlane. 'Traditional Leaders Want Title Deeds, Rights over Tribal Land', *Cape Times*, 20 February 1998, p. 1.

[172] B.N. Mdlethse, 'What Is the Fate of "Tribal Land"?' *Natal Witness*, February 20 1998 pp. 1–2.

Nevertheless, the government's White Paper on Land Policy restated its dedication to democratisation, if not individual ownership, of communally-owned land. 'Government is under an obligation to ensure that group-based land holding systems do not conflict with the basic human rights of members of such systems.'[173] This combination of thinking in terms of communities as well as individual human rights ran throughout the three pillars of the land reform process: redistribution, restitution and tenure reform. Of these, redistribution was aimed at expanding black land ownership beyond the 13 per cent of the land occupied by the former homelands by granting the most marginalised in society R15,000 to purchase, individually or with others, a house or a plot of land. Restitution, in addition to this, granted people dispossessed of their right to land after 1913 as a result of racially discriminatory measures, and their descendants, the right to claim this land via a Land Claims Commission and a Land Claims Court.[174] The third pillar, tenure reform, sought to improve general security of title by accommodating various forms of tenure, including communal tenure.

In all three pillars, the Department met more resistance from the chiefs than it cared for. In *redistribution*, for instance, many demands for land became mixed up with chiefly politics. To their dismay, Land Affairs officials saw applications pouring in from landless chiefs, traditional leaders involved in succession disputes or others who merely wanted to expand their territorial jurisdiction.[175] Also, a piece of land allocated to a CPA often turned out to be run on tribal lines: 'We created a CPA for these people and the next thing we hear is that there is a chief allocating land and demanding R250 for it, claiming it's only a *khonza* fee to allow people to join the tribe.'[176] Another example of the difficulty in disentangling land redistribution and local power politics is that of Kalkfontein,[177] where, in the 1970s, there was only a communal authority, and no chief. As part of bantustan politics a tribal authority was created and a chief imposed on the community, who immediately began to allocate land to outside supporters and to expel trouble-makers. When the redistribution programme got under way, the original community decided to pool their R15,000 grants in order to 'get away from that chief'. Once they had received a new piece of land from the government, however, the traditional leader started to claim political jurisdiction over that area as well, seeking support from the House of Traditional Leaders and the provincial premier, and causing a conflict which continues up to the present.

Similar problems were encountered in the *restitution* process. Contralesa had been opposed to the cut-off date of 1913 from the outset, stating that traditional leaders should be able to claim from 1652 – the arrival of the white settlers – onwards and many chiefs enthusiastically put in claims on behalf of their disappropriated forefathers. The Department's general response was framed by one official as:

> The chiefs are normally the ones to put in the claim. If that claim is validated, we try to break down the chief's power by creating a legal entity like a CPA. We constantly emphasise that he is only one of the claimants, and that the legal entity will have a

[173] Department of Land Affairs, *White Paper on South African Land Policy*, 3.20.2.

[174] *Restitution of Land Rights Act*. 22/1994.

[175] Interviews, Mpumalanga Land Affairs officials, 24 March 1998; Cliffe (2000:275).

[176] Interview, Mpumalanga Land Affairs official, 25 March 1998.

[177] Various Mpumalanga interviews, Chris Williams, *Mpumalanga Provincial Office Settlement Support 1997 Report*, Nelspruit: Department of Land Affairs, 1997.

> democratically elected board. Initially people protest and stand up for the chief but we explain how it works and that they can, if they want, put the chief at the head of the board. We then spread power by extending it to the whole committee. But at the end of the day a lot of claims are 'tribal' and it is proving very difficult to break down the power of the chiefs.[178]

Nevertheless, those CPAs that managed to blend the 'tribal' and the democratic seemed to function. The Makuleke land claim in the Kruger Park, for example, was considered successful precisely because of the involvement of the traditional authority.[179]

Redistribution and restitution, however, did not affect the majority of the homeland residents. Not only was the pace very slow – with only 785 out of 63,455 restitution cases settled by 2000 – but the majority of the claims were also urban. Real security in the rural areas, everyone agreed, would have to come from *tenure reform.*[180] Here, the Minister had restated the intentions voiced in the White Paper in a 1998 memorandum.[181] This stated that the government would recognise the underlying land rights of individuals or groups (for example, tribes) to land which was normally state-owned, and that it sought to vest these rights in people – as the rights holders – and not in institutions such as tribal or local authorities. These people should then decide which governance structures they wanted. Transfer of rights from the government to the people should be achieved by statute, the memorandum held, because this was the only way to ensure that:

> the legal status of millions of people is immediately secured. The alternative would be to investigate every situation on a case-by-case basis and decide to whom title should be transferred. Inevitably this opens up boundary disputes between different groups. It also opens up major disputes as to whether title should be transferred to chiefs, tribal authorities, local authorities, provincial governments, tribes, subsections of tribes, groups of people or individuals. Preliminary investigations found this route to be fraught with conflict and major disputes about power. It appears inevitable that the investigations would trigger massive instability, and also that they would get bogged down in a slow and intricate process similar to restitution.

A proposal for such a statute was introduced in 1998: the controversial Land Rights Bill.[182] Even though this did not altogether undermine the power of traditional leaders in land issues, but merely gave people a choice of how they

[178] Official, Mpumalanga restitution office, 24 March 1998.

[179] De Villiers (1998); Hannah Reid, 'Contractual National Parks and the Makuleke Community', *Human Ecology* 29, no. 2 (2001): 135–55.

[180] Marianne Merten, 'Observers Concerned About New Land Reform Policy.' http://www.mg.co.za/mg/news/2000feb2/24feb-farmworkers2.html: *Daily Mail & Guardian* electronic archive, 2000.

[181] Department of Land Affairs, *Summary of Current Events in Tenure Policy.* Pretoria: Department of Land Affairs, 19 February 1998.

[182] 'Land Rights Bill: Update on Draft Land Rights Bill, 20 July 1998', *Tenure Newsletter* 2, no. 1 (1998): 1–5. Adams et al. (1999b) states that the Bill ' will provide for the transfer of property rights from the state to the de facto owners and devolve land rights management to them. Rights would be vested in people, not in institutions such as municipalities. The proposed law would recognise the value of both individual and communal systems and would allow for the voluntary registration of individual rights within communal systems. Where rights exist on a group basis, they would have to be exercised in accordance with group rules and the co-owners would be able to choose the structures which manage their land rights. The envisaged law would be neutral on the issue of traditional authorities, supporting them where they were popular and functional, and allowing people to replace them elsewhere.'

wanted their land to be governed, reactions from the chiefs were vehement (Oomen, 2000a). Pathekile Holomisa, Contralesa spokesman and head of the parliamentary portfolio committee on land, in his capacity as an ANC MP slated Hanekom, calling the Bill a 'governmental ploy to render traditional authorities useless'.[183] There were other criticisms as well, for instance from those feeling that the Department had an idealised notion of rural communities or that the cases in which freehold title was granted would lead to 'the Kenyan scenario': large-scale mortgaging of land, resulting in land loss and even worse poverty a few years later.[184] But it was the fiery encounters with the chiefs that caused the Bill to be shelved. And some commentators also quote Hanekom's perceived attack on the traditional leaders as one of the main reasons why, after the 1999 general elections, this dedicated activist was removed to make way for a 'Africanist' minister with a tribal background: Thoko Didiza.[185]

Didiza: back to traditional communities

The first thing the new minister did was to shelve the Land Rights Bill as needing more consultation, 'kick out all the NGO people' and announce that African structures of governance should be respected, while disposal of state land to tribes should be part of policies on tenure reform.[186] A stony silence then fell on the reform issue, while Didiza concentrated on redistribution of land to emerging black farmers and general agricultural reform.

The smoke signals coming out of the – once so open – Department were far from reassuring to those concerned with rapid democratisation of the rural areas. Pressed for comment, the Minister indicated in a 2000 policy statement that 'the people who should benefit from the disposal of state land are the previously disadvantaged people, groups, communities or tribes,' and proposed the establishment of Provincial State Land Committees comprising only officials, representatives of municipalities and traditional leaders, to look into the transfer of land still held by the state.

> In rural areas, the individual family and the group/ tribe need to feel secure in their use and occupation of the land, to make permanent improvements, to graze their animals, to have access for gathering fruits, fuel, minerals and to bury their dead. They need to be able to exclude outsiders who invade their land. They require the enforcement of legal and administrative provisions to protect what is theirs.[187]

While drafting legislation, the government proposed to use the National Party's Upgrading of Land Tenure Rights Act (112/1991) to dispose of state land to tribes.[188] The Minister's sympathy for 'African solutions' also became clear in the

[183] 'Contralesa Slates Hanekom.'

[184] Cf. James (2000: 144–46); Themba Kepe, 'The Problem of Defining 'Community': Challenges for the Land Reform Programme in Rural South Africa.' Cape Town: School of Government, University of the Western Cape, 1998.

[185] 'Hanekoms' Downfall Says Much About Mbeki's Priorities', http://www.bday.co.za/bday/content/direct/0,3523,565563-6078-0,00.html: *Business Day* online, 2000. and interviews with Land Affairs officials, 1999.

[186] Louise Cook, 'Chiefs in the Dark on Land Rights Bill', *Business Day*, 7 March 2001, http://www.bday.co.za; Didiza, 'The Importance of a Successful Land Reform Programme'; 'Hanekoms' Downfall Says Much About Mbeki's Priorities'. The quote is from P. Holomisa, interviewed 19 September 2000 in Amsterdam.

[187] Minister for Agriculture and Land Affairs, *Policy Statement by the Minister for Agriculture and Land Affairs for Strategic Directions on Land Issues*, February 2000, para. 4.2.1.1.

parliamentary discussions surrounding traditional authority legislation, where she stated that, concerning land: 'ownership should rest with the traditional authority, giving it the right to decide who resides where. Governance or provision of social services will rest with the elected council.'[189]

In the end, a formal Communal Land Rights Bill was presented for public scrutiny only at the end of 2001, two years after the Minister had planned to pass the legislation.[190] At a large conference in Durban entitled 'Finding Solutions, Securing Rights', Thoko Didiza acknowledged once again the disastrous effects of tenure insecurity in the rural areas. In general, she proposed retaining 'a dual tenure system, acknowledging that we still have a freehold land tenure system in the country as well as the customary land tenure, particularly those in communal areas.'[191] There was no doubt that state land had to be given back, with rights vested in people and groups, not with institutions, in such a way that it could, for instance, be used as collateral. Land would thus be handed over to 'traditional African communities', but not to Tribal Authorities. Still, the draft Bill did allow 'traditional communities' operating under 'customary law', *and* their authorised representatives (that is, traditional leaders), to be recognised as 'juristic persons' for the transfer of state land in full ownership.[192] As a possible management structure 'to allow our elected councillors to function efficiently, effectively and harmoniously with Amakhosi in land administration in the communal areas', the Minister quoted the example of the Botswana Land Boards, which included both traditional leaders and elected councillors.

Though the broad lines of the policy proposed did not differ too much from Hanekom's – rights vested in people and groups instead of the state, an emphasis on securisation – the plans were perceived as a 'setback' for the NGOs and a victory for the traditional leaders.[193] The day after the elections, for instance, Holomisa urged the government to 'speed up the legal transfer of communal land to traditional authorities and let the people decide how best to deal with this land,' offering to include elected representatives in the traditional authority structures.[194] Rural activists, on the other hand, were shocked. ANC MP and rural resident Lydia Ngwenya fulminated: 'rural dwellers who live in the former homelands cannot understand why the rules applying to them are different from those that apply to people living in former "white South Africa".'[195] And a one-time senior consultant to Hanekom, Ben Cousins, described in an article entitled 'A return to the apartheid era?' how the lack of clarity around land and governance resulted in delays in development, because it was not clear to potential investors with whom to negotiate: central government, local government or the traditional leaders. He concluded his charge against the government's plans by stating:

[188] Ibid., para. 4.2.1.4.

[189] Mcebisi Ndletyana, 'A Report on the Public Hearings on the Discussion Document on the Traditional Leadership and Institution', Johannesburg: Centre for Policy Studies, 2000.

[190] Department of Land Affairs South Africa. 'Annual Report.' http://land.pwv.gov.za/, 1999.

[191] Didiza, 'Importance of a Successful Land Reform Programme'.

[192] *Communal Land Rights Bill*, as quoted in Cousins, (2001).

[193] Sapa, 'Minister Didiza Makes a Passionate Plea for Joint Land Tenure Reform.' ANC news briefing email service: ANC, 2001.

[194] Sapa, 'Govt Must Speed up Legal Transfer of Communal Land: Holomisa', ANC, 27 November 2001.

[195] Jaspith Kindra, 'Land Affairs Officials Push for "African Way of Life"', *Mail and Guardian* online, 2001.

> The Ministry of Agriculture and Land Affairs has had seven years to fulfil its constitutional obligation to secure the rights of millions of people.
>
> On the eve of a major national conference officials have circulated a poorly drafted document that, if it became law, would greatly strengthen the powers of unelected traditional leaders at the expense of ordinary rural dwellers. Will tenure reform create a democratic and rights-based system in communal areas, or will it recreate the 'neo-feudalism' of the apartheid era? (Cousins, 2001)

In spite of the widespread protest, the Minister continued her support for the Communal Land Rights Bill, changing relatively little in the tone of the proposals and gazetting them for comment at the end of 2002. In its preamble, the Bill recognised 'that the institution of traditional leadership played an important role in channelling the resistance to colonial dispossession of land and upholding the dignity and cohesion of the African people', reiterating that 'traditional leadership institutions and other community-based institutions should continue to play a meaningful and key role in the administration of communal land'. One of its objectives, therefore, was to 'confer legal status upon certain land tenure systems and community rules based on local custom'.[196] A novelty was the creation of Land Boards, administrative structures to manage the land, in which traditional leaders could occupy a maximum of 25 per cent of the positions. This latter innovation caused the traditional leaders also to join the concert of stakeholders rejecting the proposals, arguing that it was 'a declaration of war by the government' because 'without communal land, there is no traditional leadership'.[197]

This time their protests went unheard. When the Communal Land Rights Act was finally adopted in 2004 (11/2004), it stated that communal land registered in the name of a traditional leader should be considered as vested in the community itself.

7. The customary law debates

A third specific issue in the discussion over the relation between traditional authority and democracy was that of customary law. The recognition, within the post-apartheid dispensation, of a system based on cultural distinctiveness and group-based rights immediately raised questions concerning the relation between chiefly sovereignty and individual rights and between communalism and equality. As one expert wrote in 1991: 'customary law, which has inhabited some of the darker corners of the apartheid state, must now be thought of in relation to mainstream legal issues such as human rights, courts, legal procedures, legal formalism, the make-up of the judiciary, and of meaningful access to law' (Chanock, 1991: 53). What this could entail was summarised by another authority: 'by implicitly recognising customary law, and at the same time prohibiting gender discrimination, the Constitution has brought about a head-on confrontation between the two opposed cultures.'[198]

[196] Communal Land Rights Bill, Notice 1423 of 2002, as gazetted in *Government Gazette* 23740, 3, of 14 August 2002. The sections quoted are from the preamble and s(2).

[197] SABC news, 'Zulu king challenges Communal Land Rights Bill', 20 August 2003, http://www.sabcnews.com/south_africa/general/0,2172,64263,00.html; News24, '"Obliterating" chiefs', 24 July 2003, http://www.news24.com/News24/South_Africa/Politics/0,6119,2-7-12_1392464,00.html.

[198] Bennett, quoted in Henrard, 'The Interrelation', p. 395.

Before turning to this confrontation, it is important to re-emphasise the enormous rift that segregation policies created between 'official' and 'living' customary law.[199] Living customary law relates to the social practices of communities all over South Africa, and to essentially flexible and ever-changing arrangements concerning rights, duties and sanctions between those people living under a traditional authority. Official customary law, on the other hand, is part of the South African legal system and concerns a fixed corpus of both substantive and procedural rules that can be found in laws, judicial decisions and a wide range of text-books (cf. Bekker, 1989; Bennett, 1991; Olivier et al., 1995). Even though apartheid ideology presented official customary law as a – tidied up – reflection of 'black customs', there was often little relation between lived practices and the rules in the statute books. As the South African Law Commission (1999:2) would comment on the official customary law: 'no attempt has been made to keep it in step with changing social and legal conditions. Tainted by apartheid, and exposed by modern scholarship to be a distortion of genuine community practice, the so-called "official code" of customary law is now seriously out of keeping with current social norms and the Bill of Rights' (cf. Bennett, 1995:60).

In the course of this chapter, many of the official laws dealing with substantive aspects of customary law that formed the apartheid heritage have already been discussed: the Black Administration Act, the Black Authorities Act and all the ensuing regulations are but a few examples. The rules of customary law concerned everything from traditional authority, local government and land to family relations and inheritance.[200] They were introduced into the new order by means of two provisions in the definitive Constitution. S 2 of Schedule 6 ruled that all law that was in force when the Constitution took effect, continued to be in force, subject to amendment, repeal and consistency with the Constitution.[201] And in the chapter on traditional leaders s 211(3) provided that: 'The courts must apply customary law when that law is applicable, subject to the Constitution and any legislation that specifically deals with customary law.' In addition, new laws were added to official substantive customary law, such as those on the remuneration of traditional authorities, their representation in the provincial and national Houses, and the Customary Marriage Act, to be discussed below.

Apart from substantive rules, the new dispensation also inherited a whole procedural system of customary law. The Black Administration Act had granted chiefs the right to try both civil and criminal cases, albeit within certain limits: offences varying from treason, rape and murder to forgery, factional fighting and 'pretended witchcraft' were exempted from chiefly jurisdiction.[202] Chiefly subjects did have the right to appeal against these decisions to a magistrate's court, which could make use of the assistance of one or two assessors.[203] In

[199] South African Law Commission. 'Project 90: Customary Law', p. 24.

[200] Useful compilations of the laws that continued to apply after democratisation are F. De Villiers (1998), De Villiers and Beukman (1995).

[201] Act 108/1996. From this point on, when I speak of the Constitution, I am referring to this final Constitution.

[202] Ss 12, 20, 21A and Schedule 3 of Act 38/1927. Cf. *Chiefs' and Headmen's Civil Courts: Rules R2082.*/1967, Department of Justice, 'Legal Position: Appointment and Conferment of Civil and Criminal Jurisdiction upon Chiefs and Headmen and the Nature and Extent of Their Jurisdictions.' Pretoria: Department of Justice, 1996.

[203] *Magistrates' Court Act (as Amended up to Act 67/1998).* 32/1944, Ss 29a, 34.

addition, the 1988 Law of Evidence Amendment Act (45/1988) determined that:

> S 1. Any court may take judicial notice (...) of indigenous law in so far as such law can be ascertained readily and with sufficient certainty; Provided that indigenous law shall not be opposed to the principles of public policy or natural justice: Provided further that it shall not be lawful for any court to declare that the custom of *lobola* or *bogadi* [bridewealth] or other similar custom is repugnant to such principles.

As we have seen, the 1996 Constitution went even further than this provision: it did not simply reiterate that courts *may* apply customary law, but ruled that they *must* do so in cases where such law is applicable.

In all, the discussions over the position of traditional leaders in official customary law after 1994 would concentrate on three main issues. First, there were the general questions on the relation between 'the system' of customary law and common law, notably the Bill of Rights, which were largely up to the courts to answer. Second, there was the terrain of the legislator: the future of all those specific substantive rules inherited from the past dispensation. Lastly, debates erupted on the more procedural question of the future of chiefs' courts, and their relation to the rest of the South African court system.

Relations: customary law and the Bill of Rights

The chiefs' fierce attempts to have culture excluded from the Bill of Rights, as a separate domain shielded from threatening provisions like the equality clause, had not been successful. Even though Chief Nonkonyana had argued that the Bill of Rights would 'inflict irreparable harm on the entrenched cultural values of the indigenous people of South Africa', the right to culture had been made subject to the Bill of Rights, just as traditional leadership and customary law were only recognised subject to the Constitution.[204] Nevertheless, with the promulgation of the Constitution it was far from clear how codified customary law – with its rules on the inferior position of women, the unelected character of traditional authority, the male primogeniture in inheritance matters – would relate to constitutional provisions such as the equality clause.[205] Unless such provisions were explicitly repealed by the legislature, like the examples we shall quote in the next section, it was up to the courts to pronounce on their interrelation with the Constitution. Courts, according to the Constitution, 'when interpreting any legislation, and when developing the common law or customary law (...) must promote the spirit, purport and objects of the Bill of Rights'.[206]

The Constitution did provide courts with a few pointers on how to do this.[207] The 'horizontality clause', for instance, ruled that 'a provision of the Bill of Rights binds a natural or a juristic person if, and to the extent that, it is applicable, taking into account the nature of the right and the nature of any duty imposed by the right'.[208] This, therefore, applied to the relations between individuals: officially recognised traditional authorities, as 'vertical' organs of state, fell

[204] Cf. ss 30,31, 211 Act 108/1996. Nonkonyana was quoted in Stack (1997:6).

[205] The quoted examples come from S 11(3) of Act 38/1927 (repealed by *Customary Marriages Act*. 120/1998), Act 38/1927 *passim* and s 23 of the same Act, and their judicial interpretation.

[206] S 39 Act 108/1996.

[207] For much more in-depth discussion than space permits here see Bennett (1995); Currie. 'Indigenous Law'; De Waal et al. (1998); Kerr (1997); Sachs (1990).

[208] S 8(2) Act 108/1996.

squarely under the Bill of Rights.[209] In addition, the Constitution stated that the rights it contained, such as those of people to 'participate in the cultural life of their choice' or to 'enjoy their culture', could only be limited if such limitation was 'reasonable and justifiable in an open and democratic society based on human dignity, equality and freedom ...'[210]

The most appropriate forum for working out what these general provisions meant for specific pieces of legislation was, of course, the Constitutional Court. In its certification of the Constitution, this court had indicated that it was in favour of 'leaving the complicated, varied and ever-developing specifics' of how traditional leadership should function in the wider democratic society, and how customary law should develop and be interpreted, to 'future social evolution, legislative deliberation and judicial interpretation'.[211] The court itself, however, did not get much chance for such interpretation: in the five years after the passing of the final Constitution no cases with specific questions on the constitutionality of customary law were brought before it.[212] Nevertheless, its general approach can be deduced from cases like *Christian Education South Africa*, dealing with the question of corporal punishment in Christian schools. Here, the court ruled that one of the reasons for the phrasing of S 31, on the rights of cultural communities, was 'to prevent protected associational rights of members of communities from being used to "privatise" constitutionally offensive group practices and thereby immunise them from external legislative regulation or judicial control'.[213] Apart from viewing customary law as ever developing and subject to social evolution, the Constitutional Court also considered it to be – squarely and undeniably – subject to the Constitution.

Other courts that did hear some customary law cases in the years following the passing of the Constitution took a much more conservative stance. Their interpretation of customary law was not so much that of an open and evolving set of rules, but of a closed system, ascertainable in law. In the 1998 case *Hlope v Mahlalela a.o.*, for instance, the Transvaal Provincial Division refused to accept one expert because she 'does not or cannot differentiate between cultural practices and Swazi law,' and ruled that 'it cannot be accepted that all cultural practices are indigenous law and vice versa.'[214] A similar systems approach is found in the 1995 *Thibela v Minister of Law and Order a.o.* in which the judge underlined the duty of the court to apply customary law. He also based his

[209] S 8(1) Act 108/1996.

[210] Ss 30, 31 and 36 Act 108/1996. S 36(1) reads in full: ' The rights in the Bill of Rights may be limited only in terms of law of general application to the extent that limitation is reasonable and justifiable in an open and democratic society based on human dignity, equality and freedom, taking into account all relevant factors, including – (a) the nature of the right (b) the importance of the purpose of the limitation (c) the nature and extent of the limitation (d) the relation between the limitation and its purpose; and (e) less restrictive means to achieve the purpose.'

[211] *Ex Parte Chairperson of the Constitutional Assembly: In Re Certification of the Constitution of South Africa*, 1996.CCT, para 197 834 F/H.

[212] With the exception, possibly, of cases quoted before like *ANC v MEC for Local Government and Housing, Kwazulu-Natal and Others, Ex Parte Speaker of the Kwazulu-Natal Provincial Legislature: In Re Kwazulu-Natal Amakhosi and Iziphakanyiswa Amendment Bill of 1995; Ex Parte Speaker of the Kwazulu-Natal Provincial Legislature: In Re Payment of Salaries, Allowances and Other Privileges to the Ingonyama Bill of 1995*, 7 BCLR (1996). and *Dvb Behuising (Pty) Limited v North West Provincial Government and Another* (2000).

[213] *Christian Education South Africa v Minister of Education*, (2000), 26.

[214] *Hlophe v Mahlalela and Another*, 1 449–62 (1998), H-I.

decision on expert advice which adduced that 'according to the customary law applicable in the Pedi tribe', if *lobola* had been paid in a certain way, a child born out of former engagements became absorbed in the new family.[215] Apart from assuming customary law to be a closed and ascertainable system, these courts also presupposed its popularity. In *Bagindawo a.o.*, for instance, Judge Madlanga ruled that 'the judicial, executive and law-making powers in modern African customary law continue to vest in the chiefs and so-called paramount chiefs... This fusion of functions in one individual has ... received statutory recognition ... continues to thrive and is believed in and accepted by the vast majority of those subject to kings and chiefs.'[216]

A similar conservative position was taken in the one case that did deal explicitly with a clash between customary law and the Constitution: *Mthembu v Letsela*.[217] The issue at stake was whether a daughter in a customary union – whose father had been shot dead by the South African police – could inherit her father's estate, or whether the grandfather, as first male in line, had this right. Basing himself both on customary law text-books and the 1987 Regulations for the Administration and Distribution of the Estates of Deceased Blacks, the judge was clear on this issue: 'The customary law of succession in Southern Africa is based on the principle of male primogeniture ... in terms of this system of succession.... Tembi ..., being female, ... does not qualify as heir to the deceased's estate.'[218] The judge who looked at this case in first instance remarked on the constitutionality of this rule:

> I find it difficult to equate this form of differentiation between men and women with the concept of 'unfair discrimination' as used in s8 of the Constitution. ... In view of the manifest acknowledgement of customary law as a system existing parallel to common law by the Constitution (vide ss 33(3) and 181 (1)) and the freedom granted to persons to choose this system as governing their relationships (as implied in s 31), I cannot accept the submission that the succession rule is necessarily in conflict with s8. There are other instances where a rule differentiates between men and women, but which no right-minded person considers to be unfairly discriminatory.[219]

The judge in appeal did not counter this interpretation, but instead ruled that looking into the constitutionality of this rule was not needed, as the girl was illegitimate and would not inherit for that reason. He did, however, state that if the customary rule were to be developed, this should be done by the legislature rather than the courts, after 'a process of full investigation and consultation'.[220]

Such legislative amendments, as we shall see in the following pages, were, however, bound to be boycotted by the traditional leaders.

Rules: the Law Commission's harmonisation project

What did the legislature do? In contrast to the way in which it dealt with the institutional heritage pertaining to traditional authorities in local government

[215] *Thibela v Minister Van Wet En Orde En Andere*, SA (3) Van Dyk, R. 147 (1995).C.

[216] *Bagindawo and Others Versus Head of the Nyanda Regional Authority and Another*, (3) BCLR 326 (1998).

[217] The case was first heard as *Mthembu v Letsela and Another*, (2) SA 936 (1997), and then in appeal as *Mthembu v Letsela*, 3 SA 867 (2000).

[218] *Mthembu v Letsela*, 8.

[219] *Mthembu v Letsela 1*, 945H – 946C. Note that the Constitution referred to is the interim Constitution Act 200/1993. This view was juxtaposed by the Constitional Court decision in *Bho v Magistrate*, Khagelitsha a.o., that was passed as this book went to press.

[220] *Mthembu v Letsela*, 40.

and land, there were energetic attempts to reform the customary law legacy and bring it in line with the Constitution. The South African Law Commission put together a team headed by Professor Nhlapo and with experts like Professor Bennett on board; both are specialists on official and living customary law. The team enthusiastically embarked on the 'Harmonisation of the common law and the indigenous law' project. It identified fields in which reform was needed, such as customary marriages, the customary law of inheritance, the conflict in personal laws, the administration of estates and traditional courts. Five years and dozens of reports and discussion documents later, only one of these projects – the recognition of customary marriages – had resulted in legislative amendments. The failure of the others – such as reforming succession rules such as those quoted above – had everything to do with the chiefly protests with which we have become so familiar.

Let us start with the one successful project: the recognition of customary marriages. This was needed to remedy some of the more flagrant inequities in the inherited legislation: for one, the fact that customary unions were not recognised as fully-fledged marriages because they were potentially polygynous. There was also the provision in the Black Administration Act that a woman married under customary law 'shall be deemed to be a minor and her husband shall be deemed to be her guardian', thus making it impossible for these women to acquire property independently or to stand up in court.[221] The Recognition of Customary Marriage Act, which became legal in 2000, deleted this provision and granted spouses equal proprietary, contractual and judicial status.[222] It also recognised marriages sealed according to the 'customs and usages traditionally observed among the indigenous people of South Africa ... which form the culture of these people'.[223] The adoption of the Act, welcomed by activists, was in spite of protests by chiefs: during the consultation rounds many traditional leaders voiced their displeasure with the 'Western' and 'eurocentric' approach in the Commission's proposals, and argued in favour of retaining more duality.[224] Together with the IFP, some were amongst the 'men muttering about the law that makes spouses equal', arguing that the Bill provided for the 'slow but certain emasculation and strangulation of customary marriage'.[225]

If the traditional leaders did not manage to stop the passing of the Customary Marriage Act, they were more successful with the legislation pertaining to inheritance. As demonstrated in the *Mthembu v. Letsela* case discussed above, the official customary law departed from the notion of male primogeniture in succession. A 1998 attempt to remedy the disparity was quashed in its infancy by traditional leaders 'fundamentally opposed to the eurocentric approach which

[221] S 11(3) sub (b) Act 38/1927.

[222] *Customary Marriages Act 120/1998*, s. 6. Cf. Chambers (2000); Sapa. 'Law Recognising Customary Marriages Comes into Effect', ANC news briefing email service: ANC, 2000; L.P. Vorster, 'Traditional Leadership and the Recognition of Customary Marriages Act.' Paper presented at the SASCA Conference 'Rural Governance in the new Millennium', Port Elizabeth, 23 June 1999.

[223] Introduction and S 1 Act 120/1998.

[224] South African Law Commission (1999:1.4.3); Workshop on customary marriage reform, Pretoria, 20 February 1998.

[225] 'Maintenance Bill, Domestic Violence Bill, Recognition of Customary Marriages Bill', in *Hansard*, 7178-244, 1998, p. 7190; Mandulo Maphumulo, 'Men Mutter About Law That Makes Spouses Equal', *The Sunday Independent* 1998, p. 7.

is prevalent in [our] country'.[226] When the Law Commission timidly came up with another attempt in 2000 – including a provision exempting the inheritance of office by traditional leaders from the Act – chiefly reactions were just as militant. 'We reject the idea that our laws should be subjected to so-called common law – an imported white man's law that has been systematically used to denigrate our traditional systems of law,' as Chief P. Holomisa put it.[227] And so the Customary Law of Succession Amendment Bill was put on ice again.

Other Law Commission projects concerned the administration of estates and the conflict in personal laws. Of these, the latter was of particular importance because it dealt with the question of when customary law was applicable. The Law Commission felt strongly that, in contrast to the still-applicable provisions in the Black Authorities Act, this should be a matter of personal choice, dependent on cultural orientation and not on race or residence.[228] In a 1999 proposal for legislation it argued that parties should be 'free to agree on the law that best suits their needs', with judicial discretion applying only in case of non-agreement.[229] Also, in ascertaining customary law, the proposal held that parties should not be bound by text-books or precedents, thus allowing for a narrowing of the rift between living and official customary law. However timely and necessary the recommendations were, they had not been adopted by Parliament by 2003, making for the continued application of the old-order, race- and territory-based provisions.

Guarding the customary courts

Another process that moved much more slowly than expected concerned chiefly civil and criminal jurisdiction, and the question as to whether chiefs' courts should continue to exist. An estimated 1500 of these courts all over the country were still officially granted the right to try disputes under the Black Administration Act (Stack, 1997:14). They were severely criticised, however, because of the marginal role women played in them, the patriarchal character of the justice dispensed, their perceived bias and the lack of legal representation or legal training of the adjudicators.[230] 'It doesn't matter what your rights are, they only look at where you come from,' said one rural resident. On the other hand, the government, the Law Commission and NGOs were quick to acknowledge the advantages of these courts. As Mandela stated: 'something must be done to restore power to the chiefs. They have to have their own judiciary and their own courts. If someone has stolen a goat, there is no need to go to (a magistrate's) court for that.'[231] Not only did customary courts hold the potential of alleviating the creaking mainstream justice system, they were also considered by many to

[226] South African Law Commission. 'Project 90: Customary Law', x; Cf. Caroline Hooper-Box, 'Inheritance Laws Are a Mess of Contradiction.' *Reconstruct*, 8 April 1999, p. 9.

[227] Khadija Magardie, 'Customary Law Shake-Up', *Mail and Guardian* online, 2000.

[228] South African Law Commission. 'The Harmonisation of the Common Law and Indigenous Law: The Application of Customary Law: Conflict of Personal Laws.' Pretoria, 1999, p. 3.

[229] South African Law Commission. 'The Harmonisation of the Common Law and Indigenous Law: Report on Conflicts of Law.' Pretoria, 1999, p. 16.

[230] Cf. Samantha Hargreaves, Constance Yose, and Zora Khan, 'Make Space for Rural Women's Rights.' *Land & Rural Digest*, March/April 2000: 31–33; Nomsa Shongwe, 'Empty Justice for Women in Tribal Courts.' *Land & Rural Digest*, March/April 2000: 28–30.

[231] Nirode Bramdaw, 'Chiefs Must Have Own Courts, Says Mandela', *Business Day*, 24 October 2000, 6.

be more accessible – in terms of language, procedure and proximity – and cheaper than their state counterparts.[232]

After the debate on the subject had raged for some time, the Law Commission came up with a discussion paper on Traditional Courts and the Judicial Functions of Traditional Leaders (Law Commission, 1999). It proposed to (continue to) recognise traditional courts as courts of law in the rural areas, while recommending the establishment of democratic community courts in urban parts of the country. In contrast to the existing system, it proposed that the jurisdiction of these courts should be mainly civil, with only minor criminal cases admissible, while women should be enabled to participate freely.

In the workshops held to discuss this document, one of the most contentious issues was whether people should be able to 'opt out' of the jurisdiction of traditional leaders and take a case directly to the magistrate's court. On this issue, the Law Commission held that: 'Jurisdiction of a traditional court in respect of persons should no longer be based on race or colour but on such matters as residence, proximity, nature of transaction or subject matter and the law applicable' and hesitantly suggested giving chiefly subjects the possibility of 'opting out' and taking (criminal) cases directly to the magistrate's court (ibid.:viii.21). This idea was furiously attacked by traditional leaders all over the country: 'If people are allowed to choose where they go this will undermine the authority of the chief', was the consensus at a Lebowakgomo workshop on 11 June 1999.

In the ensuing report on 'Traditional Courts and the Judicial Function of Traditional Leaders', the issue of jurisdiction remained one of the bones of contention.[233] The report contained draft legislation aiming at the recognition of customary courts, which should be composed in accordance with customary law, but with due regard for the constitutional values of democracy and equality. According to the Commission, the courts should have both criminal and civil jurisdiction, subject to certain limits and a monetary ceiling. With regard to criminal matters, defendants should have the right to opt out in favour of another court, while in civil affairs people should be able to apply to the Registrar for Customary Courts for a transfer. The draft bill was not picked up, however, by the Department of Justice and introduced in Parliament, possibly because it wanted to wait for the general legislative framework on traditional leadership. This Traditional Leadership and Governance Framework Act, however, brought little clarity, as we have seen, merely stating that national and provincial government *might* provide for a role for traditional leaders in respect of the administration of justice.[234]

In conclusion, therefore, the customary law reform offers a mixed picture. Traditional leaders did not manage to exempt 'culture' from the Bill of Rights. They did succeed, however, in delaying the repeal of the bulk of 'old-order' customary law legislation and pleaded – often successfully – in favour of retaining a dual system of laws.

[232] On the problems with South Africa's judicial system see 'Justice for All', *The Mercury*, 13 October 1998, p. 8; 'Motsekga Hints at Community-Based Courts.' *Pretoria News*, 4 February 1998, p. 2. The advantages of customary courts can be found in South African Law Commission (1999: 3–4).

[233] South African Law Commission, Project 90, 'Traditional Courts and the Judicial Function of Traditional Leaders', 21 January 2003.

[234] B 58–2003, s 18(d).

8. Conclusion

The observers who had expected that, with the dawn of democracy in South Africa, chieftaincy would 'melt away like ice in the sun' could not have been more wrong. This chapter, which has dealt with the fate of the legal and administrative heritage concerning traditional authority, has repeatedly demonstrated the tenacity of past arrangements. The constitutional negotiations, attended by a large chiefly delegation, led to a continued recognition of the 'institution, status and role' of traditional leadership. They also left the elaboration of what this recognition meant within a democratic context up to 'future social evolution, legislative deliberation and judicial interpretation', thus leaving room for protracted tussles on the continued applicability of 'old-order' legislation and its relation with the Constitution.

It proved politically impossible, for instance, to replace the – once so hated – Black Administration Act and Black Authorities Act with new general legislation on traditional leadership. The only advances made in this field, it seemed, were those that strengthened the position of the traditional leaders: through higher remuneration and through representation in provincial and national Houses. While a White Paper on Traditional Leadership and Governance and the accompanying legislation, originally planned for 1997, were published in 2003, they failed to deal with the most contentious issues at stake. In the meantime, any attempt to curtail the powers that the apartheid state had granted traditional leaders can count on such stubborn resistance that it is sure to fail. Traditional leaders have twice managed to postpone the local government elections, have laughed away legislation awarding them largely ceremonial functions, and instead have wrenched from the President the guarantee that the 'powers and functions of traditional leaders in local government' will not be eroded, even if this means amendments to the Constitution.

A similar continuation, if not strengthening, of their formal position took place with regard to land. All attempts to reform and democratise apartheid's insecure land tenure legislation were thwarted and a minister deemed 'anti-chief' removed to make way for a more traditionalist successor who proposed to retain apartheid's duality in legislation, and spoke out in favour of tenure arrangements based on the notion of 'tribes' and their structures of governance. Similar processes were at work in addressing the customary law legacy. Traditional leaders successfully froze legislation seeking to extend the Bill of Rights to their areas by ending male primogeniture in succession matters. At the same time, they managed to retain civil and criminal jurisdiction over 'their' subjects, perpetuating duality in this field as well.

Above all, these battles fought – and won – concerned chiefly sovereignty: the right to decide the pace of democratisation autonomously within a certain jurisdiction. Much chiefly lobbying effort went into ensuring that their 'subjects' could not 'opt out' of this jurisdiction. There was the outright boycott of constitutional proposal S 32, which gave individuals the choice of opting out of customary law. There was the continued insistence that traditional authorities be the primary, and only, layer of local government within their areas. There was the Land Rights Bill giving people the right to choose which structures of governance they preferred – elected or tribal – which was unceremoniously shelved, like the proposals to allow people to bypass customary courts and go straight to the magistrate, which were heavily attacked and – by 2004 – had not made it into law. Traditional leaders, it seemed, did not want the acceptance of their authority to be democratised, to become a matter of free choice, but instead preferred to rely on the continued imposition of apartheid legislation imposing their position so that they, and not their subjects, could determine the pace of change in their areas.

This 'patchwork democracy', with its amalgam of legal and institutional arrangements allowing chiefs to decide the extent to which the new Constitution was implemented within their jurisdiction, meant that an individual's rights continued to be determined by place of residence. The apartheid criterion of race determining rights might have been deleted from the text-books, but the more technocratic regulations implementing this principle continued to exist. Behind the shiny new Constitution, with its rights for all, remained a shadow world of yellowing proclamations and old-order institutions which continued to implement an ideology which itself had long been swept away. The resulting situation was one not so much of separate legal spheres as of overlap and uncertainty, allowing power brokers on the ground to pick those rules best suited to their needs.

There is no doubt that this legal and institutional uncertainty critically impeded development in some of those areas where it was most needed all over South Africa. The uncertainty about land tenure, for instance, hampered local and external investment and led to the marginalisation of women and others without power in rural society. The clashes between traditional leaders and elected local government, often over land, stalled development projects and the delivery of houses, water and electricity. And the South African press often published reports of women discriminated against in customary courts, like the woman in the Northern Province who wanted to bring an assault charge against her husband but was turned away because she had no male representation, and was beaten to death a few days later.[235]

The pressing question is, of course: Why? Why did this legal and institutional web designed to perpetuate social and economic inequality, and based on ethnicity and patriarchy, prove so hard to unravel? Why, to quote Thabo Mbeki, was the dream deferred? To put it in the words of one observer:

> This is perhaps the most unfortunate and dangerous political development since the first democratic elections in 1994. How did it happen that the powerful ruling party could be held to ransom by this conservative clique, whose power is not based on free and fair elections but on archaic traditional and cultural systems that, in this regard, represent reactionary elements in the rural hinterlands?[236]

It is clear by now that traditional leadership, organised in 'unions' like Contralesa, managed, time and again, through late-night, last-minute lobbying to stop legislation aimed at democratising rural areas and granting their people individual rights. But the question is why the ANC, with its rhetoric of 'one-man-one-vote', 'wall-to-wall elected government' and a President whose father had once written that 'if Africans have had chiefs, it was because all human societies have had them at one stage or another' (Mbeki, 1964:47), why this ruling party fell to the chiefly lobbies. And why it deemed it so important to accommodate traditional authority that it was worth stalling democratisation for millions of citizens. It is to this question that we turn in the next chapter.

[235] Jaspith Kindra, 'Women Look for a Voice in the Tribal Courts.' http://www.mg.co.za/mg/za/africa/2000oct/03oct-women.html: *Mail and Guardian* online, 2000.

[236] Harvey. 'Chiefs Make Nonsense of Democracy.'

3. The Power of Definition
Struggling for the Soul of Custom

> Never again shall anyone tell our people and their traditional leaders what their customs and traditions should be. Never again shall anyone define the role of traditional leaders without their full participation – Nelson Mandela[1]

> What must be faced in the South African case (...) is the struggle for the soul of, and the content of, the customary law. It has proved to be adaptable, both symbolically and practically, to be a weapon in the hands of traditionalists, revolutionaries, and modernizing legalists, and it will take on its content in application from the dominant political directions and discourses (Chanock, 1991:62-3)

1. Introduction

Taking this centrality of traditional leaders in the policy debate as the point of departure, the argument in this chapter runs as follows. It was due to the specific political climate in post-apartheid South Africa that traditional leaders were able to take centre stage in discussions that affected not only them but also the 13 million or more people considered to be their 'subjects'. This political climate was tempered not only by the actors – political parties, traditional leaders, NGOs, government departments – with a stake in the process, but also by wider national and international conditions. With the fact that South Africa possessed a cultural diversity that needed to be 'recognised' as a central presupposition in the policy debate, what was essentially at issue was the contents of culture, custom and tradition. And because the traditional leaders played such a central role in these debates, they had the 'power of definition', and virtually monopolised knowledge on rural conditions, the popularity of traditional authority and the character of customary law. Thus, it was the type of culture, custom and tradition to be promoted to the 'austerity of tabulated legalism' (D'Engelbrenner-Kolff, 2001:271) that stood central in the post-apartheid power struggle, with the odds skewed heavily in favour of the traditional leaders.

We begin by briefly setting out the understanding of politics and its stakes on which this analysis draws and which is woven throughout the chapter. Policy-making can be understood as taking place in 'an arena of power, guarded by what are often very powerful gatekeepers whose interests may lie primarily in preserving or extending the symbolic capital and the status they already accumulated in that field'.[2] In this arena, both actors and the structures in which

[1] Mandela. speech at the inauguration of the National Council of Traditional Leaders, 8 January 1996, Cape Town, unpublished.

[2] Andrew Spiegel, Vanessa Watson, and Peter Wilkinson, 'Speaking Truth to Power? Some Problems Using Ethnographic Methods to Influence the Formulation of Housing Policy in South Africa' in Cheater (1999), p. 183.

they operate play a role in creating a certain balance of power. Though ontologically separable, they are intimately related: agents' actions sediment in structural conditions while structural conditions shape individual actions, which are thus neither voluntaristic nor deterministic.[3] As Marx wrote: 'men make their own history – but do not make it just as they please; they do not make it under circumstances chosen by themselves, but under circumstances directly encountered, given and transmitted from the past.'[4]

It is for this reason that I shall concentrate on both actors and structures, and their interrelation. Section 2 focuses on the important role-players in the policy process, and the interests and resources – material and symbolic – on which they were able to draw. But their discussions did not take place in a vacuum; they were shaped by, and in turn helped shape, wider structural conditions. The most important of these will be set out in section 3: the party political balance of power influenced by the lessons from the rest of Africa, the institutional heritage, the desire to be an African democracy, the worldwide tendency towards dismantling the central state and the recognition of group rights all formed part of the 'arena of power'. Thus, power, even if it concerns the ability to bring about consequences, is not something that is generated in one place. To quote Foucault:

> The analysis, made in terms of power, must not assume that the sovereignty of the state, the form of the law, or the overall unity of a domination are given at the outset; rather, these are only the terminal forms power takes. It seems to me that power must be understood in the first instance as the multiplicity of force relations immanent in the sphere in which they operate and which constitute their own organization; as the process which, through ceaseless struggles and confrontations, transforms, strengthens, or reverses them; as the support which these force relations find in one another, thus forming a chain or a system, or on the contrary, the disjunctions and contradictions which isolate them from one another; and lastly, as the strategies in which they take effect, whose general design or institutional crystallization is embodied in the state apparatus, in the formulation of the law, in the various social hegemonies. (1993:519)

If it was the 'institutional crystallisation' that was under discussion in the previous chapter, our concern now is with arriving at an understanding of the web of 'force relations' that gave rise to it.

Nevertheless, this 'institutional crystallisation', and the form it takes, says a great deal about the underlying power relations, which it reflects and reinforces. Nowhere is this more clear than in the legal recognition of 'culture'. Culture, custom and traditional authority are, as I have already emphasised, hardly fixed phenomena but widely debated, flexible and ever-changing outcomes of discursive practices. 'Culture is always relational, an inscription of communicative processes that exist, historically, *between* subjects of power.'[5] Who controls the terminology, and has the right to label and define the type of culture chiselled into the granite of law then becomes of crucial importance (Levett et al., 1997:3). For it is the definition of and the differentiation between individuals and subjects,

[3] Giddens (1993), Derek Layder, 'Power, Structure and Agency', in *Power: Critical Concepts*, ed. John Scott, London: Routledge, 1994; Brian S. Turner, ed. *The Blackwell Companion to Social Theory*, London: Blackwell, 1996.

[4] Karl Marx and F. Engels. 'The Eighteenth Brumaire of Louis Bonaparte', in *Selected Works*. Moscow: Publishing House, 1962, p. 1.

[5] James Clifford and George Marcus, 1986, quoted in Turner (1996: 362).

traditional leaders and 'rural communities', customary law and individual rights, that also serve to strengthen the power relations which gave rise to them (Wilmsen and McAllister, 1996).

What was at stake, therefore, was the *power of definition*. That this is not merely an academic consideration but was also strongly felt by the most important actors in the policy process was demonstrated over and over again in the debates. By the Eastern Cape premier Stofile, for instance, who assured the House of Traditional Leaders that 'knowledge is power' and that:

> This is a huge challenge to the House and the Institution of traditional leadership. This is so because those who speak for the institution tend to speak about peripheral things that benefit the individual rather than the institution. For instance, I have asked since 1997 that traditional leaders should assist us as we all try to transform the institution by defining, for instance, the epoch or phase in history which they use as a bench mark for defining what traditional leadership is. In previous addresses I have tried to be as forthright as possible to show how the institution was changed by circumstances over the years. Whether it was colonialism, the discovery of minerals or apartheid and its bantustan satellites, all these had an influence on the institution of traditional affairs. So there is a need, I believe, to define our threshold so that we can speak with one voice. Sometimes we tend to defend privileges that were introduced to coerce traditional leaders and miss the damage caused by these to the integrity of chiefs. We can't proceed like this even this century. We must redefine traditional authorities and restore their integrity.[6]

The discussion document on traditional leadership and its successors also acknowledged the importance of 'redefining' the institution: 'We face the challenge of restoring the traditional nature and respectability of the institution of traditional leadership. We have to redefine its focus, role and functions, and to relate it to the different spheres of government such that it is not seen as either a surrogate or an adversary of government.'[7] President Mbeki, on the other hand, recognised that government alone did not hold this 'power of definition' and that it was essentially a discursive exercise: 'both government and the institution of traditional leadership have no monopoly over defining this role. It is important therefore that we begin a national dialogue that will involve all sections of our society in defining the role of this institution.'[8]

As this discussion was far from academic, it was not without material consequences. Who was considered to be a traditional leader, what was labelled a customary marriage, how communal tenure was defined, would also determine who was entitled to a state salary, to pension benefits (as a partner in a customary marriage) and to access to land, to give but a few examples.

The contention here is that this 'power of definition' lay to a large extent with the traditional leaders who managed to ensure the perpetuation or consolidation of a number of assumptions about rural society in law. These assumptions will be discussed in section 4, and include the notions of rural-urban difference, of homogeneous communities with a coherent system of customary law and, above all, of the popularity of traditional leaders. And so a picture emerges of who, in

[6] Stofile, 'Opening Address to the House of Traditional Leaders, Eastern Cape', 18 February 2000.

[7] Department of Constitutional Development, 'A Draft Discussion Document Towards a White Paper on Traditional Leadership and Institutions.' Pretoria: Department of Constitutional Development, 2000. Cf. 'The White Paper on Traditional Leadership and Governance' and the Traditional Leadership and Governance Framework Bill, B 58–2003, preamble.

[8] Sapa, 'Address by Pres. Mbeki to the House of Traditional Leaders', Ulundi, 3 August 2001.

post-apartheid South Africa, played a critical role in the 'struggle for the soul of custom', the possible reasons for this, and what it meant for the 'institutional crystallisation' of custom, culture and tradition. Let us start with the first issue: that of the major role-players.

2. Who did the defining? The actors

In a distinct break with past secretive practices, post-apartheid policy-making has generally rested on extensive consultation and exhaustively debated discussion documents with the explicit involvement of all who consider themselves stakeholders. Decisions on the future of traditional authority have been no exception. The conferences, television discussions and parliamentary debates on the issue were invariably attended by a colourful potpourri of political parties, civic organisations, women's groups, international donors, academics, departmental officials, the Law Commission, the Human Rights Commission, the Public Protector and the media. The positions of those who would prove most important will be discussed here: the ANC and other political parties, Contralesa and the grass-roots organisations as representatives of civil society and the Directorate of Traditional Affairs as the main governmental actor.

The African National Congress

The approach to traditional authority of the party that, with an overwhelming majority, would lead South Africa's first democratic government, has always been highly ambiguous.[9] While it was generally dedicated to non-racialism and democracy, the ANC has always sought to incorporate progressive traditional leadership in these ideals and to use the institution to achieve its nationalist and unitary ambitions.

With the foundation of the party in 1912, for instance, an Upper House of Chiefs was created. There were three main reasons for this, which still ring familiar: a fear that the traditional leaders might otherwise side with the enemy, a recognition of the progressive character of some traditional leaders, and acknowledgement that a large part of the rural population still adhered to traditional authority (Mzala, 1988:39). In the course of the century, with the increased incorporation of chiefs in segregationist structures, relations became more tense: the Upper House was abolished and chiefly cooperation severely criticised.[10] However, although the ANC often emphasised that 'the people shall govern' and their 'rights shall be the same, regardless of race, colour or sex', it never totally denounced the traditional leaders.[11] It was ANC-aligned chiefs, for instance, who led the rural revolts in Mpondoland, Tembuland and Sekhukhune against the bantustan structures in the 1950s and 1960s. And Chief Holomisa

[9] The ANC obtained 63% of the votes for the National Assembly in 1994, and 66% in 1999.

[10] The Upper House had fallen into disuse by 1936 and was abolished in 1943: Jordan (1997). Mbeki (1964).

[11] ANC. 'The Character of the Anc.' http://www.anc.org.za/ancdocs/discussion/character.html: ANC, 1997, ———. 'The Freedom Charter – Vision of a People's South Africa.' 12-43, C.R.D. Halisi, 'The Place of Chiefs in Black Republican Thought in South Africa: Some Theoretical Implications.' Paper presented at the Indigenous Political Structures and Governance in Africa Conference, Ibadan, 2001.

reminisces about his contacts with the ANC in exile in the 1980s: 'they treated me with respect. I felt like an egg being incubated.'[12] Nevertheless, the 1980s, in which apartheid was at its harshest and many traditional leaders had to be protected from their subjects by the South African army, was also the period when many ANC members expected and hoped that chieftaincy would 'melt away like ice in the sun' with the dawn of democracy. They were to be severely disappointed when the ANC leadership decided to include Contralesa, the Congress of Traditional Leaders of South Africa, in its broad democratic front by the end of the decade (Van Kessel and Oomen, 1997:571-2; van Kessel, 2000:84; Maloka, 1996).

Following democratisation, the issue became highly contentious. 'On this one, we are really divided,' one ANC MP said. Two positions emerged, a modernist and a more traditionalist one, with the latter growing in strength over time. Immediately after the 1994 elections, the ANC members whose voices were the loudest were those who considered that 'chiefs and tribal authorities have provided a geographical and ideological base for apartheid' and emphasised the 'deep-rooted fear that they will bring their "ethnic baggage" with them into a new dispensation, dividing the African majority and derailing the process of democratisation and nation-building that is essential for the new South Africa' (Skweyiya, 1993:4). They echoed the party's 1992 policy principles, which stated that even if chiefs might 'continue to play an important role in unifying our people and performing ceremonial and other functions allocated to them by law,' the emphasis should be on 'non-racial, non-sexist, democratic, de-racialised and unified' local government.[13] Mandela expressed the general sentiment in 1996: 'We want to advise the traditional leaders in our country to abandon the illusion that there can ever emerge a constitutional settlement which grants them powers that would compromise the fundamental objective of a genuine democracy.'[14] Nevertheless, fault lines were visible, for instance between provincial and national politicians. While the national ANC cadres generally put more emphasis on the need to democratise local government, the provincial politicians were acutely aware of the political pressure to somehow accommodate the chiefs, and were generally more moderate.

The schism over the issue first appeared during the ANC's fiftieth National Conference, in 1997. Modernists like Peter Mokaba and Pallo Jordan made fiery speeches with titles like 'The Evolution of So-Called Customary Law' and 'The National Question in South Africa' in which they explained to the audience how traditional leaders had become 'tinpot autocrats' who, 'because their livelihoods depended on it, ... acquired an interest in fostering an ethnic consciousness by wielding the totems, symbols and other paraphernalia of a particular "culture" or practices that differentiated their subjects from those of other chiefs' (Jordan, 1997). According to them, the 1994 elections had 'entailed a degree of compromise, some concessions and postponements, many of which took account of the enemy's real strength and untapped power', but now that these had been won, the time had come for the swift dismantling of apartheid structures such as 'so-called traditional authorities' (ibid.). These radicals were, however, sternly

[12] Interview, P. Holomisa, Amsterdam, 22 September 2000.
[13] ANC. 'Policy Guidelines for a Democratic South Africa.' 1992.
[14] Nelson Mandela, 'January 8 Statement.' Cape Town, 1996 (unpublished).

and publicly rebuked by Mandela and Mbeki, who both called for continued respect for traditional leaders.[15]

It is interesting to compare the approaches of South Africa's first two democratic presidents, who were so united in curbing the 'modernists'. Both Nelson Mandela and Thabo Mbeki were direct descendants of traditional leaders – Mandela's father and Mbeki's grandfather – who had been deposed because they did not agree with government policy on chieftaincy. And both presidents had been enthusiastically reinstalled within their tribal hierarchy after the democratisation.[16] But while they each combined a traditionalist stand with a strong commitment to democracy, their motivations seemed to differ. Mandela made no secret of his enthusiasm for traditional authority, tribal governance and customary legal structures.[17] The first page of his autobiography takes the readers to the rolling hills of Qunu, where the young Nelson watched and learned from the vehement and frank discussions in the Great Place, 'democracy in its purest form' (Mandela, 1995). As president, he would address traditional leaders as 'my chiefs' and stress how 'one of the first things I did when I came out of prison was to go right around the country meeting the traditional leaders and making clear that now that the leadership of the ANC had come back we were telling our people to respect the traditional leaders'.[18]

Mbeki's motivations could be considered more strategic than intrinsic. Known as both an 'adept infighter' and a 'cautious consensus politician', the country's second president was quick to recognise the political potential of traditional leaders: 'he is clever enough to realise that he cannot wish away ethnicity and tribalism in South Africa.'[19] Mbeki's reactions to the structural factors to be discussed later, such as the fear that traditional leaders would join rival parties like the UDM or the IFP, their boycotting of local government elections and their appropriation of the notion of an African Renaissance, were very much those of a skilful power politician. He managed to walk a political tightrope, on the one hand always reaffirming the government's commitment to non-racial democracy, while, on the other, vowing not to diminish the power of the traditional leaders.[20] 'This government respects traditional leaders and nothing untoward will be done to hurt their feelings,' he continually reassured them.[21]

One way in which Mbeki could justify such seemingly contrary statements was – as many other prominent ANC members had done before him – by redefining the institution (Oomen, 1996). The ANC had long emphasised the possibly progressive and democratic character of traditional authority, for instance by

[15] Interviews, various prominent ANC members.

[16] Hadland and Rantao (1999:133), Xolisa Vapi, 'Hail Queen Graca.' *Saturday Star*, 10 April 1999, p.6.

[17] Andrew Nash, 'Nelson Mandela, the Tribal Model of Democracy and the New South Africa', Cape Town: University of the Western Cape, 1998.

[18] As during a private meeting with the Sekhukhune traditional leaders, 27 May 1999.

[19] Good (1997); Hadland and Rantao (1999); *Business Day* online, 15 June 2000.

[20] ANC, 'Anc Local Government Elections 2000 Manifesto.' anclist@lists.sn.apc.org: African National Congress, 2000; ———. 'Mbeki Address to the National Council of Provinces.' anclist@lists.sn.apc.org: African National Congress, 2000.

[21] Sapa. 'Anc Assures Amakhosi That Concerns Will Be Met.' 25 November 2000. Cf. Ntsebeza. 'Whither South Africa's Democracy? The Case of Rural Local Government in the Former Bantustans.' who feels that, since the end of 1997, the governmental pendulum seems to have swung in favour of the traditional leaders.

including many chiefs in its parliamentary delegation. Traditional leaders were depicted as servants of their people who should, above all, 'in keeping with tradition ... say what is in the best interest of their subjects'.[22] As such, they could – in Mbeki's opinion – become 'agents of change', guided by 'the wisdom and benevolence of Hintsa and Moshoeshoe, the courage, the humility, yet dignity of deportment of Sekhukhuni, Ramabulana and Cetshwayo'.[23] But, above all, traditional leaders, in the ANC's definition, formed a unifying institution – 'great visionaries (who) had come to the realisation that the disunity of the African people was at the centre of their woes'.[24] As Oliver Tambo said: 'Let the dream of Moshoeshoe who cherished a great alliance of African people to resist separate conquest come true in our lifetime.'[25] This emphasis on the unitary and nationalist character of traditional leadership was juxtaposed with the ethnicist definition of chieftaincy held by the IFP, one of the parties to which we will now briefly turn.

The IFP and some unlikely allies

Some of the most ardent advocates of a strong role for traditional leaders were Chief Gatsha Buthelezi and his Inkatha Freedom Party. The previous chapter has already set out how it was above all the need to placate the IFP that informed the concessions made to traditional leaders in the interim constitution. These concessions would prove binding for the authors of the definitive Constitution, and would thus cast their shadow far into the future. In general, the IFP's interest had to do with both pumping up its identity as a 'true traditionalist' party as well as more strategic considerations: powerful traditional structures in KwaZulu/Natal could act as a counterweight to the ANC's national majority government. It was for this reason that, after Inkatha's 1994 claim to sovereignty for the Zulu nation had failed, it continued to plead for recognition of traditional leaders as the primary layer of local government and for an important role for the Zulu monarch.[26] During the 2000 local government crisis, for instance, Buthelezi supported the traditional leaders' protests against demarcation, and, reportedly, even threatened to quit the Cabinet over the issue.[27] And in the following period, he continuously professed 'sleepless nights' over the ANC's hesitant stance: 'Now more than ever, against the backdrop of the repeated and constant showing of antagonism and contempt towards traditional leadership, it is important the government produce tangible results.'[28] Underlining his own – disputed – chieftaincy, Buthelezi threatened: 'the writing of our history is not yet finished. We have much fuel for the fire that burns in our belly

[22] 'ANC Fears Disruption to Poll.' http://www.bday.co.za/bday/content/direct/0,3523,665435-6078-0,00.html: *Business Day* online, 2000.

[23] Sapa, 'Address by Pres. Mbeki to the House of Traditional Leaders.'

[24] ANC, 'Policy Guidelines for a Democratic South Africa.', Mandela. 'Speech at the Inauguration of the National Council of Traditional Leaders.'

[25] ANC, *Unity in Action: A Short History of the African National Congress (South Africa) 1912-1982* [Internet site]. 1982 4 March 2002. Available from http://www.anc.org.za/ancdocs/history/unity.html.

[26] IFP, 'Policy Summary Traditional Leadership.' http://www.ifp.org.za/ poltldrs.htm: IFP, 1998.

[27] Sapa, 'Ifp Denies Buthelezi to Quit.' ANC news briefing email service: ANC, 2000.

[28] Sapa, 'Buthelezi Continues His Wartalk over Amakhosi.' ANC news briefing email service: ANC, 2001, ———. 'Govt Should Honour Promise to Traditional Leaders: Buthelezi.' ANC news briefing email service: ANC, 2000.

and just cannot allow government to prematurely erect a tombstone over the institution of *ubuKhosi*.'[29]

Not only was the IFP's support for traditional leadership more far-reaching than the ANC's, it also rested on a different definition of the institution. For one thing, the IFP did precisely what the ANC tried to avoid at all costs: underline a strong link between traditional leadership and – in this case Zulu – ethnicity.[30] If the institution supported nationalism, it would be Zulu nationalism, which, as King Zwelithini said in calling for a Zulu renaissance, 'embodies the purity of Africanism and all that is good and honourable within our culture and spiritual heritage'.[31] Traditional leadership was also associated, over and over again, with the IFP's core traditional values. As Buthelezi stated: 'We represent the most noble part of what our country has to offer. We are the backbone of our country's integrity, moral fortitude and the will to succeed.'[32] This entailed a much larger role for traditional leaders than the ANC ever proposed: that of the main service deliverers in the rural areas. If traditional leaders did not spearhead local government, Buthelezi told the ANC, 'the delivery of essential services to the poorest of the poor in rural areas ... will be impaired for many years to come'.[33]

One snag potentially undermining the potency of Buthelezi's traditionalist claims was his difficult relations with the Zulu king. After the 1994 reintegration of the KwaZulu bantustan, *Ingonyama* Zwelithini is alleged to have told Mandela, 'you might have been imprisoned for 27 years, I was imprisoned for 24,' and he vowed never to get involved in party politics again. He was therefore difficult for the IFP to control, although it did try. One such attempt consisted of making Buthelezi head of the provincial House of Traditional Leaders, which subsequently gave itself the right to assign and withdraw the rights, functions and duties of the Zulu monarch. For all their clashes, however, the Zulu king frequently and publicly supported Buthelezi's pledge of a stronger role for the traditional leaders, for instance by asking his people to wear more traditional clothes and to start practising traditional crafts again, and by calling for a general reappraisal of tradition: 'Since 1984 I have revived the Reed Dance, where young girls descend on one of my royal residences for a ritual of bringing reeds to the residence. This provides a forum for me to address these maidens on matters of acceptable sexual behaviour with an emphasis on the prevention of the scourge of HIV/Aids.'[34] Zwelithini also lodged a complaint with the national Public Protector against the government's hesitant stance on traditional leadership.[35]

[29] Buthelezi was appointed chief during the time of the KwaZulu bantustan, with the authorities bypassing his elder brother because they felt Gatsha would be more cooperative. After a quick rise in the homeland hierarchy, he adopted the title of 'traditional prime minister' because one of his forefathers had held that post. The Zulu 'traditional prime minister' is, however, not hereditary, and Zulu king Zwelithini has often protested against Buthelezi's self-promotion to the post. Cf. Mzala (1988).

[30] Sapa, 'Parliament Must Lead Fight against Racism: Ginwala.' ANC, 2001.

[31] Sapa, 'King Zwelithini Asks for Zulu Renaissance.' ANC news briefing email service: ANC, 2000.

[32] Abbey Makoe, Sam Sole, and Mabutho Sithole, 'Buthelezi's Local Poll Gamble.' *Sunday Independent*, 8 October 2000, pp. 1–3.

[33] Sapa, 'Buthelezi Continues His Wartalk over Amakhosi.', ———. 'Buthelezi Slams Government over Recognition of Amakhosi.'

[34] Sapa, 'King Calls on Public Protector to Protect Traditional Leaders.' ANC news briefing email service: ANC, 2000; ———. 'Zulu King Urges International Protection of Traditional Leaders.' ANC news briefing email service: ANC, 2000.

[35] Sapa, 'Amakhosi: King Asks Baqwa to Probe Mbeki.' ANC news briefing email service: ANC, 2001.

Though the IFP claimed to be 'the only party which can be trusted by urban, rural and traditional authorities and community authorities to ensure, protect and foster a healthy convergence of democracy and development and traditional ways of life', most South African parties recognised the political potential of traditional leadership (Konrad Adenauer Stiftung, 1996). The National Party, for instance, with its 50 years' experience of ruling 'through the chiefs', continued its support. More right-wing Afrikaner parties, like the Freedom Front, supported the chiefs' claims under the general banner of 'group rights', which dovetailed nicely with their own minoritarian and ethnicist ambitions. Nevertheless, neither the NP nor the Freedom Front managed to muster much support from chiefs. The situation of the UDM, founded by ANC defector and former homeland leader Bantu Holomisa and NP stalwart Roelf Meyer, was different. In the run-up to the 1999 elections this party managed to acquire substantial support from chiefs, notably in the Eastern Cape where the ANC could only regain its position by giving the traditional leaders a massive salary rise.[36] In all, even though their understandings of traditional authority – ethnic symbol, marker for group rights, service deliverer – were different, most political parties did support the institution. One notable exception was the Democratic Party, which was most consistent in its criticism of the ANC for not speeding up democratisation in the rural areas.[37]

Contralesa: chiefs in politics

If the ANC and the IFP were the most prominent political parties involved in the 'struggle for the soul of custom', the Congress of Traditional Leaders of South Africa was the most notable civil society representative in the political arena. Its success rested mainly on its chameleon character: in the course of the 1990s it transformed itself from a progressive ANC ally into a body not only representing the majority of South Africa's traditional leaders but also – so it claimed – the interests of the whole rural population.

How did this happen? The previous chapter outlined how the ANC-in-exile sought to isolate the National Party government and raise the level of organisation in the rural areas by forming a broad democratic front (van Kessel, 2000). In this context, the establishment of Contralesa in 1987 came like a gift from God.[38] Set up by progressive Moutse traditional leaders opposed to KwaNdebele independence, the organisation was firmly dedicated to ANC Charterist aims such as 'a unitary non-racial and democratic South Africa', 'fighting tribalism and ethnicity' and 'schooling chiefs about the aims of the South African Liberation Struggle.'[39] By the time Contralesa was launched nationally in 1989, the 'people's chiefs' had become one of the ANC's most important rural partners and had 'contributed a great deal to the organisation of the rural masses in the bantustans, thereby weakening the system' (Zuma, 1990b:26). It was an essentially progressive organisation, concerned with the denunciation of illegitimate

[36] Chiara Carter, 'Chiefs Welcome UDM in E Cape' http://web.sn.apc.org/wmail/issues/990226/NEWS36.html, *Daily Mail & Guardian* electronic archive (26 February 1999); Peter Dickson, 'R30m Pay Hike for E Cape Chiefs.' *Mail & Guardian*, 16–22 April 1999, p. 13, Mbhele. 'New Force Rising.' Sapa. 'UDM Accuses ANC of a Blatant Abuse of Power.' ANC news briefing email service: ANC, 2000.

[37] Sapa, 'Opposition Still Concerned About Amakhosi.' ANC news briefing email service: ANC, 2000.

[38] Maloka (1996); Ndou and Letsoalo (1994); Tanja Woker and Sue Clarke, 'Human Rights in the Homelands', in *South African Human Rights and Labour Law Yearbook*, ed. Michael Robertson, Cape Town: Oxford University Press, 1990.

[39] The Congress of Traditional Leaders of South Africa, 'Constitution.' 1987, unpublished.

chiefs who cooperated with the homeland regimes and with the winning of votes for the ANC. As Contralesa's first leader said: 'once a chief has identified himself with us, then we know that the whole tribe or the majority of the people in that area are now with the progressive forces.'[40]

All this changed after democratisation, when Contralesa's generally progressive, pro-ANC character was replaced by a more traditionalist stance. One element of the changeover was visible in the organisation's attitude to party politics. In principle Contralesa considered that traditional leaders should not be affiliated to any political party, but, as chairman Holomisa (himself an ANC MP) stated, as long as the chiefs' formal position was unclear 'it was dangerous for traditional leaders not to make their voice heard by government'.[41] Nevertheless, '*amakhosi* should all strive for a time when they no longer need to be members of political parties in order to articulate their political aspirations' (Konrad Adeneuer Stiftung, 1994:39). Until that day, Contralesa enthusiastically – and much to the frustration of the ANC – flirted with the UDM and IFP alike, and started to welcome traditional leaders of all political creeds in its ranks.[42] In fact, anyone was welcome after 1994, as long as they paid their membership fees or, like temporary treasurer Winnie Mandela, took part in fund-raising activities.[43] In addition, the war talk against illegitimate bantustan chiefs was abandoned. 'We have softened on that one, not only because it is a can of worms, but also because we see now how even illegitimate traditional leaders have entrenched themselves, even in the minds of the people,' Pathekile Holomisa explained.[44] This open attitude meant that, even though it did not disclose its membership, Contralesa swiftly became *the* party representing traditional leaders, although there were competitors like the Organisation of Traditional Leaders of South Africa. Its powerful position was reinforced in 2000, when an alliance was formed with the mineral-rich Bafokeng nation and the national and provincial Houses of traditional leaders.

Contralesa's expansion would not have been possible without its extremely agile leadership. Practically the whole executive – Holomisa, Nonkonyana, Mhinga, Mzimela – consisted of experienced politicians with a background in law and an impressive ability to slip in and out of roles: from cellphone to knobkerrie, legalism to populist rhetoric, party politics to traditional oratory.[45] For instance, Pathekile Holomisa, elected chairperson from 1989 to 2001 and once classified as 'yuppie royalty with serious sex appeal', was one of the very few ANC members to escape strict party discipline and straddle the roles of chairing the

[40] Catherine Payze, 'The Elimination of Political Opponents: The Maphumulo Assassination' in *Patterns of Violence: Case Studies of Conflict in Natal*, ed. A. Minnaar, 247–58. Pretoria: Human Sciences Research Council, 1992.

[41] During the television programme 'In Camera', SABC 1, 22 February 1998.

[42] M. Edmunds (1995) *Tension in ANC over Traditional Leaders*; Mbhele. 'New Force Rising'; Parliamentary Monitoring Group. 'Provincial and Local Government Portfolio Committee: Workshop on Public Hearings on Traditional Leadership and Institutions: Response of the Congress of Traditional Leaders of South Africa on the Draft Discussion Document Towards a White Paper on Traditional Leadership and Institutions.' http://www.pmg.org.za/appendix/000606Contralesa.htm: Parliamentary Monitoring Group,, 2000.

[43] Mduduzi Ka Harvey, 'Winnie Jumps into Traditional Leaders Row.' http://web.sn.apc.org/wmail/issues/950120/wm950120-43.html: *Daily Mail & Guardian* electronic archive, 1995.

[44] Interview, Amsterdam, 22 September 2000

[45] Cf. Simon Zwane, 'Chiefs Beat the Drums of War', *Sunday Times*, 3 December 2000, p. 15.

ANC's parliamentary portfolio committee on land as well as being the party's most severe critic on issues of traditional leadership.[46] As he himself said: '*Ubukhosi* is like a double-edged sword. Depending on the person wielding it; it can easily be used to injure and cause harm; equally it can be used to defend and therefore build.'[47]

As a result of this approach, Contralesa discourse varied. On some occasions, it took a cooperative stance, pleading for chiefly performance contracts and presenting traditional leaders as a vital element of democracy, available to 'safeguard the African value systems which are the bedrock of society'. On other occasions, it was outright threatening. If traditional leaders were forced to show the other side of the sword, 'this country could be another Burundi'.[48] As Holomisa once wrote to the government: 'it is a fact that the potential might of Contralesa is of gigantic proportions ... You, as a collective, bear the onerous responsibility of averting the creation of a Renamo or Unita in this land.'[49] At times the traditional leaders displayed breathtaking arrogance, stating, for instance, that 'politicians ... are mere subjects who have been given mandates to fulfil certain functions' and should from time to time report to the Great Place.[50] But at other times they couched their claims in purely legal terms, suing the President over the Constitution or taking the main seats in the 'technical committee on traditional leadership issues'.[51] Another facet of the hybrid organisation became apparent when Contralesa decided to form a business trust, in order to invest in mining, forestry and resorts and join in a cellphone frequency bid.[52]

For all its kaleidoscopic character, some general features of the organisation's understanding of the role of traditional leadership in South Africa can be formulated.[53] First, there is the permanent emphasis on the centrality of traditional leadership in the core values of South African society. 'A zebra should not despise its stripes,' as one traditional leader said in a discussion on the Constitution.[54] And on its popularity: 'We move from the premise that the institution of traditional leadership is rooted in the soil of Africa, of which South Africa is an integral part, as well as in the hearts and minds of all ordinary Africans

[46] 'Chief Juggles Diverse Roles with Aplomb.' http://www.bday.co.za/bday/content/direct/0,3523,715353-6078-0,00.html: *Business Day* online, 2000, Edmunds. *Tension in ANC over Traditional Leaders*; Marc Gevisser, 'That Other Holomisa.' *Mail & Guardian*, 13–19 September 1996, p. 14.

[47] Pathekile Holomisa, 'Ubukhosi the Bedrock of African Democracy.' *Mail & Guardian*, 11–17 February 2000, p. 29.

[48] Sapa, 'Election-Ld-Chiefs.' ANC news briefing email service: ANC, 2000.

[49] Gevisser, 'That Other Holomisa', referring to the opposition movements in the Mozambican and Angolan civil wars, which both strongly relied on the support of traditional leaders.

[50] Ibid., using the Xhosa term for the royal palace.

[51] *Congress of Traditional Leaders vs the President of the Republic of South Africa*. Constitutional Court, 'Contralesa Gearing up for Court Battle'; Joint Technical Committee on Traditional Leadership Issues, 'Statement by the Joint Technical Committee on Traditional Leadership Issues.'

[52] 'Traditional Leaders to Form Private Firm for Investment.' *Business Day* 2000, p. 14. This trust was also discussed at Contralesa's provincial meetings, for instance on 20 July 1999.

[53] Pathekile Holomisa, 'The Role of Traditional Leaders in Local Government', in *The Role of Traditional Leaders in Local Government*, Johannesburg: Konrad Adenauer Stiftung, 1994; Holomisa (1996); Parliamentary Monitoring Group, 'Provincial and Local Government Portfolio Committee: Workshop on Public Hearings etc.'

[54] Contralesa, 'Submission to the Constitutional Assembly on the Constitutional Role of Traditional Leaders.' 1995.

who still take pride in their history, culture, origin and identity.' While Contralesa was not opposed to democratisation, it felt that culture should be sheltered from the onslaught of Western values and left to develop at its own pace. Traditional leaders should therefore be the primary tiers of government, even if some of their councillors could be elected. They should also continue to allocate the land with which they have 'holy ties' and to settle disputes. Traditional leaders, the organisation held, 'remain the key to peace, stability and tolerance, they are the symbols of unity which political parties by definition can never claim to be.'[55]

The civics: a wilting counterweight

If there was one actor that could potentially have mitigated Contralesa's strengthening position, it was the South African National Civics Organisation (Sanco). Where traditional leaders would tell politicians that they were 'mere subjects', a civic leader once snapped at the country's traditional leaders: 'You are all residents and you are supposed to be members of Sanco.'[56] At the time of the 1994 elections, Sanco had both the constituency and the political clout to compete with Contralesa as a voice representing the rural areas. It was an umbrella body of thousands of grass-roots organisations that had taken part in the struggle for democracy, and over bread-and-butter issues like housing and water, in the rural areas. And while Sanco never wanted to do away with traditional leadership completely, it saw a severely restricted role for the institution, making it subject to job descriptions and principles of representation and accountability.[57] 'South Africa should have one law and that should apply to all the citizens of the country ... Indigenous law should not be forced upon our people.'[58] Support for traditional leaders should, above all, be voluntary, and they should not be able to tax subjects or claim representation in provincial and national Houses.

But Contralesa's reinforcement of its political position following democratisation was accompanied by loss of support for Sanco and other NGOs. One reason for this was that Sanco had never managed to become as rooted in the rural areas as in the towns. As one rural woman parliamentarian said: 'I never saw much of a role for the civics in the rural areas...They were just another group of men doing the same thing as the old chief, and just as prone to corruption.'[59] A possible exception was the Eastern Cape, where the civics' strong position led to violent clashes with traditional leaders in the run-up to the 1994 elections, with the chiefs prohibiting Sanco members from canvassing in their areas.[60] Another reason for the wilting of civil society after democratisation was the exodus of activists to positions in government, at both national and municipal levels. As one traditional leader said (with satisfaction): 'Actually, the civics in my area

[55] Ibid.

[56] 'Constitutional Assembly Public Hearing on Traditional Leaders.'

[57] Ibid, Gregory Houston, and Somadoda Fikeni, 'Constitutional Development and the Issue of Traditional Leadership in Rural Local Government in South Africa', in *Aspects of the Debate on the Draft of the New South African Constitution Dated 22 April 1996*, ed. Konrad Adenauer Stiftung, Johannesburg: Konrad Adenauer Stiftung, 1996.

[58] 'Constitutional Assembly Public Hearing on Traditional Leaders.'

[59] Interview L. Ngwenya, Amsterdam, 22 September 2000.

[60] E. Naki, 'Delay Angers Eastern Cape Chiefs'. http://web.sn.apc.org/wmail/issues/941202/wm941202-11.html, *Daily Mail & Guardian* electronic archive.

have now been reduced to one person.'[61] As well as a lack of capacity, post-apartheid civil society also suffered from a lack of funding: both national and international donors preferred to invest in the newly elected government. And so, though Sanco would remain a player in the political arena, it did not manage to take up a role as counterweight to Contralesa.

This vacuum was not filled by other representatives of civil society either. Many of the international NGOs showed a strong fascination with chieftaincy issues, and financed dozens of conferences and publications on the subject.[62] Traditional leadership, it was held, was an important part of civil society in Africa. There were only a few truly critical voices, like that of the Rural Women's Movement which called for the total abolition of traditional courts. But, in general, they did not provide a counterweight to the traditional leaders' rise to power as the gatekeepers of rural interests. One reason for this could lie in the history of the South African struggle, which was largely characterised by 'boycotts' of the official structures and elected local government; while the traditional leaders had had the chance to gain ample administrative experience under apartheid, activists at the time had explicitly refrained from participating in state structures and thus had little experience of official politics.

One slight tilt in the balance of power occurred when all the activists who had worked in the Department of Land Affairs from 1994 to 1999 and had been sacked after the 'traditionalist' Minister Didiza took over, returned to their NGOs. These organisations, such as the National Land Committee, launched vehement attacks against the government's 'undemocratic and elitist position' in the traditional leadership issue, which they considered an attempt to 'retribalise rural society'.[63] On Mbeki's 2000 'olive branch' to the traditional leaders, increasing their representation in rural councils from 10 to 20 per cent the NLC wrote: 'It is regrettable that the decision to increase representation of traditional leaders, which will have repercussions on the lives of many millions of ordinary rural women and men, was taken in the absence of any meaningful public consultation with them.'[64] It also fulminated against the fact that, at a conference on the future of traditional leadership, rural community representatives 'who do not hold positions of traditional leadership ... comprised less than five per cent of the participants'.[65] In a desperate attempt to win some of the power of definition, a group of NGOs formed the Coalition for the Transformation of Traditional Leadership, calling on the government to elicit the views of ordinary rural people before tabling legislation on the powers and functions of traditional leaders. They held that it should not be up to

> a committee comprising government and traditional leaders to resolve between themselves issues of great concern not only to the rural people of our country but to the population as a whole.[66]

[61] Interview, *kgoši* M.J. Mashile, Lebowakgomo, 9 November 1995.

[62] Cf. IMPD, 'Good Governance at Local Level.' in Konrad Adenauer Stiftung (1997); SASCA. 'Conference Proceedings'. Paper presented at the 'Rural Governance in the new Millennium' conference, Port Elizabeth, 23 June 1999.

[63] Sapa. 'NGO's Criticise Govt for Ignoring Rural People.' ANC news briefing email service: ANC, 2000.

[64] Zakes Hlatshwayo, 'Article on Traditional Leaders', *The Sowetan*, 4 September 2000.

[65] Ibid.

[66] Sapa, 'Coalition Wants Grassroots on Amakhosi.' ANC news briefing email service: ANC, 2001, ———. 'NGO's Criticise Govt for Ignoring Rural People.' referring to the Joint Technical Committee on Traditional Leadership Issues.

The Traditional Affairs officials

In the Joint Technical Committee on Traditional Leadership Issues referred to in the above quotation, 'government' consisted mainly of Traditional Affairs officials. As became apparent when discussing policy formulation, while 'government' could hardly be considered univocal in its attitude to traditional leaders, clear strands could be distinguished. The Land Affairs officials working under Hanekom, for instance, had a predominantly socialist agenda, their main aim being the democratisation of rural communities and the side-lining of tribal authorities, considered outdated relics of apartheid. The main directorate concerned with traditional leaders, Traditional Affairs, in contrast considered its mission to be 'to promote traditional institutions within a modern democracy', with the main challenge being 'restoring the traditional nature and respectability of the institution of traditional leadership'.[67]

The enthusiasm with which this mission was carried out had a lot to do with the history of the directorate. Many scholars have stressed the crucial role of its predecessor, the Department of Native (later Bantu) Affairs, in providing – together with magistrates – not only day-to-day rule in the homelands, but also an ideological underpinning for this rule (Evans, 1997; Hammond-Tooke, 1997; Posel, 1995). Under Afrikaner ethnologists such as Van Warmelo, the notion that Africans lived in ethnically distinct tribes, each with their specific structures of rule and coherent sets of traditional laws, was elaborated in dozens of studies, many of them written by people in or associated with the Department. As a result of the 'sunset clauses' in South Africa's interim Constitution, the pre-1994 Traditional Affairs officials kept their positions and thus carried this approach and legacy into the post-apartheid order. This was all the more striking because the Ministers under whom they worked could hardly be considered traditionalists. Valli Moosa, the Indian Minister for Provincial Affairs and Constitutional Development until 1999, never showed much interest in the chieftaincy issue. His successor after the elections, Minister for Provincial and Local Government Sydney Mufamadi, had been born in rural Venda and – as a traditional elder in his community – had enough first-hand experience of the institution to be strongly critical of it, stating that 'allegiance to traditional institutions co-exists with overwhelming support for democratic governance'.[68]

Although the officials stayed the same, both the official functions and the name of the directorate changed after the 1994 elections. In 1997, for instance, the Chief Directorate of Traditional Affairs was transferred from Land Affairs to the Ministry for Provincial Affairs and Constitutional Development. There, it was split into three directorates:[69] (i) Anthropology, which watched over, and computerised, the genealogies and 'tribal records' collected since 1926 and advised in the omnipresent succession disputes; (ii) Remuneration and Capacity Building,

[67] Chief Directorate: Traditional Affairs. 'Chief Directorate: Traditional Affairs'; Department of Constitutional Development. 'A Draft Discussion Document Towards a White Paper on Traditional Leadership and Institutions.'

[68] Sydney Mufamadi, 'Traditional Leaders' Role', *Sowetan*, 20 April 2000, p.12, Sapa. 'Democracy Is Here to Stay; Mufamadi Tells Amakhosi.' ANC news briefing email service: ANC, 2000; ———. 'Traditional Leaders Warn Govt over Local Elections.' ANC news briefing email service: ANC, 2000, Xolani Xundu, 'Rift Narrows on Traditional Leaders,' *Business Day*, 24 August 2000 2000, p. 2.

[69] Department of Constitutional Development. 'Organisation and Establishment.' Pretoria, 1997; ———. 'Report to the Portfolio Committee on Constitutional Development.' Pretoria: Department of Constitutional Development, 1997.

which, among other things, organised courses on 'good governance' for traditional leaders; and (iii) Leadership and Institutions, which was responsible for the preparation of policy documents like the Draft Discussion document on Traditional Leadership. Traditional Affairs also maintained a strong provincial and local presence. These provincial departments had responsibilities such as the appointment of traditional leaders, the payment of both individual chiefs and the Tribal Authority structures (offices, cars, councillors) inherited from the past, dealing with succession disputes and – as the Northern Province Director of Traditional Affairs put it – 'dealing with those traditional leaders who don't want to administer according to culture'.[70] In addition, the local Traditional Affairs officials, often with decades of experience in 'administering the locals', remained in their positions.[71] As one traditional leader said: 'these people have an interest in supporting us, otherwise they'll be out of work before you know it.'[72]

Many of these officials – nationally, provincially or locally – were old-stamp anthropologists, with a strong belief that traditional leadership and culture should not only be recognised, but also be protected against the onslaught of modernisation.[73] Traditional authorities, the official policy went, were 'mini forms of state within the broader state context', with their own identity, system of authority and exclusive customs.[74] Nationally, many Traditional Affairs officials were Afrikaners, whose sympathy could well have been fed by the fact that they came from just as patriarchal, communalist and religiously oriented backgrounds as 'their chiefs'. One such official recalled the romance of field visits, and spending nights with the chief, gazing at the stars and discussing not only the 'tribal system' but also the commonalities between their peoples. In discussing research plans with these officials the advice was invariably to work through the Houses of Traditional Leaders and to choose the most cooperative chiefs and traditional communities: 'If you want to look into the powers of traditional leaders today it would be a good idea to go to KwaZulu: you'll still find some very traditional communities there.'

The generally pro-traditionalist, structural-functionalist and legalistic approach of the Directorate towards traditional leaders was clearest in the research methods used in the process of policy formulation. It was not without reason that the Coalition for the Transformation of Traditional Leadership, discussed earlier, protested about the fact that 95 per cent of the rural participants at a departmental conference on the future of traditional leadership were traditional leaders. In assessing 'the rural condition', the directorate relied heavily on three sources: traditional leaders, the law and anthropologists. The preparation of the Draft Discussion Document is a case in point. Even though the Department did plan the involvement of provincial advisory panels of rural youth and women in the

[70] Interview, Rev. Kekana, Northern Province Director of Traditional Affairs, 6 March 1998.

[71] For example, the Northern Province Department of Traditional Affairs employed 22 officials at provincial level in 1998, and in addition had one 'traditional affairs official' per 3-5 traditional authorities in districts and regions throughout the province.

[72] Interview *kgoši* P.F. Kutama, chairperson of the Northern Province House of Traditional Leaders, 17 March 1998.

[73] Repeated interviews with Traditional Affairs officials in the National directorate, as well as in Mpumalanga, the North West and the Northern Provinces.

[74] Department of Constitutional Development, 'Guideline Document: The Handling of Traditional Institutions and Their Leaders by the Department of Constitutional Development', p. 6.

policy process, these were never established. The empirical research planned was carried out scantily by departmental officials, who said of their visits:

> We choose traditional authorities from every area as samples. We're not very scientific but we try to choose those traditional authorities that are at least functioning – some of them have almost collapsed – so that we can lift the others up instead of bringing anybody down. In an area, we speak with the tribal authority personnel, the chief, his secretary and his council. It would be good to speak to people as well, but we've never done that...[75]

But more often, instead of going on field trips themselves, the officials sent questionnaires to the Houses of Traditional Leaders. This created a methodologically dubious situation in which the only respondents to answer questions about the current powers, functions and legitimacy of traditional leaders were the traditional leaders themselves. This information, as noted in the previous chapter, was supplemented with data derived from yellowing legislation and equally outdated ethnographic textbooks.

When experts were consulted, they were often Afrikaner ethnologists or black researchers trained by them.[76] Even after South Africa became democratic, anthropology in the country continued to be divided along the lines drawn by apartheid, with a deep rift between the – mostly English-speaking – researchers who for political reasons had long shied away from issues such as 'traditional culture' and ethnicity, and their Afrikaner counterparts who had virtually reified these very same notions (Gordon, 1998; Hammond-Tooke, 1997). The 'organic alliance' between these Afrikaner ethnologists, the traditional leaders and Traditional Affairs officials, who all seemed to hold similar structuralist and idealistic notions of chiefs and their communities, became clear at a conference of the South African Association of Cultural Anthropologists in 1999. Although its title was 'Rural Governance in the New Millennium', virtually all the papers dealt with the structures, functions and powers of traditional leaders.[77] As sophisticated modern media presentations on the important role of traditional authority in rural South Africa followed one another, the many traditional leaders invited clapped and nodded in approval, while the departmental officials studiously took notes. Here, it seemed, there was agreement on how traditional authority should be defined within a democratic dispensation: as a separate sphere, to be nurtured and preserved.

3. Why could they? Signs of the times

The ANC's ambivalence, Inkatha's strong association with the traditional leaders, Contralesa's agility and assertiveness, the feeble opposition of the civics and the unwaveringly pro-traditionalist stance of the main government department involved, all form parts of an explanation for the resurgence of traditional authority in post-apartheid society. Each of these actors had an interest in reproducing a certain definition of traditional authority and customary law: the ANC emphasised the institution's unifying, people-centred and progressive character, the IFP

[75] Interview with three Traditional Affairs officials, Pretoria, 23 February 1998.

[76] Chief Directorate Constitutional Affairs. 'Development and Transformation of Policy Matters on Traditional Leadership: Evaluation and Summation of Discussions with Academics and Experts.' Pretoria: Department of Constitutional Development, 1996.

[77] SASCA. 'Conference Proceedings.'

linked it to ethnic nationalism, and Contralesa to the very soul of South African society. And while the civics relegated the position of traditional authority to that of just another stakeholder in the rural landscape, the Department of Traditional Affairs depicted it as the main representative of the rural population, a separate sphere with a coherent legal system.

The way in which these actors engaged in the 'struggle for the soul of custom', and its outcome, cannot be understood without looking at the wider environment in which it took place. The context arose from both the international and the national political climates and their interactions. South Africa, in contrast to most other African countries, can be said to have gained its independence from colonisation in the 1990s instead of the 1960s. The other countries had formulated post-independence legal and institutional frameworks guided by the stars of 'modernisation' and state-centralist thinking, but the stars had lost their brightness by the time the South African constitutional negotiators got round the table. Instead, a new moon had risen above the international horizon, with an emphasis on scaling down the state, on decentralisation but also – surprisingly – on recognising cultural difference and respecting group rights. In addition, South Africa's Constitution was not born in isolation. The negotiated character of its revolution ensured that a large chunk of the inheritance from the past would be inserted into the new order.[78] Behind the shiny, self-confident and essentially unitary new Constitution and Parliament lay more than a century of institutional segregation, with policies and practices engraved in the minds and actions of all who had grown up in them and in the thousands of institutions that had played a role in their perpetuation.

It is to these structural conditions and their influence in shaping the debate on the future of traditional leadership that we now turn. We look first at some of the salient conditions at play nationally in party-political power, the institutional legacy and the deeply-felt need for an African Renaissance. Subsequently we consider how the two global trends already discussed in the Introduction, that of 'thinking local' and of emphasising cultural rights, also influenced the South African balance of power.

Party-political power

Though the ANC was by far the majority party, both in the 1994 and 1999 elections, it remained just short of the two-thirds majority needed to single-handedly amend the Constitution. It could therefore not avoid some form of power-sharing, a conclusion that had already dawned during the constitutional negotiations and led to the formulation of sunset clauses and a Government of National Unity. Moreover, the ANC was quick to realise that it was the rural areas, with their two-thirds to a half of the national population, that formed its Achilles' heel. Essentially an urban-based organisation, both in terms of constituency as well as ideology, it had found it difficult in the 1980s to get a grip on the countryside. And it was not only traditional leaders who, after democratisation, accused the party of 'not having a clue as to what was going on in the rural areas, and not caring much either'.[79]

[78] Cf. Allister Sparks, *Tomorrow Is Another Country: The Inside Story of South Africa's Negotiated Revolution*. London: Heinemann, 1995; Waldmeier (1997).

[79] A similar criticism was made by some ANC parliamentarians, rural women and civics, in spite of the fact that after 1999 Thabo Mbeki made reviving the rural areas one of his main policy priorities.

The potential danger of neglecting the rural areas and the traditional leaders was underlined by both international and national developments. The post-independence history of many of South Africa's (distant) neighbours bore witness to the 'remarkable resilience' of traditional authorities (cf. Konrad Adenauer Stiftung, 1997; Van Rouveroy van Nieuwaal and Van Dijk, 1999; Van Rouveroy van Nieuwaal and Zips, 1998; various authors, 1996). Mozambique, well known to many ANC politicians, was one nightmare scenario. Here, Frelimo's pledge to 'kill the tribe, build the nation' resulted in 'killing the nation' and leaving the all-important rural support to the opposition party Renamo.[80] Zimbabwe provided another warning. Here, Mugabe had abolished all official traditional authority structures after independence, only to be forced to reinstall customary courts and a National House of Traditional Leaders in the 1990s (cf. De Villiers and Critchley, 1997; Maxwell, 1999). This was in line with events in other former British colonies, like Zambia, Uganda and Malawi, which had all seen some form of institutional retraditionalisation around this period (Englebert, 2001). Contrasting examples were relatively stable countries like Ghana and Botswana, where the national state had long derived legitimacy and stability from including traditional leaders in its official structures (Du Toit, 1995; Rathbone, 2000). As Mandela once said, the position of traditional leaders in countries like Angola held important political lessons: the Marxist government there had abolished traditional leaders, 'only to be faced with rebellion from tribal followers in the countryside'.[81]

The national political process also seemed to contain similar warnings. In the run-up to the 1994 elections Inkatha, with its close links with the traditional leaders in KwaZulu/Natal, had made it virtually impossible for the ANC to gain a hold on the rural areas there. In addition, there was the – at the time all too realistic – fear that if the ANC did not form an alliance with the traditional leaders in other former homelands, they would continue to support the National Party. Events in the Eastern Cape after 1994 also spooked the ANC. As noted earlier, in 1999, 20 of the province's 25 senior traditional leaders were said to support Bantu Holomisa's UDM in protest against the ANC's handling of the traditional authority issue.[82] It was only after a notable salary increase, sneered at by the opposition as an 'expensive form of political patronage', that the ANC managed to lure some of them back into its ranks.[83]

An underlying presumption in this issue was the chiefly ability to 'deliver the rural vote' and to act as gate-keeper to the rural communities. Chiefs, the general belief seemed to be, could be extremely useful if they cooperated with the ANC, but 'could be deadly opposition' as well.[84] Traditional leaders, as we shall see, were the main actors in perpetuating this image of themselves as vote-brokers.[85] As ANC-cum-Contralesa member Nonkonyana put it: 'Because my people trust

[80] Cf. Hughes (1999); F. Van Zijl Slabbert, 'The Roots of Moral Alienation and Lawlessness in South Africa: Symptoms of the Malaise.' http://www.goedgedacht.org.za/000408.html, 2000.

[81] Steuart Wright, 'A Lesson in Government as Mandela Upstages Mhlaba' 1995, accessed 18 February 2002. Available from http://www.sn.apc.org/wmail/ issues/950210/wm950210-2.html.

[82] Carter. 'Chiefs Welcome UDM in E Cape.'

[83] Eveleth. *Luring Chiefs to Democracy*.

[84] Edmunds. *Tension in ANC over Traditional Leaders*. writing on P. Holomisa.

[85] G. Houston and S. Fikeni (1996). 'Constitutional Development and the Issue of Traditional Leadership in Rural Local Government in South Africa.' in Konrad Adenauer Stiftung (1996).

me ... they will vote for my party.'[86] Nevertheless, it is far from clear if traditional leaders actually had this power. Though there were many reports of chiefs physically preventing some parties from canvassing in their areas or holding meetings in the tribal offices, the question remained as to the extent to which their party membership influenced their subjects' voting behaviour.[87] In the Eastern Cape, for instance, even though the UDM managed to muster support from 80 per cent of the province's senior traditional leaders in 1999, it received only 13 per cent of the votes. Similarly, in areas in the Northern Province where the traditional leaders continued to support the National Party, their subjects massively voted for the ANC. Nevertheless, such considerations did not appear to play a role in the ANC's policies, which seemed to depart from the notion that traditional leaders were the only tickets to the rural vote.

Path dependency

> There is every reason to expect that the current debate will take the shape of past controversies (Currie, 1994:152)

A reader of the preamble to the Promotion of Bantu Self-Government Act 46 of 1959, which states 'Whereas the Bantu peoples of the Union of South Africa do not constitute a homogeneous people, but form separate national units on the basis of language and culture', might have difficulties in distinguishing it from the classification by the Directorate of Traditional Affairs of traditional authority areas as 'mini forms of state' with 'exclusive customs' and an 'own identity'.[88] Though most South African policy-makers would vehemently deny it, there seemed to be more similarities than differences in the way the debate over traditional leadership and customary law was conducted, as well as its results before and after democratisation. This draws our attention to another wider structural condition at work, one which – borrowing a term from economics – could be called 'path dependency' (North, 1990:6-7). The term is used here to indicate the fact that past policies and practices can be so deeply and persistently engraved in both institutions and attitudes that a radical departure from them becomes virtually impossible. As Bourdieu wrote on the comparable notion of *habitus*, the past offers a system of dispositions, of structuring structures, which mean that, while a habitus contains

> an infinite capacity for generating products – thoughts, perceptions, expressions and actions – whose limits are set by the historically and socially situated conditions of its production, the conditioned and conditional freedom it provides is as remote from creation of unpredictable novelty as it is from simple mechanical reproduction of the original conditioning.[89]

As noted in the previous chapter, the recognition of traditional authority and customary law under apartheid took a distinct shape. It drew on, to borrow Scott's[90] terminology, high-modernist authoritarian state simplifications of messy local reality, and imposed these simplifications where necessary. The introduction

[86] Sapa, 'Traditional Leaders Kingmakers in Rural Vote.' ANC news briefing email service: ANC, 1999.
[87] Cf. my own experiences during the 1995 local government elections in the North-West and in 1999 in Sekhukhune, and the reports about the run-up to the 2000 local government elections.
[88] Department of Constitutional Development. 'Guideline Document: The Handling of Traditional Institutions and Their Leaders by the Department of Constitutional Development', p. 6.
[89] Bourdieu, P. (1993:482).
[90] Scott (1998).

of one uniform grid of traditional authority structures – regional authorities, territorial authorities, tribal authorities – all over South Africa is but one example. In addition, the governments of the time conceptualised rural reality in highly systematic terms: as consisting of 'tribes', each of which was a coherent entity with a closed political system and a distinct set of rules that could be asserted in law. A legalistic approach, in which customary law was encoded in laws and text-books and worked out in legal precedent, was also central to its recognition under the former regime. Strikingly, this *mode* of recognition seemed to be introduced into and perpetuated in the new order: in the dualistic approach underlying the Customary Marriage Act, the depiction of traditional authorities as 'mini forms of state' and the call for clear and uniform rules on, for instance, appointment and succession stands central.[91]

Looking through the prism of 'path dependency', various reasons can be given for this continuation and reproduction of past practices and imagery. The first lies in the actual tangible legacy of apartheid. One consequence of South Africa's negotiated revolution was the integration of 'sunset clauses' in its Constitution, which provided for the continued application of old-order legislation and guaranteed civil servants job continuity.[92] They ensured that a large part of the institutional and practical heritage arrived, prefabricated, to be inserted into the new order. But, as we have seen, past conceptions also seemed to shape the formulation of new policies and laws. Here, part of the explanation lies in the attitude of politicians, policy-makers and stakeholders alike, who all grew up in a segregated world and had that as their frame of reference. From the officials writing the policy documents to the magistrates passing verdicts and the 'street-level bureaucrats' involved in the day-to-day administration of custom, they all introduced and thus reproduced their past in their daily practices (Lipsky, 1980).

Similarly, the background of traditional leaders, main stakeholders in the policy debate, made it logical, sometimes even inevitable, for them to state their claims in terms that rang surprisingly familiar, even though, or maybe because, 'continued acceptance of imposed ethnic terms as the most appropriate vehicle for collective self-identification and social action legitimises the conditions of inequality that give rise to them in the first place'.[93] In discussing this reliance on old forms and practices, Sitas introduces the notion of 'status scripts': 'the stories, legitimations and symbolic references a social group uses to distinguish itself in its competition for resources, power or influence from others within social institutions' (Sitas, 1998:39). One of these scripts, rooted in over a century of institutional segregation, was that of custom, strongly linked to specific notions of self-determination and the preservation of 'tradition'.

There were other reasons for the resurfacing of the past in the present. One was simply the practicality of following the beaten track and retaining old institutions because of the lack of alternatives. With the magistrates' courts never being able to handle the case load of the customary courts, the elected municipalities suffering from severe undercapacity, and no viable alternative system for

[91] Department of Constitutional Development. 'Guideline Document: The Handling of Traditional Institutions and Their Leaders by the Department of Constitutional Development.' The particular assumptions underlying post-apartheid policy and legislation will be discussed more extensively in the next section.

[92] S 229 Act 200/1993; S 2 Transitional Arrangements Act 108/1996; Corder (1994:500).

[93] Edwin Wilmsen. 'Premises of Power in Ethnic Politics', in Wilmsen and McAllister (1996).

land allocation having been agreed upon, it was best to retain the existing structures. Another reason concerns the character of law itself. Law, as a system, rests on notions such as legal certainty, clear definitions, reproducible and uniform rules. Under apartheid, codified customary law had become a system that fulfilled these requirements. Attempts in the post-apartheid era to allow more flexibility and a better reflection of 'living law' within formal arrangements would not only have clashed with official attitudes and practicalities, but also with law's central premises. In order to govern, states are best served by simplifications, and this is precisely what apartheid's institutional legacy concerning traditional authorities provided.[94] What also played an important role here was the virtual lack of information on the actual 'rural condition': almost all official documents published on traditional leadership and customary law lament the lack of data on 'living law' and the current legitimacy of traditional leadership.[95] All this was not helped by the role of the press, which reported very little on the rural areas, and if it did, painted a highly stereotypical picture.

It was for all these reasons – practical, psychological, institutional – that the past *mode* of recognising traditional leadership and customary law continued to resurface after apartheid, with old forms and figures as inescapable as the grooves of a well-worn record.

The quest for an African identity

In the years after South Africa's transition to democracy, a new tradition was born. Increasingly every year, the opening of Parliament became a fashion show, a colourful exposition of the country's cultural diversity. Broadcast live on morning television, MPs and their spouses arrived adorned in meticulously woven Zulu beads, wide Muslim robes, flowing embroidered West African kaftans, Xhosa dresses or Hugo Boss clothes, with leopard pelts around their shoulders or feathered floppy Boer hats shading grey-bearded faces. The enthusiasm with which this event was adopted is symbolic of another condition at work: the deeply-felt need, reinforced by global culture, to 'localise democracy', to brand it as a home-grown product instead of a Western import, and to link it firmly to African values. This was of particular importance to the ANC, with its universal and essentially liberal agenda of individual rights and democracy. Now that communism had fallen from grace and pure neo-liberalism ran the risk of being characterised as 'too Eurocentric', the ANC had become 'a party looking for a slogan' (Ellis and Sechaba, 1992).

One of the clearest examples of this ANC search, and its attempt to reconnect the universal values it held central with the local, African heritage is found in Thabo Mbeki's breathtaking oration at the adoption of the 1996 Constitution (Mbeki, 1998:31-6). After famously exclaiming, 'I am an African!', the future president linked his being to the hills, valleys and mountains 'that define the face of our native land': 'I owe my being to the Khoi and the San whose desolate souls haunt the great expanses of the beautiful Cape... In my veins courses the blood

[94] Scott (1998); Spiegel et al., 'Speaking Truth to Power? Some Problems Using Ethnographic Methods to Influence the Formulation of Housing Policy in South Africa.'; Wilson (2000:87).

[95] Cf. Department of Constitutional Development. 'A Draft Discussion Document Towards a White Paper on Traditional Leadership and Institutions'; South African Law Commission, 'The Harmonisation of the Common Law and Indigenous Law: The Application of Customary Law: Conflict of Personal Laws'; ———. (2003).

of the Malay slaves who came from the East ... I am the grandchild of the warrior men and women that Hintsa and Sekhukhune led...I am the grandchild who lays fresh flowers on the Boer graves.' Then, sweepingly and convincingly, he presented the new Constitution – for all its uniqueness a classic liberal democratic document – as a product that could only have been grown in African soil:

> I am born of a people who would not tolerate oppression. We are assembled here today to mark their victory in acquiring and exercising their right to formulate their own definition of what it means to be African. The constitution whose adoption we celebrate constitutes an unequivocal statement that we refuse to accept that our Africanness shall be defined by our race, colour, gender or historical origins.

A similar endeavour to reappropriate universal values and concepts, blend them with the local heritage and solutions, and present them as home-grown products, was found in all other parts of post-apartheid society: law, business, health, fashion, education and the like. For instance, in abolishing the death penalty the Constitutional Court not only referred to the Constitution and universal values, but also to *ubuntu*, the notion linking one person's humanity to that of others.[96] Similarly, in the years after 1994 stacks of books on African approaches to management appeared, and outside Johannesburg a Zulu kraal was set up – by a German – for 'corporate leaders who want their staff to learn more about African culture'.[97]

In part, this 'return to the roots' corresponded, and was a reaction, to globalisation: the fact that the increased flow of capital, goods, information and ideas all over the world has often, and in the eyes of some paradoxically, led to a strengthening of local culture (Appadurai, 1996; Meyer and Geschiere, 1995; Nederveen Pieterse, 1994). Awareness of the existence of these conditions was, for instance, well demonstrated by Provincial and Local Government Minister Mufamadi who, in discussing the future of traditional leadership, referred parliamentarians to Thomas Friedman's (1999) *The Lexus and the Olive Tree: Understanding Globalization*, which sketches the twin imperatives in an increasingly globalising world: embracing modernity (the Lexus) but combining this with a reappraisal of culture, tradition, roots (the Olive Tree). Traditional leader Mnisi showed a similar awareness of the international climate when he argued that:

> Our traditional leaders have a unique system of serving our communities. We are very committed to preserving this, for we will not be blamed as a generation for destroying our culture. Even Afro-Americans come here searching for their roots and identity. When they come, they want to see chiefs. We really also have a duty to preserve them for our brothers in other countries.[98]

The desire to return to indigenous values and structures as part of democratisation went much deeper than mere performative pressure from the outside world.

> Beyond the refusal of all exterior domination is the urge to reconnect in a deep way with Africa's cultural heritage, which has been for too long misunderstood and rejected. Far from being a superficial or folkloristic attempt to bring back to life some of the traditions or practices of our ancestors, it is a matter of constructing a new African society, whose identity is not conferred from the outside. (Appiah, 1991:1, quoting Cardinal Paul Zoungrana)

[96] *State v. Makwanyane and Another*, 3 SA 391 (1995).
[97] 'A Kraal Exists on Suburbia's Doorstep.' *Sunday Independent*, 8 October 2000, p.10.
[98] Interview, *inkosi* M.B. Mnisi, Mpumalanga traditional leader, 24 March 1998.

For all its liberal democratic Constitution and the important role of 'Western' values in public discourse, South Africa is a country where a large part of the population firmly believes in core values derived from communalism, religion, and reverence for traditional authority and for the spiritual world. In this perspective, the South African philosopher Vilakazi was not far wrong when he stated that (1999:1) 'a thin layer of this (South) African population is now Western in culture and behaviour, but the overwhelming majority of the African population is not Western in culture. Their cultural orientation and assumptions are largely rooted in the principles and values of African civilization.'

This overall mood was well captured by Mbeki when he launched the 'African Renaissance'. This was principally a quest to show South Africans and the rest of the world alike that African solutions do not have to be 'pagan, savage, superstitious and unscientific ... snake-oil cures and quackery', nor did Africa have to 'remain a curiosity slowly grinding to a halt in the periphery of the world'.[99] Nevertheless, it is interesting to note the changing way in which the notion of an African Renaissance, considered an 'empty vessel' and therefore appealing to both modernists and traditionalists, has been filled in over time (Vale and Maseko, 1998). In launching the concept around 1996, for instance, Mbeki never once referred to traditional leadership as a constitutive element. Instead, his speech was mainly about the establishment of genuine and stable democracies and good governance in Africa, eliminating poverty and strengthening the economy.[100] In a 1997 speech, he emphasised cultural exchange, the emancipation of women from patriarchy, the mobilisation of youth, the broadening of democracy and sustainable development as vital areas of engagement for an African Renaissance.[101]

But it did not take long before the traditional leaders and the advocates of their cause, in another impressive exercise of redefinition, appropriated the notion and awarded traditional leadership a central place in achieving the African Renaissance. In the words of the chairperson of the National Council of Traditional Leaders: 'there is little stopping us from becoming the engine of the African Renaissance.'[102] Without traditional leadership, the chiefs claimed, there would be neither an African democracy nor an African Renaissance: 'we further believe that African Renaissance should be based on the African norms and values found only in the institution of traditional leadership.'[103] These views were echoed by the Directorate of Traditional Affairs, which in the prelude to the Discussion Document wrote that:

> The call for an African Renaissance ... is a call for the coming of age of Africa's institutions, and not for a perfect mimicry of the world's powerful societies. After all,

[99] Mbeki. 'The African Renaissance, South Africa and the Rest of the World', Sapa. *Second Oliver Tambo Lecture by Thabo Mbeki* ANC, 10 August 2000.

[100] Liebenberg (1998); Thabo Mbeki, 'Speech by the Deputy President at the Africa Telecom 98 Forum', 1998.

[101] These ideas, contained in the document 'African Renaissance, a workable dream' by Mbeki's senior political adviser Vusi Mavimbela, are quoted in Vale and Maseko (1998).

[102] 'Traditional Leaders Say No to Rural Municipalities.' http://www.bday.co.za/bday/content/direct/0,3523,544107-6078-0,00.html: *Business Day* online, 2000.

[103] Parliamentary Monitoring Group. 'Tabling the Annual Report on Behalf of the National House of Traditional Leaders.'

> it is hard to conceptualise African culture without any reference to the institution of traditional leadership and to customs.[104]

Mbeki himself followed suit in 2001, stating for the first time in an address to the National House of Traditional Members, that 'the institution of traditional leadership can and should play a central role in the African Renaissance'.

And so, while there was a deep-felt and pervasive desire in the new South Africa to look for local 'olive trees', markers of indigenous culture and symbols of an African identity, it was again chiefly political agility that put traditional leadership forward as *the* olive tree – and the only one – to be embraced.

Transformations of the state

If the search for an African identity could be considered a local reflection of a worldwide mood, this was also, maybe even more so, the case with the discussions on the shape of the post-apartheid state. While most African countries had designed their legal and institutional framework in the 1960s, the period of firm belief in central state powers in achieving a 'take-off to modernity',[105] this optimism had dwindled by the time Mandela walked to freedom. Instead, it was replaced by both an empirical establishment of state failure and a batch of normative prescriptions on how best to address the problems faced by the centralist state.

By the 1990s many observers expressed their worries about the situation of the state, especially, although not exclusively, in Africa with its colonial heritage (Chatterjee, 1993; Ellis, 1996; Leys, 1996; Mbaku, 1999; Migdal, 1998). Pestered by a lack of legitimacy, developed into an uncontrollable Moloch unable to carry out any of its central functions efficiently, geared more towards personal enrichment of its functionaries than the delivery of services, it had – in many cases – lost out as an agent of change. As Mbembe wrote:

> Almost everywhere, the state has lost much of that capacity to regulate and arbitrate that enabled it to construct its legitimacy. It no longer has the financial means, administrative power, and, in general, the sorts of 'goods' that would have enabled it to resolve politically the conflicts that have erupted in the public domain and led, almost universally, to violence previously containable in more or less tolerable limits. Having no more rights to give out or to honor, and little left to distribute, the state no longer has credit with the public (Mbembe, 2001:76)

Linked to this state failure was a strengthening, in many different forms, of both the local and the supranational spheres, a disengagement from the formal political sphere to a myriad of other spheres of influence (Baker, 1997).

This empirical observation – truer of some countries than of others – went hand in hand with a whole battery of normative prescriptions on how best to reform the state. From the late 1980s onwards, the Bretton Woods institutions, international NGOs and academics began to supplement their focus on economic development with an emphasis on 'good governance'.[106] This entailed, among other things, a down-scaling of state apparatuses to 'lean and mean' machines

[104] Department of Constitutional Development. 'A Draft Discussion Document Towards a White Paper on Traditional Leadership and Institutions.'

[105] Cf. W.W. Rostow, 'The Economics of Take-Off into Sustained Growth: Proceedings of a Conference Held by the International Economic Association' London, 1963, ———. *The Process of Economic Growth*. Oxford: Clarendon Press, 1953.

[106] Abrahamsen (2000); Konrad Ginther, Erik Denters, and Paul De Waart, (eds), *Sustainable Development and Good Governance*. Dordrecht: Nijhoff, 1995; Otto (1997); World Bank, *Governance and Development*, Washington DC: World Bank, 1992.

directed at efficient service delivery, a decentralisation of many classic central state functions to the local government level and a stimulation of public-private partnerships in what was now labelled 'governance' rather than 'government'.

While South Africa could by no means be considered a 'weak state', it did democratise within this worldwide context. And the ANC followed suit even though the party could be considered rather centralist – due to its history as a party-in-exile and its fear of the centripetal tendencies in South Africa becoming stronger than the more centrifugal forces.[107] One reason for this lay in the post-apartheid political dynamics, with parties like the IFP and the NP pleading for decentralisation and federalism in order to obtain as much decision-making power as possible in those areas where they had a large constituency (cf. Faure and Lane, 1996). But another reason lay in the multitude of international advisers and local academics and officials, trained in the jargon of neo-liberalism, new public management and good governance, involved in drawing up policies. Because South Africa democratised relatively late it could – in the dialectics of progress – incorporate all these insights in its development policies. The previous chapter showed how this resulted in, among other things, the introduction of three separate spheres of government, with relatively large competences for local government, and in a continuous emphasis on stakeholder involvement in policy-making.

These two general tendencies – decentralisation and an emphasis on participation in policy-making – created opportunities that the traditional leaders were quick to seize. Decentralisation is essentially about the transfer of functions, powers and resources to the local government level. As we have seen, traditional leaders continuously emphasised that they should be this primary tier of government, strengthened by decentralisation policies. Self-governance by indigenous authorities, as they stated and as was reiterated by many development specialists, held 'an extraordinarily large development potential' (Hofmeister and Scholz, 1997:7). It opened the way for a situation similar to that in the rest of Africa, where decentralisation has all too often led to a resurgence of traditional authority structures in the local arena.[108]

But because of the chameleon character of the institution, traditional leaders could present themselves not only as the local structures which should benefit from *public* decentralisation, but also as the ideal partners in *civil* society. Where development discourse emphasised partnerships in governance and public-private alliances, the traditional leaders stepped to the fore as the ideal partners to deal with in civil society. Thus, traditional authorities were actively involved by the state and NGOs alike in projects as diverse as the struggle against AIDS, the improvement of schools, recruiting for the army, census-taking, advising local transport boards, fighting crime and educating voters.[109]

[107] ANC. 'Nation-Formation and Nation Building: The National Question in South Africa.' Unpublished discussion document: Presented at the ANC's 50th National Conference, 1997; Wilmsen and McAllister (1996).

[108] Bierschenk and Olivier de Sardan (1998); Jeremy Gould. 'Resurrecting Makumba: Chiefly Powers and the Local State in Zambia's Third Republic'; Olivier de Sardan, J.P. (ed.), *Anthropologie et Développement*. Paris: Karthala, 1995.

[109] Thuli Nhlapo, 'Chiefs Paid by Iec to Woo Voters.' http://www.mg.co.za/mg/za/archive/2000nov/features/27nov-chiefs.html: *Mail & Guardian* online, 2000, Capt Bafana Nxumalo, 'Chiefs Meet North Western Command', *Salut*, December 1996, 40–41; Sapa. 'Mpuma Traditional Leaders Join Police to Fight Crime'; ANC news briefing email service: ANC, 2001; interview C. de Villiers, 28 February 1997.

Similar processes were at work in the administration of justice. Globally, in the late 1980s and early 1990s, the focus shifted from uniform, state-administered justice to a reappraisal of local-level community courts.[110] Again, the reasons for this lay in a combination of pragmatism and ideology. Pragmatically, community courts were considered an alternative to the overburdened state system.[111] But community-based courts were also thought to dispense a better type of justice: restorative instead of retributive, fast, accessible, cheap and close to the people.[112] Again, it did not prove too difficult for traditional leaders to capture this world-wide mood and argue that, in the South African countryside, they were the ideal – and only possible – dispensers of this 'popular justice' (South African Law Commission, 1999).

The rise of group rights

'It is hard to find a democratic or democratizing society these days that is not the site of some significant controversy over whether and how its public institutions should better recognize the identities of cultural and disadvantaged minorities,' Charles Taylor wrote in 1992 (p. 3). He captured the global mood well. Whether concerning the claims of Canadian native peoples, the opposition of Surinamese *pueblos indigenas* to gold-digging in their areas, discussions on the liberation of East Timor or greater autonomy for the pygmies in Cameroon or the Basques in Spain, the 1990s introduced a period in which politics, talk about human rights and culture became interlaced in an unprecedented way (cf. Assies et al., 2000; Gabor, 1998; Galenkamp, 1993; Henrard and Smis, 2000; Kymlicka, 1995; Preece, 1997; Segasvary, 1995; Seleoane, 1997). Again, this development was closely tied to other facets of the global situation. Take state failure, for instance: it was because the central state was deemed incapable of protecting the interests of 'cultural groups' that all sorts of sub- and supra-national communities started claiming greater political autonomy, thus in turn weakening the central state. In addition, the more tangible reflections of the nebulous process of globalisation – television, e-mail, the Internet, human rights NGOs everywhere – equipped these 'cultural groups' with the tools necessary to express and disseminate their claims: a transnational human rights discourse to suit their needs and an electronic and international platform on which to post them (Von Benda-Beckman, 1999; Wilmsen and McAllister, 1996:112).

The global attention to cultural rights that characterised the 1990s was not, of course, new. The source of this type of 'third-generation' human rights is S 27 of the 1966 International Covenant of Civil and Political Rights, which is mirrored in the South African Constitution, and declares that: 'In those States in which ethnic, religious or linguistic minorities exist, persons belonging to such minorities shall not be denied the right, in community with other members of their group, to enjoy their own culture, to profess and practise their own religion, or to use their own language.'[113] While this right is still a so-called group right – granted to *individuals* on the basis of their membership of cultural groups – legal thinking later evolved towards more emphasis on collective rights, granted to a

[110] Cf. Sally Engle Merry, 'Popular Justice and the Ideology of Social Transformation.' *Social & Legal Studies* 1 (1992): 161–76; Various authors (1996).

[111] 'Community Courts "Being Considered".' *Business Day* 1997, 6. Cf. Assies (2000:13).

[112] Mathole Matsekhga, 'People's Courts,' *Lawyers for Human Rights* 3 (1991): 39–42, Scharf (1992).

[113] As reflected in S 31 of Act 108/1996.

group as such.[114] The 1989 ILO Convention 169 concerning Indigenous and Tribal Peoples in Independent Countries was a first premonition of the upcoming prominence of 'rights to roots'.[115] It was followed in 1994 by the United Nations Draft Universal Declaration on Indigenous Rights, which recognised 'the urgent need to respect and promote the inherent rights and characteristics of indigenous peoples, especially their rights to their lands, territories and resources, which derive from their political, economic and social structures and from their cultures, spiritual traditions, histories and philosophies'.[116] In a radical departure from earlier thinking on citizen-state relations, the document stated that indigenous peoples, as collectivities, 'have the right to freely determine their relationships with States in a spirit of coexisting mutual benefit and full respect'.[117] The United Nations officially declared the 1995–2004 period the International Decade of the World's Indigenous People.

These developments in international law tallied with events in many individual countries, in which local religious, linguistic and ethnic minorities suddenly claimed – and often obtained – formal affirmation and strengthening of their position. Nevertheless, as has been set out in the Introduction, many observers considered it surprising to find South Africa so prominent among them. After all, apartheid had been developed on notions of 'cultural diversity' and group-based rights. Nevertheless, the new Constitution perfectly mirrored the international mood, with the inclusion of various cultural rights in the Bill of Rights, and their elaboration in a Commission for the Promotion and Protection of the Rights of Cultural, Religious and Linguistic Communities and a Pan South African Language Board.[118]

The most striking example of how the international mood affected local political processes was the surprise re-entry on the national stage of groups like the Griqua, the Korana, the Nama and the San. Lumped together as 'coloured' or derogatively labelled Bushmen and Hottentots, and highly marginalised under apartheid, these people reinvented themselves as South Africa's First Nations, the 'lost tribes of Africa'.[119] Assisted by international NGOs like First Peoples Worldwide and local offshoots such as the Working Group of Indigenous Minorities in South Africa and the South African San Institute, they appeared – more and more confidently as time went by – in international fora to state their claims to recognition, land and political autonomy.[120] Even if many of these movements seemed to have more leaders than followers – as experienced by the journalist who went looking for the 'real Griqua' in Griquatown and discovered only Griqua leaders, while the people all continued to identify themselves as

[114] A useful overview of the spectrum of cultural rights is provided by Levy (1997); Cf. Oomen (1999b).

[115] *The ILO Convention 169 revising the ILO Convention on Living and Working Conditions of Indigenous Populations.* See the overview in: Marquardt (1995).

[116] S 6, UN Doc. E/CN.4/SUB.2/1994/2/Add.1 (1994), prepared by the Working Group on Indigenous Populations of the Economic and Social Council of the United Nations.

[117] S 12 Draft Declaration.

[118] Cf. Ss 6, 30, 31, 185 Act 108/1996 and Henrard. 'The Interrelation', also Oomen (1999b) in which I try to set out a model of the differences in the way group-based rights were recognised before and after 1994.

[119] Barney Mthombothi, 'The Lost Tribes of South Africa.' http://www.fm.co.za/00/0107/currents/bcurrent.htm: *Financial Mail* electronic archive, 2000.

[120] First Peoples Organization. 'Southern Africa: Program Description'; 4. http://www.firstpeoples.org/southern%20Africa/southern_africa_program.htm: First Peoples Organization; Weinberg (2000).

coloured – they were highly successful in capturing national and international attention.[121] After the UN working group on indigenous people officially recognised the Khoisan as the first indigenous nation of South Africa, the South African government quickly followed suit.[122] It set up a National Griqua Forum and, in line with international jargon, a Khoisan Indigenous Nations Council, and, organised conferences which, according to deputy president Zuma, were part of 'that effort of *redefining* ourselves within the context of a democratic South Africa, wherein we promote our unity in diversity' (emphasis added).[123]

While Zuma considered the reawakening of South Africa's indigenous people to be a 'shining example of the liberating effects of democracy', it was at least surprising in the light of South African history. By 2000, for instance, the Griqua people who, for all their hardship, had benefited from their 'coloured status' under apartheid and not been deported to ethnic homelands, were clamouring for an independent state.[124] As the Griqua leader Barend Van Staden stated, his people 'were now ready to govern their ancestral land', even if they did not 'want a volksstaat, but sovereignty and independence'. In a similar twist of history, the indigenous peoples now reinvented themselves as African instead of coloured, claiming they had a vital role to play in the African Renaissance, and that their leaders should also be officially recognised as traditional leaders, in order to 'once again have a pride and dignity of origin in Africa ... We will not wish to be anything but who we truly are: Children of the African Soil.'[125]

The enthusiasm with which the global cultural rights jargon was embraced doubtless had to do with the benefits involved. International indigenous peoples' rhetoric promised, more than any other 'status script', access to land, minerals, political autonomy and government support. The UN Declaration, for instance, grants indigenous peoples 'the right to determine and develop priorities and strategies for the development or use of their lands, territories and other resources ... particularly in connection with the development, utilisation or exploitation of mineral, water and other resources'.[126] A telling example of the promises contained in international law is the Richtersveld land claim.[127] The 'indigenous' Richtersveld people in Namaqualand chose to reclaim their land – and the highly profitable mineral deposits beneath it – not only in terms of South African law, which allows restitution from 1913 onwards, but also as an aboriginal rights claim. Drawing heavily on Australian and Canadian experience, the claimants argued that this common law doctrine was also applicable in South Africa.[128]

[121] 'In Search of the Griqua...And Their Real Leader.' 6. http://www.mg.co.za/mg/news/99may2/27may-griqua.html: *Mail & Guardian* online, 1999.

[122] Sapa, 'Khoisan to Speak out on Their Future.' ANC news briefing email service: ANC, 2001.

[123] 'Interpellations: Protection of the Rights of Indigenous People.' alfk@iafrica.com, 2000, Mthombothi. 'The Lost Tribes of South Africa'; Sapa. 'Address by Deputy President Jacob Zuma to the Opening Ceremony of the National Khoisan Consultative Conference'.

[124] Sapa. 'Griqua People Request Ministerial Meeting on Independence', ANC, 30 August 2000; ——— 'Movement Set up for Griqua Independent State.' ANC news briefing email service: ANC, 2000.

[125] Parliamentary Monitoring Group. 'Khoi-San Forum.' http://www.pmg.org.za/appendix/000606Khoisan.htm: Parliamentary Monitoring Group, 2000.

[126] S 30 Draft Declaration.

[127] 'Land Claims Threaten Privatisation Process.' *Business Day* 1998, 1; Barry Streek, 'Rural Hamlet to Stage Land Battle.' http://www.mg.co.za/za/features/2000aug/29aug-hamlet.html: *Daily Mail & Guardian* electronic archive, 2000.

[128] McAllister (1997); Alexander Reilly, 'The Australian Experience of Aboriginal Title: Lessons for South Africa,' *South African Journal on Human Rights* 16, no. 3 (2000).

And even though the Land Claims Court ruled that it did not have 'the jurisdiction to determine whether or not remedies under the doctrine of aboriginal title form part of South African common law', many legal scholars believed it did, and that it was only a matter of time before the Richtersveld people would obtain an aboriginal title to their land and the riches beneath it.[129]

With such spoils to be had, it is no wonder that 'black' traditional leaders, representing an estimated one-third rather than 2 per cent of the population, were eager to hop on the bandwagon. In spite of the attempts of the Indigenous Peoples of South Africa Co-ordinating Committee (IPACC), for instance, to exclude them by definition and emphasise the 'aboriginal character' of indigenous people, their claim to specific ancestral territory linked to cultural identity and economic survival, a distinct and identifiable genealogical bloodline, reliance on natural resources, absence of concepts of individual title and a situation of non-dominance in their national economies and political systems, black traditional leaders increasingly referred to their constituency as Indigenous People.[130] King Zwelithini's support of a World Federation of Traditional Leaders and his continuous demands for international mediation in the KwaZulu case were, for instance, couched in this discourse,[131] as was the formation of a Mineral Rights Association of the Indigenous People of South Africa, in which North-West and Northern Province traditional leaders played a prominent role.[132] That this approach was successful became clear from the 2003 White Paper on Traditional Leadership and Governance, which, after reviewing international cultural rights legislation, concluded that 'the trends at an international level indicate that traditional leaders and traditional leadership institutions have a much bigger role to play as custodians of culture and protectors of custom'.[133] And so traditional leaders managed to appropriate another global mood, and to redefine it to suit their needs.

4. The assumptions

The 'struggle over the soul of custom' took place in an era which saw global and local conditions intertwined in a way which was formerly unthinkable, thus shaping actions and allowing some voices to ring out while others were muffled. Some of these conditions have been discussed above: the party-political balance of power influenced by lessons from the rest of Africa; the institutional legacy so firmly enshrined in the new order; the deeply felt need to return to an African identity; the worldwide call towards dismantling the state and granting more

[129] T.W. Bennett and C.H. Powell. 'Aboriginal Title in South Africa Revisited,' *South African Journal on Human Rights* 15, no. 4 (1999): 449–85; Chan Tung, 'Land Claims and Past Aboriginal Group Identity of the Richtersveld Namaqua.' http://www.gtz.de/orboden/capetown/cape10.htm: GTZ.

[130] First Peoples Worldwide. *Who Are Indigenous Africans?* Available from http://www.firstpeoples.org/Southern%20Africa/whatsnew/whatafrica.htm.

[131] Sapa, 'Mandela Angers Traditional Leaders.' ANC news briefing email service: ANC, 2000; ———. 'Zulu King Urges International Protection of Traditional Leaders.'

[132] 'Constitution of the Mineral Rights Association of the Indigenous People of South Africa.' 1998. Cf. Barbara Oomen, 'The Underlying Question: Land Restitution, Mineral Rights and Indigenous Communities in South Africa.' Paper presented at the Folk Law and Legal Pluralism Conference: Challenges in the Third Millennium, Arica, Chile, 2000.

[133] Department of Provincial and Local Government, *The White Paper on Traditional Leadership and Governance*, p. 11.

autonomy to cultural groups. All these conditions fuelled the ANC's ambiguity, stifled the, already weak, voices of those opposed to an important role for traditional leadership, and helped pro-traditionalist actors like Inkatha, Contralesa and the Directorate of Traditional Affairs to express their claims in a way that would have been unimaginable in other times.

But the 'multiplicity of force relations at work' did not merely favour a continued recognition and often even a resurgence of traditional leadership. It also encouraged a certain *definition* of the elusive issues at stake – culture, custom, tradition, rule, rural life. When it came to deciding which versions of these much-contested notions would be caught, fixed and frozen into the 'austerity of tabulated legalism', it was invariably the traditional leaders – and their supporters – who were passed the microphone. They received questionnaires from the Directorate of Traditional Affairs, were practically the sole invitees to conferences on their future, had late-night meetings with the President to overhaul unfavourable legislation, were the only civil society representatives in the Technical Committee on Traditional Leadership Issues and had the ear of the press. Of course, there were opposing voices. But these found the winds of change blowing against them, their cries dispersed and their approach – when heard – condemned as 'eurocentrist'.

The results of this 'gate-keeper' role for traditional leaders, who could virtually monopolise information on the rural condition, have surfaced frequently in these chapters. Nevertheless, as we head for the second part of this book, it would seem useful to enumerate them so that, when assessing the position of traditional leadership in Sekhukhune, the national assumptions on culture, tradition and the rural condition that are circulated at conferences and in political discussions and, finally, received as 'institutional crystallisation' in policy documents and the law, can provide a measure against which to check rural realities. What, then, are the most important of these assumptions? First, there is the pervasive notion of rural-urban difference, the idea that these are two completely different worlds. Second, there is the idea that communities, whether homogeneous or not, form the main building blocks of rural societies. Third, the notion that these communities are characterised by, among other things, a coherent system of customary law(s) that can be ascertained and reproduced keeps surfacing in the national debates. And fourth, there is the persistent assumption that traditional leaders enjoy great legitimacy, and are the ideal spokespeople for their communities. Let us briefly take a closer look at each of these notions.

Rural-urban difference

One of the ideas woven throughout the policy debates and omnipresent in White Papers and subsequent legislation was that of an irreconcilable difference between 'rural' and 'urban' areas. Traditional leaders, government officials, politicians and civil society alike would frequently underline this difference and its consequences for the type of local government, land administration and justice needed. Until 2000, for instance, different legislation applied to metropolitan and 'rural local government'.[134] Similarly, the land tenure discussion was larded with references to the need in rural areas, for a different system of tenure from the

[134] *Local Government Transition Act (209/1993): Repealing of Proclamations Nos 10/1995, 30/1995: Establishment of Northern District Council: Bosveld District Council and Transitional Councils in the Northern Province.* Pietersburg: Government Printer, 1995.

freehold title characteristic of the rest of South Africa. And the South African Law Commission recommended the establishment of traditional courts in the rural areas and community courts with elected members in 'urban and peri-urban areas'.

Though the term 'rural areas' was used frequently, it was unclear which parts of the country were being referred to. It often seemed to be used as a politically correct synonym for the former homelands, or traditional authority areas. The White Paper on Local Government was one of the few to point out the 'the very different contexts which are classified as rural': dense rural settlements, villages, agri-villages and dispersed settlements.[135] Nevertheless, most of the imagery evoked was surprisingly homogeneous: that of poor but still subsistent economies, governed by a completely different morality from that of the cities, which could be considered a shrine of Africanness and should therefore be shielded from onslaught by urban-based, Western intellectuals.

Rolling hills, scattered adobe cottages and ample green grazing fields for well-fed cows is the way in which rural areas often came to be represented in the public imagery. Even though such places do exist all over South Africa, the 'rural slums' created by homeland policies are easier to find: overcrowded and polluted corrugated iron shacks, with a few scrawny goats desperately trying to find a tuft of green between the dirty plastic bags that lie scattered over the eroded commons. The Municipal Demarcation Board, for instance, estimated that traditional authority areas had a population density of 199 people per square kilometre, as opposed to 19 in the rest of South Africa,[136] the majority of them without access to water, electricity, telephones or sanitation, and certainly without access to land (Beinart, 1994:198).[137] Nevertheless, the image of rural areas has remained that of places where people live off the land, as became apparent in an interview with government officials:

> We're coming to realise now that a rural area doesn't necessarily have to be a wide open space, some of them are actually quite densely populated. But they are rural because they're quite far removed from the towns. And the people's main activities, of course, are rural. Subsistence farming and that sort of thing...[138]

Another persistent image has rural societies ordered completely differently from the urban areas. 'The high level of peace, orderliness, stability and tolerance you will find in the rural areas, as opposed to the cities, are dual [sic] in no small measure to the customs and traditions which underpin the system of traditional leadership.'[139] The assumption seemed to be that central to this order were notions such as rural communalism, traditional leadership, a close link to the land and to indigenous value systems like *Umuntu umuntu ngabantu* – a person is a person through other people.[140] This meant, observers argued, that rural people

[135] Ministry for Provincial Affairs and Constitutional Development. *The White Paper on Local Government*, 2.1.

[136] Parliamentary Monitoring Group, 'Provincial and Local Government Portfolio Committee: Traditional Leadership and Institutions Discussion Document: Hearings.'

[137] Ibid., which estimates the backlogs in water, electricity, telephone and sanitation provision in traditional rural communities as follows: Eastern Cape – 50–60%; KwaZulu-Natal – 60–80%; Northern Province – 70–90%; Mpumalanga – 40–60%; North-West – 40–60%; Free State – 20–30%.

[138] Group interview, officials Directorate of Local Government, 20 February 1998.

[139] Contralesa, 'Submission to the Constitutional Assembly on the Constitutional Role of Traditional Leaders.'

[140] Herbert Vilakazi, 'Traditional Leaders and Modernity', unpublished, 1996. The Sepedi equivalent of this saying is: *motho ke motho ka batho.*

might not even want the same democratic system as the rest of the country: 'The entire process of democratization and modernization, so far, has been a ruthless imposition upon rural people of the values and culture of urban elites ... for in rural cultures, competition and haggling in public of individuals over votes may seem vulgar, ugly, and unbecoming.'[141] As the female Zulu traditional leader-cum-medical-doctor S. Zungu once warned Parliament (1995):

> City people should be careful not to impose upon rural people institutions and cultural processes which go hand in hand with city life, where clans and kinship groups are no longer coterminous with city neighbourhoods and city blocks. Anonymity is the rule in cities. Neighbours, by and large, are not known personally to one another. City life knows nothing of community... Students of cultural and social change in pre-industrial communities have too often witnessed brand-new tractors abandoned, left to accumulate dust and rust, while people tilled the soil with traditional tools. Are we not running a similar risk in buying for rural African people new democratic institutions and practices born in the anonymous urban milieu? Will we not find these new gadgets also, a few months later, piling up dust and rust, unused, abandoned on the landscapes of rural communities?

Not only was a dichotomy created between urban, individualist thinking and a rural, communalist way of life; the former was also classified as a Western import, while the latter was considered 'authentically African'. In the African village, the rhetoric went, lay the shrine to African morality, the well of African identity. The prominent philosopher H. Vilakazi copied W.E. Du Bois in stating that 'the African village is one of Africa's precious gifts to humanity':

> As humanity first emerged in Africa, the African Village contains all, or the now broken parts of all, the precious gifts Africa developed and moulded for humanity. The age-old wisdom, the philosophy, the music and dance and other arts, the religion, the poetry, the medicine and other sciences, the knowledge of human nature, the respect for nature – all these gifts were moulded and developed in the African Village. Other civilizations boast of precious knowledge and culture that developed in cities. African civilization boasts of precious knowledge and cultures that developed in her villages. ... The African village was the shell, as in the shell of an egg, within which was contained the gift of Africa to humanity... All this is part and parcel of the challenge of Africanization, the African Renaissance. (Vilakazi, 1999:3)

A logical consequence of this type of thinking was a condemnation of the supposed urban onslaught on pastoral rural life, and a plea for the continued recognition of rural areas as separate spheres which were to be governed differently from the urban areas.

Community-think

'The view that somehow rural people are different and that they should behave and live differently..(and that).. their desires, needs and aspirations should be different from those of urban people' also found expression in another assumption: that rural society was made up of *communities*.[142] This community-think, again, slotted in nicely with global trends in, for instance, development discourse (Tapscott, 1995). Policy-makers, having shunned communities as obstacles to development for decades, now enthusiastically embraced their warm fuzzy logic

[141] Ibid.

[142] Salim Fakir, 'Community Projects Drown in Ideology', *Mail & Guardian* 1999, p. 36.

and implicit connection with notions such as trust and social capital.[143] The old *Gemeinschaft–Gesellschaft* dichotomy was reintroduced in policy documents which, if they bothered to define 'communities' at all, considered them 'social networks with a high degree of homogeneity, a closely-knit organisation, stooled normally on tradition and more often than not with an own territory',[144] or stated that communities occur when 'a set of people share beliefs, preferences, membership is stable and relations are multiplex' (Singleton and Taylor, 1992).

The circle of people enthusiastically reintroducing the notion into the South African policy debate was much wider than those supporting traditional leadership alone. The Reconstruction and Development Programme, for instance, rested squarely on what Bähre has labelled a 'naïve notion' of 'homogeneous and peaceful communities'.[145] Land Affairs also took communities as central building blocks for its reform programmes. Commentators warned that 'restitution is based on an idealistic attempt to invoke a romantic image of life characterised by a degree of social cohesion that no longer existed due to fragmentation caused by removals' and that 'communities reclaiming land may desire rapid, urban-style material advancement while their urban-based development partners envision them as committed to communalist ideals and simple, rural-style and "appropriate" technology'.[146] But the Department continued to couch its policies in 'characteristically communalist rhetoric', in which it sometimes seemed as though 'community' was nothing more than a politically correct synonym for the tainted notion of 'tribe'.[147]

Coherent systems of customary law

Another deeply rooted assumption was, as we have seen, that these rural societies consisted of ethnic groups each of which had coherent systems of customary law, with specific and ascertainable rules on land, marriage, succession and all other aspects of life. These rules, it was assumed, were known within the communities and could be identified, written down and reproduced within the formal legal system. The South African Law Commission's project (1999) on the Harmonisation of the Common Law and Indigenous Law, for instance, was all about ascertaining which rules applied to which people in certain fields of law, and subsequently harmonising these rules with the Constitution. It also made a distinction between the 'customary legal systems' of various ethnic groups: 'Because South Africa does not have a single, unified system of customary law the courts may have to decide which of two or more systems of customary law apply to the facts of any given case.'[148] Similarly, magistrates would refer to the customary law systems of the Tswana, the Pedi or the Zulu when ruling on cases brought before them.[149] This approach was echoed by the traditional leaders, who proudly spoke of 'our traditional systems of law' which contained the

[143] Keebet, von Benda-Beckmann and Andre Hoekema (eds), *Over De Grenzen Van Gemeenschappen: Gemeenschap, Staat en Recht*. 's-Gravenhage: Elsevier bedrijfsinformatie, 1998, p. 2.

[144] Ibid.

[145] Erik Bähre, 'Housing the Urban Poor in Cape Town: A Post-Apartheid Dream or Nightmare?', *Global Built Environment Review* 1, no. 1 (2001): p. 36.

[146] Brown et al. (1998); James (2000:148).

[147] James (2000:146) speaks of this characteristically communalist rhetoric.

[148] South African Law Commission. 'The Harmonisation of Customary and Common Law: Conflict of Personal Laws,' Pretoria, 1998, p. 127.

[149] Cf. *Hlophe v Mahlalela and Another, Thibela.*

'entrenched cultural values of the indigenous people of South Africa' and had to be protected from eurocentric onslaught by, for instance, the Bill of Rights.[150]

Although there seemed to be consensus on the existence of ascertainable systems of customary law, actors disagreed on the extent to which official customary law – that of codes and text-books – still reflected living law. In many courts codified customary law was taken as the customary law to be applied, with contrary evidence being shunned: 'It cannot be accepted that all cultural practices are indigenous law and *vice versa*', as the judge in *Hlophe v Mahlalela* stated. The Law Commission, in contrast, took a much more progressive approach: 'Many of the customary rules currently used by the courts are not only in conflict with the principle of equal treatment but are also out of step with social practice.'[151] The general popularity of customary law and the fact that 'the majority of the population in the country is rural and conceivably still wedded to tribal lore and culture' were not, however, subject to doubt. Even the Law Commission frequently stated how customary legal systems were 'deeply imbedded in South Africa's cultural tradition',[152] and that extensive research was therefore needed to collect and record information about these systems. It wrote, with regret: 'It is unfortunately not possible, as many people have requested, to mount a nation-wide survey in order to establish which customs are still observed and which serve the interests of the African community.'[153]

Chiefly legitimacy

A final striking aspect of the way in which culture, custom and traditional authority were defined in the 1990s discourse concerned the legitimacy of traditional authority. A more pervasive presumption flourishing in the post-apartheid arena of political power was that traditional leaders enjoyed great popularity in the rural areas. 'To this day, the majority of South Africans, especially (but not exclusively) in the rural areas, continue to owe allegiance to the institution of traditional leadership', the Draft Discussion Document on Traditional Leadership stated in its introduction. The rural difference was thus defined as located not only in the existence of, more or less, homogeneous communities with distinct legal systems, but also in their adherence to traditional leadership. Traditional leaders enthusiastically fuelled this widespread conception, underlining that 'traditional leaders, as far as rural communities are concerned, are the only form of government they know'.[154]

Buttressing these ideas was the lack of statistical data on the legitimacy of the institution.[155] The few polls conducted indicated that a majority of South Africans

[150] Magardie. *Customary Law Shake-Up*, Stack (1997:6).

[151] South African Law Commission. 'Project 90: Customary Law', p. xv.

[152] Ibid.: 1.4.8: R.B.G. Choudree, 'Traditions of Conflict Resolution in South Africa.' *African Journal on Conflict Resolution* 1, no. 1 (1999): 9–28.

[153] South African Law Commission, 'The Harmonisation of Customary and Common Law: Conflict of Personal Laws', 2.3.11. The Law Commission went on to say, 'The time and resources are not available to engage in such an immense research project. Even if it were possible, the legal status of the findings would be bound to be controversial, and, no matter how sensitively done, any such statement of law is soon overtaken by changes in social conditions.' Cf. Magardie. 'Customary Law Undermines Constitutional Rights' for a similar call for research.

[154] Contralesa. 'Submission to the Constitutional Assembly on the Constitutional Role of Traditional Leaders.'

[155] Marna De Lange, Dumisani Magadlela, Annie Sugrue, and Chris Stimie, 'Rural Women's

were in favour of the continued existence of traditional leadership, but did not specify what role the institution should play – in the eyes of the people – and how it should relate to elected local government.[156] Most research, however, was qualitative and had traditional leaders as its main respondents. Naturally, they were quick to stress their own importance in rural affairs and their popularity with their subjects. And even though there were voices hinting that 'it may well be that chiefs, because they are unable to meet their obligations to their subjects and are no longer mystical figures, have lost the allegiance of their "subjects"', these opinions never made it to the centre of the policy-making stage.[157]

It was in this fashion that traditional leaders came to be considered the gatekeepers of rural communities. The White Paper on Local Government, for instance, asserted (para 4.1) that traditional leaders are not only 'symbols of unity' but also 'the spokespersons generally of their communities'. And *nkosi* Holomisa frequently emphasised: 'traditional leaders have always been a link between the community and the government.'[158] The flow of information, both into and out of 'communities' thus came to be channelled through the chiefs. They were used to disperse information on such disparate issues as development, crime prevention and voter education among 'their subjects'. Conversely, they controlled the information on the rural condition, and the position of custom and traditional authority communicated to the outside world. Thus, a circular process became visible: it was because of their assumed popularity that traditional leaders were granted the 'power of definition', and the right to represent their communities, which in turn allowed them to define a rural reality in which they were central.

5. Conclusion

> Was not the key change wrought by colonialism in the sphere of 'customary law' to privilege a single authority – chiefs – as the source of custom, thereby sanctioning an authoritarian version of custom as law? In a context where there had been multiple sources of custom – not only chiefs, but also clans, women's groups, age groups – and no single authoritative source in all social domains, was not the effect to silence every contrary version and expand the authority of the chief to every social domain? (Mamdani, 2000:5)

While the previous chapter discussed *how* traditional leaders retained such a strong role in local government, land allocation and customary law in the former homelands, our concern here has been *why* this could be so. We have seen the interplay of actors and more structural conditions at work, none of them determinant or even dominant, but together creating a political climate in which continued recognition of traditional leadership seemed the most logical policy

[155 cont.] Association: An Assessment of the Success Factors and Sustainability: Draft Report April 1999,' International Water Management Institute, 1999.

[156] Cf. Pillay and Prinsloo (1995), who state that 64.8% of all South Africans are in favour of the continued existence of traditional authority.

[157] 'Traditional Leaders: Reinventing Their Roles,' *Sowetan*, 17 July 2000, p. 9.

[158] Parliamentary Monitoring Group, 'Provincial and Local Government Portfolio Committee: Traditional Leadership and Institutions Discussion Document: Hearings.'

option. This interplay led to the ANC's ambiguity being fuelled by the lessons from the rest of Africa and the deep-felt need to 'return to the roots'; the negotiated revolution meant that the same officials and magistrates as before could continue to refer to the same laws; and the quick-thinking chiefs found it relatively easy to seize on the global mood of decentralisation and cultural rights and turn it to their advantage.

What was essentially at stake in this political game was the power to define custom. All the actors were well aware that the subject-matter under debate – culture, traditional authority, custom – was malleable enough to suit anyone's needs, but that, once it had been frozen into 'the austerity of tabulated legalism', it could have important consequences for the power landscape it claimed to mirror. This is why the ANC always underlined the unitary and progressive character of traditional leadership, and how it could complement democracy. Inkatha, on the other hand, opted for an ethnic representation, firmly linking the institution to Zulu identity. And the traditional leaders depicted themselves as 'the stripes of the zebra', the very soul of South African society. Those opposed to a powerful institution of traditional leadership joined in the scramble over definition by calling for more research and even forming a 'Coalition for the Transformation of Traditional Leadership'. Their voices, however, remained dispersed.

For – as we have seen over and over again – if there was one winner in this struggle over the right to define custom, it was the traditional leaders. The prominence of chiefs in the policy arena had as much to do with their political agility as with the feebleness of their opponents, and the fact that they had the winds of the times comfortably behind them. Thus, of all the possible depictions of 'rural reality' in the national debate, traditional leaders held the remote control and decided which version would be watched in the national arena and would finally make it into law. The Joint Technical Committee on Traditional Leadership Issues, with only government officials and traditional leaders determining whether the powers of traditional leaders had been diminished and what could be done to remedy the situation, could be considered a perfect model for the rest of the policy process. In that sense, for all the alterations in the wider political climate, not much seemed to have changed since the days when Native Commissioners sat down with Tribal Chiefs on their field visits for a dialogue to draw up a system of customary law that suited both parties.

Now that we have some idea of how and why these particular notions could flourish in the national policy debate, two sets of questions remain. The first, of course, is: to what extent does this public imagery correspond to 'rural reality'? How big is the difference, in terms of democratic aspirations, between rural and urban areas? How coherent are communities, how ascertainable their laws and how popular their traditional leaders? The second set of questions then concerns the constitutive effects of a particular statal representation of custom and culture. If the way in which traditional leadership and customary law are recognised is not a mere reflection of rural reality, but a politically derived product of the national power relations in a given era, what does this mean locally? It is with these questions in mind that we now turn to the dusty plains of Sekhukhune, one of the poorest areas in South Africa, the cradle of rural revolt in the 1980s, but also the home of famous traditional leaders like the legendary Sekhukhune I.

4. Sekhukhune
The Institutional Landscape

1. Introduction

> 'Re buswitše! *We are being ruled again!,' shrieked a praise-singer in animal skins, his feet kicking up the red Sekhukhune sand. It was 19 December 1998, and in front of him sat the newly enthroned Billy Sekwati Mampuru III, king of the important Pedi lineage of Mamone. Behind him the thousands assembled roared in agreement, women in colourful attire ululated shrilly, the trumpets of the khaki-clad Zionist Christian Church marching band sounded, old men hymned songs from the initiation schools, disco music pumped and against the clear blue sky a helicopter full of VIPs prepared to land. The whole cacophony of sound seemed to add up to one message, voiced by an old man standing next to me: 'The Mamone Pedi are going back to their roots.'* Re buswitše! (see Photo 4, p. xiii)

For some outside observers, it was not enthusiasm but wonder that prevailed. Was not Sekhukhune the area where, over a decade before, youngsters had 'toyi-toyi-ed' (danced in protest) around burning palaces, throwing stones and calling for a new order without the chiefs? Still, the exuberant festivities surrounding Billy Sekwati's coronation were not unique, but rather exemplified a much more widespread and deep-running process already described when discussing the national debate: the reconfiguration and, often, reinforcement of traditional authority within the new democratic context. It is to the local manifestations of this process that we now turn our attention. Nevertheless, as we move from the national to the local level, the questions remain the same: What was the relation between the legal and the socio-political positions of traditional authority and customary law in post-apartheid South Africa? Why was this so? What can this teach us about the relations between law, power and culture in the post-modern world? Comparing national and local perspectives will enable us to draw conclusions about the interaction between national and local dynamics in determining the power of traditional authority and the position of customary law.

This first section serves as an introduction to Sekhukhune and its local power configuration. Although it is about the whole area, much of the narrative is structured around the coronation of Billy Sekwati and subsequent events. This is not because I would want in any way to suggest that Mamone exemplifies Sekhukhune's 56 chieftaincies. No traditional authority area could. But the mere fact of the coronation, its extensive guest list and the ensuing debates on what is expected of a new king constitute a clear example of some of the processes, institutions and debates found, in various guises, all over Sekhukhune: the restoration of traditional authority, its alliances with other institutions and the debates on the definition of local rule. It is this process that I am seeking to describe, using Mamone as a point of departure. For it is often in a period of flux that arguments are put most pointedly and the underlying processes are most visible.

Before turning to the approach taken in this chapter, it is necessary to take a closer look at what the name Sekhukhune encompasses. Any name chosen for the area concerned, the shrubby lowlands cradled between the Strijdpoort and the Sekhukhune mountains, and Oliphants and the Steelpoort river, with the Leolo range cutting through it, requires justification. This justification is, in a way, an introduction to local politics, in which the naming of an area and the establishing of its boundaries can be considered one of the central stakes (cf. Berry, 2000; Herbst, 2000). I have chosen the term Sekhukhune, or Sekhukhuneland, for a number of reasons. First, it is probably the name most inhabitants of the area would come up with if asked for *gaê*, their place of origin. Consensus over a term, however, is not necessarily an indication of consensus over its meaning. Asked for a definition of boundaries, people will come up with vastly different descriptions. By Sekhukhune, I mean the area that is principally inhabited by Bapedi and ruled by leaders who are politically linked to the Maroteng paramountcy, and which for that reason has a common political heritage.[1] Its centre of government is then the Mohlaletse *mošate*, the large brick-faced royal palace currently inhabited by acting *kgošikgolo* K.K. Sekhukhune. This link to chiefly politics – our central concern – is the second reason for speaking of Sekhukhune instead of the corresponding local government or magisterial entities. At the same time it poses the first problem: some of the traditional authorities in the area, like the Mamone Bapedi with Billy Sekwati III as their newly enthroned leader, would prefer to refer to *Bopedi* – the homeland of the Pedi instead of the synecdochical Sekhukhune.

The name Sekhukhuneland has, over the past century, been subject to a process of redefinition that teaches us much about the power relations of the times. Once the British had conquered the Pedi polity they divided it into magisterial districts, with 'Sekhukhuneland' as a severely condensed version of the former territory. The centre of government of this magisterial district became Schoonoord, the parochial building in which a succession of magistrates and Native Commissioners – later Bantu Affairs Commissioners and today Traditional Affairs officials – epitomised administrative rule in the area. Were we to redefine our choice of the traditional authority area of Sekhukhune in magisterial terms, it would comprise Sekhukhuneland and parts of the bordering Praktiseer, Nebo and Thaba Moopo magisterial districts. Another terminological option became available with the introduction of elected local government in 1995, when the bulk of Sekhukhune as described above was redefined as the Greater Ngwaritsi-Makhudu/Thamaga Transitional Local Council (with an estimated population of 200,000 on 1100 km^2),[2] with some traditional leaders finding themselves in the Tubatse/Steelpoort and the Nebo North TLCs. With this new demarcation a new centre of rule arose: a tiny local government office crammed between a record store and a café in the Jane Furse shopping mall. These three TLCs were, together with five others, united in what was first called the Southern District Council but was renamed Greater Sekhukhune after the 2000 local government elections.

[1] Cf Delius (1983: ix). The estimated population of this area is 85,000 (Interview, K.K. Sekhukhune and council, Mohlaletse, 16 December 1998.

[2] Alastair McIntosh, 'Rethinking Chieftaincy and the Future of Rural Local Government: A Preliminary Investigation,' *Transformation* 13, pp. 100–1.

In this area, as in the rest of South Africa, the period after the first democratic elections can be considered historic in that it brought a profound reconfiguration of the institutional – but not the socio-economic – landscape. It saw, for instance, the introduction of elected local government, and the rise of the powerful vigilante organisation *Mapogo a Mathamaga*. But what changed, and especially what did not, can only be understood by looking at aspects of continuity, which is why, in section 2, we shall first trace the historical experience of Sekhukhune. Section 3 will explain the impact this had on the power of traditional authority. While policies of indirect rule and segregation left traditional authority tainted and transformed, we shall see in section 4 how traditional leaders were able to strengthen their position in three different spheres, each with its own vernacular and rationale: palace politics, bureaucracy and party politics. Power is, of course, relational, and in order to strengthen their position traditional leaders form alliances with, or foster antipathy against, a variety of other institutions involved in local rule: elected local government, government agencies, civics, vigilante organisations, churches, business-linked organisations and migrants' organisations. Section 5 will map out this institutional landscape and the way in which it is rooted in wider socio-economic conditions, to provide a picture of law and governance in an area like Sekhukhune. Section 6 will focus on the fact that the situation is one of not only legal, but also institutional, pluralism. At stake is control: over resources, over boundaries, over people and over meaning. It is this model of local power relations in Sekhukhune that will lay the foundation for the analysis of the legitimisation of rule and the role of law in later chapters.

2. From Bopedi to Lebowa

Back to the coronation of Billy Sekwati Mampuru III. A glossy multi-colour programme was handed out; on the back of it was a genealogy of the Bapedi, tracing the young *kgoši's* roots as the paramount chief of all the Pedi. This was yet another move in a succession dispute which has raged in the area for over a century, and which started when the two sons of Sekwati I, Mampuru and Sekhukhune I, fought over their father's inheritance. While a succession dispute was nothing new among the Bapedi, the context in which this was played out was. The end of the nineteenth century saw the violent conquest of the mighty Pedi polity and its incorporation into a succession of wider political entities. From this time on, outside influences would significantly affect local politics, which is why it seems a good starting point for a brief history of Pedi royalty and the forces determining its position over the past century.[3]

When King Sekwati died in 1861, he left behind a large and relatively stable polity in the Pedi heartland, cradled comfortably between the Strijdpoort and the Sekhukhune mountains. Since their settlement in the area around 1650, the Maroteng people had steadily built up a paramountcy over various surrounding chiefdoms, especially through an intricate system of marriage, politics and intermediaries. Although it was a time of profound change – Sekwati died on the day the first missionary service was held in the area – the weapons earned by

[3] By far the best history of the Pedi polity in the nineteenth century is Delius (1983). Other accounts are Hunt (1931); Mönnig (1967).

migrant workers since the 1840s had allowed them to fight off the persistent attacks from the Zulu, Swazi and Boer armies.

On the day that a loud wail announced Sekwati's death and – with the benefit of hindsight – a new era, it was not his designated heir, Mampuru, who sped to bury his father and thus claim the throne, but Sekhukhune I, the headstrong eldest son of Sekwati's first wife. It was he whose name would come to be dreaded by the British, and after fending off attacks by Swazi, British and Boer forces, he would finally lead the Bapedi into the war in which they were to be bludgeoned into submission.[4] 'His struggle against the rising tide of White occupation and rule was as hopeless as, in those days, it was inevitable,' one commentator has written (Hunt, 1931:303). Still, it was not the British who would ultimately kill Sekhukhune I but his half-brother Mampuru, who as the sociological son of the tribal wife had a claim to the throne and, together with the Swazi, fought alongside the British.[5] Mampuru was unceremoniously hanged for murder by the government of the day, and recovering his bones was to become one of the major projects of the Mamone Bapedi in the late 1990s. 'That skeleton is out there somewhere and might even be used for a biology class,' Billy's mother told me.[6]

Following the British tradition of indirect rule, a Native Commissioner was sent to the area, and he appointed yet another offspring of the old Sekwati from a more remote house, Kgolane, as a regent in the Maroteng paramountcy. Commenting on this choice of a not very logical but cooperative candidate for chieftaincy, one of his successors would muse: 'It is not clear why Abel Erasmus did this: as Native Commissioner he must have known that it would be quite unacceptable to the tribe. Perhaps he did it purposely to weaken the tribe by creating a division among them ... ' (Hunt, 1931:307). Whatever the reasons, this decision meant that the Bapedi paramountcy entered the twentieth century with three major chieftaincies: the successors of Sekhukhune I, considered by the majority of the Bapedi to be the paramount lineage, and who would remain settled at Maroteng; the line of Mampuru, who moved to Mamone and would continue to claim – in the late 1990s with Billy Sekwati Mampuru III – to be the rightful paramountcy deprived of the position by Sekhukhune's forceful intervention after their father's death; and the line of Kgolane who had been given land and recognition by the British in return for his cooperation.

The century they entered would be characterised by ever-encroaching imperial forces, and shaped by a combination of capitalism, bureaucratisation and segregation. Whereas the maintenance of order and the extraction of resources and labour at the beginning of the century was carried out by blatant force, a slow and essentially bureaucratic and legal redefinition of power and property relations would largely replace the tax raids and lashings that were the main modes of command by the British in the period immediately after the Boer war. Nevertheless, the first signs of this English form of warfare – by 'papers' and

[4] Delius (1983:2); Johannes August Winter, 'The History of Sekwati,' *The South African Journal of science* 9 (1912): 229–332.

[5] The Sekhukhune system of succession, in which the bridewealth for one of the chief's wives, the tribal or candle-wife, is paid by the whole community, is discussed extensively in Chapter 6. There I shall also explain how both chief and candle-wife can have not only biological children, but also children born from other mothers (for instance, the candle-wife's sister, if the wife is barren) but sociologically considered theirs.

[6] Interview, Mohumagadi Sekwati Mampuru, Mamone, 25 May 1999.

agents and courts – and through indirect rule, were there from the beginning.[7] For instance, an assessment of Billy Sekwati's grandfather sent to the Native Affairs Department in 1910 read: 'Young Sekoati ... is a very promising youth and with careful handling ... should make a very useful chief.'

The redefinition of property relations, which was the nub of the colonial project, started in Sekhukhune immediately after the 1879 defeat. Virtually overnight, writes Delius, the Bapedi found the independent Pedi polity transformed into Crown lands, mission lands and privately owned farms, often sold unseen to outside speculators, with three small locations set aside as reserves (Delius, 1996:10). Redefinition continued with the 1913 Natives Land Act, but the heaviest and most widespread attack came with the implementation of the 1936 Native Trust and Land Act, which vested all location and reserve land in the South African Native Trust (ibid., 55). Much to the discontent of the Bapedi, who considered the land to belong to them anyway, the then Native Commissioner Hunt urged them actually to pay for some of it, and established a fund with which they could do so. Many Bapedi would continue to carry their proof of payment of these taxes in the new South Africa and show crumpled pieces of paper stating that they had paid '1 rand for the land, 25 cts per cow and 5 cts per chicken'. By the 1950s, Sekhukhune had become a patchwork of scheduled lands, released for 'native occupation' on the basis of the 1913 Land Acts, trust lands bought and held in trust by the government, and tribal farms.

This continued curtailment of the Pedi living space was increasingly accompanied by optimistic official ideology on how to make the most of their pitiful parcels of land. By the 1930s, many of the former paternalistic Native Commissioners had been replaced by technocratic officials clutching development manuals and spouting a rhetoric of 'betterment', 'modernity' and 'development' (ibid.:51). In what has been dubbed 'one of the most virulent varieties of modernism', lines were drawn, areas for grazing and living planned and cattle culled, the latter causing horror in an area where 'live-stock is a type of property set apart from ordinary simple commodities by cultural rules which establish a one-way barrier between livestock and money and a prestige complex centering on the domain of property so defined' (Ferguson, 1994:151; Thornton, 1996:141). As one old man in the Leolo mountains reminisced years later: 'The Boers would come on horseback and then point out a place where our cattle had to be slaughtered, and then kill those who produced a lot of milk. We had to pay levies for cattle and even for dogs and donkeys. You even had to pay for being a human being.'[8]

A modernised chieftaincy would spearhead this developmental revolution. Although chiefs had always been central to the implementation of colonial policies, it was only after the National Party's victory in the 1948 elections that the *volkekundiges* at the Native Affairs Department decided unequivocally to invest in traditional authority as the major mode of rule in the reserves, and to unleash 'the latent power of the Bantu's own system ... to play a leading part in the programme for the development of the Bantu community'.[9] After property relations, it was now the turn of relations of power to be redefined. The Bantu

[7] John Mackenzie quoted in Comaroff and Comaroff (1997:370).
[8] Interview, *nkosi* Joseph Nkosi and *bakgoma*, Hoepakranz, 11 January 1999.
[9] 'Promotion of Bantu-Self-Government,' *Bantu* 5 (1959): 14. Cf. Evans (1987:56–85).

Authorities Act of 1951 envisaged traditional leaders as embedded in Tribal Authorities, who would 'assist and guide the chief in the administration of the affairs of the tribe and in the performance of his other functions, which are to maintain law and order, disperse unlawful assemblies, and ensure the enforcement of regulations such as those relating to public health, the collection of taxes, registration of births and deaths, the prevention of animal diseases, occupation and use'.[10] The Minister of Native Affairs realised that many of these functions had not existed before, and recommended that traditional leaders 'interest themselves in education and in exercising judicial functions according to Native law and customs'. Chiefs were offered special courses on law and administration, agriculture, forestry, Bantu Education and Bantu Authorities.[11]

Just as Bantu Authorities focused on a redefinition of traditional authority, so did the response to it. Protest organisations that arose among migrant workers – who had become a well-entrenched category in Pedi society and through their work on the Reef were linked to the ANC and the Communist Party – emphasised that *kgoši ke kgoši ka batho* (a chief is a chief by the people) and brought the traditional leaders presents to demonstrate that this was not the prerogative of the Afrikaner officials (Delius, 1996:133). And the direct catalyst that turned the rumbling unrest against the Bantu Authorities in Sekhukhune into a fully-fledged and bloody revolt in 1958 was the replacement of the uncooperative Pedi paramount Morwamotše Sekhukhune by a remote cousin who happened to be a retired policeman. This affront to Pedi identity led to clashes between the *Marangere* – named after the Rangers, the hated agricultural assistants – who were in favour of the Bantu Authorities, and the *Voortrekkers* who paradoxically had adopted Boer terminology to symbolise their attempt to fence off further outside interference (Sansom, 1970:65). The Sekhukhune revolt, one of the most important rural revolts in 1950s South Africa, was quelled harshly, with police swarming in and arresting nearly 300 people.

The 1958 revolt led to fragmentation of the Bapedi traditional leadership, the effects of which are still felt today. While the Native Affairs Department realised the fatal mistake it had made in overtly tampering with the paramountcy and brought back Morwamotše, it simultaneously developed an alternative strategy: former headmen, especially those deemed useful and cooperative, were appointed as fully fledged chiefs and their areas turned into Tribal Authorities. As these leaders also needed followers to complete the image, the period saw a 'general reshuffle of the tribes in the north-eastern Transvaal..., the object being to reassemble the scattered portions of tribes'.[12] Government officials complained about the 'untidy state of affairs' and 'the pattern of settlement that is as mixed up as the spots on a guineafowl', but did their best to cram unruly Sekhukhune reality into the official moulds.[13] By the end of the 1960s, the three Sekhukhune chieftaincies had burgeoned to 56.[14] Retribalisation led to the clearance of 'black spots' outside the planned Lebowa homeland and increasing pressure on the land

[10] South African Institute of Race Relations. *Annual Report 1956-1957*, Johannesburg: SAIRA, 1957:55.

[11] SAIRR, *Annual Report 1954-1955*, pp. 58, 62.

[12] SAIRR, *Annual Report 1956-1957*, p. 55.

[13] Bothma (1976); Central Archives, BAO, No. 5/386, Ref: F54/1608/11: letter of the Native Affairs Commissioner dated 21-6-1958. Cf. Joanne Yawitch, *Betterment. The Myth of Homeland Agriculture*. Johannesburg: South African Institute of Race Relations, 1981, p. 68.

[14] Bothma (1976:179); Delius (1983:141) speaks of 54.

inside it. Following the rationale that people 'no longer fit for work or superfluous in the labour market ... are expected to return to their country of origin or the territory of the national unit where they fit ethnically even if they were not born and bred in the homelands', people who had never followed a traditional leader were unceremoniously dumped under one and – by law – ordered to respect him.

This period also demonstrated the different responses chiefs could make to the redefinition of their role. The Maroteng and Mamone chieftaincies did promise to go along with the new system, but managed to drag out actual implementation for over a decade. Conversely, *Kgoši* Kgoloko in Madibong enthusiastically embraced the Bantu Authorities and was stabbed to death by an angry mob led by Madinoge, the tribal wife. Following the advice of former government ethnologist Van Warmelo that 'a drop of honey attracts more flies than a barrel of vinegar,' the bait used by the government to lure traditional leaders into becoming Tribal Authorities varied from developmental promises such as schools and clinics to more gaudy spoils like cars and televisions sets (Delius, 1996:79). Eventually, most leaders did give in, although they often did not consider this a surrender but rather a temporary alliance, meant to retain as much independence as possible (Ritchken, 1990a:15; Sansom, 1970:295). Billy's mother recalls the period as one of playing along with the authorities until the arrival of better times: 'We were suddenly given big *bakkies* with our totem painted on it, and a television. At the same time we were totally powerless, being called to Pietersburg three months a year to be told the new laws, and forced there to write down the names and numbers of all the cattle in our district.'[15]

Even more than before, rule was by administration and decree. An enormous number of proclamations and regulations attempted to regulate every aspect of life in the Lebowa homeland. For instance, every Tribal Authority was proclaimed in a separate decree. The Pedi of Mamone were defined as a Tribal Authority by Government Notice 2275 of 1969, which determined the number of councillors to be 30 and described precisely which tribal and trust lands fell under their jurisdiction. Centres of rule were the magistrate's offices at Schoonoord and Nebo, where the magistrate held tribal trust accounts, paid the traditional leaders, and supervised the implementation of administrative regulations. These administrative offices were also the portals out of the Pedi homeland, outside which people stood waiting for hours for their passes. Protest against apartheid often specifically took the form of protest against this bureaucratisation, against Bopedi being subdivided and fenced in, its people subdued and every aspect of life regulated. As the men sang outside pass offices: 'Take off your hat. What is the name of your home? Who is your father? Who is your chief? Where do you pay tax? What river do you drink from? We mourn for our country' (Sansom, 1970:28).

After the naked force as a mode of rule at the beginning of the century, and the increasingly administrative dominance that followed it, the 1970s brought a new element to legitimise homeland rule: parliamentary 'democracy'. As before, the Lebowa legislative assembly was strongly directed from the outside and reliant on traditional leaders; it consisted of 60 chiefs and 40 elected members. Playing along again seemed to be the most viable strategy, as Billy's mother cheerfully explained. As a regent for her son, 'I was in the Lebowa parliament, that's what got me the money to buy my house. We really had fun, just shouting

[15] Interview, Mohumagadi Sekwati Mampuru, Mamone, 25 May 1999.

'voetsak voetsak' at everything that was introduced. But we never allowed homeland leaders like Pathudi onto our grounds.'[16]

Nevertheless, the ostentatious cooperation of the chiefs with the bantustan structures, their increased absence from their areas, the high levies charged in their name and their recasting as bureaucrats armed with guns severely damaged their legitimacy.[17] As the grim 1980s arrived and life inside and outside the homelands became increasingly harsh, with a land shortage, repression and extreme poverty as recurrent themes, revolt rumbled, a revolt which would propel Sekhukhune onto the front pages all over the country just like the one in 1958. But this time it was not the migrants who were the main actors, nor was retention of the old order of traditional authority what was at stake.

'Comrades, wake up, remake the world. Our parents' hour has passed away. This hour belongs to the youth. We, the comrades,' chanted the young people who took to the streets, singing and burning enemies and their property, calling not only for the abolition of apartheid but also for a complete reversal of the social order (Ritchken, 1995:312). Although the 1986 Sekhukhune youth revolt was linked to the nationwide protests that took place largely under the umbrella of the United Democratic Front (UDF), it fell into long-standing local conflicts and was played out in a particularly local vernacular (Van Kessel, 2000:75–149). One of its main targets was the chiefs, some of whom were burnt, chased away or killed. Chief Kgoloko, for instance, almost suffered the same fate as his father, as Madibong *mošate* was set on fire and he had to flee to Botswana. Other victims also associated with the old and divisive order were people accused of witchcraft. In the village of Apel/GaNkoane, for instance, 32 'witches' were killed in the February–April 1986 period (Delius, 1996:192). The identification of witches was only one of the functions that the youth wrested violently from the older generation; they also started to try disputes in people's courts and to allocate land. And although the revolt was once again quelled harshly, with SADF soldiers and tanks rolling into the area and surrounding schools and palaces, the scars left by this war of youth against elders could be felt long into the post-apartheid era.

It was in this setting that the last days of the homeland administration ticked away, with the army all over Sekhukhune, deep confusion and fear running through its communities and the homeland administration becoming more and more unabashed in its display of wealth. The administration of Ramodike, the last Lebowa Chief Minister, was considered distinguished by 'incompetence and corruption on an epic scale', symbolised by the R10 million government buildings in the homeland capital Lebowakgomo, where sprinklers watered lush gardens and cows stared thirsting beyond the fences.[18] As the new order dawned and black, yellow and green ANC flags came to wave triumphantly all over the longtime stronghold of Sekhukhune, there was a last-minute scramble by some of the homeland bourgeoisie to squeeze as much as they could out of the old order by, among other things, transferring land to the names of individual chiefs.[19] But

[16] Ibid. Cedric N. Pathudi was Lebowa's Chief Minister from 1973 to 1987, when he was followed by M. Nelson Ramodike.

[17] National Land Committee, *Bantustans in Crisis*. Johannesburg: National Land Committee, 1990, p. 16.

[18] Ibid., p. 208; SAIRR, *Annual Report 1988-1989*; 1989, p. 129.

[19] SAIRR, *Annual Report 1993-1994*, p. 225. Parliamentary Monitoring Group. 'Minerals and Energy Portfolio Committee: The Abolition of Lebowa Mineral Rights Trust Bill: Discussion'. http://www.pmg.org.za/minutes/000926pcmin.htm: Parliamentary Monitoring Group, 2000.

these were the final spasms of an old order; the 'entire bantustan edifice' collapsed and in 1993 Lebowa was reintegrated into South Africa.[20]

On paper, that is. In practice, the differences between the impoverished former homeland and the surrounding areas were still – and would remain – all too clear. In changing from Bopedi to part of Lebowa, the Pedi polity had turned from being a relatively fertile and self-supporting land to an overcrowded and impoverished dust bowl, a labour reserve largely dependent on income earned in the cities and welfare (cf. van Kessel, 2000:87). The figures for the Southern District, the administrative area that covers most of the former Lebowa, are unambiguous.[21] The area has an estimated population density of 135 people per sq. km. as opposed to 41 in the rest of the province. A staggering 70 per cent of its population are under the age of 30. In 1990, absenteeism was estimated at 49 per cent of the economically active males, and most of the income was derived from migrant work and old-age pensions. Nevertheless 81 per cent of the people earned less than the calculated minimum level and 56 per cent had no formal employment whatsoever. Schools were overcrowded, with a 40:1 pupil/classroom ratio and the highest matric (high school) failure rate in the country. The majority of the population had no access to tap water, electricity or a sewerage system. Although most households grew vegetables around the house, there was a severe shortage of arable as well as grazing land.[22]

But the difference between surrounding South Africa and the Sekhukhune area of the former Lebowa lay not only in the abrupt changes experienced when crossing the borders: from watered green pastures to sandy patches, from cricket fields to barefoot children in ragged school uniforms crammed into corrugated-iron school buildings, from mega-malls to women walking for hours carrying wood or water on their heads. For all its poverty, the area remained the centre of Pedi identity. Whatever the fate of the homeland over the past century – integration into a range of wider polities, a redefinition of its central institutions, an increased dependence on outside capital – it would, in the eyes of many, always remain Bopedi. This difference was, and would remain, conceptualised in a vastly different way by outsiders and locals: the former would, for instance, equate 'rural' with agricultural, while the latter took it to mean a lack of jobs. 'Do you also have rural areas back home, where people just hang around and do nothing?' I was often asked. But it was not only the former policy-makers who conceived of Sekhukhune as a separate sphere, as Sansom found when doing research in the areas in the 1960s, at the height of the repression, when a villager told him: 'Young man, if you want to bother us with many questions you must catch us in town. Here we just rest. Even the Afrikaners first go past the chief when they come here' (Samson, 1970:9).

[20] *Revocation and Assigment of Powers of Self-Governing Territories Act*. 1993.

[21] The following figures are taken from McIntosh, 'Rethinking Chieftaincy and the Future of Rural Local Government', which draws heavily on the October 1995 CSS household survey, and thus reflects the situation in the period after the reintegration of Lebowa into the Republic of South Africa. Since then, unemployment has gone up. Good statistics on the role of migration and the composition of household income, if only for two areas, can be found in Rupert Baber, 'Current Livelihoods in Semi-Arid Rural Areas of South Africa,' in Lipton et al., 1996. Cf. Development Bank of South Africa, *Statistical Macroeconomic Review Northern Province*.

[22] André De Villiers, 'Land Reform Options for the Northern Province,' in *Rural Land Reform Issues in Southern Africa: Lessons for South Africa's Northern Province*. Pietersburg: Land Management and Rural Development Programme, University of the North, 1997.

Traditional authority was, and would remain, the central icon of this separate identity, the structuring principle in the name of which wars were fought, as in the 1950s, or against which resistance was formulated, as in the 1980s. Nevertheless, the traditional leadership had also undergone a massive transformation since the days of Sekwati I. The paramountcy, with its network of subservient chiefs and enough power to keep invading armies at bay, was splintered into bureaucratised, autonomous chiefdoms whose power was crucially linked to the outside world. It is on this transformed traditional authority that I shall now focus, in an attempt to assess the world into which Billy Sekwati III was inaugurated on that sunny day in December 1998.

3. Traditional leadership and its spheres

As Lebowa was dismantled and a new order loomed, it was far from clear that this order would include traditional leaders. The songs of the comrades '*nako e fedile, nako ya magoši*' (the time is over, the time of the chiefs) still reverberated through the area, as did the promise of wall-to-wall elected local government (Delius, 1983). How could it be that by the end of the first decade of democracy thousands of people would flock to enthrone a new chief, and government officials, elected councillors and other politicians would enthusiastically pay their respects? Various pieces make up this puzzle: chiefly agency, the alliances sealed, and the people's perception of traditional authority. We focus first on the traditional leaders themselves. One legacy of the inclusion of the Pedi polity within first segregated and, later, democratic South Africa is that traditional leaders have come to operate within three distinct but overlapping spheres: that of *palace politics*, the *bureaucratic sphere* and that of *party politics*. It was in these differing spheres, each with its own rules and rationale, that the articulation of authority and the reproduction of power by traditional leaders in the post-apartheid era would take place.[23]

This approach, describing what traditional leaders are by concentrating on what they do and in what context, allows us to distinguish some common features of traditional authority in Sekhukhune today without having to essentialise or generalise what is, by all standards, a widely disparate group. The active genealogical engineering left post-apartheid Sekhukhune with 56 officially recognised traditional leaders and a multitude of contenders and headmen who felt that they should be chiefs in their own right.[24] While the majority of these chiefs were not very highly educated males who worked full-time as traditional leaders, there were also university graduates. Four of the leaders were women acting as regents for their sons and some spent their days working in town or obtained an income from a bottle shop or a cinema back home. Devout Christians alternated with people never seen in church, leaders with a large and faithful following with others who might have been known at the financial department of Traditional Affairs but not among the people they were supposed to rule. And although all Sekhukhune leaders were active in the spheres described below, the extent and success of this participation differed. Mamone forms our leitmotiv

[23] There is a long tradition in political anthropology of seeing politics as a game with rules; one of the classic works in this field is Bailey (1969).

[24] Information supplied by the Department of Traditional Affairs.

again, not as a generic example of Sekhukhune traditional leadership in general but more as a paradigm case: a strong, well-established chieftaincy where Pedi political tradition is exceptionally clear and can be contrasted with other, more *hlakahlaka* (mixed-up) chieftaincies at a later stage (Mönnig, 1967:vii).

Palace politics

> This was a power landscape in which the basic units were not citizens but rather a set of different, and fundamentally unequal, kinship statuses bound together in a diffuse but inescapable moral net of general mutual obligation. (Crehan, 1997:87)

The day that Billy Sekwati Mampuru III was inaugurated, seated on his royal throne with a leopard pelt round his shoulders, he looked distinctly unhappy. Half a year later, when we finally got to talk alone in the villa with black marble floors and elaborate gold chandeliers which the community had built for him, he would explain why.[25] He recounted how he had grown up outside the area and attended a separate school for chiefs' sons. Though his father Sekwati II had once referred to his destiny, he only fully realised what this entailed after the community had decided to select a candle-wife, a mother of the future heir, for him in 1992. 'Those things are very difficult because you are married at your uncle's place, and suddenly have to say "sweetheart, lovely" to your cousin.' He did manage to father a son by her before she died, and afterwards married a young nurse of his choice, but now feared – with good cause – that the community would select a new candle-wife for him. In addition, he felt isolated among his closest advisers. 'I don't know these *bakgoma* and *bakgomana* and I don't trust any of them; I fear that they are trying to bewitch me.' He had discovered that ruling was difficult: 'You can't really control the Bapedi. If they want something, they'll use force. And if they say "the nation said", there is nothing you can do. I am really ruled by them.'

The frank discussion showed with exceptional clarity the net of ties and obligations circumscribing individual traditional leaders. In *Sepedi*, three issues form the main strands of this net: marriage politics, various advisory bodies and the links with sub-clans through *batseta*, intermediaries.

A traditional leader, following the principle of *kgoši ke kgoši ka madi a bogoši* (a chief is chief by the blood of the chiefship), is the son of the former chief and the candle-wife. This candle-wife (*lebone la setšaba*, candle of the nation/community or *mmasetšaba*, mother of the nation/community) is a central institution in the Pedi political system, and typical of it (Mönnig, 1967:255-61; Bothma, 1976:193-4; Delius, 1983:51-2; Harries, 1929:29–35; Prinsloo, 1978: 34-9). Candle-wives invariably come from another royal family, and are often the daughters of the brother of a former candle-wife, who might be the chief. Their *magadi*, bridewealth, is paid by the whole community and villagers would say when meeting Billy Sekwati: 'Here is the person for whom we paid the bridewealth.' Many Sekhukhune chieftaincies would 'take' as their candle-wives the sisters and half-sisters of the paramount chief in Mohlaletse, and this has been a way of sealing political ties with those of kinship for over 200 years (Bothma, 1976:193). The Mohlaletse royalty said of these candle-wives: 'These women are our eyes and ears in the different communities, and they are especially trained for this job by a team of royal advisers.'[26] Although chiefs

[25] Interview, *kgoši* Billy Sekwati Mampuru III, Mamone, 22 July 1999.
[26] Interview, *kgošikgolo* K.K. Sekhukhune and council, Mohlaletse, 16 December 1998.

generally married in the same place – the Sekhukhune leaders at Mpahlele, the Mamone Bapedi at Magakala – there were exceptions: Billy's mother was a sister of Rhyne, the contender for the Sekhukhune paramountcy. The candle-wives are very important: they not only organise the initiation schools but they also often act as regents for their sons. Lebowa, in contrast to other areas, officially allowed them to do so, which gave them an even more important political position. Billy's mother, for instance, Lekgolane III, was a formidable matriarch who ruled Mamone for 14 years after Sekwati's death in spite of some protests that *tša etwa ke e tsadi pele, di wela ka maopeng* (if a woman leads, the nation goes astray).

As the candle-wife was often one of the last wives married by a chief, it frequently happened that he did not succeed in begetting an heir by her. There are many cases in which the *magadi* had already been paid, but the chief died before the candle-wife arrived. In that case – and this is what happened in Mamone – a blood relative of the late chief would 'raise seed' with her. Another scenario is that the candle-wife does not succeed in giving birth to a son, in which case one of her sisters stands in as a *seantlo* (she who goes to the hut) or, if she is barren, *hlatswadirope* (cleaner of ties) (Prinsloo, 1978:38). A combination of stand-ins for the chief and candle-wife also occurs: Sekhukhune III, for instance, was born out of a such a combined sororatic and leviratic union.[27]

There are thus elaborate but negotiable rules about what procedures have to be followed to marry the rightful candle-wife, who can be a candidate and which members of the royal family can raise seed or stand in for the candle-wife. These, combined with the fact that many designated heirs are not welcomed out of fear of witchcraft, make it possible 'to remove incumbents and to redefine genealogical relations without violating either the ascriptive ideology or its underlying logic' (Comaroff and Roberts, 1981:39). An example could be seen in Mamone six months after the coronation: when Billy did not perform as some community members wished, gossip suddenly surfaced about him being fathered by a school principal and his more active brother being the true heir. In addition, history has seen many, often older, half-brothers born to other chiefly wives take the throne. A classic way to do this is by burying the deceased leader – after exhuming him, if necessary – as tradition holds that the person who buries the former chief is his successor. The lingering dispute between the Sekhukhune lineage at Mohlaletse and the Mamone Bapedi started this way, with Sekhukhune

[27] It is characteristic of the fissure between national legal discourse and local practices that the human rights aspects of these arrangements hardly received any attention in post-apartheid South Africa. There was severe pressure on girls as well as traditional leaders to accept their designated marriage partners, to whom they had often been betrothed at birth. 'If a girl doesn't go, she will bring scandal to the whole family, and her father is responsible for making her go.' (Interview, *kgošikgolo* KK Sekhukhune and council, Mohlaletse, 16 December 1998) One candle-wife recounted with horror how she had to sleep with an old man who did not seem to know what a bath was and would visit her smeared with *muti*. 'Luckily I fell pregnant with a boy soon and was left alone after that.' (Interview with an anonymous *lebone*, Pietersburg, 9 February 1999.) There was elaborate discussion on the subject among the South African Law Commission members when they prepared the discussion document on customary marriages (Meeting in Lebowakgomo, as recounted by Teshell Shikwambane, Traditional Affairs official). One of the issues raised was whether in such a union, essentially between the community that paid the bridewealth and the candle-wife, only the community or only could the chief can call for a divorce. None of the discussion appears to have made it into the final discussion document: South African Law Commission. 'Project 90: The Harmonisation of the Common Law and Indigenous Law – Report on Customary Marriages.' Pretoria: South African Law Commission, 1998.

I as the oldest son of the first wife burying his father and thus seizing the throne from Mampuru, the son of the candle-wife.[28] Another group of typical contenders are the male regents who stand in for their brothers or cousins and find it difficult to give up the throne when the latter are old enough. Mamone, for instance, was torn apart by violent fights between supporters of *rangwane* (younger brother of the former chief) and the *mohumagadi* (the queen-mother) in the early 1980s.

The same combination of ascriptive, supposedly fixed but debated rules and space within these rules for achieved status determines the composition of the *sehuba (*lit: breast), the body that advises the chief on all facets of palace politics. This body – all over Sekhukhune – consists of the *bakgoma* and the *bakgomana.* The *bakgoma* are the family members closest to the chief: his brothers who share the same mother and thus belong to the *kgôrô ya mošate* (chief's kraal). Among them, the *mokgoma wo mogolo* holds the most important position: often the younger brother of the late chief, he functions as the main adviser to the chief and chairs meetings in his name (cf. Mönnig, 1967). The chief's sisters, if they are married, also have the advisory status of *bakgoma* and are called *kgadi.* The *bakgomana (*small *bakgoma)* are either the children of the other royal wives or the heads of the agnatic sub-clans called *dikgôrô,* the *borradikgôrô.* All this is the ideal, as it exists only in theory.[29] In practice, who actually is invited to advisory meetings and the essentially kinship-based *sehuba* appears to be affected by the territorial Tribal Council structure (see below). In addition, while people agree that there are definite rules on who can be *bakgoma* and who cannot, the content of these rules is heavily debated. In Mamone I witnessed a protracted discussion on the question of whether a certain uncle was a *mokgoma.*[30] But whatever its composition, the *sehuba* is not called breast for nothing. It is the closest layer around the chief, which simultaneously protects and restricts him. In the words of a Mamone *mokgomana*: 'He is our child, we put him there. He rules us and we rule him. We teach and guide him, especially now that he is still young.'[31]

The *dikgôrô* are a central organising unit in Pedi politics. They have been described as 'corporate units consisting each of a core of agnatically related men with their wives and children', who do not have to live together and basically consist of people with the same surname (Bothma, 1976). Although this is the basis, there was a tendency for *kgôrôs* to become territorially organised, and people with different surnames can join a *kgôrô* in the area where they live or choose to become members of the *kgôrô ya mošate.*[32] Still, the essence of *dikgôrô* remains agnatic, and can thus be contrasted with the *metse*, villages. A large area like Mamone had about 30 *borrametse*, representatives of villages, and 50 *borradikgôrô*, who in various ways and in various fora advised the traditional leader.[33] Essential in linking these various territorial and kinship-based sub-units is the system of *batseta*, intermediaries. Originally the term indicated the repre-

[28] In fact, there is also discussion as to whether Mampuru's mother, Malekutu, was the rightful candle-wife. Burial is often carried out by a group of *bakgoma* and *bakgomana.*

[29] For extensive if essentialist and not very up-to-date discussion of the Pedi political structure see: Bothma (1976: 184–93); Mönnig (1967: 249–99); Prinsloo (1978: 182–97).

[30] Meeting Mamone Commission on the Tribal Constitution, Mamone, 11 July 1999.

[31] Meeting Mamone Tribal Council, Mamone, 15 June 1999.

[32] Interview, *Bakgoma* and *bakgomana*, Mamone, 15 December 1998; Interview, Emily Magabe, Madibong councillor, 8 April 1999. I am aware that this contrasts with the descriptions of Bothma (1976:184) and Mönnig (1967:224).

[33] Interview, *Bakgoma* and *bakgomana*, Mamone, 15 December 1998.

sentatives of certain *kgôrôs* that coordinated relations between the chieftaincy and other *kgôrôs* and played an important role in dispute resolution. For example, the Malaka clan would always approach the royal house through the head of Matubeng (Bothma, 1976:189). Although by the end of the twentieth century *batseta* had become an umbrella term for all forms of intermediaries, the importance of the go-betweens and circumspection in approaching the royal house as well as other sub-clans persisted.

The vernacular of palace politics is thus one of kinship, mutual obligation and *setšo*, tradition. Nevertheless, the system has always left space for individual agency, to allow achievement to appear as ascription, whether it concerns the selection of chiefly candidates, their wives or their advisers. The bureaucratic sphere, within which traditional leadership operated for over a century, ruled by rationale and simultaneously confined and 'froze' these flexible arrangements but also – by creating alternative fora – enlarged the space for political action. It is to this process that we now turn.

Bureaucracy

> *RESOLUTION: COMPULSORY LEVY*
> *.....................Tribal/Community Authority*
>
> *At a duly constituted meeting of the ....tribe under chief/chairman.......on the ....day of ....19 ... there being present Mr.........Departmental Representative, ...chief/chairman and ....members of the tribe/community it was resolved that:*
> *The tribe/community being desirous to collect money for the purpose of covering administrative expenses as well as projects of development....*
> *(iv) the said levy shall be paid at the rate of R .... per annum per taxpayer*[34]

Immediately after Billy's mother had draped the leopard pelt around his shoulders, the director of the provincial Department of Traditional Affairs handed him a large red cylinder containing a certificate conferring on him jurisdiction to settle disputes, as well as a stamp with a porcupine, the totem of the Mamone Bapedi. 'The Northern Province Executive Council has accepted and approved the installation of Sekwati as *kgoši* of the Bapedi Tribal Authority,' he stated.

This Tribal Authority is synonymous with the bureaucratic sphere in which traditional leaders have operated for over a century, the lived results of apartheid planning that simultaneously strengthened traditional authority and drastically transformed it. In contrast to the stifling net of kinship ties, its main *modus operandi* is through laws, decrees and regulations and its main rationale is legal-rational, as manifested in bureaucratic power (Weber, 1993). The crucial importance of 'administration' as one of the ways in which the apartheid state lumped law, administration and force into one instrument of control has often been described (cf. Evans, 1997; Mamdani, 1996; Hammond-Tooke, 1975). It is important to reassert that the stated aim of bureaucratised Tribal Authority, as conceived by the apartheid government, was not conservation but, on the contrary, 'modernisation' and 'development'. Tribal Authorities were expected to 'assist and guide' the chief in a variety of local government functions, and even

[34] Regulation 22(4), General Regulations for Tribal and Community Authorities R2279 of 1991.

largely to take over these functions from him: the role of the chief was more legitimising than executive.[35]

As we have seen, the host of laws, regulations, proclamations and decrees defining Tribal Authorities and their functions remained in force after the advent of democracy.[36] The introduction of an alternative local government, the Transitional Local Council, would transform the political playing field, but it is sufficient for now to emphasise the remarkable continuity in the flow of funds to, and administrative support, for the bureaucratised Tribal Authorities after democratisation. This support formed, and would continue to form, the essence of Tribal Authority rule. If chiefs had come to operate as clenched fists during the period of segregation, the arm that linked them to the statal body was that of the administrators (cf. Mamdani, 1996:23). It is therefore logical that any overview of the bureaucratic sphere should start with these administrators and then continue with the local, fractured reflection of the pyramid of rule introduced by law: Regional Authorities, Tribal Authorities and Headmen.

Although the days were long gone when magistrates, as local-level administrators, were responsible for the day-to-day contacts with the traditional leaders in Sekhukhune, the Traditional Affairs officials who had taken their place in Schoonoord in the 1990s were still called 'magistrates'.[37] And when small girls danced in the mountains one of their favourite songs was still: 'I am scared to go to Schoonoord, for I am still small.' A day spent in the 1950s-style brick-faced complex, which included a sleepy magistrate's court, a jail and the Traditional Affairs Department, revealed the central role the department continued to play in ruling the area even after democratisation. Traditional leaders sat in line outside the small office of the Traditional Affairs official, waiting to withdraw money from the 'tribal trust fund', the 'school fund' or one of the other funds kept by him, complain about border and succession disputes, and hear about new policy measures. As a 'little king', the official would send out letters demanding that traditional leaders come to see him, often at very short notice (Mbeki, 1964:34). With yellowing proclamations corrected by hand and Van Warmelo's 1935 *Survey of Bantu Tribes* as the only reference work, he determined what the traditional leaders should and should not do.

The main functions of the Traditional Affairs officials are settling disputes, administering tribal funds, supporting the Regional Authority and acting as intermediaries between Tribal Authorities and the government. As 'street-level bureaucrats', most of these officials have a considerable degree of autonomy and

[35] SAIRR. *Annual Report 1956-1957*, p. 55.

[36] As determined in S 229, Act 200/1993. The most important ones in the former Lebowa are: *Black Administration Act 38/1927*; *Black Authorities Act 68/1951* and the ensuing regulations and proclamations, such as 'Third Schedule: Offences Which May Not Be Tried by a Chief, Headman or Chief's Deputy under Subsection (1) of Section 20 of 1955; 1. Regulations for Bantu Tribal Authorities in the Area of the Lebowa Territorial Authority 2. Regulations for Regional Authorities in the Area of the Lebowa Territorial Authority 3. Regulations for the Lebowa Territorial Authority 4. Rules of Procedure, Lebowa Territorial Authority.' Cape Town: Government Printer, 1969, *Regulations Prescribing the Duties, Powers, Privileges and Conditions of Service of Chiefs and Headmen (as Amended, for Northern Province) Procl. 110/1957*; *Land Regulations Proclamation R188/1969*.

[37] The description here is largely based on the Traditional Affairs Department office in Schoonoord, which covers the Sekhukhune magisterial district and is thus the one that most Sekhukhune traditional leaders deal with. Mamone, most of which lies in Nebo district, falls under another Traditional Affairs Department ofice which has just been moved from Nebo to Monsterlus. However, the conditions are largely similar.

strongly sympathise with their main clients, the traditional leaders (cf. Lipsky, 1980). The officials come under the Directorate of Traditional Affairs in the provincial Department of Local Government and Traditional Affairs.[38] In this department, apart from general administrative and financial issues, one of the main activities is advising on the appointment of traditional leaders, and the Directorate has a special anthropological section for this. Although state ethnologists are no longer involved in spotting and monitoring 'useful' chiefly candidates, this section continues to play a crucial role in determining who is appointed as a chief, often with genealogies and old anthropological studies as the only guides.[39] For instance, when I was visiting one of the state anthropologists, the Sekhukhune Traditional Affairs official stopped by to ask for advice on a case where a 30-year-old chiefly successor was available but the people wanted to appoint his mother. He was sent back with a resolute 'Impossible. That goes against their custom.'[40]

The Traditional Affairs officials also act as secretaries to the Regional Authorities, of which there were twelve in the former Lebowa at the time of this study. The largest one in Sekhukhune, the Leolo Regional Authority with 37 traditional leaders, was formally responsible for wide-ranging developmental issues such as the establishment of educational institutions, maintenance of roads, stock control and health issues.[41] While meetings were still held quarterly and were well attended, development was not on the agenda. Rather, Regional Authorities constituted a forum for the Department to communicate policies to the traditional leaders and for the traditional leaders to voice their concerns. The future of tribal land, for instance, was high on the agenda in the years after the elections, as were the remuneration of traditional authorities and the formation of a union of tribal clerks. It is possible that the attendance allowance explains the enthusiasm to hold meetings: in 1996 the Directorate even called a moratorium on Regional Authority meetings, as they were held 'at random, and the rate at which some traditional leaders claim is alarmingly high'.[42]

Below the Regional Authorities in the hierarchical pyramid, superimposed on pre-existing structures in all the former homelands, were the Tribal Authorities. The Mamone Tribal Authority was typical: not far from the royal palace and the traditional open court surrounded by *mafata* (ragged branches), stood a large Gothic-style new tribal office, staffed by two full-time tribal clerks, two tribal

[38] The Northern Province had a special Commissioner for Traditional Authorities up to 1997, when all the special Commissioners were abolished, and Traditional Affairs was placed under the newly formed Department of Local Government and Traditional Affairs. Above the local officials there are regional officials for Local Government and Traditional Affairs.

[39] Hammond-Tooke (1997:112). The genealogies have been computerised by now.

[40] Meeting state anthropologist, Department of Traditional Affairs, Pietersburg, 4 March 1998.

[41] *General Regulations for Bantu Tribal and Community Authorities : Cessation of Effect in the Area of the Lebowa Territorial Authority / General Regulations for Bantu Regional Authorities: Cessation of Effect in the Area of the Lebowa Territorial Authority / Further Amendment of Government Notice No R. 1274 of 1962, as Amended: Repeal of the Regulations for the Lebowa Territorial Authority*. Proclamation No R. 114. The size of the Leolo RA was determined by Government Notice 879, *Government Gazette* 2418 of 30 May 1969, where the 37 traditional leaders in it are listed. Also, a RA is established in terms of s3 of Regulation N115 of 1969 and its duties, according to Schedule A, are establishment etc. of educational institutions, construction and maintenance of roads etc., stock control, health issues, improvement of farming methods and afforestation.

[42] Northern Province Commission on Traditional Authorities, 'Letter Concerning Moratorium on All Regional and Executive Meetings.' Pietersburg, 1996.

cleaners and a driver. How these staff were paid varied. Sometimes their salaries came from tribal levies imposed by decrees like the one quoted at the beginning of this section, and administered by the Traditional Affairs official. In other cases, the necessary funds would come from the Directorate or payment for sites and administrative tasks. Whatever the source, this income was always low, with clerks paid around R600, drivers R450, tribal policemen R350 and cleaners R230 a month.[43] It is for this reason that the tribal secretaries formed TUSAA, the Trade Union of South African Authorities (TUSAA) and demanded 'higher wages, housing and car funds, medical aid, a pension fund, maternity leave, sick leave, study leave, normal leave, overtime and leaving wage'.[44]

The still applicable 1957 *Regulations Prescribing the Duties, Powers, Privileges and Conditions of Service of Chiefs and Headmen* (as amended for Northern Province) show the tribal office to be a typical local government body, often operating in liaison with government agencies, although it can hardly be said to follow the law. Public health (s9)? 'The community collects funds for clinics and then contacts the hospital through the tribal office.' Registration of births and deaths (ss9b/c)? 'It still happens sometimes, but people normally go directly to Home Affairs.' Conducting a census? 'The government.' The eradication of animal diseases through cattle dipping (s 9e)? 'This is the Department of Agriculture, we just write letters to warn the people.' The building of fences (9g)? 'Road signs are under the Department of Traffic. Graveyards do fall under [the] *mošate* (the palace); the chief will ask people to make the fences and then give them traditional beer.' Preventing crime (9h)? 'The police come by here every week.' Overseeing labour resources and the influx of blacks in urban areas (9l/j)? ' Ha, those days are over.' Preservation of flora (9l)? 'Yes, we do still give permits to cut trees, but many people disobey them.' Protecting public property (9m)? 'That is the responsibility of the community and the *kgoši*.' Soil erosion (9n)? 'This should be the government and Public Works.' 'Anyway', tribal clerk S. Mampuru concluded after having studied the law determining his job description, 'we don't have all these laws. We just do what is needed. The government never gave us any job description whatsoever.'[45]

Bureaucratisation, as a term to describe this sphere of traditional leadership, should also be understood in the sense of an excessive emphasis on documents and stamps. Many tribal offices still keep a chief's record book, in which the names of troublesome people are entered. Also, they have meticulously written lists of who has paid tribal levies. But the most important, and lucrative, administrative function of the tribal office is the issuing of Permissions to Occupy land, for which locals in Mamone would pay R60 and strangers R400.[46] As we shall see later, this function is carried out together with a variety of other actors: the Department of Agriculture demarcates and the magistrates and sometimes even the TLC have to give approval. But the final say rests with the *mošate*, as embodied in the tribal office.

Land use is also a central point on the agenda of the actual Tribal Council meetings, which in Mamone are held every fortnight. Although an aged copy of

[43] TUSAA meeting, Tafelkop, 6 June 1999; Interview, Elias Sepodumo, Traditional Affairs official, Schoonoord, 13 March 1998.

[44] TUSAA. 'Memorandum Handed to the Mec for Local Government.' Pietersburg, 1999.

[45] Interview, S. Mampuru, Mamone Tribal Office, 22 July 1999.

[46] *Land Regulations Proclamation.*

the proclamation establishing the Mamone Tribal Authority and determining its number of councillors hangs in the tribal office, many more people than the ten allowed attend the meetings.[47] At the time of my research, the chairman, vice-chair and the secretary all came from Mamone village. There were always a number of *bakgoma* and *bakgomana*, and about a dozen headmen representing the villages that fell under the Mamone jurisdiction. This was a typical mix for village council meetings generally, combining illiterate elders and educated young men (Kuper, 1970:61). The headmen, the foreignness of their position indicated by the Zulu title *indunas*, formed the lowest echelon of the Tribal Authority hierarchy established under apartheid. Some were elected, others had inherited the position from their fathers, some formed part of a local council or elected committee, while others worked on their own. Being headman was a lucrative position. Even if the former Lebowa headmen were not paid – a long-standing complaint – they shared in the R18,000 which the Mamone Tribal Authority received annually for running costs. In addition, they could demand money for allocating sites and settling disputes.

The bulk of the Tribal Council agenda was, in Mamone as elsewhere, filled with discussion over land allocation, development projects and the resolution of disputes. One meeting can serve as an example.[48] After the ubiquitous opening with a prayer, a traditional dance group came in, looking for a site to practise but also wanting to discuss in-fighting within the group. Then came applications to start a clinic, to build a holiday resort and to start a hospital with traditional cures for AIDS. A village headman asked permission to hold a *koma* (initiation school) but was told that that was impossible because of the mourning for the late candle-wife. Community groups asked for a site to start a poultry project and a businessman wanted a permit to open a general dealership.

Striking in the discussion here – and I often witnessed a similar process in other Tribal Councils – was that the sole unofficial purpose of the meeting seemed to be to reinforce patriarchal and chiefly rule and generate income for the Tribal Authority.[49] Women were told to be quiet, remain seated and to send their husbands instead. The villagers who had plans to put forward were not questioned about the developmental or organisational aspects of the projects, but merely whether they were known to the chief and had paid the R100 tribal levy raised for the coronation and the building of the chief's villa. 'We want development, but we can't have people not paying their dues,' one councillor grumbled. The poultry project, for instance, was initially denied a site because one of the participants was 'not in the chief's books' and others had not paid the levies. It was only after the 'stranger' had agreed to pay a staggering *bonthule* (stranger's fee) of R650 and his colleagues had paid their levies that a site was allocated. These practices led many people to regard the Tribal Councils as 'an apartheid structure that will give our land away for nothing and does not represent us at all'.[50] While similar complaints surfaced all over Sekhukhune, the solutions varied. In some areas, like Madibong, the Tribal Councils were revamped in order to include more progressive and popular members. In others alternative structures were created. This was the case in Mamone, where the

[47] The number was reduced from 30 to 10 in the 1980s.
[48] Meeting Tribal Council, Mamone, 15 June 1999.
[49] This was especially striking in Madibong, Mohlaletse, Ga-Masha and Ga-Matlala.
[50] Interview, *bakgomana*, 6 June 1999.

kgôrô (meeting) under the thorn-tree was re-instated after Billy's coronation, and claimed a legitimacy that the Tribal Council did not have: being in line with Pedi tradition (see photo 2, p. xii).

What was the role of individual traditional leaders in these Tribal Councils? It differed sharply from area to area: in some the traditional leader would chair the council meetings and be its most active participant, in others, he (or she) would hardly ever show up, leaving the day-to-day running of affairs to the councillors. But in all cases, as we have seen with the web of kinship, individual traditional leaders were simultaneously confined and redefined in the bureaucratic sphere. For instance, a large part of the council meeting described above was dedicated to discussing Billy's endorsement of one particular headman in Jane Furse, while the council preferred another candidate. Also, Billy's absenteeism was irritating the councillors. Even though 32-year-old Billy was, as palace members and councillors alike kept underlining, 'a young child who just needs some grooming', this pattern of leaders caught up in wider traditional and bureaucratic structures with little space for individual action could be found all over Sekhukhune. In this sense, the bureaucratic sphere and that of palace politics differed vastly from a third sphere, in which there appeared to be much more space for the agency of individual traditional leaders: that of party politics.

Party politics

I am not sure whether the yellow, green and black umbrella that shielded speakers from the December sun during the Mamone coronation was chosen deliberately in the ANC colours. What is clear, however, is that the parade of speakers that passed under it emphasised the political character of traditional leadership, and introduced the multitude of institutions that allow individual traditional leaders to campaign for a better position. Speakers, for instance, included the chairman of the House of Traditional Leaders – 'I greet you in the name of the African Renaissance' – and representatives of the ANC and its obstinate sibling Contralesa. As the political activities of traditional leaders in Sekhukhune largely took place within these fora, it is on them that we shall now focus.

If the advent of the Bantu Authorities in the 1950s led to increased bureaucratisation, it was the homeland regime which introduced traditional leaders to party politics, to operating on their own in parliament, far from their communities and with little need to consult with them. As the Northern Province premier said: 'Traditional leaders were politicised by the former administration, and it is very difficult to turn back the clock.'[51] To some, the provincial House of Traditional Leaders was the continuation of the homeland parliament. This House consisted of 36 members, and was established only after a protracted discussion on the division of seats between Sjangaan, Venda and Sotho traditional leaders.[52] Although its official task was to advise on legislation affecting traditional authorities, reading through the minutes revealed that discussion was

[51] Interview, N. Ramathlodi, Moria, 4 April 1999.

[52] Northern Provincial Government: Ministry of Land, Housing and Local Government. 'Status of Local Government.' Pietersburg: Ministry of Land, Housing and Local government, not dated, p. 16; Legislature of the Northern Province. 'Hansard Verbatim Report.' Pietersburg, 1996; *Northern Transvaal House of Traditional Leaders Act*, 1994. as amended by *Northern Transvaal House of Traditional Leaders Amendment Act*, 1995 and *Northern Province House of Traditional Leaders Amendment Act*. 5.

mostly about stipends and salaries, and questions such as whether members would receive cell phones and business cards.[53]

The House's advice to traditional leaders not to ostentatiously join political parties was followed by most Sekhukhune traditional leaders. Even though the area was traditionally an ANC stronghold, and leaders like those of Sekhukhune and the Sekwati had a long-standing alliance with the party, they did not flaunt their preferences and allowed everyone to campaign in their areas. Surprisingly – or perhaps not – it was those leaders who in the 1980s had the closest links with the homelands and underwent the heaviest clashes with their communities, who – often after trying a few other parties – became active in the ANC. A good example is *kgoši* Kgoloko. Not only was he the son of the chief who was killed by his community for supporting the Bantu Authorities, he also murdered five comrades himself in the 1980s and subsequently had to flee to Botswana. In the early 1990s, the ANC executive went to great pains to reconcile him and his community, with the result that *kgoši* Kgoloko joined the ANC in early 1999 and was voted into the national Parliament soon afterwards. There, in his own words, his main task was to protect the interests of traditional leaders, even if parliamentarians grumbled that 'no-one knows why he is there. If he has to make a speech he just gives some praise-songs in deep Sepedi which even the translators can't understand.'[54]

If fellow parliamentarians were puzzled by the positions suddenly offered to former homeland leaders, community members were baffled. The young comrades who had spent years fighting the *magoši* suddenly found their former enemies being given the political jobs they had hoped for.[55] 'Our chief was a money-monger and a political monger, and now we suddenly had to respect him. That change in policy was really, really difficult for us.'[56] But although the Northern Province ANC was far from unambiguous in its approach to traditional leaders, the provincial cadres felt it strategically advisable to include them within its broad alliance. 'When we protested against the inclusion of chiefs, we'd be told that "this one can't be changed, it is strategic".'[57] When Mandela visited Jane Furse before the 1999 elections, he spent over an hour talking to the Sekhukhune chiefs, before making a ten-minute appearance in front of the roaring masses. During the meeting, from which journalists were excluded, he told the chiefs: 'My leaders, one of the first things I did after my release was to go around the country, meet with traditional leaders and tell the people that now the ANC was back we were telling them that they must respect their chiefs.' And that whatever the Sekhukhune traditional leaders wanted, be it cars or other spoils, they just had to ask him and he would try to help (see photo 7, p. xv).[58]

Another forum many Sekhukhune traditional leaders chose to join in order to improve their position was Contralesa. This organisation had been active in the Northern Province since the late 1980s and its provincial chairman, the lawyer Thobejane, came from Sekhukhune. During Billy's coronation he emphasised the two main concerns of the organisation in the province: land and minerals. 'The

[53] Minutes, Northern Province House of Traditional Leaders, Department of Traditional Affairs; *Northern Province House of Traditional Leaders Act*, s. 6.

[54] Interview, Parliamentarian, 19 September 2000.

[55] Interview, councillor, Jane Furse, 6 April 1999. Cf. Delius (1996); Van Kessel (2000).

[56] Interview, civic members Ga-Moloi, ANC office, 14 June 1999.

[57] ANC activist on the Madibong situation, Jane Furse, 5 May 1999.

[58] Meeting Sekhukhune traditional leaders with N. Mandela, Jane Furse, 27 May 1999.

land has been stolen from the *magoši* and the government shouldn't forget that it belongs to us.' Whether the Northern Province Contralesa wanted land to be given back to individual traditional leaders, or to leaders on behalf of their communities, was a question that it preferred to leave unanswered, but the idea was that 'if you give land back to the people they won't be under our authority any more'.[59] Apart from taking a vocal stand on all political issues concerning the position of traditional leaders, Contralesa also sought to further the business interests of the chiefs and to capitalise on the 'Africanist' value of its constituency. For example, as already noted, it became a trust in 1999 in order to join a mining consortium and even to be able to bid for cell phone frequencies.[60]

A working day for Billy Sekwati Mampuru and many of his Sekhukhune colleagues could thus consist of a discussion on customary law in one of the thatched rondavels around the *mošate* and whispered witchcraft accusations with his *bakgoma* and *bakgomana*, followed by a meeting on development projects in the tribal office, after which he would drive, alone, to a Contralesa discussion on mineral rights. Although the three spheres overlap, each has its own rationale and vernacular, and requires a specific form of agency. While the webs of kinship and bureaucracy allow chiefs very little room for manoeuvre and encapsulate them in structures – be it the *sehuba* or the Tribal Council – that essentially seek to redefine traditional authority in a way that strengthens their own position, party politics and interest groups such as Contralesa leave space to further their individual interests.

Although the advent of democracy did not crucially alter the existence of these spheres of operation, it did create ample opportunities for entrepreneurial traditional leaders to strengthen their position in each of them. In the bureaucratic sphere, for instance, the introduction of the elected local councils reduced the pressure on traditional leaders to deliver development, while the flow of funds and administrative support to the Tribal Councils continued. And the unbanning of the ANC and its pro-chief strategy, combined with the formation of Contralesa, provided the traditional leaders with legitimate fora to further their interests. Thus part of the reason why traditional leaders stayed on and even staged a surprise come-back lies in their agility in adapting to the new times in each of their three spheres of operation. But another part lies in their capacity to forge alliances with other important actors in Sekhukhune. Even though the underlying socio-economic conditions remained the same, the 1990s saw an important reconfiguration of what I call the Sekhukhune institutional landscape. It is to these new allies and adversaries in local government that we now turn.

4. The institutional landscape

After the Traditional Affairs official had handed the young king the certificate conferring jurisdiction on him, a parade of assorted authorities followed on the platform. There was Abraham Mafiri, mayor of the Greater Ngwaritsi Makhudu-Thamaga local government, followed by John Magolego, leader of the popular vigilante organisation *Mapogo a Mathamaga*, who gave Billy a whip and promised assistance in ruling the area. The khaki-clad marching band of the Zionist

[59] Interview, S. Thobejane, Pietersburg, 1 October 1999.
[60] Contralesa Central Region Meeting, 20 July 1999, Lebowakgomo.

Christian Church played and leaders of various church denominations called down blessings on the young leader. All these speakers, I would argue, were representative of the kaleidoscopic Sekhukhune institutional landscape at the end of the 1990s.

In order to understand the power that traditional leaders held and the role of law in the Sekhukhune institutional landscape it is necessary to map out the other institutions involved in the production of local, living law, the norms they came up with, and their sources of legitimisation. The mapping, as we shall see later, should be taken quite literally in that there are important geographic aspects to local power relations: the rules that apply in the townships are different from those that apply around the *mošate* (De Sousa Santes, 1992; Thornton, 1996). Before starting to draw the map, three caveats should be issued about its use. First, in stating that various institutions are involved in creating local law and governance, I am not in any way suggesting that these are 'coherent systems locked in a structurally determined struggle' (Wilson: 2000). On the contrary, I follow Wilson in regarding them as 'actors and collective groups ... engaged in the reflexive self-production of society'. Next, this institutional map is not only specific to Sekhukhune, it is also intended as the location of one set of actors, the traditional leaders, and thus puts the emphasis on these leaders and the institutions with which they interact most. A final warning concerns the rootedness of institutions in the broader socio-economic conditions of Sekhukhune and the surrounding world; any attempt to describe the institutional landscape without reference to the social categories that characterise Sekhukhune society and its economic conditions would be futile.

Some of the features of Sekhukhune that need to be re-emphasised in this context are its poverty, its reliance on migrant labour, its demographically and agriculturally undeserved classification as a 'rural' area, its patriarchal character and the importance of religion in making sense of events in daily life.[61] Also, there is the paradoxical importance of 'communities', which are a central point of reference for people but whose cleavages are often more obvious than their coherence. One of the most profound and significant cleavages, and one without which it is difficult to understand the institutional landscape, is that between youth (*baswa*) and elders (*batswadi*). We have seen how the 1980s youth revolution overturned what many people considered the rightful, patriarchal social order. Restoring rule in the 1990s was often crucially about restoring this social order: of elders over youth and men over women. It is in this context that the rule of the most important institutions, together with the traditional authority, can be classified: the elected local governments and the civic organisations as exponents of the youth revolt, government departments, the vigilante organisations, the churches and business and migrant organisations. Let us look briefly at each of them and their relations with traditional authority.

Elected local government

Before his election as mayor of the Greater Ngwaritisi Makhudu/Thamaga Transitional Local Council (TLC), Abraham Mafiri was the driver of *kgoši* Kgoloko. After his election, he and his eleven co-councillors ran an area of 91

[61] Teresa Kathleen Connor, 'Conflict and Co-operation: Gender and Development in a Rural Settlement of Sekhukhuneland, Northern Province.' MA thesis in Development Studies, Rand Afrikaans University, 1998; Delius (1996); James (1985); Ritchken (1990b).

villages and 1100 sq. km. with 28 traditional leaders and a population of 200,000.[62] They were formally responsible for development in this area and had a colourful mix of functions in the fields of health, education, welfare and trade.[63] Many of these functions, of course, fell under the Tribal Authorities before democratisation. As the jurisdiction of these Tribal Authorities was never officially repealed, nor the support for them withdrawn, and they maintained the power to allocate land, the introduction of the TLCs in 1995 marked the beginning of a protracted struggle over jurisdiction. 'We now have two bulls in a kraal' is an expression that always seemed to crop up when discussing Sekhukhune politics.

The handicaps under which the TLC started this power struggle became clear immediately after a visit to the office of this elected local government. In contrast to the large well-staffed tribal offices, the TLC had a tiny space in the Jane Furse shopping mall, with one clerk, a broken-down car and no other administrative staff. Most of the twelve councillors – all ANC members – were teachers, and they had to work during the day to supplement their monthly stipend of R1300. The ten men and two women were all former comrades who had spent the 1980s in the struggle and had very little experience in local administration. As 32-year-old mayor Mafiri said: 'We really had to start from scratch and learn everything.'[64]

Nevertheless. the Greater Ngwaritsi Makhudu/Thamaga TLC was considered relatively successful compared with those surrounding it, where, in the worst case, the councillors never showed up again after having heard how low their stipends would be, and just went back to work in the mines. In its first five years, the GNMT TLC saw a large-scale electrification project and the building of a hospital, a library, work on water reticulation, a large shopping centre, various boreholes, sports facilities and a large housing project.

An explanation for this contradiction between the extremely limited capacity and the relatively high level of achievement is that it was not the TLC itself that carried out these projects. Many of them were implemented by government departments which either fell directly under the provincial government or under the Northern District Council. The vital role of District Councils, factually and legally a fourth government layer between the province and local government, has received very little attention in the literature. But these councils, in the post-apartheid era, were formally held responsible for most of the local government functions and had a far larger administrative capacity than the TLCs whose funds they held.[65] As mayor Mafiri put it: 'The District Councils don't build capacity, they want the TLCs to remain dependent on them.' What the TLCs did do is set priorities for development, for instance through the land development objectives.[66] And, as good political logic required, it did try to take the credit for all the development projects carried out by others. In fact, many of the wrangles

[62] District Coordinating Team, 'Situation Analysis of the Ngwaritsi-Makhudu-Thamaga-Tubatse-Steelpoort District (Nmtts), Northern Province.' Jane Furse: District Coordinating Team,, 1998; McIntosh, 'Situational Analysis: Status Quo Report for the Setting of Land Development Objectives for Ngwaritsi TLC.'

[63] *The Constitution of the Republic of South Africa* 108/1996, Ss 152, 156 ; *Municipal Structures Act* 117/1998, Ss 83-84.

[64] Interview, A. Mafiri, Jane Furse, 8 December 1998.

[65] Proclamation 51/1995. This situation has not really changed since 2000.

[66] *Development Facilitation Act* 67/1995.

between the TLC and traditional leaders were over who got to 'stand in the limelight' for delivering basic services.[67]

In spite of the TLC's achievements in Sekhukhune, both councillors and voters were quickly to become seriously dissatisfied with the elected local government. One main frustration for the councillors was the low stipend they received, 'while your whole family suddenly stands on your doorstep expecting you to support them'.[68] The lack of support from the government was also a sore point. Another letdown was the in-fighting between councillors: in the TLC concerned, eight of the twelve councillors represented wards, while four were voted in through proportional representation. The ensuing pressure resembled that from family members: ward representatives were under a great deal of pressure to steer developments back home. Many of them seemed to yield to the pressure, and this caused tensions as well. But the greatest frustration of the councillors was the lack of support from their people. 'We, as councillors, have inherited an illiterate mass, silent and suspicious, but susceptible to manipulation.'[69] The elders, according to the councillors, would often be manipulated by the traditional leaders, 'who claim the divine right to rule the people'.[70] That people continued to obey the chiefs was, in the eyes of the councillors, the result of a culture of fear sown under apartheid, and a general and regrettable 'tribalism'.[71] But the youth, peers of many of the councillors, could not be trusted either: 'Ah, the youth. They expect everything to come from the government. And they are very dangerous; if you make a mistake they'll burn you.'[72] Councillors would also complain about witchcraft accusations, which might be why there was a photocopied warning on the wall of the TLC office that 'Jealousy kills'. The people, in turn, were disappointed because they hardly ever saw those they had voted for. Allegations of corruption were rampant, as was the accusation that 'these boys are more committed to supporting their family than delivering.' In addition, the age of many councillors was perceived as a problem: 'The TLC is only about young boys driving around in flashy cars, failing to deliver but undermining *magoši* at the same time.'

The TLC's relation with the traditional leaders lay at the heart of many of its problems. In the GNMT TLC, as in 90 per cent of the Northern Province, the *ex officio* clause which would allow traditional leaders to participate in the TLC was never implemented. There was an offer to allow four of the 28 traditional leaders to attend meetings, but the *magoši* refused because they all wanted to be represented.[73] In a neighbouring TLC two traditional leaders, one of whom was K.K. Sekhukhune, did officially take part in meetings, but councillors would complain that they were never there. The two were selected by vote, and *kgoši* Thobejane, who was also from the area, was so angry to be excluded that he claimed

[67] Jubie Matlou, 'Amakhosi Stick to Their Guns.' http://www.mg.co.za/mg/za/archive/2000nov/features/27nov-amakhosi.html: *Mail & Guardian* online, 2000.

[68] Councillor, 20 May 1999.

[69] Interview, Members of the Executive of the Northern Province Local Government Association, Pietersburg, 19 March 1998.

[70] Ibid.

[71] Interview, A. Mafiri, Jane Furse, 8 December 1998.

[72] Interview, A. Mafiri, Jane Furse, 20 May 1999.

[73] The *ex officio* clause was implemented in only 3 out of the 36 rural TLCs in the Northern Province: Elandskraal, Louis Trichardt, and Fetakgomo. Information from the Department of Local Government.

afterwards that no-one could represent him anyway. This is only one of the problems linked to letting individual traditional leaders sit on local councils. Billy Sekwati voiced another: 'If you as a chief get into politics, you'll lose your respect. People can just chase you there and throw stones at your door if they don't want something. Because you'll just be like any other councillor.'[74]

The absence of formal links between councillors and traditional leaders did not mean that there was no contact between them. On the contrary, the seemingly opposite positions were somehow reconciled in the day-to-day running of the area. Tribal offices grew accustomed to disseminating local government information, the Tribal Councils sent large and potentially lucrative business applications to the TLC, and the elected council paid substantial sums into the tribal coffers to be able to build on tribal land. Mayor Mafiri estimated that he got on well with 80 per cent of the traditional leaders in his area, because he was 'a local boy' and knew the correct procedures to follow. But the relationship remained inherently tense, an issue to which we shall return when discussing, in the next sub-section, what was actually at stake in the struggle for local control.

Government departments

As part of the reconfiguration of local power relations, the period before the 2000 local government elections saw an ongoing attempt to move the Department of Traditional Affairs officials to the TLC building and to bring them under the jurisdiction of elected local government. Understandably, the traditional leaders did not like being housed 'with the other bull'. But the most vehement protest came from the officials themselves, who feared a loss of autonomy. Having taken over the 'administration of traditional authority' from the magistrates in 1994, they had become 'little kings' like their predecessors, with much of the final responsibility for the local government functions still carried out by traditional leaders.

Other government departments that had been a local presence for a long time and were intimately connected with the traditional leaders also perceived the TLCs as a threat. The Department of Agriculture is the most prominent example. Its officials had played an important local role since the days of the betterment schemes. They demarcated sites and were involved in land planning, putting up fences and advising on livestock use. Even though the traditional authorities actually allocated the sites, they did much of the preparatory work and provided the tribal offices and headmen with the maps to use in allocation. Another example is the Department of Justice. Even though the magistrates were no longer responsible for 'administering the traditional leaders', they continued, as we shall see in the next chapter, to send 'tribal cases' concerning land and family matters back to the traditional courts, thus substantially strengthening the power of the chiefs.

Other government departments considered the Tribal Authorities to be easy 'one-stop shops' through which to contact and deal with communities. They called meetings in the tribal offices, made use of their networks of tribal offices to disseminate information, and relied on the authority of the leaders to add credibility to proposals and policy measures. Thus, in Mamone, a parade of officials

[74] Interview, Billy Sekwati Mampuru III, Mamone, 22 July 1999.

from Departments such as Tourism, Health and Welfare, Safety and Security, or Public Affairs would regularly visit either the Tribal Council or the *mošate*, the chief's palace. It is this type of day-to-day interaction which, perhaps more than other forms of official governmental recognition, reinforced the position of traditional authorities *vis-à-vis* the elected local government.

The civics

Civic associations (civics), as a generic category, could be found in practically every Sekhukhune traditional authority area. These activist organisations could be considered the institutional outcome of the 1980s youth revolt, when the ANC and the UDF saw them as a means to mobilise people around local bread-and-butter issues (Van Kessel, 2000:27). Although they shared some common features, such as a strong association with the 'youth' and 'development' and an antagonism towards traditional authority, they took on widely different forms in different localities.

Generally, civics in Sekhukhune can be said to have gone through two phases. The first phase was in the years prior to the 1995 local government elections, when civics were established all over Sekhukhune as a direct challenge to traditional authority. Young men, often with university degrees and a history in the struggle, started to apply for development projects, allocate land and settle disputes. This affront to the old order led to violent clashes in some cases, and to a renegotiation of jurisdiction in others, where developmental issues – often no priority of the traditional leaders anyway – would be left to the civics.[75] But the atmosphere was always tense, with traditional leaders protesting about the youngsters wanting to do what they had 'been doing since times immemorial anyway'.

The 1995 elections slightly altered the power relations. The civics had formed an ideal breeding ground for local councillors, and many collapsed after all their members had been voted into local government. Others, often the activists who felt left out in the elections, continued to organise the electricity supply, start gardening and poultry projects, open soccer fields and carry out a host of local government functions which often led to increasingly strained relations with their former comrades and a rapprochement with the traditional leaders. While some of these organisations brought a lot of benefit to the communities they claimed to serve, others were, often rightfully, accused of the same profit-seeking and patronage politics they had once charged the chiefs with. Their progressiveness was also questioned by women, who pointed out that 'the civic is dominantly represented by young men who are deeply rooted in the world of male domination'.[76]

Two examples demonstrate how one might see the same patterns of institutionalisation of authority all over Sekhukhune, but how they were played out in vastly different ways depending on local agency. In Madibong, where there was a rapprochement between *kgoši* Kgoloko and the ANC, the former appointed the young head of the civics as chairman of the Tribal Council. During its meetings,

[75] McIntosh and Vaughan (1994:22); K. Van der Waal, 'The Rhetoric and Practice of Participation in Rural Development: Anthropological Perspectives from South Africa.' Rand Afrikaans University: unpublished research paper, 1997, p. 14.

[76] This position, taken by many women I spoke to, is also expressed in Transvaal Rural Action Committee. *The Rural Women's Movement: Holding the Knife on the Sharp Edge*. Johannesburg: TRAC, 1994, p. 34.

the old tribal councillors could be heard deferentially asking this comrade Phaahla for 'directions', at which the young boy would sometimes sigh 'I have to run a *kgôrô* with pensioners here, it is so difficult.'[77] In the neighbouring Mamone, however, things were played out differently. In one of its villages, Eenzaam, a violent clash erupted between civics and the representatives of the traditional authority over a housing project. The active civics, who had already started to give out land free of charge and stimulate development through a brick-making project, a sewing project and a community garden, had applied for the project without the permission of the *mošate*.[78] In the ensuing debates, Billy's headman would prompt the villagers to 'Think: what have these young boys done for you?'[79] And in the Mamone *kgôrô* the old men spent months furiously denouncing the youngsters 'who think the soil belongs to them'.[80]

The civics were not the only form of organised civil society. Even the smallest village abounded with water committees, electricity committees, development fora, village development councils, community policing fora and a colourful collection of other fora that sought – often with little success and dwindling enthusiasm – to improve local life. This abundance of what were often called 'structures' shows how people were not only forced to take local development into their own hands, but were also prepared to do so. This sector of the institutional landscape was, in that sense, formed out of necessity and shaped by the absence and the malfunctioning of the government. The same – even though it concerned security instead of development – went for another institutional actor propelled to the fore in the 1990s: the vigilante organisation *Mapogo a Mathamaga*.

Mapogo a Mathamaga

The institutional landscape we are seeking to map out consists of those actors that hold power locally, are involved in local rule and in a variety of day-to-day interactions weave a local normative framework, reinforce these norms and seek to legitimise this process. Even though this analysis is separate from the state, it is an idealised version of this same state that is at the very centre of it, and forms its key sounding board: the non-governmental institutions described carry out those functions that we have come to associate with state power.[81] Providing citizens with security through its monopoly of violence is at its core, which is why an analysis of the organisation that largely took over these functions in 1990s Sekhukhune shows us the relevance of such a broader approach to understanding local law, governance and power.

'If you think you're a leopard, I'll turn into a tiger,' is what the idiomatic expression *Mapogo a Mathamaga* means (see photo 8, p. xv).[82] And in late 1996,

[77] Tribal Council meeting, Madibong, 9 June 1999.

[78] For a more detailed description of this case cf. Oomen (2000a).

[79] Visit to Billy Sekwati Mampuru and Councillors, Eenzaam, 14 June 1999.

[80] Kgoro, Mamone, 30 June 1999.

[81] One commonality between legal positivists and legal pluralists, although the latter are hesitant to admit it, is that the state remains at the centre of their analysis: either as the sole entity to produce 'law' or as a point of reference to explain why other normative frameworks should also be considered as law. Cf Von Benda-Beckmann (1996).

[82] For the sake of brevity I focus only on *Mapogo a Mathamaga*, as the main vigilante organisation in Sekhukhune. It should be emphasised, however, that this phenomenon is neither new nor unique. Many vigilante organisations have been recorded in the history of South Africa, formed against stock theft or as a counterweight to liberation movements. Cf. Nicholas Haysom, *Mabangalala: The Rise of Right-Wing Vigilantes in South Africa*, ed. Centre for Applied Legal Studies. Vol. 10, *Occasional Papers*.

when a crime wave peaked with the brutal murder of eight local shopkeepers, the Sekhukhune businessmen turned into tigers. The Business Shield they formed was propelled on to national front pages when a mob of its members whipped two alleged criminals to death with sjamboks and assaulted six others, among them two drunk policemen.[83] In the years that followed the 'sjambok vigilantes of the North' would continue to make the headlines, and newspapers splashed pictures of businessmen in T-shirts carrying small bottles of the *Mapogo* 'medicine' in one hand and a whip in the other, bleeding victims dumped in front of the local police stations and the ever-smiling *Mapogo* leader Magolego who never tired of explaining that this was the 'traditional African way of solving problems'.[84]

For all the anarchy alluded to by the press, *Mapogo*'s most striking feature could well be its high level of organisation. In the 1996–2000 period, Monthle Magolego built up an organisation with a Jane Furse headquarters larger than the police station, an estimated 55,000 members who paid between R60 and R10,000 for their annual protection, and 90 branches in all the major Northern Province and Mpumalanga cities and also in more distant provinces. The characteristic protection sticker with the two tigers could be seen behind most shop windows and farm fences in the area, and Mapogo had become a household name to 80 per cent of the Sekhukhune population.[85] As is typical of vigilante organisations, it possessed defined goals, rules and regulations: it had its own constitution and code of conduct.[86] This 1996 constitution, for instance, set out its motivation in a preamble:

> As the state and its political rulers do not have the ability to stop the crime wave that specifically targets businesspeople...and the police are understaffed, ill-equipped and demoralized, all good men and women must now bond together to show the criminals that there are men and women in these areas who are no longer prepared to take the situation lying down and ... to suffer injuries, humiliation and loss of life and property

[82] (cont.) Johannesburg: University of Witwatersrand, 1986; Ritchken (1995:368). In Sekhukhune another important vigilante organisation is the herdsmen united in *Badiši re timeletšwe*, the organisation formed by the youth to oppose *Mapogo Maputla re tla ja kae* and *Mapogo* split-offs such as *Sekhukhuni se bonaa ke Sebataladi.*

[83] Over the years, there have been many newspaper articles about Mapogo. Some worthwile articles are: 'Lashing out at Crime.' *Saturday Star*, 2 May 1998.; Decca Aitkenhead, 'Rough Justice.' http://www.mg.co.za/mg/news/2000may2/29may-vigilante.html: *Daily Mail & Guardian* electronic archive, 2000; Tangeni Amupadhi, 'Sjambok Vigilantes of the North.' http://www.mg.co.za/mg/news/97feb1/17feb-vigilante.html: *Daily Mail & Guardian* electronic archive, 1997; Chris Barron, 'When Fighting Crime Depends on a Vigilante.' *Sunday Times*, 2 August 1998; Kathu Mamaila, 'Businessmen "Assault" 20 Burglars,' *Sowetan*, 27 November 1996, 4; 'Provinces Adopt Conflicting Stances on Mapogo Vigilantes.' *Business Day*, 10 October 1998, 5; Kathu Mamaila, 'Vigilante Group Changes Its Name – Mapogo a Mathamaga Now Calls Itself a Community Shield.' *Sowetan*, 26 August 1997, 4; Mungo Soggot, and Evidence Wa ka Ngobeni, 'We Must Work on Their Buttocks.' http://www.mg.co.za/mg/news/99may1/14may-vigilante.html: *Daily Mail & Guardian* electronic archive, 2000. Cf: Oomen (1999a).

[84] Interview, John Magolego, president *Mapogo a Mathamaga*, Glen Cowie, 8 December 1998; Soggot, and Wa ka Ngobeni. 'We Must Work on Their Buttocks.'; Evidence Wa ka Ngobeni, 'Vigilante Group Sweeps the Suburbs.' http://www.mg.co.za/mg/news/2000jan2/25jan-vigilante.html: *Daily Mail & Guardian* electronic archive, 2000.

[85] Cf. Aitkenhead. 'Rough Justice.'; Wa ka Ngobeni. 'Vigilante Group Sweeps the Suburbs.'

[86] On comparable vigilante organisations in the US, Haiti, Brazil, China, Philippines, and Tanzania see Les Johnston, *The Rebirth of Private Policing*. London: Routledge, 1992; also Abrahams (1996); Jeroen Cuvelier, 'La Privatisation de la Sécurité au Kwazulu-Natal : Le Chantier Remis à L'ouvrage.' Antwerp: International Peace Information Service, 2000.

> by these swaggering criminals... This constitution is agreed to in order to teach these criminals the meaning of the idiomatic expression *Mapogo a Mathamaga*.[87]

'Teaching criminals the meaning of the expression *Mapogo a Mathamaga*' typically meant driving up to a suspect's house with a squad of cars, dragging him out into the open and publicly flogging him until he was senseless or – in at least ten cases – dead. When *Mapogo* celebrated its first birthday it boasted that it had taken action in about 1000 cases of theft, 500 of armed robbery, 80 of hijacking, 30 of murder and 30 of rape.[88] Among its members it counted not only large companies but also white farmers, schools, clinics and regional government offices.[89] It had also developed an increasingly sophisticated legitimisation discourse, with the emphasis on *sepogo (*the *Mapogo* way of doing things), the 'traditional' character of corporal punishment, the incompetence of the police and the swiftness and effectiveness of the *Mapogo* medicine.[90]

An emphasis on its community-based character also formed part of this process of legitimisation: in 1997 *Mapogo* changed its name from Business Shield to Community Shield.[91] It held large festivals and supported soccer teams and cultural dance groups financially. Like many vigilante organisations, it had an essentially élitist base, of shop-owners, concerned parents and church-goers whose frustration with state incapacity and police corruption had reached a stage where they felt it necessary 'to break the law in order to uphold it'.[92] By tapping common concerns about security and the breakdown of norms it could form a conservative hegemonic block, seeking to re-establish a certain, patriarchal and often even biblical moral order (cf. Gramsci, 1971). This explains the organic alliance with Afrikaner farmers, many of whom joined and even became branch leaders, stating that 'It's better than having a guard dog outside.'[93]

A close alliance with the traditional leaders also formed part of the legitimisation discourse. On the day of the coronation of Billy Sekwati Mampuru, *Mapogo* leader Magolego gave him a sjambok and a cheque and told him to 'just relax, *Mapogo* will do enough for you'. Magolego also boasted of having put unpopular traditional leaders back in the saddle: 'The *magoši* suffered from all these young chaps toyi-toyi-ing around. In the Mashishi tribe at Driekop there were so many people against the *kgoši* who were undermining his territory. But when he joined hands with *Mapogo* things started to pick up again and now he is a well-respected *kgoši*.'[94]

Mapogo's ability to put the youth back in their place is one of the main reasons that 55 per cent of the Sekhukhune people in general, and elders in

[87] Mapogo a Mathamaga Business Shield, 'Constitution,' 1996.

[88] Barron, 'When Fighting Crime Depends on a Vigilante'. Having lived next door to the *Mapogo* head office for over a year, and visited many of the organisation's branches, I do not regard this claim as unreasonable.

[89] Evidence Wa ka Ngobeni, 'Vigilante Group Faces Split.' http://www.mg.co.za/mg/news/2000may1/9may-vigilante.html: *Daily Mail & Guardian* electronic archive, 2000.

[90] On *sepogo*: the prefix se- in Pedi stands for an overall, encompassing quality: Sepedi, for instance, is Pedi culture. Even though there are no official statistics to prove it, the overall popular perception is that crime plummeted in Sekhukhune after the formation of *Mapogo*.

[91] Mamaila, 'Vigilante Group Changes Its Name – *Mapogo a Mathamaga* Now Calls Itself a Community Shield.'

[92] Johnston, *The Rebirth of Private Policing*, p. 13.

[93] Barron, 'When Fighting Crime Depends on a Vigilante.'

[94] Interview, John Magolego, president *Mapogo a Mathamaga*, Glen Cowie, 8 December 1998.

particular, appreciated the organisation.[95] 'We don't have to be afraid of naughty children coming to demand our pensions any more.' In a country with the highest rape statistics in the world, women had an extra reason to like the organisation: 'At least we can move around freely in the evenings again.' In addition, 'people should go on their knees and pray that God gives Magolego some extra miles' because the *Mapogo* leader restored confidence in property ownership. 'We now dare to buy cars and big houses without being scared of our children.' By restoring faith in ownership and parental and chiefly power, *Mapogo* had, its supporters felt, 'healed the land'.

It comes as no surprise that much of the 'youth' had a strong sense of being targeted by *Mapogo*: 'They don't want the youth to be alive.' The complaints against the organisation centred on the unconstitutionality of the public beatings, but also on the randomness of the procedures. 'They start by beating suspects without even having proof and might only realise their mistakes afterwards.' In addition, accusations abounded of *Mapogo* members using the organisation for personal gain: 'they are criminals themselves.' It is true that an institution like *Mapogo* might arise and derive its success from common socio-economic concerns all over Sekhukhune, but that part of its strength – as is the case with the civics – lay in its ability to take on a variety of local forms. As such, it merely functioned as an organising principle for long-standing local social tensions which could be articulated in a variety of ways. In these struggles, *Mapogo* members were sometimes known to steal, throw foes into a crocodile-infested river, tie them behind cars or apply electric shocks to their genitals.[96]

The furious government reaction that might have been expected in the face of such provocation was absent. The Northern Province Department of Justice was acutely aware of the problems of credibility suffered by the police, and of the void filled by *Mapogo*. While denouncing its methods, the department tried to stay on speaking terms with the organisation, and to sign agreements about its conduct.[97] The case filed against the *Mapogo* members involved in the initial murder of two businessmen in 1996 was to drag on for years. In addition, there were many reports of policemen and other government agents tacitly approving of, or even explicitly joining, *Mapogo*. The most severe clamp-down occurred after *Mapogo*'s president, Magolego, who in 1994 had campaigned for the NP, joined

[95] Of 607 respondents 90% knew *Mapogo*. Asked whether they thought the organisation was doing a good job, 549 answered as follows:

	Like *Mapogo*	Don't like
General	55%	45%
Under 20	32%	68%
20-30	48%	52%
30-40	46%	54%
40-50	59%	41%
50-60	77%	23%
60 +	75%	25%
Men	49%	51%
Women	62%	38%

[96] Soggot and Wa ka Ngobeni. 'We Must Work on Their Buttocks'; reports, Department of Safety and Security: correspondence, ANC branch Eenzaam.

[97] This is in contrast to Mpumalanga 'Provinces Adopt Conflicting Stances on Mapogo Vigilantes.'. Cf. press statements 1996–9, Department of Safety and Security.

the UDM: police cars swarmed into Sekhukhune to arrest the leader and 35 senior *Mapogo* members.[98] They were, however, released soon afterwards.

The churches

The hesitance of the Northern Province politicians, many of them Bapedi, to clamp down too hard on the popular organisation seemed to show sound judgement of local political dynamics. As Northern Province premier Ngoako Ramathlodi said when we were discussing politics, religion and tradition in his province; 'It is a tapestry, a mat with many different strands interwoven.'[99] As we spoke we looked out over a million people dressed in yellow/green, khaki and bright blue: it was the Easter congregation of yet another important actor in the Sekhukhune institutional landscape – the Zionist Christian Church.

It is impossible to look at local law, governance and power without examining the crucial role of religion. A staggering 93 per cent of the Sekhukhune population interviewed claimed to be church members, and religion permeated every aspect of daily life and the meaning given to it. In the next chapter we shall look at the – ambiguous – role of religion in legitimating traditional authority. But a description of the institutional landscape is not complete without emphasising the role of churches, as institutions, in local law and governance and in the alliances formed between churches and traditional leaders.

On an average afternoon in Sekhukhune, one could see members of a multitude of denominations on their way to worship: the Apostolics (19 per cent of all the people interviewed); the classic mission churches such as the Dutch Reformed, known as NG (Nederlands Gereformeerd) (10 per cent), Roman Catholic (9 per cent) and Anglican (7 per cent); and the fast-growing Born-Again (8 per cent) and Pentecostal (5 per cent) churches. But by far the largest was the Zionist Christian Church (30 per cent), whose members characteristically wear a green badge with a dove or a star, depending on which of its two branches they follow. This church shot to popularity because of its ability to combine classic 'Christian' and 'Africanist' discourses, and to include in its theology and practice ancestors, traditional healers, witchcraft beliefs and traditional leaders.[100] It is for this reason that I shall, for now, concentrate on what is commonly known as the ZCC.

The ZCC's main message is obedience, not only to God but also to the laws of man. This approach resulted in much criticism in the 1980s when Bishop Barnabas Lekganyane told his followers to obey 'the laws of the headmen, the homeland governments and the government of the RSA'.[101] After democ-

[98] B. Lubisi and S. Makgotho. 'Mapogo Plunged into Crisis.' *City Press*, 16 April 1999. They were released on bail and tension lessened after it turned out that Magolego had not been a candidate for the provincial parliament.

[99] Interview, Ngoako Ramathlodi, Northern Province premier, Moria, 4 April 1999.

[100] The ZCC increased from an estimated 200,000 members in 1970 to over a million in 1980 and a self-estimated 3 million at present. Cf. Beinart (1994). The 1 million people from all over Southern Africa who attend the annual Easter celebration are indicative of the ZCC's large support. On its theology, see: Naude (1995); Miriam Motlala, 'The Relative Influence of Participation in Zionist Church Services on the Emotional State of Participants,' in *Afro-Christian Religion and Healing in Southern Africa*, ed. G.C. Oosthuizen, Lewiston, NY: Edwin Mellen Press, 1989; Allan H. Anderson, 'The Lekganyanes and Prophecy in the Zion Christian Church,' *Journal of Religion in Africa* 29, no. 3 (1999): 285–312.

[101] Martin Murray, *South Africa: Time of Agony, Time of Destiny*. London: Verso, 1987, p. 291, quoted in Van Kessel (2000:94).

ratisation, the bishop continued, whenever possible, to stress that 'South Africa does not need problems ... it is the responsibility of all Christians to work tirelessly in the eradication of lawlessness in our communities... God expects us to be industrious and practical in our faith.'[102] Part of this message of obedience is also to see things as they are by nature, and to 'respect the categories in society'.[103]

One such category is, obviously, traditional leadership. The many *magoši* who are ZCC members receive a respectful welcome at the annual Easter celebrations, where they are housed separately and sit inside the church and dine with the bishop, while the uniformed masses wait outside. Many services are held at *mešate*, and through these meetings the ZCC often comes to support one candidate in a succession dispute. The church not only supports traditional authority but also seeks to redefine it. As the bishop once said at a prayer meeting:

> To chiefs and tribes, the Lord giveth each of you special talents. Chiefs are assigned special duties of ruling and serving their tribes to the maximum effectiveness. This is the NATURE of chiefs. No chief can achieve this mammoth task of a job unless he has love for his tribe... As a Church we are here this afternoon to pray for chiefs to concentrate on their traditional and assigned duties of effectively serving their tribes and that is the only way to maintain their nature.[104]

There was thus often an organic alliance between the churches and traditional leaders, played out differently in different settings, within the Sekhukhune institutional landscape. The same can be said for the next and last actor we shall look at: organisations of business and migrants.

Business and migrant organisations

In post-apartheid Sekhukhune, most household income was earned by migrant workers, with government pensions as a second important source of earnings.[105] One-third of the male population was absent, working in the mines or otherwise in *makgoweng*, the place of the whites.[106] There was, however, also a local élite that managed to make a living out of the taxi industry, general dealing, bottle shops, petrol stations and other businesses, in spite of the fact that apartheid legislation had long hampered economic activity and forced the Sekhukhune population to spend its money in the bordering white villages – essentially conglomerations of shops around a Dutch Reformed or NG church – and despite there still being plenty of structural constraints on local investments.[107] Because

[102] Barnabas Lekganyane, 'Sermon Delivered by His Grace the Right Reverend Bishop B E Lekganyane at the Royal Kraal of King Makhosokhe II before a Congregation of the ZCC on 7.3.1999', *The Z.C.C. Messenger* 43, Easter 1999 (1999): p. 12. Cf. sermon on 22 November 1998 at Ga-Moloi.

[103] Interview Mra Khutoane, ZCC general secretary, Moria, 2 April 1999.

[104] B.E. Lekganyane, 'A Sermon in Giyanie, June 1993, at a Prayer Meeting of Chief P.P. Hlungwane at Malamulele,' in *Wisdom*. Pretoria: Olyfberg publishers, 1993, p. 42.

[105] Baber. 'Current Livelihoods in Semi-Arid Rural Areas of South Africa', p. 297 states that in Mamone, which still has a reasonable agricultural base and job opportunities in Jane Furse, 37% of the income derives from migrant remittances and 15% from pensions. In a more impoverished area like Rantlekane these figures are 66% and 16%.

[106] Development Bank of South Africa, *Statistical Macroeconomic Review Northern Province*, p. 70. These are 1991 figures. Due to the slump in the South African economy and retrenchments throughout the 1990s, male absenteeism was probably reduced in the years after the publication of this report.

[107] The insecurity of land tenure, to which we shall turn in the next section, is the most important constraint. Another example quoted to me by a shopkeeper is the fact that insurance companies refuse to insure assets of shops in the former homelands (!).

of their influential role in the Sekhukhune economy, the migrants, businessmen and institutions in which they are organised also had a large impact on local power relations.

Let us start with the migrants. It is precisely because they are absent most of the year, incorporated into the urban economy, that these men (as the majority are) have an interest in maintaining and pursuing a particular form of local law and governance, based on *setšo* (tradition), chiefly authority and male dominance, in their home areas. The urban experience frequently leads to the reformulation and strengthening of 'ethnic' identity and the need to emphasise and actively contribute to the construction of difference between the urban and the rural (James, 1999). Underlining 'ethnic' difference, often by means of all sorts of invented traditions, is a way of maintaining oneself in the insecure and at times threatening urban setting. Simultaneously, traditional authority structures are considered particularly well equipped to keep an eye on spouse(s) and property during the long periods that the migrants are away. And although the relation between migrant organisations and traditional authority is complex and has changed over time, many meetings held by Sekhukhune migrant organisations in town were dedicated to traditional politics, and *go lotša* (greeting the chief with money or a present) was often still part of the ritual of home-coming.[108] Conversely, important local political issues were saved for discussion until times such as Christmas, when migrants came home and could participate in meetings.

The role that the migrants played in the coronation of Billy Sekwati Mampuru is instructive. The Commission on Kingship, which organised and found funding for the lavish coronation, consisted largely of migrants, typically dressed in yellow T-shirts with Billy's picture. At a meeting in Witbank, one of the drab mining areas, six months after the coronation, the Commission organised a report-back (feedback meeting) for the Bapedi migrants' organisations based in all the important mining cities.[109] 'People of the porcupine,' the chairman opened the meeting in the company boardroom, straightening his jacket as if he were addressing the *kgôrô.* He proceeded with a financial report on the coronation, showing that – while the mining company had paid for the lavish dinner – the migrants had borne the costs of the leopard pelt, the limousine and much of the other infrastructure. The meeting then proceeded to discuss the lack of agricultural fields in Mamone, the rules that needed to be drawn up for the young king, and the idea of setting up an advisory committee for him: 'This is our village, we need to govern from here.' Also, high on the agenda was the application to the Department of Traditional Affairs to have Billy Sekwati recognised as a paramount chief: 'There is a lot of money in that, and it could lead to a lot of jobs.'

Like the migrants, businessmen formed an important force in Sekhukhune. Most of them were organised in *Mapogo*, with all its necessary links to traditional authority, for businessmen depended on the support of the tribal offices for business sites. Many other forms of organised business also fostered such links. Take the taxis. Although they were known as a 'wild-west industry' because of the bloody wars fought over the lucrative right to transport migrants to the cities, the taxi businesses cherished their relations with the traditional leaders: they needed local patronage, customers from the traditional authority areas and land

[108] On the evolving relations between migrants and chiefs see Delius (1990). Migrant organisations often take the form of stockvels (rotating credit associations) such as burial groups.

[109] Meeting, Witbank Douglas Colliery, 20 July 1999.

on tribal grounds for the taxi-ranks. This was why the taxi industry, at a time when the Mamone *kgôrô* had to go to court, offered to take them there free of charge.

The institutional map thus drawn bears little resemblance to what might have been expected when studying official texts and policy documents. In contrast to the assumption disseminated nationally, of traditional leaders as the sole form of local government, landmarks in local rule proved to include not only chiefs and councillors, but also civic organisations, churches, fiercely independent government agencies, a vigilante organisation and people not even living in the area. Drawing it up took me through the same process as when I was trying to compare the large-scale topographical map I had bought in Pretoria with the Sekhukhune I knew (cf. Scott, 1998). Large settlements I drove past every day were not mentioned at all, others seemed misplaced or misnamed: the official map showed a large disjuncture with local reality. The same was true of the institutional map. It was not just that the institutions one would expect to find looked different locally, or had somehow adapted to local circumstances. The actual power landscape, when studied from 'below', was formatted in a vitally different way and on different premises from what one would expect from a national perspective. Of course, there are complex interlinkages between the national and the local, to which we shall turn in subsequent chapters. But for now our concern is with understanding local rule.

One final remark needs to be made. Having sketched the most important local institutional landmarks and the way in which they have their foundations in Sekhukhune's socio-economic situation, it is important to re-emphasise the combination of fixedness and fluidity that characterises Sekhukhune legal and political life. While institutions like the churches, *Mapogo* and the civics might seem fixed and representative of a certain worldview and categorisation in society, part of their strength lies in their ability to take on a variety of different shapes locally. Actors also switched between institutions with remarkable ease. Mr Mafoko from Ga-Maphopha is an example: the soft-spoken ZCC member was the chairman of the local *Mapogo* branch, after having headed the civics for a few years. In addition, he had lodged a land claim through which he also – as a remote member of the royal house – hoped to claim chieftaincy over the area concerned.[110]

This puts the importance of institutions into perspective. A mere mapping of the institutional landscape cannot help us to fully understand what law and governance are about in Sekhukhune and how traditional authority fits in. For that, we need to turn to the next building block in our argument: what is at stake.

5. Asserting control

Now that we have mapped out the playing field and the main players, it is time to look at the basic rules of the game and the prizes to be won. Up to now, I have been talking generally about the struggle for local power, understanding

[110] Meeting Mapogo, Ngwaabe, 30 September 1999.

power as an essentially relational phenomenon that concerns the ability to ensure compliance against resistance (Foucault, 1993, 1994). It is about regulating and controlling local activity, and I would hold that the struggle for power in Sekhukhune takes the form of attempts to assert control in four different, if overlapping, spheres: over *resources*, over *boundaries*, over *people* and control over *meaning*. It is to attain such control that 'seemingly anomalous' alliances are made between chiefs and councillors, churches, civics and others and that rules are invented and renegotiated to legitimate their claims (Ritchken, 1990:393).

Control over resources

Of the various resources at stake in local power struggles, land is by far the most important. Control over land is vitally linked to authority, and the institution governing land allocation also controls people, boundaries and meaning.

The insecurity over land tenure can be illustrated by the case of Mr Moela, who was tried under the Mamone thorn-tree for illegal land occupation some time after Billy's coronation.[111] The trembling old man told the Mamone villagers how he had arrived one day from the Leolo mountains and asked the first person he met where to apply for a plot of land. Unfortunately for him, he was sent to one of the contenders for chieftainship, who scribbled a Permission to Occupy on a piece of paper and after receiving R60 directed him to a piece of land. The Mamone *kgôrô*, which heard such cases practically every week, reacted angrily and sentenced Mr Moela to pay *bonthule* (a stranger's fee) of R400 as well as a contribution to Billy's house and coronation.

Rules concerning land allocation were permanently debated, and shaped within local power relations (Goheen, 1992). Not only did various institutions and authorities fight over the right to allocate land; but the register of potentially applicable rules also varied depending on who was applying for the plot of land, on its formal legal status, its geographical location and the purpose for which it was acquired. Let us take the residential sites as an example.

Of all the authorities involved in what could be called the scramble for the scarce local land, the traditional leaders are the best placed. Not only did they often still hold the right to allocate land in the post-apartheid era, but 76 per cent of the Sekhukhune people also felt that the chief, as *mong-wa-naga (*owner of the land), was the right person to do so.[112] This feeling was not, however, unconditional, but linked to the idea that traditional leaders hold land on behalf of the people, combined with the fact that the majority of people would have liked to have a 'title deed' for the land on which they resided.[113] In addition, demarcation and allocation of land were often a communal effort, with the tribal office, the headmen, the agricultural affairs official and the magistrate all

[111] Kgoro, Mamone, 14 July 1999.

[112] The legal position of land tenure in traditional authority areas was, as stated earlier, insecure. Legislation like the *Land Regulations Proclamation*, based on the *Black Authorities Act* 68/1951, continued to be applied in spite of the existence of the *Abolition of Racially Based Land Measures Act* 108/1991. Cf. Adams et al. (1999a), a law which according to Meer (1997:19) should have abolished them. On the respondents: N = 592 asked 'who, in your opinion, should allocate land?': 74% said *kgoši*, 7% democratically elected council, 11% government, 4% TLCs, 2% don't know, 2% other. These findings contrast sharply with Levin (1994), who finds 85% of the people in the Eastern Transvaal Central Lowveld against chiefs allocating land.

[113] 52% of the people interviewed wanted a title deed, 37% were not interested.

involved. As noted earlier, the authority to give out land was contested by the civics, and was at the centre of the argument between traditional leaders and TLCs. In 1999, for instance, a Northern Province government circular suddenly surfaced stating that TLCs, which were suffering from undercapacity, should allocate residential sites, but this was not followed at all in Sekhukhune[114] in contrast to other areas in the province, where the TLCs were stronger and the chiefs weaker, and traditional leaders could be found transferring land to the TLCs.[115]

Whether a Sekhukhune resident has access to land and on what conditions also depends on who he or she is. Generally, men have more chances of being allocated a plot of land than women, married men are favoured over single candidates, local people have more chance and receive land under better conditions than strangers, and any connections with the traditional authority are helpful.[116] This patriarchal system was enforced by official law: the forms for the PTOs, the Permissions to Occupy given out by the tribal office, not only required the recommendation of the headman, the chief, the local agricultural officer and the sectional head of development, but also needed to know how many wives the applicant had and whether he had paid his tribal levies. As the Mamone Tribal Clerk explained: 'A man can't apply for a site if he's not married. What will he do at night? Here, in Mamone, local people pay R60 for a site, and strangers pay R400 extra.'[117] That a woman would be allocated a site in the village of Mamone was unthinkable.

A few kilometres down the road, however, completely different rules seemed to apply. The densely populated 'township'-like area still fell under the Mamone traditional authority, and people still had to apply for a PTO. Yet women, unmarried men and strangers without letters from their chiefs could apply for such permission, provided they were prepared to pay whatever the headman asked. Such a 'geographical aspect' to authority was frequently found in Sekhukhune. Rules in the 'traditional' villages differed from those in the 'new stands', areas demarcated with lines (*malaeneng*) often once meant as betterment villages but now considered places where 'the youth live', and the grip of the chiefs was slightly less than in areas closer to the *mešate*, royal palaces.[118] Part of the explanation for this geographical variance – although not all of it – lies in the differences in official legal status. As explained earlier, an area like Mamone consists of a patchwork of trust land, tribal land and land proclaimed as a 'location', the township. On the trust land, which the South African Native Trust and Land Act No. 18. of 1936 made reserve land to be held in trust by the government, the government has always had a larger say than on the tribal land actually bought by communities.

If there was uncertainty about who got to decide what concerning residential sites, grazing land and business sites, the situation was even worse when it came

[114] Interview, P. Mphahlele, Agricultural Extension Official, Mokwete, 24 July 1999.

[115] Meeting, Executive Council, Northern Province Local Government Association, Pietersburg, 19 March 1998.

[116] Cf. Baber, 'Current Livelihoods in Semi-Arid Rural Areas of South Africa', p. 285; Ngqaleni, Malijeng, and Moraka Makhura. 'An Analysis of Women's Status in Agricultural Development in the Northern Province,' in Lipton et al., 1996; Oomen (1999c).

[117] Stephen Mampuru, tribal clerk, Mamone, 4 June 1999.

[118] Cf. Interview, *Kgosi* Madinoge, Ga Maila, 10 December 1999; Interview, Sophani Matsomane, ANC office Ga-Moloi, 14 June 1999.

to land destined for large-scale development projects. In order to start housing projects and build hospitals, taxi-ranks and shopping centres, the departments and developers concerned often demanded a secure title to the land. Proclaiming land as a township, and thus for sale by means of a 'tribal resolution', was a way to create such a title. The law required that this be done according to the 'custom and usage of the community', entailing a meeting with the majority of the rights holders, but this often boiled down to deals sealed between the *mošate* or the Tribal Council and the TLC.[119] How much money was involved, and where it went would remain unclear.[120] In other cases, parties could not reach agreement and the project simply did not go through.

Land is only one resource inextricably linked to authority, bound up with power struggles and allocated according to shifting rules that are essentially an outcome of these struggles. Similar processes could be seen with regard to access to minerals, water, firewood, development projects and all other 'resources' available in the impoverished area. Taxes are an example. Nearly every traditional authority imposed some form of tribal levy on its 'subjects'. Although the days when people were prepared, and could be forced, to pay a fixed yearly amount had ended with apartheid, most traditional authorities imposed levies for specific projects: a school or a clinic but also a new house or car for the chief. In addition, traditional leaders often received more 'traditional' tribute as *sebego* (lit: beer, but also tribute in general) and *lehlakori* (special cut of beef) and demanded financial compensation from those women unable to carry out their 'traditional duties' such as hoeing and collecting thatch for the chief.

Control over boundaries

As we have seen when discussing the national debate, the traditional authorities project could be understood essentially as an ongoing attempt to single out a sovereign sphere that could be governed as a separate nation, to transform *setšaba* (community) into *setšaba* (nation) (cf. Gellner, 1983:24). Far from proceeding from a preconceived plan, it was about the processes of demarcation and inclusion and exclusion that formed part of the day-to-day interactions between the local actors. But the importance of drawing boundaries and defending a sphere of 'traditional rule' became clear when the demarcation of municipal boundaries through traditional authority areas led to violent clashes all over South Africa.[121]

In Sekhukhune, the ubiquitous *trekpas* was the most symbolic example of this process of drawing boundaries and determining the conditions of access and the rules applicable in the territory demarcated. Essentially a residue of apartheid, this pass was remarkably resilient. A typical example of such a letter would read:

> From Mabhedla Royal Kraal to whom it may concern on 6/7/97. Mr X is allowed to stay anywhere he wants. He is a man who respects the law, anything that the

[119] *Interim Protection of Informal Land Rights Act 31/1996*, s 2.

[120] In Mamone this occurred with two housing projects, a shopping mall, a hospital and a clinic. In surrounding chieftaincies similar processes could be witnessed.

[121] Cf. 'Demarcation Issue a Sticking Point, Say Traditional Leaders.' http://www.bday.co.za/bday/content/direct/0,3523,634144-6078-0,00.html: *Business Day* online, 2000; 'Government to Review Local Boundaries.' http://www.bday.co.za/bday/content/direct/0,3523,550986-6078-0,00.html: *Business Day* online, 2000; 'Municipal Demarcation Expected to Be Completed by Month-End.' http://www.bday.co.za/bday/content/direct/0,3523,645400-6078-0,00.html: *Business Day* online, 2000.

> community agrees with as long as it means progress. Mr X respects tradition (culture) and customary law. He was under the leadership of AM Nkosi from Hoepakranz. We'll be glad if he'll be accepted anywhere he wishes to stay.[122]

These passports and testimonials were often needed to obtain a plot of land and had to be produced in traditional court sessions. Conversely, they could also stand for exclusion. The Afrikaans expression 'giving someone a *trekpas*' had become synonymous with sending people away, for instance for not respecting traditional authority or because of witchcraft accusations.

'Let's give him a trekpas,' was an expression frequently heard in Mamone in the months after Billy's coronation. The presence of a new chief led to fierce attempts to restore chiefly power and to mark out the boundaries of traditional authority. One of those given a *trekpas* was a follower of one of Billy's contenders who still allocated plots. The man was brutally dragged from his home, beaten up, tied to a thorn-tree and smeared with Vaseline to make him extra attractive to red ants. The ensuing court case resulted in a stand-off between the magistrate and Billy's supporters, who filled the courtroom, waving branches, singing traditional anthems and complaining about the audacity the man had shown in running to the police. After a debate on the subject in the *kgôrô*, I witnessed the scene recounted in the Introduction which well illustrates how important control over boundaries is. One old man, shaking his head, drew a circle on his hand and said: 'Mamone is not like this, a separate nation where the laws of the land don't apply.' His friend did not agree: 'Of course we are, why else should we have a chief?' (cf. Oomen, 2000a:9).

Control over people

The continued existence and use of *trekpasses* shows the importance of control not only over boundaries in the local power struggle but also over people. Although traditional leaders could no longer control the 'influx of blacks to the urban areas' – one of their main power bases under apartheid – they would continue to control people in many different ways. Let us look briefly at two of them: dispute resolution processes and labour extraction.

A few family members in a homestead, hundreds of men seated in a circle under a thorn-tree, the tribal councillors in the Gothic office: disputes in Sekhukhune were resolved in a variety of fora. The staple of these meetings was family fights, land disputes, small theft, witchcraft accusations and other forms of insult. In a later chapter, we shall look extensively at the contents of customary law and the debates surrounding it. For now, we only need to emphasise how chiefly power was reinforced in these spheres. The subjects of traditional authorities often had little choice but to take their problems to the *kgôrô* (traditional court); not only was the magistrate far away, but 'if we shoot there he will send us straight back to the chief'.[123] The rule enforced in these meetings – if contested – was patriarchal, with a strong emphasis on respect for chieftaincy. And although only a few traditional authorities with a private prison were left in Sekhukhune, the administration of corporal punishment was a matter of routine.[124]

[122] Administration Mabhedla Royal Kraal, Hoepakranz, translated from Sepedi. The word *culture* was written in English.

[123] Dozens of respondents, confirmed by M.Z. Ramotwala, magistrate, Nebo, 17 June 1999.

[124] Magistrate M.Z. Ramotwala (Nebo, 17 June 1999) stated that many traditional leaders still have prisons, I know of only two.

Another important way in which traditional leaders controlled people was through the extraction of labour. As with customary law, women are the most important subjects to get to 'hold the knife on the sharp edge'.[125] They were often still expected to hoe for the chief, collect thatch for his house, brew beer for festivities or perform other 'customary' functions. If they were not able to perform these duties, they had to pay money as compensation. 'This is a thing from before the chiefs got paid, but we are still doing it and no-one is paying us,' one Mamone villager complained.[126]

Control over meaning

'Without *bogoši* we were like leaves flying in the wind; now we are back in tune, proclaimed a Mamone royal during Billy's coronation. The most important form of control exerted by traditional leaders might well derive from their role in influencing how people define themselves and make sense of everyday events. In Sekhukhune, both religion and ritual are linked to traditional authority in manifold ways. Part of the political project of traditional leaders was to emphasise and strengthen these links, while their foes sought to downplay them.

The relationship between traditional leaders and religion is ambiguous, as we shall see when considering sources of legitimisation. On the one hand Christianity was associated with 'softness' and a break with 'tradition'. Leaders who belong to churches critical of initiation schools, like the Born-Again Christians, the dovish wing of the ZCC and the NG Church, were often accused of being too cowardly and faint-hearted to be strong leaders.[127] On the other hand, traditional leaders emphasised their role as God's representatives on earth. Billy's councillors would, for instance, often introduce him by quoting from Proverbs 8:15: 'By me kings reign and rulers make laws that are just. By me princes govern and all nobles who rule on earth.'

Many important life-cycle rituals were linked to traditional authority, often in conjunction with *dingaka*, the traditional healers: the *magoši* spoke at funerals, received tribute at weddings and conducted rain-making ceremonies. But perhaps the most important ritual during which traditional authorities got to exert and expand control was the *koma*, initiation school. The majority of Sekhukhune boys and girls visited these schools, and organising them was considered one of the most important chiefly functions.[128] In the past, the young people used to set out for the mountains for their initiation in either the cold winter months or during the December holidays, and only in those years when a chief's son had reached the right age – between 12 and 18: age groups remained an important building block in social and political organisation (Mönnig, 1967:107-28; Delius, 1996:29-30; Harries, 1929:63-76). However, as part of a broader process that could be called the 'commodification of tradition', the *koma* became a lucrative

[125] Transvaal Rural Action Committee, *The Rural Women's Movement: Holding the Knife on the Sharp Edge*.

[126] Meeting, Commission on the Tribal Constitution, Mamone, 11 July 1999.

[127] Interview, Pauline and George Nkosi, Hoepakranz, 1 February 1999.

[128] Of the people we spoke to (N= 579) 67% had gone to initiation school. Out of ten possible chiefly functions, 4% found it the most important function, 20% the second most important, and 42% the third (after dispute resolution and land allocation). The role of traditional leaders in organising *koma* is reinforced by the *Northern Province Circumcision Act*. 6/1996, which gives them – together with the premier – the sole right to issue permits for initiation schools.

business and many traditional leaders insisted on organising one every year.[129] The purpose remained the same: apart from circumcision for boys and, in some cases and completely neglected by politicians, clitoridectomy for girls, the initiation period taught youngsters 'respect for parents, respect for authority, protocol'.[130]

6. Conclusion

The exuberant festivities surrounding the coronation of a senior Sekhukhune traditional leader, Billy Sekwati Mampuru III, formed our point of departure for a *tour d'horizon* of the power traditional leaders wield in this part of the Northern Province. There are two ways of looking at the lavish enthronement. On the one hand, it was what the genealogy at the back of the glossy programme made it out to be: merely another episode in an ongoing saga of palace politics, in the struggle over control of *Bopedi.* The post-apartheid era might have brought different foes and allies, but the stakes were essentially the same. On the other hand, the coronation was extraordinary in that it seemed to symbolise not only business as usual, but also a return to the roots, the restoration of an old order. If anything, the advent of the democratic era in Sekhukhune seems to have led to a retraditionalisation.

How did this happen, and why? This chapter has laid part of the foundation for an explanation. It has pointed, first, to the agility of traditional leaders in playing different registers, that of palace politics, bureaucracy and party politics. The coronation ceremony, where leopard pelts and praise-songs alternated with sjamboks and army vehicles, stamps and official rhetoric and overtly political petitions, showed how these spheres might be analytically distinguished but are all knotted together in day-to-day politics. The second part of an explanation is the alliances sealed with other local actors, making up a web of power in the local institutional landscape. Traditional leaders formed a hegemonic block, in various different ways in various localities, in conjunction with government officials, *Mapogo* and other vigilante organisations, churches and sometimes even the civics, and thus strengthened their position (Gramsci, 1971).

These alliances took on their particular salience because they were able to tap into a deep desire on the part of various powerful factions in society to restore local rule after the turmoil of the 1980s. Democracy had been announced in Sekhukhune in the form of young boys in T-shirts, toyi-toying through the villages chanting slogans, setting fire to *mešate* and generally wresting power from their parents. The chiefs, businesses, churches and elders in general

[129] People pay between R200 and 1500 for a few weeks in initiation school, and the prices for 'non-villagers' are much higher than for local children.

[130] Girls are much more hesitant to speak of initiations, as those who do so are automatically labelled 'witches', with all the consequences this may have (various respondents). The abundant literature on the subject also only deals with men (see above). However, nurses at Jane Furse hospital told me how they admit girls suffering from failed clitoridectomies every year. Cf. Jane Barrett, *Vukani Makhosikazi: South African Women Speak.* London: Catholic Institute for International Relations, 1985, p. 99. The quotation is from the discussion of the Northern Province Circumcision Act in the legislature, where, again, there was no attention whatsoever for this aspect of initiation and the discussion focused on chiefly power and the danger of boys being infected by AIDS. Legislature of the Northern Province. 'Hansard Verbatim Report.'

considered it in their interest to 'go back to the roots', to restore a patriarchal, hierarchical and essentially ascriptive form of local rule. In addition, the institution could draw on its essential strength: the ability to take on different roles, to present itself as the epitome of civil society, on the one hand, and as a separate nation, a circumscribed polity, on the other.

While this is the broad pattern, woven through every sjambok session of *Mapogo*, every meeting under the Mamone thorn-tree and every clash between chiefs and TLC councillors, attention also has to be drawn to local variance. The overall process of restoring rule was played out differently in various Sekhukhune localities, depending on local agency and historical trajectories. Similarly, while the need to 'restore rule' was voiced all over Sekhukhune, by chiefs, businessmen and church leaders alike, the actual contents of this rule were subject to ongoing debate, and determined within local power relations.

This fluidity of local rule and the constant debate and negotiations surrounding it can be understood by means of the notion of an institutional landscape. The plurality of institutions created fundamental insecurity over not only the substantive contents of rules but also procedural questions as who sets and administers them. Here, it should be noted that many actors had an interest in this basic insecurity. The 'political instrumentalisation of disorder', in which political actors seek to maximise their returns on the state of confusion, uncertainty and even chaos described for other African polities, kept cropping up in Sekhukhune politics (Chabal and Daloz, 1999: xviii, 155) For example, the agricultural extension officer who, after he had explained the anarchical situation pertaining to land allocation, sighed resignedly and concluded optimistically: 'When there is a fight at the top, we at the roots can enrich ourselves.'[131] And the Mamone *bakgomana* who were trying to fix land rules but ended up observing cynically that: 'the *mošate* does not want to be a part of this, because they benefit from this confusion'.[182]

Part of the process of retraditionalisation in Sekhukhune – the part symbolised by Billy Sekwati's opulent enthronement and the long line of dignitaries present – can be understood through the model presented above, which considers traditional leaders as important actors in a wider institutional landscape, who tried to regain and strengthen their control over resources, people, boundaries and meaning through alliances with other actors, and who could tap into a general desire to restore order in the process. Nevertheless, another part – the roaring masses and those villagers who are conspicuously absent – requires further scrutiny. How do people perceive traditional leadership? How do traditional leaders legitimate their claims? To what extent is their power based on popular support and to what extent is it founded on state recognition? It is these types of questions that we need to answer in order to arrive at an understanding of the interplay between local and national dynamics in determining the power of traditional leaders in contemporary South Africa. The next chapter is, therefore dedicated to these questions.

[131] Interview, P. Mphahlele, Agricultural Extension official, Mokwete, 24 July 1999.

[132] Meeting, Commission on the Tribal Constitution, Mamone, 11 July 1999.

5. 'Walking in the middle of the road'

People's Perspectives on the Legitimacy of Traditional Leadership

Kgoši ke kgoši ka batho, batho ke batho ka kgoši, ba swanetše go kukišana morwalo o boima wa bophelo bjo – A chief is a chief by the people, a people are a people by the chief. Together they have to carry the heavy load of life (Sotho saying)

1. Chieftaincy and legitimacy

'We don't really have a chief,' says a middle-aged man who lives in a densely populated settlement called Riverside. 'I know of a headman Manala who is supposed to be working on behalf of the traditional leader, but I have never seen him.' Nevertheless, he is enthusiastic about the institution of traditional leadership. 'That thing is really part and parcel of our black culture; it should be retained. Even if some of us originally grew up on farms outside the tribal areas.' Paying the traditional leaders, however, would be overdoing it. 'These people are just like us. They should go out and look for a job. After all, they are not really serving us with anything and just demand tribute from the community.'

A woman of the same age-group from Ga-Molepane says: 'This whole thing should be thrown in the dustbin, or they should just rule those people who still honour them.' After all, 'they are ripping off our parents left and right. Remember that our mothers have to work at the palace while our fathers are taxed. Surprisingly, our parents still love them. Even if the chiefs do nothing for them.' Also, the institution discriminates against women. 'Ha, I would like to see my mother go to the traditional court one day without being represented by my uncle. Or show up there in trousers...'. The court does, however, seem to be a good institution. 'Generally the people adjudicating there are very old and relaxed, and they make wise decisions.' Her main problem is the lack of development. 'No water, no electricity, dirt roads, schools with broken windows. All those people we elected never set foot in our village again afterwards. I'll never vote again.'

'Without traditional leadership, there would be no community,' says a male pensioner from Ga-Masha. 'It is like tea without water.' He feels his chief is doing his job very well. 'Through him our women now have poultry and garden projects, which in turn sustain our families.' The problem, according to him, is that the elected leaders seem to undermine the chiefs. 'The world is upside down today and respect is a thing of the past.' Also, the government should pay all the traditional leaders, not just some. 'They are civil servants and, like any other workers, should be paid.' Although he has never attended a sitting of the traditional court, he likes the idea. 'Everyone gets a free trial and is judged by many people, unlike at the magistrate's court where only the judge and the lawyer communicate.'

A young woman from the same village sees the traditional court differently. 'How do you expect old, uneducated men without any woman present to come up with a fair judgment?' Traditional leadership, she feels, 'should be exhibited in a museum. Today people need mayors and municipalities. I think they are tired of working at the royal palace.' Still, the elected councillors are not much good either: 'They are young and more committed to supporting their families than to delivering services to their communities.' She sums up her dilemma: 'The traditional leaders are not capable, the elected councillors not reliable and the government is far away and doesn't listen to us. So for now let's just keep the traditional leaders.'

How do people feel about their traditional leaders? Why do they feel that way? What does this mean for the legitimacy of the institution? These questions, which often seem to be at the core of academic and policy debates on traditional leadership, are said to be 'grossly underresearched' and undertheorised'.[1] Still, an understanding of the degree to which chiefly power is 'rooted in local societies' should be the first step in any assessment of the present-day role of traditional leaders (Geschiere, 1996:307)

The lack of empirical data on the legitimation of traditional leadership does not mean that nothing has been written on the subject. In the academic literature as well as the policy debate, assumptions abound concerning the extent and nature of popular support for chieftaincy within the present democratic context. These assumptions are often striking in their simplicity, and can be classified into two categories. The first is that people 'continue to owe allegiance to the institution of traditional leadership', which is 'deeply rooted in the social fabric of African communities' and enjoys a cultural legitimacy.[2] The second is equally absolute, and holds that traditional leaders in South Africa have lost all legitimacy because of their involvement in the apartheid government.[3]

The scant evidence available seems to contradict the second assumption but tells us little about the validity of the first. In 1994, for instance, nearly 2000 South Africans from all over the country were asked whether traditional authorities should continue to exist. Almost two-thirds (65 per cent) of the respondents answered affirmatively, but the people were not asked why they felt that way (Pillay and Prinsloo, 1995). Another rare study on the topic looked into attitudes towards traditional leadership in the former homelands and found that 38 per cent of the people saw a ceremonial role for traditional leaders, 24 per cent saw no place for them, 20 per cent were in favour of more power and 16

[1] Gould, 'Resurrecting Makumba: Chiefly Powers and the Local State in Zambia's Third Republic', p. 3; Ray and Van Rouveroy van Nieuwaal (1996:33); Falk Moore (1973:81). An exception is Williams (2001).

[2] The first quotation is from the Department of Constitutional Development. 'A Discussion Document Towards a White Paper on Local Government in South Africa.', the second from Tapscott, 'Institutionalisation of Rural Local Goverment.'

[3] Cf. Jabu Sindane, 'The Future of Traditional Leadership, *Ubuntu* and Nation-Building,' in *Traditional Leadership in Southern Africa*, ed. Konrad Adenauer Stiftung. Johannesburg: Konrad Adenauer Stiftung, 1997; Zuma (1990a).

per cent thought that they had to be accommodated.[4] Again, the research failed to investigate what these opinions mean for the way in which people actually support traditional leadership and what their motivation is for doing so: whether legitimation takes place in terms of culture or on a different basis.

Most local-level research on the subject concentrates on chiefly agency: the way in which chiefs obtain power and manage to retain it. There is a broad range of excellent classic studies on leadership structures in kinship-based societies in which the national state does not play a role.[5] In addition, many recent works do explicitly focus on the co-optation of traditional authority by the nation-state, and describe the way in which traditional leaders have come to draw on different sources of legitimation in their role as 'hinge points' between the state and their community (cf. Hammond-Tooke, 1975; Rathbone, 2000; Van Rouveroy Van Nieuwaal and Van Dijk, 1999; Van Rouveroy Van Nieuwaal and Ray, 1996; Vaughan, 2000). They describe the creative way traditional leaders interweave 'traditionalist' legitimising discourses with reliance on state support and the interplay between 'chieftaincy politics, elite formation, communal identities and the struggle for state power' (Vaughan, 2000:2).

This chapter seeks to add to this ample body of literature by taking up the popular perspective and considering the way in which people see traditional leadership in an institutionally plural landscape. Sekhukhune, as described in the last chapter, can be considered a political arena in which an assortment of authorities compete over, and collaborate in, local rule. Apart from traditional authorities, there are newly elected municipalities, vigilante organisations, government agencies and other authorities involved in creating and maintaining a local normative framework. The way in which the Sekhukhune Bapedi view this framework and the role of traditional leaders in it became clear from the 607 questionnaire interviews on traditional leadership, land, local government and customary law that Patson Phala, Tsepo Phasha and I conducted in Sekhukhune in 1998-9.[6] All the data and quotes in this chapter derive from these interviews,

[4] L. Schlemmer (1996), quoted in Gregory Houston, 'Traditional Leadership and the Restructuring of Rural Local Government,' in *Traditional Leadership in Southern Africa*, ed. Konrad Adenauer Stiftung. Johannesburg: Konrad Adenauer Stiftung, 1997.

[5] Cf. Gluckman (1965); The works by J. Comaroff on the Tswana (Comaroff, 1975); Comaroff and Roberts (1981), which deal explicitly and perceptively with issues of legitimation, also pay surprisingly little attention to the way in which inclusion within the homeland of Boputhatswana and the South African state affected these issues.

[6] N = 607, of which 52% female, 48% male; 5% under 20, 28% 20–30, 22% 30–40, 19% 40–50, 14% 50–60 and 12% 60 +; 20% no education, 21% up to standard 6, 42% standards 6–10, 7% matric, 7% technicon, 3% university; only 27% formally employed. This is more or less representative of the Sekhukhune *adult* population as a whole, cf: CSS (1995): Statistical Release P0317.'; Development Bank of South Africa. 'Statistical Macroeconomic Review Northern Province.' and based on Probability Proportionate to Size samples in the three field-work areas (N=367) and other Sekhukhune traditional authority areas (N=240) (see on PPS-sampling Russel Bernard (1995)). The interviews were conducted by Tsepo Phasha, Patson Phala and myself or by two of us, usually in Sepedi, in personal, face-to-face interviews based on a Sepedi questionnaire with 45 closed and open-ended questions, which would typically take 1-2 hours and have been translated into English by the interviewers. The data in this chapter derive from uni-, bi- and multivariate analysis in SPSS. Unless mentioned otherwise, the data presented are the valid percentages. The quotations in this chapter are, unless mentioned otherwise, drawn from these anonymous interviews, which is why speakers remain nameless. Neither the set-up of the quantitative parts of the research nor the analysis of the data would have been possible without the unwavering assistance of Herman Lelieveldt, for which I am deeply grateful.

of which about half took place in Hoepakranz, Mamone and Ga-Masha, the three areas in which I also did extensive field research, and can thus be embedded in more qualitative information. As stated in the Introduction, I am slightly familiar with some of the areas in which the other interviews were conducted, and will provide additional information here and there, but this is inevitably of a more anecdotal nature.

Before turning to my understanding of the legitimacy of traditional leaders, I need to describe what is meant by the concept. Notoriously difficult to define, legitimacy implies an acceptance of the 'right to rule' of the authority concerned, and a compliance that is more or less voluntary.[7] In order to assess the legitimacy of traditional leaders – the institution and the office-holders – in Sekhukhune, I have operationalised the term as *justified support.* Although support does not completely equate with voluntary compliance, I argue that it does form a reasonable and measurable indication of whether people will comply when told to do so. The notion of justified support has two elements. First, the support itself, which can be material or immaterial – framed in actions or verbal – and can entail anything from tribute paid to adherence expressed. A second element is that of justification. Legitimacy, as Weber has observed, can be seen as the way in which people think of, speak about and justify the way in which institutions and organisational arrangements obtain their authority (Hatt, 1996:123).

This chapter is in three parts. First, an examination of the nature and extent of popular support for traditional leaders: *how* do people support traditional leaders? Second, an attempt to ascertain which variables determine support for traditional leadership: *who* supports chiefs? And ultimately an investigation into how this support is justified and what this means for the strategies traditional leaders use to gain legitimacy: *why* do people support chiefs and what does this mean for local politics? The argument runs as follows. Although immaterial support for traditional leadership is high in Sekhukhune, I shall show that material support is *limited*. It is also *issue-related*: people support traditional leaders on certain topics. In addition, it is not *exclusive*, but exists jointly with support for other authorities. Moreover, it is *dynamic*, and can change over time. Apart from these four general features described in section 2, the nature and the extent of the support also depend on three sets of variables: the characteristics of the *community* (section 3), the features of the *chief* (section 4) and the *personal characteristics* of the people concerned (section 5).

After having thus unpacked the notion of support for individual leaders and shown how this also largely determines how people think about traditional leadership as an institution, I shall look at its justification. Why do people support traditional leadership, and what is the relation between support for chiefs – as individuals – and for chieftaincy – as an institution? There are four realms of justification, related to tradition, the performance of the traditional leadership, the governmental recognition of the institution, and the default need to have some form of governance (section 6). The fact that people justify their support in all these realms, in turn shapes the strategies used by traditional leaders to obtain

[7] The approach is, of course, Weberian: Max Rheinstein (ed.), *Max Weber on Law in Economy and Society*. New York: Simon and Schuster, 1967, pp. 334–7; Weber (1973); Connolly (1984). Legitimate power is referred to as authority. Cf. Hammond-Tooke (1975:48–9); Hamnett (1975:22). Note that in line with common usage, I use authority both in the sense of 'legitimate power' and to indicate the institution surrounding the individual traditional leader.

and legitimate their power. Thus, the parameters and modalities of the ongoing local dialogue between rulers and ruled become visible.

2. How do people support chiefs?

A staggering 80 per cent of the people in Sekhukhune, including three of the four people quoted at the beginning of this chapter, say that they support (*go thêkga*) a traditional leader. The majority of them speak positively about their chief, with 38 per cent saying that he is performing his job well and 22 per cent that he is performing it very well: 'he is the answer to all our problems'; 'the aspirations of the community are achieved because of him'; 'he rules us with patience'.[8] Immaterial support, in other words, is very high. Material support, on the other hand, is more limited. The majority of the people have never paid tribute to the traditional leader in the area where they live, and among those who have there are many who did not do so voluntarily. In the following paragraphs I shall briefly look at the kind of support people give to traditional leaders, and argue that it is not only limited but also related to specific issues, far from exclusive and dynamic in nature.

Within limits

A 20-rand note handed over in the tribal office and the sum duly scribbled into an exercise book; a contribution to the school fees of the chief's son; a calabash full of home-brewed beer or a day spent harvesting maize under the hot Sekhukhune sun: material support for traditional leadership can be shown in a myriad of ways. The majority of the people in Sekhukhune (56 per cent) have never shown any such material support, but the rest have. In order to underscore their relation with the traditional authority they paid tribal levies, or gave presents to the traditional leader, or offered 'traditional tribute' such as *sebego* (home-brewed beer) or *lehlakori* (a special cut of beef), or worked for their traditional leader, or did a combination of all of these.

Demanding tribal levies was one of the prerogatives traditional leaders acquired under apartheid. Taxation is, of course, central to every form of power, and long predated the colonial recognition of traditional leadership (cf. Ellis, 1996:264). Under the homeland system, however, the government-appointed chiefs could ask the Traditional Affairs officials for permission to impose taxes, after which the money would be kept in the 'tribal trust fund' for building schools and other community projects. With the end of apartheid this practice came to a halt in some communities, mostly because the people simply refused to pay and the central authorities would no longer provide the soldiers, tanks, guns and other forms of force to back up chiefly demands. In other communities it continued on a more voluntary basis, for example in Mohlaletse where the tribal clerk still dutifully noted every R20 paid in an exercise book in the tribal office.[9] Also, levies were often imposed for specific purposes, like payment for the bright-red Ford Thunderbird that stands outside *kgoši* Madihlaba's palace in Ga-Moloi;

[8] 25% is neutral, 11% says he is bad and 4% that he is very bad (of the valid percent). N= 606.

[9] R20 is an amount often noted in other communities as well, although there are also reports of people paying as much as R250–300 annually.

the glitzy brick-face villa full of baroque furniture in Mamone or the Jaguar given to K.K. Sekhukhune; or the fees to pay the lawyer representing this traditional leader in a succession dispute.

The number of people who paid any of these levies is small: only 24 per cent of the Sekhukhune population. As with all forms of support, it is difficult to distinguish between 'inner justifications' and 'external means' to ensure support (Weber, 1993:121). Nevertheless, it is clear that many of the people who pay tribal levies do not do so voluntarily. 'Once, I needed the chief's signature for an identity document and was told that my parents had not been paying tribal levies: I had to pay R250,' says a woman from Nchabeleng. Similar extortion can take place when someone wishes to acquire a plot of land, or to obtain administrative support from the Tribal Authority. Even if payment is not forcible, it is often far from spontaneous. Take the reactions in a Mamone village a few months after the coronation of the new traditional leader, when his councillors admonished the villagers who had flocked to see their new chief: 'Don't you attend weddings any more? Anyone visiting a wedding should pay R100 to the *mošate* (the palace). This money goes straight there, you won't get a receipt. The headman will write down the names of those who don't pay, and there will be severe consequences after the wedding.' This caused many of the villagers to leave the meeting, shaking their heads and grumbling that there are limits to what a chief can expect.

Another material way to show support is through the presentation of gifts. Gifts, as the classic anthropological insight goes, form a way to establish and affirm relations and to create debt.[10] Only 11 per cent of the people had ever affirmed their relationship with 'their' traditional leader in this way. In line with this theory, it is especially those people who are physically removed from the traditional leader who feel the need to emphasise their links with him. In Hoepakranz, for instance, a mountain village which will be introduced in more detail, nearly a third of the inhabitants support *kgoši* Kgolane, who lives elsewhere. Because this support does not follow the usual – although not systematic – territorial logic, it has to be reaffirmed continually: instead of the standard 11 per cent, 63 per cent of the villagers gave this 'non-local' chief presents, 67 per cent worked for him, and 52 per cent paid tribal levies. Another group of people who seek to compensate for physical absence by presenting gifts are migrant workers. Many of these men, although not a majority, show their appreciation of the fact that the traditional leader simultaneously symbolises and maintains the 'traditional' local order while they are away. Thus, at Christmas many mine and factory workers visit the royal palace with some cash, a tape recorder, a micro-wave oven, a cell phone, or smaller consumer items.

Sebego and *lehlakori* are gifts that lie more in the realm of 'tradition', and are offered somewhat more often: by 20 per cent of the people. *Sebego* is the thick, delicious beer brewed from sorghum sprouted on cow dung spread out in the sand, brought to the palace by women carefully balancing calabashes or buckets covered with cool leaves on their heads. *Lehlakori* is its solid counterpart: the three prime and four small beef ribs of a beast slaughtered for a special occasion. Offering *sebego* and *lehlakori* can be – but not always – part of marriage and

[10] Marcel Mauss, *The Gift: Forms and Functions of Exchange in Archaic Societies*. New York: Norton, 1925; Piot (1999:64).

funeral rituals. Again, the voluntariness of these gifts can be questioned: they are often presented to thank the traditional authority for a positive decision in a running dispute, or in the hope of obtaining such a decision, or to acquire a stand (a plot of land on which to live). But, as one young man says: 'It is not right. This is a very big piece of meat for which you'll pay R50 if you get it at the butcher's. So why give someone R50 when he'll charge you R250 for a stand afterwards?'

In addition to the power to extract tribute and to present this as a just state of affairs, the ability to recruit free labour is another classic litmus test of authority. Traditional leaders in South Africa's national debate often pride themselves on the fact that the women in their villages still enthusiastically hoe their chief's fields or help with his annual harvest, and that the men also pay tribute to their chief by working for him. Nevertheless, this type of support is limited: only 16 per cent of the women and 10 per cent of the men in our sample ever worked for their traditional leader.

To sum up, material support for traditional leadership is much smaller than immaterial support: 54 per cent of the people had never shown any of the material support listed above and were content not to do so. A chief who does not 'bother' his subjects too much can count on a great deal of appreciation. 'At least we don't have to do personal duties for him like with other traditional leaders' and 'we like him because he doesn't demand anything from us like paying tribal levies'. This is also why 68 per cent of the people feel that the government should pay the traditional leaders. 'We can then stop paying levies. And the *kgoši* might employ some of us to plough his fields.'[11]

The fact that more than half of the people had never shown any form of material support for their traditional leader does not, in theory, mean that they had never had anything whatsoever to do with the chief . They could have asked him to settle a dispute, allocate a plot of land, fill in a form or sign a document, or admit them to the initiation school. However, this type of support is limited as well. Most of the people in Sekhukhune (82 per cent) have never taken a case to the traditional court or even attended one (67 per cent). These figures do not differ much from those for the magistrate's court, in which 9 per cent of the people have been tried and 19 per cent have attended a hearing. The same goes for land: only 17 per cent of the people have acquired the land themselves and nearly half of these did so through the traditional leader. By far the majority live on plots of land that have been in the family for a generation or more. In addition, these chiefly functions are even less of an indication of voluntary support for traditional leadership than the material support expressed, as they are often just as much imposed by 'external means' as they are 'internally justified' – although a combination of both is well possible.

This interfusion of voluntary and externally reinforced support is found in land allocation. Although the legal situation is unclear, with a variety of overlapping legislation, traditional leaders are still massively perceived as *beng-wa-naga*, the leaders of the land. Many of the people believe this to be rightfully so: when asked who *should* allocate land, 75 per cent of the Bapedi name the traditional leader.[12] Then, again, they do not have much choice. Those people who arrive in one of

[11] The Sepedi term for traditional leader and traditional leadership is *kgoši* (plur. *Magoši*). *Bogoši* represents the institution and the values associated with it.

[12] This contrasts sharply with Levin (1994).

the Sekhukhune villages and occupy land without informing the traditional leader, or who go to a weak competitor, run the risk of being fined heavily or beaten up.

Initiation schools are an exception to the limited role traditional leadership plays in the lives of ordinary people – whether it is about showing material support, asking for land or going to the traditional court. Every year, when winter arrives and the school holidays start, long lines of girls can be seen, topless, in the villages, with buckets of water on their heads to take to the mountain camps. Like their male peers, who go through weeks of tribulation, a painful circumcision, and learning praise-songs and 'how to be family heads', they come back to the villages as heroes. Two-thirds of the population have attended initiation school, but this participation, again, is not entirely voluntary.[13] Not only is there considerable moral pressure to do so, especially among peers who tease the uninitiated 'boys' mercilessly, but the winter months are also characterised by boys being physically chased in the streets, to be 'abducted to the mountains'. When a shopkeeper in Ga-Moloi, for instance, refused to take his son to initiation school, the chief filed a case against him, and his house and shop were burnt down under the slogan '*go nyatša kgoši go go tlôga* – if you don't respect the traditional leader you'd better leave'. He ended up going to Lebowakgomo, 'where you don't need a chiefly permission to stay'.[14]

Nevertheless, although going to initiation school might often not be a matter of choice for a Sekhukhune youth, there is what one might call a 'choice of chiefs'. Traditionally, initiation groups would be formed around the chief's sons and daughters. Now that the *koma* has become a lucrative business, and traditional leaders can charge more than R1000 for a few weeks on little food in a self-built mountain hut, many traditional leaders hold one annually and also welcome youngsters from outside their own area. And since a 1996 provincial act required that any headman or ward-head wanting to start his own *koma* had to have permission from the officially recognised traditional leader, this is another source of income – and, of course, external reinforcement of the power of traditional leaders.[15]

On the face of it, the notion of the chief as the physical centre of local life does not seem to match day-to-day reality completely. 'I have never seen this guy,' many respondents say. Of course, this does not preclude an important role in the moral landscape, or that people do know the headman in their village. But for now, we can conclude that even those issues on which it is difficult not to involve chiefs, such as land allocation and dispute resolution, have not arisen in the lives of the majority of the Bapedi interviewed. It is with this in mind that we turn to a second feature of support for traditional leadership: its issue-related character.

Issue-related

Acceptance of chiefly authority is not total but related to certain issues, the three most important of which have already been introduced above: settling disputes, allocating land and presiding over the initiation school.

[13] It could well be that the average rate of initiation in Sekhukhune is higher than 67%, as 128 of my cases are from Hoepakranz, which has a large Swazi population which does not go to initiation school. If these are filtered out, the percentage rate is 80%.

[14] Group interview, Ga-Moloi, 14 June 1999.

[15] *Northern Province Circumcision Act 6/1999.*

'When lions are fighting, they can even be beaten by an injured buffalo' (*ditau tša hloka, seboka di šitwa ke nare e hlotša*) is an oft-quoted saying on what is conceived of as the most important function of traditional leaders. 'How can we stay here alone? Without a leader the community will fight over every petty issue;' 'a chief is like a protector, stopping people from jumping at each other's throats'; and 'no herd of cattle can take care of itself'. Eighty-one per cent of the people consider settling disputes to be the most important function of traditional leaders. A good chief is someone who 'judges wisely without looking at where you come from' and 'builds up the community'. This goes further than the mere settling of disputes: it also concerns the role of the traditional leader as the symbol of the existence of a 'community'. This is why some chiefs are sneered at for 'creating fights and factions' and 'allowing the faces of the royal advisers to be bought'.

But even though people deem settling disputes to be a central function of traditional leaders, certain disputative issues are considered out of bounds. People feel that traditional leaders should concentrate on 'family matters' (71 per cent), 'witchcraft' (68 per cent), 'petty theft' (67 per cent), and 'land issues' (62 per cent). Other subjects are best left to the magistrate, such as large theft and maintenance cases which only 9 per cent and 19 per cent, respectively, of the people would take to the traditional court. These opinions are, of course, as much a result of the legislation limiting the judicial powers of traditional leaders to precisely those subjects that scored so highly in the survey and stipulating that maintenance cases should be tried directly by the magistrate. Even when people were asked 'which cases do you feel the traditional leader *should* try?', most of them echoed the present dispensation, showing the constitutive effects of cultural rights legislation.[16] A notable exception is witchcraft, which does not exist in the South African official mind but is such an important element of Sekhukhune reality that people would prefer to have witches tried by the traditional leaders.[17]

Land allocation is another issue that is felt to fall squarely in the realm of traditional authority, without implying absolute or unchecked powers for the chief. Within national discourse in South Africa, there are many misunderstandings about the nature and practice of land tenure in the tribal authority areas. The dominant image is one of abundant land, handed out for a nominal fee, to which everyone has access and the occupation of which is understood in the 'warmly persuasive' ideology of communalism (Crehan, 1997). None of this even remotely describes the Sekhukhune reality. Although there are some wide stretches of green and hilly land, most of the area is arid and dusty and unable to provide subsistence for its population. The extreme pressure on this land has forced prices up, especially in fast-developing areas where the new era has brought the much-sought-after electricity and tap-water.

The spoils to be had in this market situation have led not only to an upsurge of self-appointed leaders and to even more vehement fighting about chieftaincy

[16] For a discussion of the notion of the social effects of law see J. Griffiths, 'Une législation efficace: une approche comparative,' in *La Création du Droit en Afrique*, ed. Dominique Darbon and Jean Du Bois de Gaudusson. Paris: Karthala, 1997.

[17] *The Witchcraft Supression Act 3/1957*, as amended by the *Justice Laws Rationalisation Act 18/1996*, rejects the belief in witchcraft and makes witchcraft accusations a criminal offence. The *Local Government Municipal Structures Amendment Bill 4223/2000* suggested that 'matters relating to witchcraft' be tried by traditional leaders, but was never enacted.

and headmen's positions than before, but also to a situation in which the highest bidder gets the land. 'In our area locals are now being driven out because foreigners offer much better prices,' an inhabitant of one such settlement told us. In other areas it is not the highest bidder but only married men, preferably those related to the traditional authority, who have access to building and grazing land. The legal title under which this occurs – Permission to Occupy, nicknamed Permission to Lose – offers so little security of tenure that it stops people from investing in building houses. A government minister, for instance, spoke of the enormous problems he had in selling the brick-faced building where he had his medical practice. Nevertheless, in spite of this legal insecurity, people have a strong sense of ownership.

The support for traditional leaders is thus related to specific issues. The organisation of initiation schools, for instance, is considered by 20 per cent to be the second-most important function of the traditional leader and by 40 per cent to be the third-most important function. Other high scorers are the registration of marriages, ensuring community participation, the handing out of state pensions and the foundation of schools. These issues are not considered to be the sole responsibility and prerogative of the traditional leaders, however. Support for traditional leadership, as we shall see below, is far from exclusive.

Not exclusive

'You cannot have two bulls in one kraal' is the well-worn expression used to describe the relations between traditional leaders and elected local governments – on which policy-makers discuss abstract scenarios of 'a bull and a sheep' or 'two sheep' in the kraal. This demand for exclusive rule might be understandable from the point of view of the traditional leaders; it is less so from the popular perspective. People do not mind, to retain the metaphor, having access to a whole barn full of authorities. After all, even though the institutional pluralism described earlier can lead to legal insecurity, it also offers opportunities for forum-shopping and for holding more institutions responsible for bringing development to the poverty-stricken areas. Thus – even if 49 per cent of the people acknowledge the lack of cooperation between chiefs and councillors – there is hardly any correlation between support for a traditional leader and the way in which people rate the TLC (Transitional Local Council). Of the 65 per cent who have heard of the TLC, 32 per cent are negative about its performance, 20 per cent are neutral, and 48 per cent are positive. These figures do not differ significantly for the people who also support a traditional leader: if anything, people who do not support a traditional leader are also negative about the TLC.

When asked who should be responsible for which of the functions legally reserved for the elected local government, a diffuse picture arises. The answers people gave largely arose from the situation in their particular village: in communities where the traditional leader had actively collected money to build a clinic, the chief was considered the authority responsible for clinics. In general, the people we spoke to had no strongly held ideas about which authorities should do what, but just hoped that things would get done in their area. In their opinion, a plurality of institutions increased the chances of development, especially if these institutions cooperated with each other.

All this does not mean that people only look to the official authorities, be it the TLC or the traditional leader, to bring development. In addition to the ubiquitous civics, many villages have a variety of other self-help organisations. The 500 people in the tiny mountain village of Hoepakranz, for instance, were organised in the Baditaba Development Forum, an electricity committee, a water committee, a roads committee, a health committee, the 'Cowherds Against Stocktheft', the Hoepakranz Youth Development Forum, various school building organisations, an active local ANC branch, a village development committee and many other 'structures' – with a varying degree of success. People who are active locally often combine membership of many such organisations and change easily from one role to another. The chief's son in Hoepakranz, for instance, chaired the ANC and some of the development fora. And in Madibong the head of the civics also presided over the Tribal Council, while the chief's former chauffeur became mayor of the TLC. This role-switching also motivates people not to support one authority exclusively, but to lay claims wherever the chances of success are highest.

Table 5.1. Responsibility for carrying out local government functions (%)

	TLC	Traditional leader	Political parties	Civics	Government	Others/ combination
Democratic government	24	30	25	16	2	3
Services	32	23	19	21	1	4
Socio-economic development	39	13	32	9	3	4
Safe environment	14	18	11	53	1	3
Involvement of communities	16	33	23	23	1	4
Pre-schools	33	15	6	41	2	3
Electricity	57	15	10	10	3	5
Clinics	46	21	8	16	3	6
Tourism	40	15	14	23	3	5
Water	49	15	6	23	2	5
Roads	54	14	9	15	3	5
Trading regulations	30	31	15	16	3	5
Building regulations	17	48	5	23	3	4

A similar approach of forum-shopping characterises people's attitude towards the courts. While traditional leaders have an interest in presenting themselves as the only first-tier court, as the only portal to other forms of justice, their subjects do not share this interest. Although they believe the traditional court to be substantially better for many cases, they do appreciate it if their chief facilitates access to the magistrate's court in others: 'At least he writes us a letter to go to the magistrate when we need it.' They'll also take problems to other forums. In Hoepakranz, again, many community fights are discussed in the ramshackle school on top of the hill instead of the traditional court, or under a tree with members of the Community Policing Forum or the 'Cowherds Against Stocktheft'.

Dynamic

A last feature of the support for traditional leadership that needs to be mentioned is its dynamic character. As we shall see in the following section, support for traditional leadership is influenced by community, and by chiefly and personal, characteristics. All these can change. Communities can grow in size and other institutions can successfully take over chiefly functions. Chiefs can become better leaders, or worse ones: 'He is all right now, but I am afraid he will turn against us in the future,' says one respondent. Or, 'He is still young now, we still have to see his true colours.' And as people earn more or get a better education, their ideas about traditional leadership are, as we shall see, likely to change.

In addition to the above, there is a widespread perception – often noted with surprise – that traditional leaders have managed to reinforce their position in the period following the first democratic elections of 1994. 'We had really expected these *magoši* to disappear with the liberation. In the days of the struggle we were very much opposed to them, they tried to kill us and we would burn their palaces. But now they are back, and we are working together well.' There are multiple reasons for this 'surprise come-back': the continued government support for traditional leaders, the lack of capacity of the elected local governments, but also the fact that traditional leadership can provide a sense of identity in a fast-changing world.

The dilemma voiced by many Sekhukhune people was well summed up by Lydia Ngwenya, a veteran of the struggle, who commuted between the Cape Town Parliament and her mud house, with no electricity or tap-water, in the red and dusty Sekhukhune village of Tsimanyane.

> Traditional leadership is our culture, you can't run away from it, even though it must change. It's like a branch where you have to slice away all the bark and buds until you are left with a new lean walking stick. Still, I never saw a big role for the civics in the rural areas. These guys all became just as corrupt as the traditional leaders. And they're all-boy choirs, discriminating against women and leaving them out. It seems to me that it's better to have the devil you know than the devil you don't ... You know, rural people see the insecurity of the ANC on traditional leaders and don't know where to lean. They see the weakness of the TLCs, they see the weakness of the *magoši* and don't know who to support. They're just standing in the middle of the road where they can get hit from both sides.

Support for traditional leaders is thus limited, related to certain issues, not exclusive and dynamic. It also depends on a number of variables, to which we shall turn in the following section.

3. Support at community level

After having considered, in general terms, *how* people support traditional leaders, we can now turn to the next question: *who* supports chiefs? An analysis of the survey responses shows that the factors determining support lie at three different levels: those of the *community*, the *chief* and the *individual* concerned. This section focuses on the community characteristics. It introduces the three areas in which I did field research and considers how their specific features influenced people's opinions on traditional leaders.

Before moving to the lush hills of Hoepakranz, the sandy plains of Ga-Masha and the busy Mamone taxi-rank, it is necessary to say a few words about the evanescent and often ill-defined concept of 'community'. If one takes as a definition of community a 'group of people who share beliefs and preferences, of which membership is stable and in which relations are multiplex', none of the three groups I describe would qualify (Singleton and Taylor, 1992).[18] As we shall see, even the most bounded of the three communities, Hoepakranz, tightly woven together by kinship ties, was torn apart by chiefly succession disputes and generational cleavages and had as much experience of forces holding people apart as of those keeping them together. The same issues played a role in Mamone and Ga-Masha, which also had many inhabitants with no kinship ties at all, since they had recently moved to the area or been dumped in it as part of the apartheid forced translocations (Schirmer, 1996:213).

Why, then, not drop the term 'community' altogether and replace it with a territorial alternative like 'area'? One reason is that the notion, even if it is not grounded in empirical fact, does play an important role in discourse, for outsiders and insiders alike. Nationally, at a point when the notion of 'tribe' was discredited, the idea of 'community' seemed to take its place to conceptualise life in the rural areas. NGOs and government officials hold 'community' meetings and seem to depart from the notion of homogeneous groups that can, for instance, be represented. In doing so, of course, they reinforce this very notion. But local people also speak of their 'communities', notably when discussing traditional leadership, which is considered to play a central role in ensuring social cohesion and stability. '*Setšaba ke setšaba ka kgoši* – a community is a community because of the chief,' is a well-known variant of the Sotho saying quoted at the beginning of this chapter. The notion of communities might thus be fictitious, but it is important in the local and national conceptual landscape, which is why I shall follow suit.

With this out of the way, let us now look at three vastly different Sekhukhune communities, at the role traditional leaders play there and how this influences the way in which people think about them.

Hoepakranz: out on the mountains

Tucked away high in the rugged Leolo mountains that form the backbone of Sekhukhune, at the end of a virtually inaccessible road through wild green pastures dotted with yellow lilies, with an infrequent herd of cows watched by a youngster in ragged clothes, an adobe homestead or an orchard full of apricots, lies Hoepakranz, a 'classic out-of-the-way place' where the people, according to the rest of the Bapedi, 'live like monkeys on the mountains', without electricity, tap-water or any other form of development.[19] The approximately 500 inhabitants are knit together by kinship ties (they share five surnames), and even if they came from Swaziland in the nineteenth century, intermarrying with Bapedi has

[18] Cf. T. Kepe (1998). 'The Problem of Defining "Community": Challenges for the Land Reform Programme in Rural South Africa.' Cape Town: School of Government, University of the Western Cape.

[19] As Charles Piot has pointed out, the reasons for 'remoteness' often lie as much in wider, 'global' forces as in local factors. One such external reason why Hoepakranz remains so inaccessible is the marijuana fields that also lie hidden in the lush mountains and undeniably tie the village to a much wider economy: Piot (1999).

led to a population that is *hlakahlaka* – a mixture.[20] The most important link with the outside world is through the migrant workers, many of whom work as grave-diggers or in the mines in the metropolitan areas and climb the mountains twice a year to visit their wives and families. Apart from that, remoteness is the area's principal feature. No government vehicle has ever made it up the mountains. The villagers even had to go down to fetch examination papers for the matriculants because government officials refused to 'wear out their cars on those stones and rivers'.

The institutional landscape tallies with this image of remoteness. The ward councillor elected to the far-away TLC was never seen again in his village and did not bring any development. There is a high degree of self-organisation, as described earlier. On an average day, one could look around the village and see a meeting of the Youth Development Forum in the valley among the maize fields, of the women's savings club with their tin money-box under the cluster of wild fig trees on the mountains, and of the School Building Committee on the rocks behind the school. The school generally forms the centre of public activity, and most community meetings, whether they concern disputes or general development issues, are held in it. One reason for the centrality of the school is the long-standing succession dispute between the two local traditional leaders, which renders it impossible to have community meetings in one of the palaces even though both leaders have a *kgôrô*, where disputes can be discussed.

We shall look at the omnipresent succession disputes in Sekhukhune and the way in which they are argued in the next chapter. For now, suffice it to remark that this rift has not led to a decline in the appreciation of traditional leadership. A staggering 94 per cent of the people in Hoepakranz support a traditional leader, a much larger percentage than in the two other communities; 87 per cent have shown some form of material support to the traditional leader or attended a hearing at the traditional court. People also give their traditional leader the highest rating of the three areas: only 4 per cent view him negatively, 9 per cent are neutral, and 87 per cent evaluate him positively. Even if one takes account of variation related to the characteristics of the chiefs and community members involved, these figures are still very high. Why, *at community level*, is support for traditional leadership so high in this tiny, bounded mountain village?

Part of the explanation can be found in the cultural orientations of the people in Hoepakranz.[21] This village comes as close to a 'community' with stable membership, shared beliefs and multiple relations as one can get in Sekhukhune, even if a wide rift divides the supporters of both chiefs, and the village school-children frequently go on strike to show their dissatisfaction with their parents and teachers. It is also a status-based society, in which men and women sit separately in meetings, children are smacked by their mothers if they are too cheeky, and people are 'considered in their categories'. Land is ample and fertile, and the chiefs generally do not demand too much of the people. Respect for traditional leadership, as the apex of an order installed by the gods and the

[20] An important difference between Bapedi and Swazi people is that the latter, normally, do not attend initiation school (there are exceptions). The Sepedi and Swazi people in Hoepakranz, however, do not differ significantly in their opinions on traditional leadership, so I will make no further mention of this issue.

[21] I agree with Van Binsbergen that 'cultures' as such do not exist, and that it is preferable to use the term 'cultural orientations': Van Binsbergen (1999:12).

ancestors, fits within such kinship-based social organisation and status-oriented cultural orientations.

Nevertheless, this does not mean that people are opposed to the notion of development or that they do not support alternative institutions. They yearn for a road, 'so that we can go down the mountains and sell clay pots there', and 'we'll have clinics and shops and many nice things'. The civics are widely appreciated for making it possible for old-age pensioners to collect their government pensions at the local school instead of having to be 'carted down the mountain in a wheelbarrow'. A school was built and paid for by the community, a feat that one woman credits to the involvement of women: 'Before we were led by men, and there was no progress. Now women are involved, and look what has been achieved.' The support for traditional leadership is thus combined with support for all institutions willing to assist in the development of the village.

The main reason for the exceptionally high material and immaterial support does, however, seems to lie in the complete absence of alternative public institutions. 'We are staying far away from the government,' as one old woman said. Other community members agreed: 'There must be some authority in the land' or 'how can we stay without a *kgoši*? What if a conflict arises; where shall we take it?'. Sixty-nine per cent of them never heard of the TLC. A young woman explained: 'In the mountains we still pay respect to the *magoši* because they are closest to us. We still have to see the importance of these elected people.' In section 6 I shall argue that there are four reasons why people (do not) support traditional leadership. These lie in the realm of: tradition or culture, state support for traditional leadership, its performance and a default 'need for rule'. Half of the people in Hoepakranz legitimate their support for traditional leaders by referring to the 'need to be ruled.' No herd of cattle, it was often reiterated, can take care of itself.

Another related reason is that traditional leaders are perceived to be the only stepping-stones for access to the state. '*Bogoši* is the main road to all government. They are useful to politics and can engage local structures,' said one man. Another agreed: 'The chief is the eye of the government. If something goes wrong, he is the one to report it to them.' Even if the traditional leaders in Hoepakranz are not paid by the government, this image is reinforced in contacts with various state institutions, in particular the magistrate. 'At the magistrate's you'll always have to produce an identity letter from the palace'; 'you can't take a case there directly, they'll always ask if you have been through the *mošate* first' and 'many letters still need the approval of the *kgoši*'. This outside reinforcement of the power of traditional leaders brings to mind Piot's observations of how boundedness and 'traditional' cultural orientations are, even in the most remote villages, as often a result of wider forces as they are local productions of meaning (Piot, 1999; Meyer and Geschiere, 1999).

Ga-Masha: one step away from riches

The high Leolo mountains form the backdrop to the potholed tar road that cuts through Ga-Masha and leads – past dilapidated bottle shops, an old garage, a general dealer with a Coca-Cola fridge next to a generator and women selling tiny pyramids of tomatoes outside – out of Sekhukhune and into the former 'white' South Africa. Along this 20 kilometres of road, five 'officially recognised' traditional leaders and a plethora of headmen claiming to be recognised were clumped together with their subjects or people who had never followed a chief before, as part of the forcible homeland removals in the 1950s and 1960s. Of the three communities under consideration, the approximately 5000 people in Ga-Masha are the poorest. The ramshackle adobe and tin-plate houses, the eroded soccer field covered with plastic bags, the single scrawny goat scurrying across it, all reinforce an image of desolation. Only 27 per cent of the people have access to an eroded field on the Steelpoort river, between cacti and ant-hills. Below the sparse trees sit many men with their yellow mining helmets still on their heads, but a retrenchment letter in their pockets.

Still, all this could change. Ga-Masha is one of the few communities that has a real chance of its socio-economic situation improving drastically within the next few years. Not only does a claim for land on the opposite side of the tar road from which the Masha people were removed in 1940 have a good chance of succeeding; underneath that land lies a rare reserve of vanadium, the mineral used to give plasticity to both tweezers and buildings, the mining rights to which have been leased by a large company. Recent years have thus brought a flurry of meetings between the 'community' and the Land Claims Commission, government departments, the mining company's lawyers, and non-governmental organisations.

In all these contacts, two questions prevail: 'who gets to represent the community?' and 'if there are spoils to be had, whose are they?'[22] The struggle of the 1980s and the area's turbulent history had already turned Ga-Masha into a divided community, with two chiefly contenders, their supporters and an active civic organisation fighting bitterly over the power to speak on behalf of 'their people'. This struggle has now worsened. 'I have never attended a meeting of this community in which they didn't fight,' complains the representative of a mineral rights NGO. And the project manager of the mining company recounts how they began their dealings with the community: they drove in, asked for the traditional leader and got her to sign a cooperation agreement, only to find that neither the supporters of the other chief, nor the youth organised in the civics, felt bound by it. The Land Claims Commission officials ran into similar difficulties when they proposed the election of a Land Claims Committee but stipulated that the traditional leaders should be excluded. As one of the civic members said: 'Which committee to elect, that's our problem. Who should sign? And if there is some money, who will get it?' Thus, committees are chosen, contested and rechosen, all delaying the decision-making process.

How does such a divided community regard traditional leadership? An overwhelming majority (82 per cent) still support a traditional leader, although this is fewer than in Hoepakranz. However, most of them (83 per cent) have never shown any material support for their traditional leader. People are also more critical of traditional leadership: even though the majority of respondents were neutral about the performance of traditional leaders, opposition to the institution is vehement, with many youngsters saying that 'this institution must be thrown in the dust-bin because of its greed' or 'it is oppressive and should be shut down immediately'. Only 56 per cent of respondents want to retain the institution, sometimes with changes such as 'people should start voting for their

[22] B. Oomen, 'The Underlying Question: Land restitution, mineral rights and indigenous communities in South Africa'. Paper presented at the Conference on Folk Law and Legal Pluralism: Challenges in the Third Millenium, Arica, Chile, 13–17 March 2000.

traditional leaders'. The reasons why people support traditional leadership also change; in this fast-changing community, there is a much higher emphasis on its 'cultural' and 'traditional' character, on the one hand, and its intimate relationship with the government, on the other. As we shall see in the next section, when looking at chiefly characteristics, this also has to do with the way in which chief Johannes Masha persistently and actively seeks government reaffirmation of his position.

What community characteristics explain the fact that support is lower than in Hoepakranz but higher, as we shall see, than in Mamone? The shortfall can be explained partly by cultural orientations. Even if 93 per cent of the – practically completely Bapedi – population have been to initiation school, only 44 per cent of the people living here are married customarily, and of those who are single 92 per cent would not follow the Pedi custom. A third of the people were born elsewhere and there is much closer contact, by men and women alike, with the nearby towns. At the community level (so with chiefly and personal characteristics set aside) the main variable explaining the high support again seems to be the institutional make-up. Here, it is not the absence or presence of elected local government but its complete failure that has ensured continued support for traditional leadership. The Transitional Local Council under which Ga-Masha falls – a different one from that of the two other communities – completely collapsed a year after its election, with the councillors going back to work in the towns. While 77 per cent of the people know about the TLC, 81 per cent condemn its performance as bad. 'We elected some guys but unfortunately they went into hiding' and 'those people promised us heaven and earth, but nothing has happened at all.'

Thus, it is again a combination of cultural orientations and the performance of alternative access paths to the state which, at community level, explains how people think about traditional leadership. In the third community to be discussed, Mamone, there is a TLC which operates more or less effectively. Let us see how this has affected support for traditional leadership.

Mamone: retraditionalisation in a fast-changing world

Even more so than Hoepakranz or Ga-Masha, Mamone defies easy characterisation. There is the township of Jane Furse, with its flashy shopping centre, bustling taxi-rank and brand-new hospital. Just a few kilometres down the road, in Mamone village, lies another world, with traditional Pedi homesteads around the royal palace on the hill and the traditional court under the thorn-tree. And there are also the eleven 'satellite villages', some of which lie more than 50 kilometres of dusty dirt road away from the palace, and where life revolves around maize fields and cow-herding, at a much slower pace than in Jane Furse. Within Mamone's population of about 40,000 – nearly ten times as large as Ga-Masha and a hundred times as large as Hoepakranz – there are groups that could be considered 'communities', but this does not apply to the whole.

Although the degree to which parts of Mamone have experienced development differs, the post-1994 period has brought some changes to the area as a whole. 'At least there is a shopping centre and some clean water, but we still need jobs.' Electric wires now seem to spin a web above many Mamone villages, and all the local institutions – from the ANC to the traditional leaders, and the TLC to the civics – seek to take the credit for having brought this government service to their communities. The reason for this area having seen at least some progress since 1994 seems to lie in the fact that the TLC, which covers 28 chieftaincies, has its office in Mamone. 'Those TLC guys only take care of their own areas,' people from other villages complain. Although the council does not have the capacity actually to implement projects itself, it can decide to which area resources are channelled. As a result, 54 per cent of the Mamone people feel that their standard of living has improved.

Another post-1994 development is the coronation of a new chief, Billy Sekwati Mampuru. As we saw in the previous chapter, this led to vehement debates on the functions of a traditional leader, and a process that might be labelled 'retraditionalisation' (cf. Oomen, 2000a). The traditional court has been revamped, the Mamone Bapedi discuss 'going back to the roots', and a 'road-show' starring the new chief and some of his advisers tours the satellite villages to persuade people of the advantages of supporting a traditional leader – materially and immaterially. Not only is traditional authority strengthened, other government institutions are also cautioned to keep out of Mamone business. Whether it is the TLC, the state magistrate or the police, when they interfere in what are deemed Mamone affairs they are told, 'this is where Sekwati rules'.

How do people in such a heterogeneous area feel about traditional leadership? While the number of people supporting a *kgoši* remains high, it is down to 73 per cent. People are also more critical about traditional leadership than in the other two areas: 27 per cent find the institution to be bad, and 37 per cent are neutral. Most of the Mamone people have never seen 'their' chief, let alone done anything for him: 'I would like to talk to him first before I can tell you what I think of him.' Only 61 per cent want to retain the institution, with the rest saying things like 'this is now a very old toothless animal that should be buried for good'. What is particularly interesting is the shift in the justification for retaining traditional leadership. Now that the TLC has become active as an alternative governmental institution, the performance of the traditional leader has become much more important. But even more important is the 'traditional and cultural' character of the institution: traditional leadership has moved from a 'main road to government' and 'a form of rule' to an institution celebrated because of its unique, local character. This, as we shall see in section 6, spurs the traditional authority to actively underline this difference and emphasise its 'traditional' character.

Again, an amalgam of community-level variables appears to determine this outcome. Mamone is considered 'traditionalist', much more so than Ga-Masha. Even if fewer people have been to initiation school (70 per cent), people say: 'Those Mamone Bapedi can go to Johannesburg for years, but they will always retain their accent, and long to return to their area.' Nevertheless, there are more non-Pedi speakers in this area than in the others (11 per cent), nearly half of the people (48 per cent) were born elsewhere, and 65 per cent do not have fields. Another reason for the decrease in support might be the relative increase in appreciation for the TLC: While half of of the people are still negative ('how can these boys drive around in fancy cars?' and 'the province should send in their anti-corruption squads') and 37 per cent neutral, the rest do say things like 'traditional leadership is finished as we now have TLCs'.

It would seem from these three examples and the comparative Sekhukhune material that support for traditional leadership falls slightly in larger areas that

Table 5.2 Support for traditional leadership in 3 study villages (%)

Question	Hoepakranz (N=133)	Ga-Masha (N = 100)	Mamone (N=121)	All (N=598)
Have you ever heard of the TLC?				
Yes	31	76	68	66
No	69	24	32	34
Do you support a traditional leader?				
Yes	94	82	73	80
No	6	18	27	20
How would you rate the institution of traditional leadership?				
Very bad	1	11	0	3
Bad	3	11	27	14
Neutral	9	49	37	23
Good	44	22	26	36
Very good	43	17	10	24
Do you think traditional leadership has a future?				
Yes	76	56	61	65
No	23	44	39	35
For which reason would you (not) want to retain traditional leadership?				
Culture, tradition	10	28	36	24
Link with government	22	32	11	23
Their performance	18	21	35	27
Default: need some rule	50	19	18	26

are more developed and where the TLCs are accepted as an alternative government institution. Also, it changes in character, with the emphasis more on the 'cultural and traditional' aspects than on its instrumental character. The degree of support is highest in small communities with less contact with the outside world and no 'governmental' alternatives to the traditional leaders. These, of course, are only general community characteristics. The features of the chiefs and the people concerned also determine their support for traditional leadership.

4. Support dependent on chiefly characteristics

There are two royal palaces in the lush valley that cradles Hoepakranz. One belongs to Abel Nkosi, an old soft-spoken unmarried man with a shy demeanour but a great deal of wisdom. He heads the local NG Church and acts as a chief together with his identical twin brother who used to be the school principal (whose existence we were not aware of at first, causing us to wonder at Abel's omnipresence). His opponent in the local succession dispute, Joseph Nkosi, is a much younger, uneducated, brash bearded man with three wives, a tractor and a collection of guns in his house. Then there is the 'non-local' traditional leader, Kgolane, who presides over another village but can count on a great deal of support in Hoepakranz: he is a young man who has only recently acceded to power, likes drinking and girls, but also actively stimulates development in his area.

In Ga-Masha, the picture is just as diverse. Johannes Masha is a fierce-looking man who spends most of his time going around government departments seeking recognition of his claims. Mante, his contender, is a warm-hearted, grey-haired lady, who leaves ruling to her advisers and prefers to look after her grandchildren. In Mamone, Billy's ascension to the throne put out of action the uneducated but shrewd uncle who had contended with Billy's mother for over two decades. The new *kgoši* himself is a born-again Christian with a college education, who feels threatened by the community he is supposed to rule.

This small portrait gallery demonstrates the differences that can exist between traditional leaders. The fact that not only the Sekhukhune paramountcy, but nearly every chieftaincy position in Sekhukhune is contested, allows us to compare how *chiefly characteristics* impact on the way in which people who live in one community and share the same personal characteristics regard traditional leadership. Before turning to people's assessment of their individual leader, however, let us look briefly at the relation between support for a traditional leader and for traditional leadership. How do the ways in which people think about the office and the incumbent relate to each other?

Supporting chiefs, supporting chieftaincy

In a seminal and still often-quoted article on the Tswana-speaking Barolong boo Ratshidi, John Comaroff describes how they make a distinction between their evaluation of the office of chieftainship and of its holder (Comaroff, 1975, 1974) When speaking about chieftainship, the people will use a formal code and laud the virtues of the institution. Speaking about their individual chief, on the other hand, they use an evaluative code which can be highly critical (Comaroff, 1975). The same distinction is made in Sesotho culture. As a school principal, ANC member and member of the Mamone royal family said:

> The whole system of *bogoši* is a way of trying to keep stability in the community, to keep the community together. It is central in determining where people find themselves. All our customs and traditions are enshrined in *bogoši*. Where there are *magoši* you will find respect... The moral fibre of the whole society rests on *bogoši*. It encompasses religion, tradition, governance, customs, everything... This system of governance is in our blood. They are above all politics and should be a symbol of unity.
>
> This is why it's very annoying if a *kgoši* is bad. Especially if the whole community has put their trust in him. But this is never, never a reason to do away with the institution. Instead, we should try to empower the institution instead of the person. If the *kgoši* is bad, you can always still discuss with someone else in the institution.

This delinking in *political oratory*, in local debate, of people's thoughts on chieftainship from their thoughts on individual chiefs could easily suggest that their *opinions* on the two are also not linked: that they might, for instance, hold chieftainship in high esteem while being critical of their individual chief.

This is not the case in Sekhukhune. There is an exceptionally high correlation between how people rate their traditional leader and their rating of traditional leadership.[23] Thus, the young man who says 'my chief does not respect his status as a chief and is a drunkard' will also say '*bogoši* must come to an end'. Similarly, the person who states that 'this guy is a chief because of his royal blood but does not have leadership abilities' feels that 'this whole thing must just be dispersed'. Conversely, the woman who feels that 'my chief is fair and works together well with his people' states that 'our chiefs must remain the way they are'. And the young man who feels that 'our *kgoši* leads us well and gives us all the reference letters and stamps we need' also reasons that '*bogoši* is good and progressive.' The causal relation between the two variables is demonstrated by the fact that people who are uncertain about their leader hesitate over what they should say about traditional leadership. In this vein, the old lady quoted earlier as saying that Billy Sekwati 'is still young, we still have to see his true colours' considers traditional leadership neither good nor bad.

People's feelings about *bogoši* are clearly influenced by their evaluation of their *kgoši*. In the following section we shall briefly consider how people evaluate their leader, and what criteria they use to do so.

Virtues and vices of traditional leaders

As Hammond-Tooke has pointed out, an elaborate set of premises of 'good government', of which consensual decision-making was the most important, was traditionally used to evaluate chiefly performance (Hammond-Tooke, 1975; Kuper, 1970; Comaroff and Roberts, 1981). This is also well documented in other areas: 'The greater the degree to which a chief (and his supporters) can achieve a *convergence* between the public evaluation of his incumbency and the stated criteria of good government, the greater the extent to which he may expect to wield legitimate power' (Comaroff, 1975).

What are the criteria of good government in present-day Sekhukhune?[24] Most of the 600 responses to the open question 'What do you think of your traditional leader?' concentrated on aspects of traditional leadership that can be classified into five categories: accountability, initiative, wisdom, achievements and restraint. This was true for both positive and negative responses.

'He is an obedient person,' is how many people positively evaluate their traditional leader. Accountability is deemed a central virtue of a traditional leader, and the degree of control people feel they can exert over a chief determines their appraisal of him. 'We work together well,' villagers say contentedly, 'he respects the people and his constituency' and 'he does exactly what we want'. The sense of ownership, of a good traditional leader operating on behalf of the community, was voiced by an old man in Ga-Mashabela: 'A chief is there for the people. He must work through our mandate and can't act on his own. If he is bad, the community is bad as well.' This means that a traditional leader perceived to 'take unilateral decisions' and 'undermine his advisers' will be

[23] Kendall's tau_b = 0,710 (N = 450). Respondents were asked, 'How do you feel about your traditional leader?' and 'How do you feel about traditional leadership?' as two open questions, but were also asked to rate their chief and the institution on a scale from 1 (very bad) through 3 (neutral) to 5 (very good). In 73% of cases, people felt the same about the institution as they did about their traditional leader.

[24] For a general discussion of the evanescent notion of good governance in development cooperation, see Otto (2001).

severely criticised, like the brash and individualistic Johannes Masha, who was accused of 'being a young, ambitious fellow who just wants everything for himself'.

While accountability is an important virtue, it should not be overdone. The ability to take initiative is deemed important: a traditional leader should also have 'leadership qualities' and 'a vision of where the community is going'. Courage and bravery are deemed as important today as ever, but traditional leaders are also respected for 'having stood up for us in the dark days' of apartheid. While listening to councillors is regarded as vital, a traditional leader should take decisions independently (Otto, 1987:297). The supporters of Mante Masha, a soft-spoken docile leader, complain that 'her advisers use her like a tool; she just rubber-stamps anything' and 'she is a passive person and not vocal at all'. A traditional leader, it appears, should dare to take responsibility for individual decisions, even if they are unpopular.

Wisdom and fairness are deemed other important attributes, as becomes clear from satisfied responses like 'he listens attentively to our community', 'he handles our issues with care', 'by being patient he is like a parent', and 'he is very soft, he understands us all'. On the other hand, one of the most common complaints against traditional leaders is their bias. 'He will always judge in favour of his relatives' and 'in the traditional court they'll only look at who you are, where you're from and what you've taken with you'. This has an impact not only on the assessment of traditional leaders, but also on how people feel about traditional courts. For instance, nearly 90 per cent of the supporters of traditional leaders like Abel and Joseph Nkosi and K.K. Sekhukhune also liked the traditional court, while the figure is only 50 per cent in the case of Johannes Masha: 'In that place you will find some very greedy and discriminatory minds together.'

The achievements of a traditional leader are another important variable determining how people feel about him. Such achievements can include bringing 'projects' to the village, one of the reasons why Johannes Masha, who was criticised before by some, is popular with other villagers. 'At least this guy is trying to create jobs for us' and 'he has brought a poultry farm and a community garden to the village'. Even if, in this case, it was not the traditional leader but an NGO which took the initiative for the project, J. Masha managed, in the classic role of gate-keeper, to reap the benefits. It is also appreciated if a traditional leader facilitates access to (other) government institutions: 'He gives us all the letters and stamps we need.' A traditional leader who 'fails to do anything for us' or 'has never delivered at all' can count on a negative assessment. The least a traditional leader can do, people feel, is to not 'disturb progress by refusing all sorts of development projects'.

This is in line with a final feature valued in traditional leaders: restraint. 'This guy doesn't give us any problems' and 'we don't have to work in his fields or pay tribal levies'. 'He is not oppressive' and 'he has never chased anyone from his village' are some of the reasons why people appreciate their chiefs. The traditional leader who 'is an oppressor of underprivileged people by squeezing money from dry land' or 'beats people while they're naked and throws cold water over them' can count on little sympathy. Leaders should be 'soft', and patient, which is why Christian traditional leaders are valued highly by some of their subjects. Others, however, doubt their ability to lead initiation schools and to 'really stand up for the community'.

These are thus the criteria by which Bapedi evaluate their traditional leaders and that influence their support for them and consequently, as we have seen in this section, their appraisal of traditional leadership in general. The fact that people assess their individual leaders, the office holders, by a yardstick that runs from accountability to restraint does not say anything about the way in which they legitimate their support for the institution of traditional leadership: this will be discussed in section 6. Here, we are merely concerned with the question of why certain people enthusiastically support traditional leaders materially and immaterially and others do not. Part of the answer, we have seen, lies in the community they live in and the chiefs that rule it. But an important part also lies in their individual circumstances. It is to those personal characteristics that we now turn.

5. Support at the individual level

A municipal labourer from Mohlaletse told us how he took the case of his neighbour's goats feasting on his corn fields to the traditional court, and the *kgôrô* decided in his favour. 'I like our *kgoši* because he settles disputes fairly, without looking at where you come from.' In his opinion, traditional leadership should be respected, unlike the TLC which 'does nothing for us'. In another interview we conducted, sitting on a rock with chickens scurrying at our feet, an old lady told us why she wanted to retain traditional leadership: 'If my husband beats me up again, there is at least someone close I can turn to.' A few hours later, we sat in the shade on an adobe porch meticulously polished deep red, talking to a woman who saw no need for the government to retain, let alone pay for, traditional leaders: 'Why? What are they doing? If they were doing something for us it would be a good idea, but I see nothing.'

Having discussed how the community to which people belong and their chief have an impact on their support for traditional leadership, we now turn to those variables that *at the individual level* account for (a lack of) support. For all the personal motivations and life-stories that inform individual opinions on chieftaincy, some clear patterns can be determined. The young people are more critical than the elders, men are a little more critical than women, and support also decreases as education and income rise. We shall look at these variations, and the possible explanations for them.

'This is a thing of our parents': the youth and the elders

In every dusty Sekhukhune village – the groups of youngsters hanging around outside schools and beer-halls where kwaito music thumps out of the speakers – girls in tattered black-and-white school uniforms with babies strapped on their backs and lanky boys in tight T-shirts (with Che Guevara and reggae prints) and floppy hats – might well comprise the group that has lost out most in the new South Africa. During the Sekhukhuneland revolt of 1986 the generation before them marched in protest against the old order, throwing stones, burning down palaces and generally trying to wrest power from their parents (cf. Delius, 1990, 1996; Van Kessel, 2001). However, far from bringing a new dawn, the new South Africa has brought youngsters much of the same: congested and broken-down classrooms, teachers with sjamboks under their arms, and a demoralising

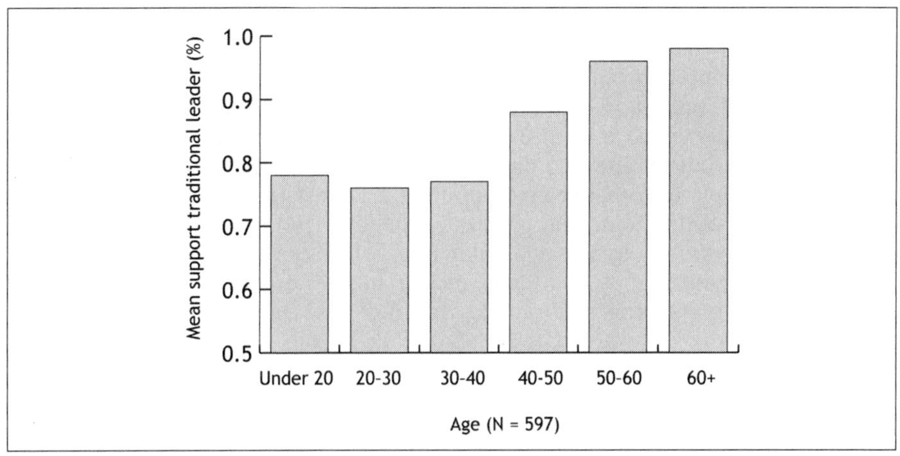

Figure 5.1 Support for traditional leadership by age cohort

lack of job opportunities. A few former comrades might now 'drive a Mercedes Benz and have flashy girlfriends' but, for the majority, life has inescapably slipped back into the rural humdrum.

In Sekhukhune, as we saw in the previous chapter, 'youth' is very much a generic category, roughly used to designate those groups of people associated with the civic organisations and resistance to traditional authority. This is why the same people who spearheaded the local revolutions in the 1980s can still be referred to as the 'youth' of today, even if they are now grey-haired family heads. When asked whether they feel they can participate in community affairs, many pensioners will grumble that 'all this standing up and talking about democracy is something for the youth'. 'Youth' is a category associated with the uninitiated, those not yet socialised into Bapedi 'tradition' and symbolic of resistance to it, or with those people who remained jobless after the struggle, failed to jump on the 'gravy train' of the new times, and thus failed to become 'real men' supporting families.

The image of 'youth' as anti-traditionalist is reflected in the opinions of the youthful Bapedi on traditional leadership. While support is still high, only 78 per cent of the people under 20 support a traditional leader. This figure rises steadily to a staggering 97 per cent of those over 60: only one of the 72 pensioners we spoke to did not support a *kgoši* (see Figure 5.1). The youth are also more critical of their traditional leader than their parents are. 'For what good reason should I support a chief? I don't know him and I really don't care whether he knows me,' as one boy said. The comrades from Ga-Moloi stated, in the same vein, 'Our chief is a power-monger and a money-monger who changes colour whenever he feels like it.' The youth also, to a much larger extent than their elders, legitimate their (lack of) support for traditional leadership by pointing to chiefly performance. Of the people aged under 30, 38 per cent gave a performance-based reason to (not) retain traditional leadership, varying from 'he does good things for us' to 'he is anti-development'. Of the people over 50, on the other hand, only 9 per cent considered chiefly performance to be the reason for maintaining the institution, while 38 per cent gave a 'cultural' form of legitimation (as compared with 15% of the youth).

The critical approach of the youth is also echoed in the way Bapedi under 30 rate their traditional leader. The mean rating on a one-to-five scale was about 3.6 for people under 20 and rose to nearly 4.2 for the population over 60. A possible explanation for the two dips in Figure 5.2 is the fact that the formative years of the people aged between 40 and 50 occurred at the very height of the implementation of the homeland policies in the late 1960s and early 1970s with traditional leaders playing an unpopular role, while the youth between 20 and 30 were the ones who marched to the *mešate*, torches and stones in their hands. Also, there are many migrants among the men between 30 and 40, and they tend to be more positive about traditional leaders than their peers who remain behind in Sekhukhune.

The youth, as both young and old agree, have less respect for traditional leadership than the elders do. 'As youngsters we seem to be forgetting about our culture by not respecting *magoši*,' said one boy. An elderly community member said, with reference to the vigilante organisation that forcibly helps traditional leaders back into power: 'We need *Mapogo* to beat these young tigers and teach them some respect because they are claiming to be mature.' Traditional leadership as an institution systematically favours the elders, as a man from Mohlaletse acknowledged by saying that traditional leadership is needed 'to know who is young and who is old, who is who in the land'. Following the premise that those people will support traditional leadership who can expect to get something out of their support, the critical attitude of the youth can be understood. Conversely, the pensioners who have grown up with traditional leadership, sit in the traditional courts and have much more to expect from this institution than from the young elected councillors, are overwhelmingly positive: 'We were born to find chieftaincy, so I think it is better left alone.'

The paradox of the women

The opinions young people hold are easily explained by looking at how traditional leadership, generally speaking, treats them. Women's opinions cannot be explained so obviously. In the South African debate on the 'future of traditional leadership', critics invariably point to the discriminatory character of the institution.[25] They are right in arguing that rural women 'hold the knife on the sharp edge'.[26] An average Sekhukhune woman will wake up at dawn to sweep the yard, feed the children maize porridge cooked on a wood fire, walk long distances with a jerrycan of water or spiky branches of firewood on her head, work in the fields, all this time hoping that an absent partner will send back some money for the school fees. While there is a high degree of self-organisation among women and they are represented in many village 'structures', their access to chiefly politics is often limited. In many villages – like Mamone and Ga-Masha, but not Hoepakranz – they are not allowed to act as adjudicators, and even if they bring a case against someone they have to remain

[25] Meer (1997); Pillay and Prinsloo (1995); Sibongile Zungu, 'Traditional Leaders' Capability and Disposition for Democracy: The Example of South Africa,' in Hofmeister and Scholz, pp. 161–77.

[26] Transvaal Rural Action Committee, *The Rural Women's Movement: Holding the Knife on the Sharp Edge*.

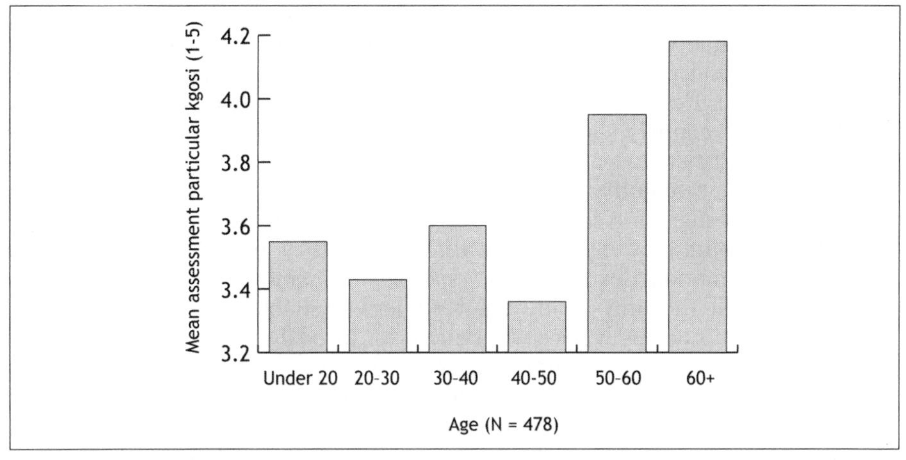

Figure 5.2 Women's assessment of traditional leaders by age cohort

seated on the ground, their head covered and their eyes downcast.[27] As it is the women who usually stay behind when their husbands leave to work in the towns, they do the bulk of the chores for the traditional leaders: brewing beer, hoeing the fields and even scraping together the tribal levies.

For all these reasons, one would expect women to be much less enthusiastic about *bogoši* than men. The opposite seems to be the case: there were slightly more women (83 per cent) than men who supported a traditional leader. These women also rated their traditional leader slightly higher than male villagers did, with an average of 3.74/5 as opposed to 3.55. 'They should continue what they're doing, we appreciate their work,' said one old woman. And when a chief enters a village it is the women who ululate, kicking up sand during traditional dances with brightly coloured feather-dusters, and – if they are lucky – get to say *direto*, praises of the chief in high Sepedi: 'I see the man who wears the leopard-skin and I stand shivering; before we were moving through thick bush, now we see light.'

Does this female support for traditional leadership mean that women feel the institution does not discriminate against them? The answer is mixed: 42 per cent of the women, as opposed to 28 per cent of the men, felt *bogoši* discriminates against women, but the majority did not. 'Everything goes well and we can participate in all activities'; 'if we want to say things we can do so in the school and other places'; 'even if I as a woman come to the *mošate* with a problem they will listen to me;' 'maybe women can't stand up at the *kgôrô*, but that is not discrimination; it's just our culture.' Some women went even further, to say that '*tša etwa ke e tshadi pele, diwela ka leopeng* – if a woman leads, the nation goes astray.' Nevertheless, many others did have problems with their role in the institution. 'If there is one place I really don't like, it is the *mošate*: women sit in a separate corner and can't even stand up' and 'the *kgôrô* doesn't listen to women, no matter how truthful their story is'. The larger and more 'developed'

[27] Cf. Janet Small, 'Women's Land Rights: A Case Study from the Northern Transvaal.' In Meer (1997) p. 49.

the area in which they live, the more critical women become: while only 29 per cent of the women in the small village of Hoepakranz felt discriminated against by traditional leadership, the figure was 39 per cent in Ga-Masha and 54 per cent in Mamone. Here, more and more women say things like: 'We live in a free and democratic country, but at the *mošate* a woman can't raise her voice or stand up against her husband. It is very peculiar.'

The fact that a majority of the Bapedi women support traditional leadership and even feel it does not discriminate against them can be explained, not only by cultural orientations, but also by the interest they have in supporting the institution. Traditional leadership is, especially in remote villages like Hoepakranz, often still the only form of government available, and the only portal through which to access wider state structures. In addition, it can be controlled more easily than remote governmental structures. Even if women have no official role in the traditional authority – apart from that of candle-wife and possible regent – there are all sorts of informal ways in which women can exert influence over the authorities in their midst. Lydia Ngwenya's observation that it is better 'to have the devil you know than the devil you don't' comes to mind. The proximity of traditional leaders also means they can function as a check on abusive husbands: 'At least if I'm lashed at home I will know who to turn to,' quite a few women say, although others remark that 'a woman is not always supported at the *kgôrô* if she is beaten by her husband'.

Moving up, moving out: education and income

The above shows that age as well as sex determines support for traditional leadership – the first strongly, the second marginally. Two other correlated variables for which this is the case are education and income: as socio-economic status rises, support for traditional leadership falls. Thus, while 92 per cent of the people without an education supported a traditional leader, the figure was only 53 per cent among university graduates (Figure 5.3).[28] The same relation is found between income and support for traditional leadership: among people with the lowest incomes, 89 per cent supported a traditional leader, while the percentage was 71 per cent in the highest income group (Figure 5.4).[29]

To take one example out of many, a relatively rich Mohlaletse taxi driver was critical of traditional leadership: '*Bogoši* has failed to do anything for us. It is really is not managed well, so it should not be allocated means by the government.' Such a cynical approach is not taken by all people with a high income. A man who has spent most of his life toiling in the Benoni mines and earns more than most other villagers mused: 'This is our history and heritage. They build the community and encourage unity.' Thus, his opinion did not differ much from that of the old illiterate man in the Leolo mountains, whose self-proclaimed profession is 'guarding the village from monkeys' and who stated that '*Bogoši* is our proof of being human. Also, we just found this thing to be here; where else would we go with our problems?'

People with a higher income or education are not only – relatively – less inclined to support a traditional leader, but also more critical of that leader: the

[28] Educational figures are as follows: no education 21%; up to standard 6 20%; standard 6-10 42%; matric 7%; technicon 7%; university 3%.

[29] Household monthly income figures are as follows: under R500 27%; R500–1000 34%; R1000–2000 22%; R2000 + 17%.

1.0
0.9
0.8
0.7
0.6
0.5
0.4
0.3
0.2
0.1
0.0
Mean support kgoši (%)
No education
Until Standard 6
Standard 6-10
Matric
Technikon
University
Education - highest level (N=591)

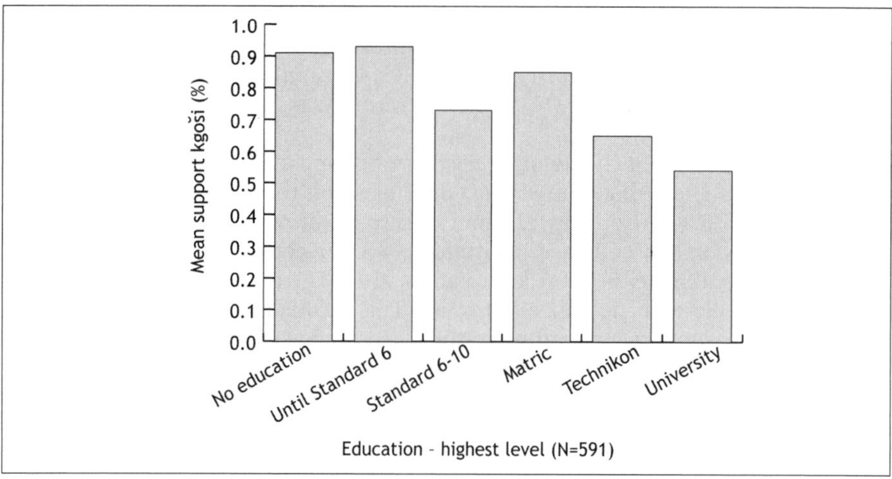

Figure 5.3 Support for traditional leadership by education

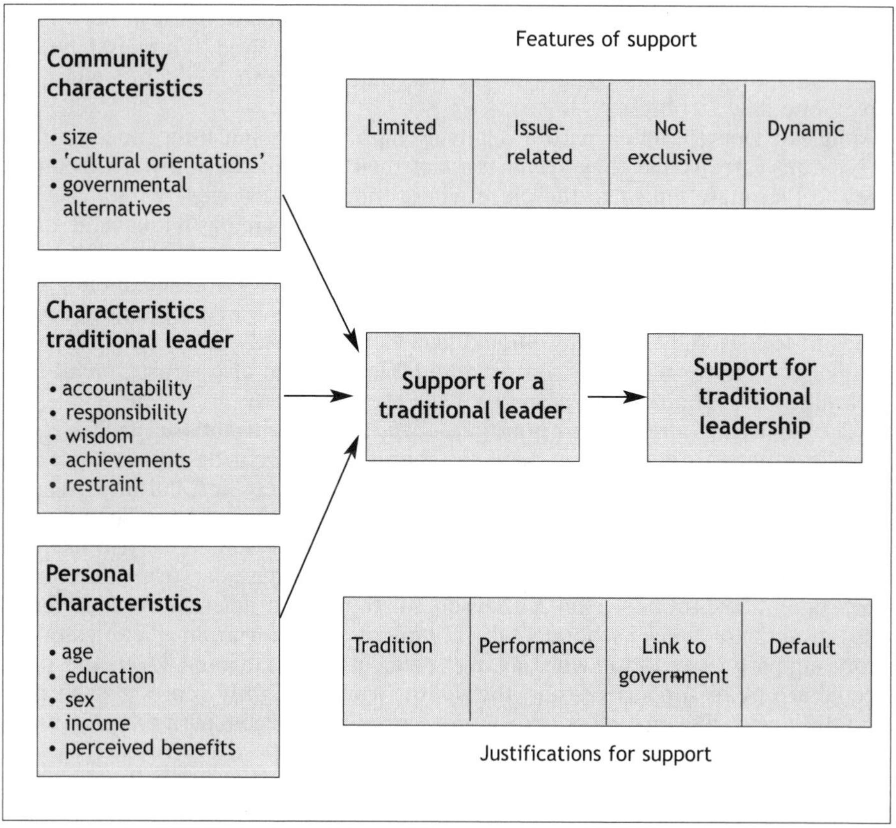

Community characteristics
• size
• 'cultural orientations'
• governmental alternatives
Characteristics traditional leader
• accountability
• responsibility
• wisdom
• achievements
• restraint
Personal characteristics
• age
• education
• sex
• income
• perceived benefits
Features of support
Limited
Issue-related
Not exclusive
Dynamic
Support for a traditional leader
Support for traditional leadership
Tradition
Performance
Link to government
Default
Justifications for support

Figure 5.4 Justified support for traditional leader(ship) in Sekhukhune

mean support among people without an education was 4.04/5, while it dropped to 3.10 among university and technikon graduates. The same applies to income differentiation: people who earn less than R500 monthly gave their traditional leader an average rating of 4.04, while the rating was 3.15 among people in the highest income bracket.

How can we explain this relative decrease in support? The first reason is that people with a higher education are less dependent on the chief, and can therefore afford to be critical. Also, they are more likely to know about alternative forms of government and to compare institutions: 85 per cent of the people who had completed secondary education knew about the TLC, as compared with 27 per cent of the people with no education at all. This means that they will more often legitimate their support by pointing to the performance of traditional leaders than people with no education at all would do. Another reason lies, again, in whether people have an interest in traditional leadership and perceive it to be beneficial to their personal situation. Let us take the example of land tenure; 45 per cent of the people with a low income appreciate the system in which communal land is allocated by the traditional leader, because – arbitrary and insecure as it may be – it provides them with a better chance of obtaining a plot of land than a market-based system. With the people in the highest income brackets, the figure is only 30 per cent. The relatively rich would often want to invest in brick-faced houses and businesses on the land they had already acquired, but considered the quit-rent tenure too insecure, with the risk that 'the *kgoši* might just chase me away one day' too high.

Migrant workers, often with a relatively high income but little education, are a separate case. While they spend most of their time in the mines or factories, they feel strongly linked to the place where they have left their wives, children and fields. During their meetings in dance groups, savings clubs and other organisations they will spend a great deal of time discussing affairs back home and, according to those left behind, 'it is those migrants with their money who really run this place, even if they are hardly ever here'.[30] This group generally tends to feel strongly about traditional leadership: not only do they consider it a symbol of their rural identity, but traditional leaders can also – instrumentally – look after their families and property while they are away.

The answer to our second question – *who* supports traditional leaders? – is therefore that this depends on personal characteristics, chiefly performance and community characteristics – a mix of individual interest and cultural orientations. Some general trends can be distinguished on the basis of the Sekhukhune data. People who live in large, fast-developing areas are somewhat less likely to support a traditional leader than those in small villages, far from alternative government institutions. And if they do so, they have different reasons for it. Also, traditional leaders who meet the criteria of 'good governance' can count on more support than those who do not. And, at the individual level, the older people are more supportive than the youth, women slightly more so than men and those with less income or education more so than people with a higher socio-economic status.

In looking at *who* supports traditional leaders, we have also some of the answers to our third question – *why* do people support traditional leaders(hip)?

[30] For an interesting discussion on how migration strengthens and reconstitutes ethnicity and forms a way of interacting with people within the 'world of work and city', see James (1999).

What we have not yet addressed is the *justification* for that support, the way in which people legitimise their ideas about local rule. It is this issue that we deal with in the next section.

6. Why do people support traditional leaders?

If, five years into the 'new' South Africa with its democracy and elected local government, 80 per cent of the people in a dusty and remote corner of the country still support traditional leaders(hip), how do they justify this support? While most of the literature on the subject points to the cultural or traditional legitimacy of traditional leadership, all of the above suggests that support is justified in other ways as well (cf. note 3 and Konrad Adenauer Stiftung, 1997; Wilson, 2000: 84). These various forms of justification can be understood by looking at the patterns in people's answers to the open question 'How do you see the position of traditional leadership in the new South Africa?' While 65 per cent thought that *bogoši* still had a role to play, their motivations varied from 'traditional leaders represent our ancestors and should be protected' to 'the government must pay the *magoši* so that you have a meeting of government and tradition'.

For all their variation, the bulk of the answers seemed to fall into four reasons to (not) see a future for traditional leadership and thus four spheres of justification for supporting the institution. The first lies in the realm of tradition, of culture and of the links the institution has with the ancestors. When recoded, 24 per cent of the people came up with reasons like '*magoši* represent our culture and they are from God'.[31] The second form of justification was used by 27 per cent of the people who pointed to the performance of the institution: 'Let's abolish it. They have governed us for all those years but do you see any progress?'. A third realm of justification points to the governmental recognition of traditional leadership: 23 per cent of the people said things like '*bogoši* is not good, the government should replace it' or 'they are guarding us on behalf of the government'. Finally, 26 per cent of the people seemed to justify traditional leadership by default, not because of the merits of the institution but because of the lack of alternatives: 'We are living very far away from the government so we just have this thing.'

Naturally, these four spheres – tradition, performance, governmental recognition and the default need for rule – are intertwined, and people can legitimate their support in more than one way. But they do demonstrate that 'cultural legitimacy' is only one of the sources of justification that traditional leadership can draw on. We shall now go on to look at the four forms of legitimation and how they differ from area to area and how they shape the strategies chiefs use to obtain and retain power.

[31] The question can, of course, be answered in various different ways and we had never expected the open answers to provide such clear information on why people feel strongly about the institution. Still, 477 of the 606 valid answers could be coded this way. This is in line with theories on legitimacy being evaluative: Seymour Martin Lipset, 'Social Conflict, Legitimacy and Democracy,' in Connolly, p. 88. The other 129 said things like 'it should just be kept' and did not provide reasons.

'These are our roots': traditional legitimacy

'*Bogoši* is our culture and should therefore be protected and promoted'; 'traditional leaders are precious gifts from God and we must take care of them;' 'this is about royal blood, you can't abolish that'; '*Bogoši* should be kept as a symbol of unity and pride in black culture'. About a quarter of the Sekhukhune population primarily legitimise their support for traditional leadership by referring to culture, tradition, the ancestors or God. The essence here is that present arrangements are justified by reference to the past, the 'established belief in the sanctity of immemorial traditions and the legitimacy of those exercising authority under them' (Weber, 1978: 215).

This, of course, does not mean that the arrangements and practices referred to actually existed in the past. Life in Sekhukhune is full of 'invented traditions', from the 'traditional Pedi dances' in red checked skirts that arose out of an armed encounter with a Scottish regiment in the nineteenth century, to the leopard pelt around the shoulders of a newly inaugurated chief bought in a Johannesburg shop a week before (cf. Hobsbawm and Ranger, 1983; Ranger, 1993). Even where present practices do echo the past, the potpourri of history offers enough ambiguity to legitimise practically every form of order, and it often depends on present power relations which and whose version is successful.[32]

Of our three case studies, the people in Mamone, the largest and most developed of the three areas, were most active in the reinvention of traditions. This is not by chance. As studies of ethnicity and identity formation have shown us over and over again, the underlining of difference that is central to ethnic identity originates over boundaries, in contact with others (Barth, 1969; Clifford, 1988l Vermeulen and Gorens, 1994; Wilmsen and McAllister, 1996; Young, 1993b). In such encounters, the ostentatious exposition of ethnic markers and the performative aspects of culture become increasingly important, as if to convince the encroaching world of the uniqueness and difference of the people involved (van Binsbergen, 1999). The fact that in Mamone 36 per cent of the people legitimise their support for traditional leadership by pointing to culture or tradition, while this is only 10 per cent in the 'traditional', out-of-the-way mud-hut village of Hoepakranz, is precisely because of Mamone's encounters with the outside world. The active TLC, the televisions flashing in the new shopping centre, the foreigners coming to live in the area, all question the existing order and force it to legitimise itself in terms of its distinctiveness. The centrality of traditional authority to this process of asserting identity is clear from motivations such as: '*Bogoši* is a good instrument to reinstall our tradition'; 'it is about consolidating our roots' and 'without it we would not have a community'.

Thus, while the traditional leaders in Hoepakranz wear old business suits and continue to hold court in their yards under the leafy mango tree, or on the flat rock outside, the Mamone chief and the structures around him have taken on an increasingly 'traditional appearance' over the years of rapid change since the 1994 elections. The tribal office has been repainted with a colourful 'tribesman' and the Mamone Bapedi totem of the porcupine, there is talk of opening a museum, and the slumbering conflict over the missing skeleton of the first Sekwati, who was hanged by the Boers a century ago, is once again high up on the agenda. The performative character of this 'retraditionalisation' became clear

[32] This is one of the central points in the next chapter, which looks at the power of definition of custom and culture, which is why I shall not elaborate on it now.

on the day when girls from an expensive boarding school who were reading the Sepedi classic *Kgôrông ya mošate* visited the Mamone Traditional Authority (see photos 5 & 6, p. xiv). After the male elders had patiently answered dozens of questions on the reasons for paying tribute, marrying candle-wives and having a chief, the children were conducted to the palace. There, under a banner with 'welcome to the Mamone Bapedi' spray-painted on it, sat the unhappy-looking chief with a leopard pelt around his shoulders – its tail between his legs – on an ornate chair surrounded by yellowed portraits of his forefathers, reed baskets, tortoiseshells and divining bones with silk flowers scattered between them.

The Mamone respondents, but others as well, also show how traditional legitimacy is increasingly blended with reference to God. Ever since the first missionaries arrived in Sekhukhune in the 1860s, the relationship between Christianity and chieftainship has been tense (Delius, 1983, 1996). At that time, *Bakristi* (the people of Christ) were often seen as antithetical to tradition because of their rejection of initiation schools and ancestral beliefs. However, as the century rolled by and more and more chiefs became Christians while the churches incorporated elements of the local cosmology, this distrust vanished, although some people still protest that their chief is 'too soft, too Christian' and therefore not fit to rule.[33] They are in the minority; many others see a future for traditional leadership because 'God said that at the end of life chiefs will shine like stars – how, then, can we talk about their fate?' and 'God made the chiefs and they should be there as long as God is alive.' Accordingly, the Mamone traditional councillors urge people to support their traditional leader by quoting freely from the Bible: 'if you fight your leader, you fight God.'[34]

'They do good things for us': performance as a source of legitimation

If tradition, culture and religion together form one important source of legitimation, chiefly performance is another. As we have seen above, it is not only values and wider conditions like cultural orientations that guide people in their assessment of traditional authority, but also self-interest.[35] Twenty-seven per cent of the people evaluated traditional leadership in terms of performance, varying from 'let's abolish them, they were corrupt before and are still corrupt' and 'they have delayed progress in the community' to 'they are the people who bring development'.

There is, again, a relation between the presence of alternative government institutions – be it the TLC, the magistrate's court or other government departments – and an increase in this form of legitimation: while in Hoepakranz 18 per cent of the people legitimated their support by pointing to chiefly performance, the figure was 21 per cent in Ga-Masha and 35 per cent in Mamone. People in the two larger areas compare the traditional authorities with other government institutions, and judge them accordingly, which in turn also shapes chiefly strategies. Followers of Johannes Masha, for instance, see a future for traditional leadership now that their chief has brought a poultry project and a communal

[33] In 1970 Sansom still wrote that he knew of only two Christian chiefs in Sekhukhune; this number has multiplied today. On the relation between chieftainship and Christianity in general, see Comaroff and Comaroff (1997); Maxwell (1999).

[34] When asked, the councillors said they were referring to Proverbs 8:15. 'By me kings reign and rulers make laws that are just. By me princes govern and all nobles who rule on earth.'

[35] Cf. Habermas (1984:149) speaking of the performance ideology.

garden to the village. And in Mamone, Billy Sekwati is lauded for his attempts to bring in tourism, and to start a computer project in those areas with electricity.

This attitude of comparing institutions – without, as I have emphasised before, its leading to absolute and exclusive support – is particularly prominent in regard to the traditional courts. The majority of the Bapedi believe the traditional court to be substantially better than the magistrate's court – because of its accessibility, the number of people present, the restorative justice promoted, the judgment by acquaintances and the absence of lawyers. 'Cases are solved correctly locally, in the way it should be done.' Traditional authorities, especially those faced with competition, emphasise these unique features of traditional courts, – people do not only shop for fora, but fora also shop for people (K. von Benda-Beckman, 1984). In Mamone, for example, after a long day of settling disputes and with calabashes of beer in prospect, the audience was given a summary of the many cases heard in the past weeks: 'They were all solved amicably and all those people have come back to praise us. At least we try to build up people here, instead of the magistrate's court where you never know what they'll decide.'

It is not surprising that, when compared with alternative state institutions, traditional leaders are often ranked first. They are close to the people and can thus involve them in a decision-making process that often seems more democratic than casting a ballot once every five years never to see the candidate again – unless at a distance in a brand-new Mercedes Benz. Chiefs are local, and thus controlled more easily than councillors: 'My chief is an obedient one.' But, as we saw in the last chapter, they also have access to many more resources than the TLCs: from the chiefly salaries pouring in to state-sponsored tribal offices with entire administrations. This continued government support for traditional leadership has in itself become a source of legitimation for the institution, as we shall see in the next sub-section.

'They guard us for the government'

Large stacks of literature describe exhaustively how colonialism and apartheid cast traditional leaders in a precarious balancing act between the bureaucratic demands of their new rulers and the – often opposed – interests of the populace. The information on how this system of 'decentralised despotism' influenced people's perspectives on traditional leadership is more tentative, and generally suggests a sure loss of legitimacy for the institution (Mamdani, 1996:24). The evidence from Sekhukhune does not support this view. Quite the contrary: inclusion in the government seems to have provided traditional leadership with an extra, 'legal-rational' claim to legitimacy. In this vein, people say that 'the government should solve all these succession disputes'; '*bogoši* is in the hands of government departments'; 'I hear the government has built them a House of Traditional Leaders'. Or, alternatively, 'the government should stop buying the faces of these *magoši* and dissolve this structure'.

The extent to which many people associate traditional leaders with the government becomes clear from how they motivate their response when asked whether the government should pay the *magoši*. It should, according to 68 per cent of the people, and apart from pointing to (lack of) performance and the poverty of the community, many say things like: 'the chiefs are the ears and the mouth of the government'; 'they work for the government just like any other civil servant'; or even 'of course; they are the government'. In these cases, traditional leaders do not derive their legitimacy from their antagonism to, but rather their association with, the state. The traditional leader is considered the 'main road to the government' without whom access is impossible. 'There is no way we can go straight to the magistrate, we will always have to go via the mošate.'

It is of course hardly surprising that more than a century of inclusion of traditional leadership in wider state structures has left its imprint on how many people see their chiefs – as 'government workers' and 'civil servants'. Nor does it come as a surprise that all the laws and decrees compelling people to respect and obey the Tribal Authorities, from the Natives Land Act to the recent recognition of traditional leadership, have resulted in support for traditional leadership also being legitimated in legal-rational terms, with reference to their role in the government. Although often deprecated, these are some of the inevitable social effects of legislation on customary law and traditional leadership.[36] Traditional leaders, in turn, emphasise this government support, for instance, as we shall see in the next chapter, when it comes to succession disputes.

The degree to which traditional leaders can claim legitimacy as 'portals to the government' depends not only on chiefly agency but also, again, on the presence of alternative governmental institutions. Thus, there are two possible explanations for the fact that 32 per cent of the Ga-Masha community legitimate their (non-) support for traditional leadership by pointing to government support for the institution. The first is the personality of one Masha chief, Johannes, who keeps stressing that 'I am the umbrella of the community, everything must go through me' and actively presents himself as the intermediary between the government and the community. The second is the lack of alternative institutions: as we have seen earlier, the TLC in this area was a dismal failure and did not achieve any development. In Mamone, in contrast, where the TLC office stands a few kilometres from the tribal court and has an active presence, only 11 per cent of the people legitimate their support for traditional leaders by pointing to their inclusion in government.

'What else is there?: default legitimation

During the interviews in the adobe homesteads in Hoepakranz, people gave one reason for retaining traditional leadership that went beyond the traditional roots, performance or government support for the institution: namely, the lack of alternatives. Here, the legitimation for support did not lie in the merits of the institution or the values associated with it, but in the complete absence of other options. Half of the people said something like: 'You see, we are living far away from the government, that's why we only have this thing'; 'it should remain: where else could I go if I am fighting with someone?' or 'you need to have some authority in the land'.

On the other hand, there were people (18 per cent), mostly in Mamone, who saw the installation of the TLCs as the inevitable end of traditional leadership. They argued that '*bogoši* is a thing of the past, we now have elected leaders, so we can throw them out if they are out of order'; '*bogoši* should be given a rest and TLCs given a chance to see what they can do'; and '*magoši* are not important anymore, we are governed without them now'. From this perspective, there is no

[36] Griffiths. 'Une législation efficace: une approche comparative.'

essential difference between the TLCs and traditional leaders: both are thought of as a form of local government, and there is no need to have both.

As people legitimate their support for traditional leaders in different ways, this also shapes chiefly strategies to obtain, and retain, power. The more a traditional leader manages to draw on various sources of legitimacy, the greater his power will be; organising development projects, seeking government recognition, and underlining the unique features of tradition and the absence of alternatives, are not mutually exclusive sources of legitimation; on the contrary, they potentially reinforce each other.

7. Conclusion

In the light of South African history in general, and the Sekhukhune past in particular, the thrust of this chapter is surprising. How could it be that in 1999, five years after the last remnant of the artificial homeland edifice had been pulled down and the first democratic local and national elections had been held in the area, a staggering 80 per cent of the Bapedi said that they still supported a traditional leader? How could it be that the traditional leaders, instead of making the silent retreat envisaged for them during the 1980s youth revolt against the older order, in which traditional leaders were chased, their houses burnt down and their role as 'puppets of apartheid' ridiculed, not only stayed on but even seemed to be reinforced?

A large part of this chapter has been dedicated to a qualification of this high degree of support, and a debunking of many of the assumptions held nationally about the way in which rural people support their traditional leaders. It has shown how support is, first of all, limited: it is mostly immaterial, and very few people actually do something for their *kgoši*, be it giving presents, paying levies, or working for him. Also, if support is given, it is not always voluntary but is often enforced by external means. Support is also related to certain issues – dispute settlement, land allocation and the organisation of initiation schools – while other issues are thought better left to alternative governmental structures. These structures can well coexist with traditional leadership: support is not exclusive and the fear of having 'two bulls in a kraal' seems more a chiefly than a popular preoccupation. Far from being stable, support is also dynamic, the result of an ongoing dialogue between rulers and ruled, a permanent weighing of interests and alternatives.

The benefits people see in their association with traditional leadership guide them in their assessment of and support for the institution. Although there are some general patterns that surface, with variables at the individual, chiefly and community levels determining support, their basis lies in these individual motivations. The woman who feels the chief can protect her from her abusive husband, the migrant worker for whom he symbolises home, and the young boy who feels excluded, come to mind. But even as people get richer or more educated, or spend a larger part of their lives in town, most of them will continue to support traditional leadership, albeit in a different way – with more emphasis on performance and culture.

Even if the above partly explains the (extent of) chiefly resilience, it is the comparison between Hoepakranz, Ga-Masha and Mamone and the way in which support for traditional leadership is justified in these three case studies that enable us to understand the potential of the institution in the new South Africa. They seem to present three scenarios out of the many that are possible. In the mountain village of Hoepakranz, where the new South Africa has caused mere ripples and certainly no progress, chiefly power is rooted in the lack of alternatives. In Ga-Masha, in contrast, Johannes Masha bases his power on, and derives legitimacy from, his association with the government, from insisting on being 'the umbrella of the community', the main road to the government. This scenario, a reverberation of the apartheid situation with the traditional leader as the 'clenched fist', the sole authority in the area, works because of the early collapse of the TLC and the continued government support for traditional leaders (Mamdani, 1996:23).

Mamone, the third case study, offers us one possible scenario of what *can* happen once the promises of democracy do materialise locally, be it through active TLCs, development projects or an increased exposure to the outside world. Here, the traditional authority no longer presents itself as an extension of government, but has reinvented itself, and is accepted as an alternative to the government. It has become more performative, underlining its unique features and its otherness, in discourse – 'we solve disputes better' and in display: the museum, the leopard pelt, the revamped traditional court. If such a traditional authority also succeeds in bringing tangible benefits, its potential is high: after all, it embodies a form of rule deemed local, within reach and thus control, a focal point for identity formation, a locally grown support to hold on to as rivers of change swirl on.

Together, the three cases demonstrate the essential potential of traditional leadership: its ability to slip in and out of roles, to arrive on stage as the messenger of the state one day and as its most powerful rival, heavily cloaked in tradition, the next. In its dressing-room stands a colourful collection of attributes to endorse this role, from symbols of tradition to faded piles of legislation, a long track record and – if needed – guns and sjamboks. The attributes displayed, and the role played, are determined in a permanent dialogue with the people. As John Comaroff wrote about the Tswana: 'the chief and his subjects are thought to be involved in a permanent transactional process in which the former discharges obligations and, in return, receives the accepted right to influence policy and command people' (1974:41).

Traditional leadership, like the customary law that determines its authority, is not a fixed institution but is subject to ongoing debate and negotiation.[37] This became clear from the Sekhukhune villagers who said: 'chiefs are all right but they should just be workshopped [educated in workshops] about these transitions'; 'it would be better if we were to start voting for our traditional leaders'; 'this thing should be retained, but only with some changes'. These debates on the contents of customary law and traditional authority, the way in which they take place within the local power relations and how traditional leaders draw on various sources of legitimacy, form the subject-matter of the next chapter.

[37] Cf. Williams, *Blurring the Boundaries of Tradition: the transformation and legitimacy of the chieftaincy in South Africa.*

6. Negotiated Laws, Relational Rights
Power, Authority & the Creation of Local Law

> ... customary law was an established system of immemorial rules which had evolved from the way of life and natural wants of the people, the general context of which was a matter of common knowledge, coupled with precedents applying to special cases, which were retained in the memories of the chief and his counsellors, their sons and their son's sons, until forgotten, or until they became part of immemorial rules ... (Bekker, 1989:11)

> 'Do you have some books on customary law for us?' – Madibaneng councillor

1. Introduction

The South African Constitution recognises the 'institution, status and role of traditional leadership, according to customary law'. The previous two chapters have described the institution, status and role of traditional leadership in Sekhukhune as that of an important actor in the institutionally pluralist rural landscape. This actor was able to strengthen its position within the new dispensation through its organic alliances with other important actors, vigilante organisations and churches alike, and its access to various sources of legitimacy – traditional, governmental and others. In this final chapter on Sekhukhune, the time has come to consider the last element in the constitutional provision: customary law. What do the Bapedi consider to be the customary law determining the position of traditional leadership?

A first issue to look into is the meaning of 'customary law'. As described in an earlier chapter, the South African Law Commission distinguishes between 'official' and 'living' versions of customary law.[1] The 'official' customary law is a sub-category of South African state law, and consists of laws like the Black Administration Act (38/1927) the Black Authorities Act (68/1957), the Recognition of Customary Marriages Act (120/1998) and the large corpus of ensuing decrees and regulations and court judgments as well as the customary law text-books to which they refer.[2] These in turn draw heavily on – often apartheid-inspired – ethnographic text-books such as the *Laws and Customs of the Bapedi and Cognate Tribes*, *The Pedi* and the Afrikaans *Indigenous Public Law in Lebowa* which lists rules of customary law worded like the Ten Commandments. This 'official' customary law is, in the words of the Law Commission, 'frequently consulted as the most readily available source' but is 'often inaccurate and misleading'.[3] The

[1] South African Law Commission. 'Project 90: Customary Law', p. 24.

[2] For an overview of the legislation see De Villiers (1998); Text-books are Bekker (1989); Bennett (1991); Olivier et al. (1995). Court judgments can be found in, *inter alia*, the South African Law Reports.

[3] South African Law Commission. 'Project 90: Customary Law', p. 24.

Commission laments that, in contrast, little is known about the 'living' customary law, which 'rests squarely on the existing and generally accepted social practices of a community' and is 'imprecise, flexible, and liable to constant and subtle change'.

This 'living law', and its interaction with the other registers of law, form the subject-matter of this chapter. For the analysis, it is useful to refine the Law Commission's dichotomy to distinguish four registers of law, each embedded in separate discourses and discernible through a distinct research methodology.[4] First, there is South Africa's common law, the composite of laws, legal precedents and doctrine, with the Constitution as its umbrella text. The 'official' customary law is a species of the generic common law, its recognition couched in a specific discourse but its substance essentially also discernible from the text. A third distinction is that of 'stated customary law', the idealised rules often retrieved through interviews with traditional leaders or village elders. Not long ago, this was accepted as the prime way to 'assert' customary law. Even today, after numerous commentators have emphasised how this method often does not lead to statements of what local law is – if that is at all possible – but of what respondents would like it to be, it continues to be the prime research tool of many South African legal researchers and policy-makers.[5] One reason for this is that its favoured 'hit-and-run method' – driving into a village, getting the village elders together, confronting them with a questionnaire and then speeding off – makes it more cost-efficient than the participatory research of the *longue durée* associated with the fourth register, living law. This term, first coined by Ehrlich and with synonyms such as 'local law', 'folk law' and 'law in action', serves to indicate law as lived in day-to-day life and the norms and values it draws on.[6] While discussion on the appropriate research method – should the focus be on rules or processes, troublesome cases or trouble-free cases? – is a staple topic in the anthropology of law, there is consensus on the necessity of long-term field research to understand the nature of 'living law'. Although the four registers are distinct, they influence and draw legitimacy from one another. In Sekhukhune, for instance, the contents of the Constitution have reached the Bapedi since the advent of democracy through the radio station *Thobela FM*, booklets and

[4] Many comparable distinctions have been made. Bennett (1997:86) speaks of the official code, ethnographic texts and living law, quoted in Costa (1998:534). D'Engelbronner (2001:26) basing herself on Roberts (1984) even distinguishes seven categories of customary law in Namibia: 1) pre-colonial customary law; 2) the survival, transformation and displacement of this pre-colonial customary law during the period of colonisation; 3) the colonial customary law; 4) lawyers, anthropologists, colonial administrators and missionaries, who retrieved and wrote down the law; 5) the living law of today; 6) the law currently applied in the customary courts; 7) the customary law as applied by the post-colonial government.

[5] The best-known and most detailed description of how 'customary law' was created in a dialogue between policy-makers and local rulers can be found in Chanock (1985). Cf. Costa (1999a). The South African Law Commission, in its project on the harmonisation of the common law and indigenous law, held numerous workshops with traditional leaders, who were able to put forward 'the' rules of 'their' communities. In academia, this rule-centred approach is still favoured by the Centres for Indigenous Law at the University of South Africa and the University of Pretoria, which issued a 'Handleiding by die Optekening van Inheemse Reg' (Guide for the Assertion of Indigenous Law).

[6] Ehrlich (1936:493). Cf. Griffiths (1986); Hellum (1999:62). See also the remarks on legal pluralism in the Introduction to this study. One main objection against Ehrlich has been that his definition of law was too broad and could include any social norm. As stated earlier, this can be remedied by adopting Tamanaha's non-essentialist definition of law: 'law is whatever people recognize and treat as law through their social practices', Tamanaha (2000:319).

newspapers. Traditional authority officials and tribal offices have yellowing copies of proclamations such as the 'Regulations Prescribing the Duties, Powers, Privileges and Conditions of Service of Chiefs and Headmen', and village elders invoke idealised norms – all influencing living law.

While the fissure between this official customary law and the living law has been well described in the literature, its depth dawned on me only during the first customary court case I attended in Sekhukhune. Still in the process of selecting research sites as well as a research assistant, I visited Madibaneng in the company of a Pedi law student who had recently taken a course entitled 'African Customary Law 203' at the University of the North. As case after case was discussed by the councillors squeezed on to the school benches of the 'tribal office', he could not stop shaking his head in intense frustration: neither process nor substance complied with what he had just been taught. Cases were discussed by male *and* female councillors, on opposite sides of the room. The councillors were not royals, they told us, but elected because of their 'active mind and ability to come up with innovations'. Instead of having a group discussion, people were appointed – in a clear imitation of penal cases in the magistrate's court – as either *prosekutora* or *magistrata.* The *kgoši* himself was absent, but youthful representatives of the civic organisations had been invited to give their opinion.

One *molato* (case) concerned a child who had stolen a pump part. The parties agreed that in different circumstances the thief would have had to stay behind to sweep the floor of the tribal office, but that this would amount to *child labour* (in English) here, and that it would be preferable to ask the mother to pay a fine. The longest discussion was about the reclamation of a plot of land. 'Aha, revindicatio', the law student whispered in delight. But far from being about the simple exertion of an ownership right, the discussion seemed to focus on the social and political status of the absent claimant. Had the man merely gone to town as a migrant labourer or been sent away by *kgoši* Phahlamohlaka? If the latter, did Phahlamohlaka have the right to do so or did the land fall under *kgoši* Mohlala? And what was actually known about this man who wanted to resettle in the village? Even if the land had once belonged to him, the consensus seemed to be that, for now, there was no reason to give it back to him. At sunset, after the councillors had patiently answered our questions on customary law, one of them escorted us back to our car and said: 'Actually, we're just doing something [muddling along] here. Couldn't you send us some books on customary law?'

As the research continued and I teamed up with another research assistant, who knew little about codified law but a lot about local social and political relations, I learned that the Madibaneng customary court – with its elected councillors, division into prosecutors and magistrates and involvement of the civics – was far from typical. In fact, there hardly existed such a thing as a typical customary court. On the other hand, some of those early lessons were constantly reaffirmed: the importance of the local political arena in the creation of living law, the willingness to invoke state laws and procedures in some cases and set them aside in others, the essentially negotiated character of local law and its embedment in social and political circumstances in a way that cannot be caught in terms such as 'revindicatio'.

These lessons, which will be elaborated more fully in the course of this chapter, call for a specific approach. First, they require a revision of the term 'customary'. Terms such as 'stated customary law' and 'living customary law' typically refer to the – supposed – living law in areas with a traditional authority. In the previous two chapters, Sekhukhune has been shown to be such a field, but also abounding in institutions involved in the creation of local law. In addition, as with the legitimation of support for traditional authority, local law draws on a variety of sources ranging from the 'loosely constructed repertoire' of custom to constitutional and developmental values (Comaroff and Roberts, 1981:18). It is for this reason that I shall generally speak of 'living law' or 'local law' instead of 'customary law' when discussing what *molao (*law) entails locally.[7]

Secondly, the central viewpoint that this living law is negotiated within ever-fluctuating social and political settings, which it simultaneously reflects and shapes, precludes the possibility of neatly listing the Bapedi rules concerning the succession to the throne, the choice of candle-wives, the structure of the traditional authority and the extent of and limits to the powers of traditional leaders.[8] Even if ideal norms can be stated, and do have an importance in that they reflect worldviews and moral claims, they more often than not turn out to be exceptions rather than rules. What is more useful, then, is an investigation of the forces that determine which rules are invoked, why and by whom at a specific moment, and on which sources they draw. This requires a continued analysis of the Sekhukhune legal culture, defined in Bierbrauer's terms as the 'socially derived product encompassing such interrelated concepts as legitimacy and acceptance of authorities, preferences for and beliefs about dispute arrangements, and authorities' use of discretionary power' as well as the forces that shape it (Bierbrauer, 1994:243).

With this in mind, section 2 will describe the main characteristics of living law in Sekhukhune. Following on from earlier chapters, it will describe the plurality of fora to which Bapedi can take disputes and how this access to alternatives forces customary courts to come up with socially acceptable settlements. I introduce the notion of *negotiated law* to draw attention to the degree to which law is crucially shaped within political relations, and how these relations determine which norms, out of a large possible pool, get accepted. Within these negotiations, state law as well as tradition can be considered resources, potentially drawn into and reaffirmed within the local arena. Apart from reflecting and shaping the political, living law also acts as a 'motor and flywheel' of social relations.[9] The term 'relational rights' indicates how the claims an individual can make are tied up with his/her status in society. The fact that the political and social landscape is in a constant state of flux – caused by wider national trends, local shifts of power which can even be caused by affirmation of certain positions in law – creates the need for rules and rights to be permanently renegotiated and adapted. This leads to a legal culture that is much more *processual* than the common law with its reliance on absolutes and legal certainty.

After this general introduction to living law and legal culture in Sekhukhune, the way these affect the power and authority of traditional leaders is discussed in two contrasting case studies. Again, my central concern is the interaction of

[7] In the literature, both terms are used. Cf. Hellum (1999:62); Von Benda-Beckmann (1989).

[8] These can be found in Harries (1929); Mönnig (1967); Prinsloo (1983).

[9] The term is Sklar's: Richard Sklar, 'The Premise of Mixed Government in African Political Systems.' Paper presented at the Indigenous Political Structures and Governance in Africa conference, Ibadan, 2001.

the local and the national in determining the position of traditional leaders, this time viewed through the prism of the law and the interaction between its four registers: common law, official customary law, idealised customary law and living law. In section 3, the first case study looks at succession disputes in Sekhukhune and the way in which traditional leaders can at times gain a decisive advantage in the permanent search for local legitimacy through drawing in state law, with its certificates and lifetime appointments. The next case, in section 4, focuses on the negotiation of a 'tribal constitution', in part to deal with the powers of the Mamone *kgoši*, and shows how state law can also be invoked by the more marginalised sections of a community. One consequence of the notion of law negotiated within local political relations is that those in power benefit from legal uncertainty and a large repertoire of conflicting rules and values to call into disputes, while the relatively powerless benefit from codification of, for instance, the rights and privileges of traditional leaders. For all their contrasts, both cases demonstrate the importance of the local political arena, in which state law is merely a resource in what are essentially local struggles, even if it can, sometimes crucially, affect the balance of power. The theoretical implications of this viewpoint will be discussed in section 5.

2. Living law and legal culture in Sekhukhune

To illustrate the central claims of this section, let me start by recounting one case out of the 50-odd discussions of *melato* (problems) I witnessed in Sekhukhune – in official customary courts, the yards of *magoši*, headmen and family heads, the offices of the vigilante organisation *Mapogo a Mathamaga*, the local government office, many schools and the magistrate's court: the fight over teachers' trousers in Hoepakranz.

> Built on one of the undulating hills surrounding the tiny village of Hoepakranz, the small school constitutes a symbol of community solidarity and local aspirations for 'a better future for our children', as well as a visible encounter with elements of the outside world like the Department of Education. It is also the one forum in which all members of this community, which is torn apart by a succession dispute between two chiefs, find common ground. One winter morning in early 1999, the school was packed with men and women assembled to discuss the fact that the female teachers had gone on strike because the School Policy, recently drawn up by the principal and one male teacher, forbade them to wear trousers. All the local 'structures' were represented – the two chiefs, the School Governing Body (SGB), a competing School Forum, the ANC branch – as well a great many villagers. The school principal, one teacher, the head of the SGB and a royal adviser chaired the heated meeting and controlled the agenda chalked on the blackboard (1- opening, 2- rollcall, 3- words of the chairperson, 4- issues to be discussed, 5- closure). The lengthy and heated discussion began with criticism of the fact that only part of the community had been involved in drafting the School Policy. Nevertheless, *kgoši* Joseph Nkosi remarked, 'Women who wear trousers solicit rape'. The female head of the pre-school protested: 'Our new Constitution says that anyone can wear what they want.' The brash young head of the ANC agreed, waving a newspaper with an explanation of the South African Schools Act. In contrast, a male teacher told how he had once attended a meeting during which the Minister of Education had ordered a teacher to take off his baseball cap. The head of the traditional dance group angrily asserted that 'teachers should be recognised as teachers. Some people at this meeting have read so well that they want to bring outside policies to our

> school. If you say this is following apartheid policies, so be it. We'd rather do that than be free with all sorts of funny ideas.' Another prominent villager agreed: 'We send our children to school to learn about respect, because that is something we value.' Some women tried to suggest exceptions to the proposed rule: could women teachers wear trousers if they wore long-sleeved shirts, or only when doing exercises? One of the teachers involved proposed a vote, by all present and by the students. She was hissed down: 'We are not allowing votes; the youth have no say in this matter.' One of the *kgošis* concluded: 'I am saying this for the last time: ladies should not wear trousers. I don't care about votes – we have many youth and if we vote they'll outnumber us.' Upon which the principal closed the session: 'We have now agreed that ladies are not allowed to wear trousers.'

This case, as typical as any, shows how rules and rights are discussed not only in magistrates' and customary courts, but in other fora as well, and how the participation of as many local stakeholders as possible renders its decisions legitimate. This plurality of fora and their consequences will be discussed next. We then go on to see that it also demonstrates how law can be considered negotiated rather than adjudicated, complete with counterbids ('only during exercises') in which the political relations often essentially determine outcomes. We then examine how state laws and policies can be invoked – often with contrasting examples – as a resource in these negotiations, as can such traditional values as 'respect'. This is followed by a sub-section on relational rights, focusing on the fact that the rights of female teachers are related to their position in society. Thus, the legal culture can be considered processual, rather than binary, as the final sub-section will show.

Plurality of fora

The pluralism that characterises the Sekhukhune institutional landscape is reflected in a plurality of fora for the settlement of disputes. For analytical purposes, a distinction can be made between the magistrates' courts, official customary courts, unofficial customary courts and other fora involved in dispute resolution.

'This is the most boring place to work in you can imagine,' one of the four (African) Sekhukhune magistrates said. 'People solve their cases at home. *Mapogo* does the criminal cases these days and customary cases remain with the chiefs. I only have one sitting a week, in which I predominantly deal with assault and theft.'[10] Like his colleagues, he told people who brought cases deemed 'customary' – land disputes, family fights, insults – to go back to their chief. 'Many people don't want to be subject to their chief and rush to us. But cases should start at home, then be taken to the chief, and only then to us.' It is rare for Sekhukhune citizens to reach this last stage: in the period 1994–9 the Sekhukhune magistrate's court registered only six appeals from the official customary courts: two demands for dissolution of a customary union, return of the bridewealth and custody of the children, one case concerning grave insults, a land dispute and two cases in which cattle given in custody had died.[11] The magistrates generally try these cases according to 'official' customary law; during our discussions they always had a copy of Seymour's *Customary Law in Southern Africa* ready for consultation.

[10] Interview, 9 September 1999.

[11] Sekhukhune magistrate's court, file 'appeals from chiefs' courts', consulted 9 September 1999. These appeals are lodged ex *Chiefs' and Headmen's Civil Courts: Rules R2082/1967*, which in turn is based on s12 of *Black Authorities Act 68/1951*.

Table 6.1 Responses regarding who should try cases (%)

Subject	Kgosi	Magistrate
Marriage matters	53	57
Family matters	71	22
Petty theft	67	19
Maintenance cases	19	77
Land issues	62	35
Assault/bodily harm	49	38
Large theft	9	90
Witchcraft	68	35

People have various reasons for not taking disputes to the magistrate's court. First, they too acknowledge the systematic reinforcement by the state of the customary courts: 5 per cent of the 606 people asked to comment on customary courts said something like: 'If you shoot straight to the magistrate he will send you straight back.' A much larger number (42 per cent) also had substantive reasons to steer clear, if possible, of these state courts. They pointed to the adversarial character, lengthy procedures, corruptibility, costliness, unintelligibility in terms of language and procedure and the fact that the magistrate is far away, 'doesn't look at who you are or where you come from', has the power to imprison and 'just decides on his own'. 'One ear cannot hear....', goes an oft-quoted saying. Some cases, however, are deemed best solved by the magistrate, in particular those concerning maintenance and large theft (see Table 6.1).[12]

The official customary courts are those of chiefs recognised by the state on whom jurisdiction has been conferred by s 12(1) and 20(1) of the Black Administration Act (38/1929).[13] Official customary law only states which cases these courts cannot try – from faction fighting to perjury to 'pretended witchcraft'.[14] Formally, these courts are obliged to report all their decisions to the magistrate through a so-called B502 form where they can list the names of the plaintiff and the defendant, the particulars of both the claim and the defence, and the judgment. In practice, hardly any of Sekhukhune's 34 official customary courts files such reports: the 84 cases that were reported in the 1994–9 period should therefore be treated with circumspection, but do offer some insight into the types of cases that are ruled on.[15] Thirteen cases involved couples fighting

[12] This table contains the answers to two separate closed questions: 'Which cases do you feel the *kgoši*/magistrate should try?' Respondents could choose more than one answer.

[13] Proclamation 961 of 1992 assigned the power to confer civil and criminal jurisdiction on traditional leaders to the Minister of Justice.

[14] The full list forms Schedule III of the *Black Administration Act 38/1927* and includes treason, murder, rape, robbery, assault with intent to do grievous bodily harm, abortion, sodomy and extortion.

[15] File with the B502 records in the Sekhukhune magistrate's court, consulted on 14 September 1999. The majority of the cases were reported in Sepedi and translated by the author. In total, 19 traditional authorities had reported cases, of which the Koni Maloma (15), Tau Mankotsane (15) and Koni Legare (10) did so most frequently. This is a very small portion of the cases ruled on. One reason not to regard the subject-matter of these cases as representative is that many of them (35 out of 84) seem to have been reported because the *kgôrô* alleged disrespect. On the other hand, the predominance

and wanting to separate, including demands for return of the bridewealth, transfer of property and custody of the children. Nine cases were about often severe instances of domestic violence, in which the battered wife usually received the support of the *kgôrô*, sometimes with judgments like 'the court found Mr Maripane guilty of assaulting his wife with a stick without adequate reason'. Cases that started with an insult, varying from 'she said my children would be eaten by ants' to accusations of witchcraft, are just as frequent. Other recurrent topics are land disputes (7), small theft (8), lack of respect for the *kgôrô* (8) and breach of contract, particularly in supplying building materials (7).

Cases in the official customary courts are often appeals from unofficial customary courts, those not recognised by the state but associated with the 'traditional authority hierarchy', and varying from courts convened by traditional leaders who do not have state recognition but are recognised by their people, to courts convened by headmen or ward-heads, or even *ka setšo* (traditionally), *mo lapeng* (in the yard) or with the larger family. In general, courts that are considered appeal courts, like those of traditional leaders or headmen in large areas, are more bureaucratised than the lower-level fora: they take place in a 'tribal office' or a designated space surrounded by *mafata* (ragged branches), and at times the 'tribal secretary' even takes notes. Nevertheless, the procedures are similar: both parties and their supporters can state their case, after which the opinions of all present are collected, followed by a period of *go aga* (building) and searching for a solution. Men wear a jacket and stand up when speaking, while women cover their heads and remain seated.[16] The procedure is thus a mixture of adjudication and negotiation, in which the adjudicator can be the *kgoši*, headman or family head, alone or with some councillors, who have either inherited the function or been elected or appointed. The involvement of women varies as well: in some courts women can only be witnesses or silent listeners, in others they have won the right to present a case themselves or even to adjudicate in the role of *kgošigadi* or councillor (regent).

On the whole, Sekhukhune citizens prefer customary courts to those of the magistrates: Sixty-five per cent of the respondents were positive about the *tseko ya kgoši*. The majority of them gave reasons related to procedure and performance: the fact that cases are usually decided within a day, and are debated 'by many heads' in Sepedi, that the debate is easy to follow and aims to achieve harmony and consensus, and that the case is decided 'by people who know who you are and where your come from'. Some also emphasised the cultural and traditional character of the dispute resolution process: 'This is how our parents did things and we will hand it on to our children.' There are also other voices: the 35 per cent of respondents who were less positive emphasised that the courts' embedment in local politics and social relations cause them to be biased: 'They will always look at who your family is and what you have done for them.' The lack of education of those involved is also considered a problem: 'How can these old, illiterate men pretend that they are the magistrate?'

Other fora involved in local dispute resolution often use the same procedures and invoke the same values as customary courts. Even if the form and content

[15 (cont.)] of couples fighting, domestic violence, land issues, insult, and petty theft in the customary courts was confirmed during my field research.

[16] This was considered by many of the women interviewed as one of the most discriminatory aspects of the traditional authority.

differ, most powerful local institutions are at times asked to settle disputes. In the 1980s, the heyday of the protest against traditional authorities, the young agitators were often confronted with old men and women asking them to settle marriage matters or land disputes. The mighty *Mapogo*, notorious for the violent public flogging of criminals, is also often confronted with parties that show up in the organisation's offices looking for a mediated settlement. The same goes for the community policing fora, the Transitional Local Council and organisations such as 'People Against Stocktheft'.

The parallel existence of all these courts – with a varying degree of formality – allows a certain degree of forum-shopping among the Bapedi. It also stimulates dispute resolution fora not only to come up with negotiated settlements acceptable to all parties, rather than decisions that benefit only one side, but also to legitimise their own position and at times actively 'solicit cases' (cf. K. von Benda-Beckmann, 1984:37ff). The way in which many official customary courts have reinvented themselves in the post-apartheid era is a good example. Even if the magistrates continued to send 'chiefs' subjects' back to these courts, the state's support of official chiefs, councils and courts by means of guns and tanks had withered away, obliging these courts to reposition and legitimate themselves within the fast-changing institutional landscape.

The trajectories by which this happened differed. Take the neighbouring communities of Madibong and Mamone, comparable in size and population. In Madibong the apartheid Tribal Council was revamped, with the head of the civics as its chairman and two female ANC councillors among its members. While the procedures and substance of dispute resolution hardly changed, this relegitimised the council in the eyes of the people. In Mamone, conversely, the inauguration of Billy Sekwati Mampuru III led to the dismantling of the Tribal Council – 'an apartheid structure, which is not representative and can't be controlled' – and the refounding of the 'traditional' *kgôrô*, held under a tree surrounded by *mafata*, at a stone's throw from the Tribal Office. 'The owner of the house has returned,' the royal advisers told villagers, urging them to take their problems to the *kgôrô*. After the lengthy court sessions, Billy's brother would from time to time practise a bit of public relations and recount with gusto all the cases already solved amicably: 'All those people came to us crying and left satisfied, praising us for our wisdom.' At the same time – the stick and the carrot – plaintiffs who came to the *kgôrô* because they had been sent back by the magistrate or were not happy with decisions taken elsewhere, were severely reprehended. 'This man isn't happy with the decision of the Tribal Council and now he comes running to us, he is playing with fire.' Nevertheless, as we shall see in the next sub-section, the plurality of fora stimulated negotiated and widely accepted settlements.

Negotiated law

All the fora described above invoke and create a tissue of norms and values best described as *negotiated law*.[17] This term draws attention to the fact that law-

[17] The notion of dispute settlement by negotiation was put forward by Gulliver, who took it as a procedural feature and contraposed the notion of adjudicated dispute resolution when writing about the Arusha tribunal in Tanzania (Gulliver, 1979, 1963). Recently, the term 'negotiated' has also been coined for the rules and rights themselves, especially in the field of conflict resolution and property rights (cf. Berry (2000); Bierschenk and Le Meur (1999); Gérard et al. (1996); Lund (1999); Ben Kwame. 'Changes, Ambiguities and Conflicts: Negotiating Land Rights in Buem-Kator, Ghana.' PhD Thesis, Baltimore, MD: Johns Hopkins University, 2000; Bernhard Venema and Hans van den Breemer,

making, for all its reference to rules, takes place squarely in the context of local power relations, and is crucially shaped by them. While the distinctive influence of the social and political landscape on the legal has long been widely acknowledged, there has been considerably less attention to what this means for the character, procedure and substance of local law.[18]

First, it is important to consider briefly the place of dispute resolution, for instance in fora such as customary courts, in a specific social field like Sekhukhune. While I agree with Marilyn Strathern (1985) that dispute settlement takes place in a continuum, and that court cases merely form part of the social processes in which people are involved, customary courts should also be considered as symbolically and materially distinct social spaces (cf. Griffiths, 1997). They provide well-defined, singled-out fora with a specific vocabulary, roles and procedures in which issues can be brought up that would be unheard of outside; there are various forms of punishment at hand; and power relations are laid bare and norms and values explicated and potentially reaffirmed. Apart from mirroring the rules and relations in wider society, they also shape them. This is why (customary) courts and the cases they hear merit their continued centrality in studies of the local (re)production of law, bearing in mind that the role of 'troublesome cases' cannot be understood without looking at 'trouble-free cases' and the way in which they are rooted in the wider institutional, political and moral landscape.

Just as this wider moral landscape involves permanent negotiation of status – *vis-à-vis* others, the ancestors, the invisible world – court sessions can also be considered essentially as bargaining processes, though based on reference to an amalgam of rules, facts and values. In this process the relative importance of speakers plays a great role in determining how their arguments are valued. A typical case will begin with an outline by the adjudicators – the chief, 'official tribal councillors ', *bakgomana* or an elected council – who thus set the tone and delimit the range of topics to be discussed. Subsequently, the family members and other supporters of the parties give their opinion, after which the floor is open. The elderly speak first, and if women and uninitiated men are allowed to speak at all, it is right at the end. In the next stage, the councillors and royal advisers themselves pose questions and give opinions, and in so doing already put forward the contours of a solution. Arguments deemed valid are met with explicit appraisal: cheers, murmurs of approval, clapping. Only then will the adjudicators decide, sometimes after retiring to consider the issues. In general, they will follow the argument presented by the most influential villagers, although their prominent position does give them some leverage to mitigate or aggravate the solution proposed. Let us take an average case decided at the Mamone *kgôrô* as an example:

The Magakalas v. the Monagedis[19]

Mr Magakala had threatened to kill his wife 'by rope or knife', in a letter taken to the *mošate* (the palace) by his wife's family, the Moganedis. The protracted discussion

[17 (cont.)] eds. *Towards Negotiated Co-Management of Natural Resources in Africa. African Studies*. Vol. 12, Muenster: Lit Verlag). Regrettably, most of these books offer little explicit analysis of the notion of negotiated rights and what this means for the relation between law and politics. I shall try to address this issue and posit the notion of negotiated law in a wider theory on the interaction between state and local law in the Conclusion.

[18] Notable exceptions are Bronstein (1998) and Falk Moore (1978).

[19] Heard in the Mamone *kgôrô*, 26 May 1999.

> involved issues such as whether both families had followed the right procedures, whether the man had been unfaithful to his wife, fights between the wife and her mother-in-law and how the parties had first tried to resolve the conflict in the church, by means of a ZCC dance. All sorts of norms were invoked to underline that the man's conduct had been wrong: 'Even in the Bible it says that men and women should live in harmony', 'we don't beat our wives either', 'if you are a man and you've built your own house you should treat your wife with respect'. The chief's brother structured the discussion, allowing *directions, follow-ups, concerns* and *questions* (all these words in English) and emphasising and acclaiming certain points. After hours of debate, Mr Magakala was asked whether he accepted guilt and *molao wa Maroteng* (the law of the Maroteng). 'I will accept whatever solution you come up with,' he said. After guilt had been established, excited bargaining took place on the punishment. 'Five strokes on his buttocks', 'a cow or a goat', '100 Rand'. The royal advisers retired for a while and came back with the verdict: payment of R200 to the court.

Adjudication and negotiation thus exist side by side. The fact that the accused had to accept explicitly and agree with the verdict is but one example of this: in cases where one of the parties refused to accept the verdict, talks would continue until there was consensus. Although the emphasis on 'harmony', 'building' and 'bringing people together' is a central and recurrent aspect of the Sekhukhune processes of dispute resolution, the unequal power relations in which it is embedded should not be underestimated. To quote Gulliver (1963:2-3): 'a party's agreement to a settlement does not at all imply that the party likes it in any absolute way, but rather that it is accepted as the most advantageous one which can be obtained in the total circumstances.' Behind harmonious decisions there often lurches, implicitly or explicitly, the threat of force: a thrashing, bewitchment, expulsion from the community, the wrath of the ancestors or of God.

What can be said now of the law invoked and produced in these fora? While there is no such thing as a 'system' of customary law, there is a pool of shared values, ideas about right and wrong and acceptable sources of morality that are commonly acknowledged and rooted in local cultural orientations. These include the importance of tradition and respect for the local order, the ancestors and for God, but also of development, unity, participation, discipline, justice in general and, at times, obedience to the state system. Behind these general values lies a whole pool of often contradictory norms and rules that can be, but are not always, invoked. Thus, while respect for tradition is generally accepted as important, its contents can be seriously debated. The local process of dispute resolution is about mixing and matching rules that refer to culture, common sense, state regulations, the Constitution, precedent and a variety of other sources hardly considered contradictory. As one Mamone councillor said: 'Actually, we're just using our heads and doing something. Don't you sort out your children fighting in the same way?' The fact that local law is 'combined law', engendered in many places but woven together in one specific spatial and temporal moment, explains why the notion of 'legal pluralism' does not capture the essence of the local-level dispute resolution process.[20]

Rules might be the language in which disputes are argued, but they do not determine their outcome. While this observation about the differing contexts of discovery and of justification has often been made concerning the judicial

[20] The term is Fitzpatrick's quoted in F. Von Benda-Beckmann (1984:31). The notion of legal pluralism is briefly discussed in the Introduction. See Fitzpatrick (1983:168).

procedure in state courts in Africa and the West, it takes on an extra dimension in customary courts.[21] Here, the range of norms able to be invoked is infinitely larger and the legal much more intimately caught up in the social and political, in the knowledge litigants and adjudicators have of one another and the interests many of them have in specific outcomes. Naturally, rules can also check power and delimit the range of possible outcomes. They are, as we shall see in the next sub-section, important resources in the negotiation process.

To sum up, the intimate relations between law and power as well as the rule-making capacities of the customary courts are demonstrated by a discussion held in the Mamone customary court. After having finished the actual adjudication, the chief's brother suggested that it was time to 'go back to our tradition of not working in the fields on Wednesday, as this is the day for settling disputes'. A discussion ensued on the limits of this rule: would it also apply to people guarding their fields against monkeys, and to working in community gardens? And what would be the penalty for transgressors? R120, for the informer and half for the royal house? Interestingly, all through the discussion the old men protested, saying things like: 'I've never heard of this rule. I know for sure that my father would go to the fields on Wednesdays, as would my grandfather. What tradition is this?' Their words were not taken into account. After a protracted discussion, the chief's brother, fatigued, hammered on the ground with his walking stick and belched: 'Let's close this discussion. This is our tradition, we're going back to it now and who does not follow will be fined.'

State law as a resource

The local stakeholders who are, collectively and individually, involved in the negotiation of local law can be considered to have potential access to a variety of resources: reference to tradition, the Bible, common sense, development ideology, laws, the Constitution, but also the threat of force, privileged access to information and status in society.

> 'Resources' is, in fact, a loose concept intended to cover anything that, in context, offers potential power in the negotiations. Thus resources range over economic and physical assets of many kinds, the relative status of the disputant and his supporters and their skills and experience, the degree of support that a disputant can recruit and the unity in purpose and policy of the party so formed, the support of influential outsiders with their own interests and values, and normative correctness vis-à-vis society at large, particular sectors or individuals within it and the opposing party in particular. No useful purpose is served by an attempt to enumerate or classify the full range of possible resources, not only because the range varies a good deal cross-culturally but also because available resources depend so heavily on the context of a particular dispute. (Gulliver, 1979:202)

With Gulliver, I feel that norms, whatever their source, should be considered a resource drawn on by litigants together with all other resources that can

[21] Cf. Falk Moore (1978), who makes a similar argument and then writes: 'Many of the Chagga cases alluded to in this paper referred to norms. But given what we know of the political setting in which they were made, it would seem that the norms were sometimes more justifications than reasons. The most venal of Chagga chiefs making the most self-interested of decisions usually did so while invoking accepted, or at any rate, politically legitimated principles of conduct.' See also: Vedeld (1997:344).

further their position. State law, whether common law or codified customary law, can then be considered a potential resource in the negotiation of local law.

To what extent and in which form state law is invoked in the local arena depends on mediators, often those people who have privileged access to organs of state such as the Department of Traditional Affairs, to the ANC and to newspapers, and who derive distinct bargaining strength from this access. The ambiguous character of the messages sent out by the state – through overlapping legislation and contradictory policies – makes it easy for mediators to select those aspects of state law deemed useful, and set aside those that will not further their interests.[22] Schapera (1969:244) described long ago how important the personality of traditional leaders is in deciding the local applicability of 'missionary and similar norms', but the same goes for headmasters, local politicians, civic leaders and other brokers with a local following and – sometimes monopolistic – access to state information. As with development projects, local mediators will deconstruct state law and retain those elements deemed useful.[23] One result is that the local process of dispute resolution can borrow and derive legitimacy from the state legal system and has thus become more and more like it, while simultaneously retaining an 'exit option', the freedom to underline its difference.[24]

A discussion with Mohlaletse tribal councillors on the changes since 1994 illustrates this feature of customary courts. 'There have been some changes with the new Constitution. For instance, we are not allowed to give corporal punishment any more. They also say that women have equal rights to land now, but we don't apply that one: it seems to be too fast. Sometimes we ask the magistrate for advice, but he does not always understand our custom.'[25] The way in which state law is invoked can vary: in an area close to Mohlaletse an unmarried woman was granted a plot of land for the first time by referring to the new Constitution as explained on the radio and amassing support among her uncles for this position (see Oomen, 1999c). As a resource, state law cannot only be deconstructed but also reinterpreted, invented, presented as tradition or plagiarised in terms of procedure. Let us consider examples of each of these processes.

'The social life of norms' and the way in which state law is subject to persistent reinterpretation can be illustrated by the 'tribal resolutions'. A 'tribal resolution' is a community decision to sell a plot of 'tribal land', for instance. Although various state definitions are ciculating, the most commonly cited one comes from the Upgrading of Land Tenure Rights Act of 1991:[26]

> 'tribal resolution', in relation to a tribe, means a resolution passed by the tribe democratically and in accordance with the indigenous law or customs of the tribe: Provided that for the purposes of this Act any decision to dispose of a right in tribal land may only be taken by a majority of the members of the tribe over the age of 18 years present or represented at a meeting convened for the purpose of considering such disposal, of which they have been given sufficient notice, and in which they had a reasonable opportunity to participate.

[22] The most notable example of overlapping legislation is the continued existence of the Black Administration Act and the Black Authorities Act and old Lebowa legislation, together with the Constitution 108/1996 based on the principle of equality for all South Africans. Cf. Fleming (1996:57).

[23] Olivier de Sardan (1986), discussed in Geschiere (1989:8).

[24] Cf. Collier (1976) who described a similar process for the Zinacantan.

[25] Group interview, 16 December 1998.

[26] S1 of Act 112/1991 as amended by Act 34/1996.

In Mamone, however, tribal resolutions to alienate community land – destined, for instance, for building a hospital, a library or a shopping mall – were generally taken by the Tribal Council on its own, without informing the community members about the large portions of land it was 'signing away'. When in 1999 a vehement dispute erupted in the Mamone village of Eenzaam over a housing project on a plot of community land about which the traditional authority had not been informed, it turned out that the 'tribal resolution' alienating the land to the Department of Housing had been signed by a representative of the Department, the contractors, one elected councillor and *one* person representing the Mamone tribe, who could not be found anywhere. As the contractor said, 'That guy said he was signing on behalf of the *kgoši* and the community, and who were we to question him' (cf. Oomen, 2000a; 2000b; Von Benda-Beckmann, 1989:134).

In addition to the reinterpretation of state law, there is also its invention. During the introduction of B. Sekwati Mampuru to the satellite villages, the new Mamone *kgoši* was often accompanied by a representative of the Department of Agriculture, who told the assembled villagers:

> The land on which you live is a Trust Farm, which is why we have given all of you a Permission to Occupy. Before you would pay R10 a year for this to the magistrate. Now people think this has changed, and they don't have to pay any more. But this is not true: your yearly contributions should now go to me as representative of the Department of Agriculture...[27]

Even if this 'legal rule' had no empirical basis whatsoever, and would in all probability only benefit the official concerned, its apparent backing by the traditional authority and the absence of alternative voices caused most villagers to agree to pay the new annual fee.

State law can also be presented as tradition by parties seeking to strengthen their position. While, for instance, the revamped Madibong Tribal Council, referred to earlier, included two female councillors, these found it difficult to attend meetings as they were always held during the week, when they both had to work in two different NGOs. When asked why they did not meet at weekends, the *bakgomana* (royal advisers), who were far from content with the changes introduced by the chief, stated that it was an ancient Madibong tradition to meet during the week: 'We have done this since time immemorial.' In actual fact, although possibly unknown to the *bakgomana*, the weekdays meetings had been introduced by the homeland administrators during the 1970s, as a measure to ensure that only the conservative old villagers, instead of the often more radical migrants, would be involved in the local decision-making process.[28]

Another way in which 'people create their own legality by using the forms and symbols of state law', is by borrowing procedural elements from the state legal process. (De Sousa Santos, 1992; quoted in Merry, 1988:80). The striking emphasis on bureaucratic symbols and procedure in Sekhukhune customary courts has been referred to earlier. Every traditional leader has a stamp with the 'tribal totem' and the name of the authority to add weight to written summonses and letters such as 'the Ga-Maphopha tribal authority orders Mr Malaka to give back the black bull to Mr Mogadi'. As noted earlier, some courts are divided into

[27] Eenzaam, 14 June 1999.
[28] This was explained to me by Ga-Maphopha councillors, 16 September 1999.

prosekutora and *magistrata*. And in courts like Mamone, villagers who want to give their opinion must indicate whether they are putting a 'question' or a 'point of order'.

State law can thus be invoked, reaffirmed, or put at stake in local processes of dispute resolution. But if the person who invokes it is relatively powerless and cannot rally enough support for his/her position, it is often set aside. An example from the Kgatla area, with its predominantly Tswana inhabitants, illustrates this point. A widowed Jehovah's Witness refused to follow the customary procedure of washing her hands and sprinkling herbs after her husband's death. When senior male community members, angered by her disregard for custom, threatened to keep her locked up in the house for a year, her son called in the South African Human Rights Commission, who supported her claim by pointing to the constitutional freedom of movement. Even though the chief was publicly humiliated, it did not help the woman much. Not only had she already been locked in the house by the time the decision was made, she also faced the threat of expulsion by the traditional leader who lashed out at her 'disobedience', stating: 'I don't know what makes this woman think that her rights will take precedence over those of the tribe.'[29]

Relational rights

Just as the political landscape leaves its imprint on local law, so social relations crucially determine which rights (*ditokelo*) a person has in practice. Whether someone is male or female, royal or a commoner, married or unmarried, supporter of one chiefly contender or another, initiated or not, Bapedi or foreigner, all these factors determine his/her rights to marry, to own property, to settle disputes, etc. The kinship-based Sekhukhune moral landscape, in which status is highly valued, makes it hard to conceive of such a thing as an absolute right (to rule, to own property); rights are determined in relation to others, and can change with shifts in these relationships. How people are situated within kinship networks also influences their power to negotiate, and social identities are reflected in the legal (Griffiths, 1997:1,12).

Land ownership is a classic example of this relative and relational character of 'individual rights'. 'Throughout Africa, where rights of access to land depend on social identity...social identity and status have become objects as well as instruments of investment' (Berry, 1989, quoted in Goheen, 1992:44). In Sekhukhune, one's social, financial and political status determines the rights to land one can expect to acquire and keep, even if the way this is played out differs by chief, area concerned and over time. The Mamone citizen who staunchly supported a chiefly competitor and had been allocated a plot of land by him serves as an illustration: once the competitor's support decreased, the citizen was arrested by the Mamone *kgôrô* for unlawful occupation of land and fined heavily. On the other hand, a female member of parliament remembers how 'my chief told me that women are not supposed to own land unless they have a degree or are divorced. So my land was first put into my young son's name, and only transferred to mine after I had got a degree.'[30]

It is important to emphasise, as has been done in the anthropological literature of the past few decades, how personhood in kinship-based societies is relationally

[29] As recounted by Human Rights Commissioner P. Tlakula, 14 January 1999.
[30] L. Ngwenya, 22 September 2000.

defined, and the self can be depicted as 'enmeshed in a web of influences, a field of relations with other people, spirits, and natural phenomena, none of which are set apart from the self as static and objectified states of being and all of which are linked to the self in terms of continuous strands of influence' (Comaroff, 1980:644). *Motho ke motho ka batho:* a person is a person through other people, goes a well-known Bantu saying in Sepedi.

But there is more. This relational state of being means that people combine various identities, and are actually different people in different relationships. Instead of people having a fixed social status, it is the specific relationship that determines who one is, and thus what rights one has at a given point. 'Persons,' as Marilyn Strathern observed about other kinship-based societies, 'are frequently constructed as the plural and composite site of relationships that produced them' in which, to give one example, female and male elements can coexist.[31] Although there is insufficient space here to go into the legal consequences of this insight,[32] its importance can be illustrated by one example: that of woman-to-woman marriages.

As in many other parts of (South) Africa, gynaegamical marriages are relatively frequent in Sekhukhune.[33] In what is essentially a socio-economic arrangement which can take many forms, a woman who is affluent, powerful, or childless, or all three, will marry and pay the bridewealth for another woman, who is then expected to conduct typically female tasks, such as cooking, working in the fields, cleaning the house and giving birth to children. As with the famous rain-queen Modjadji, the biological father of these children often remains anonymous, while the more powerful woman will become, in the eyes of the community, the social father (Krige and Krige, 1943; Krige, 1974). This status has legal consequences, as was demonstrated by a case before the Mamone customary court:

Mrs Matjageng and her wife

This case was heard twice by the Mamone *kgôrô.* During the first hearing, Mrs Matjageng (the female husband) told how she had married a younger woman because she was childless. After she had paid the full bridewealth of two goats, the 'wife's' children became hers and took her family name. After a while the relationship turned sour: the female 'husband' complained that the young wife insulted her and refused to cook for her, while the young wife accused her 'husband' of not maintaining the children. For this, the female 'husband' was severely reprimanded: 'If you marry a wife, you are not a woman any more, but just like a man. These are your children now, take them in and maintain them. If you don't, your wife can take you to the maintenance court.' Divorce, the councillors agreed, should not be allowed: the women were told to go home and make it up.

A month later the two were back in court, hurling accusations at each other. During the heated discussion, the female husband even wanted to stand up, causing the male councillors to cry out in outrage, 'Don't you know that we don't allow

[31] Marilyn Strathern, *The Gender of the Gift: Problems with Women and Problems with Society in Melanesia.* Berkeley, Los Angeles and London: University of California Press, 1988, pp. 13–14. Cf. Piot (1999).

[32] Part of such an analysis can be found in Comaroff and Comaroff (1997:370–404).

[33] See Oomen (2000c); Cf: Melville J. Herskovits, 'A Note on "Woman Marriage" in Dahomey,' *Africa* X, no. I (1937): 335–41; Denise O'Brien, 'Female Husbands in Southern Bantu Societies,' in *Sexual Stratification*, New York and Guildford, Surrey: Columbia University Press, 1977; Elisabeth Tietmeyer, *Frauen Heiraten Frauen: Eine Vergleichende Studie Zur Gynaegamie in Afrika.* München: Klaus Renner Verlag, 1985.

> women to stand up in this court?' However, when the female husband indicated that she saw no other solution but divorce, she was told: 'You are just like a man. And if it is the man who wants to divorce, he must leave the house taking only his jacket with him. Also, he must continue to maintain the children.'

The way in which a person's – compositely gendered – identity influences her rights is clear: *vis-à-vis* the young woman, Mrs Matjageng was a 'man', with all the rights and duties attached. But when she attempted to stand up in the customary court, she was severely reprimanded: as a 'woman' she did not have the right to stand up in a court full of men.

A processual legal culture

The combined notions of a plurality of fora, negotiated law, state law as a resource and relational rights all draw our attention to the intimate relation of Sekhukhune legal culture to the social and political landscape. This relation is double-sided and dialectic: not only is the legal grafted into social and political relations and oscillates with them, it can also act to check abusive actors and strengthen social positions, thus reshaping them. Law, it has already been said, is both motor and flywheel, both sword and shield. The fact that legal culture is so closely related to, and constitutive of, the wider Sekhukhune social order endows it with a final feature I should like to discuss here: its processual character.

South African state law, like most formalised systems of law, consists largely of 'absolute' rights and puts a high premium on legal certainty. A central notion is that of legal subjects who can, from one day to another, attain a certain status (being married, being the owner of property, being a traditional leader), which automatically endows them with a number of rights and duties. After parties have fulfilled the formal requirements to marry and signed the marriage register, a number of legal consequences automatically and irrevocably set in. The owner of a plot of land can leave the country for years, but has just as much right to his property upon his return. And a chief, according to the Black Administration Act, can be appointed by the President and will then 'enjoy the privileges and status conferred on him by the recognised customs and usages of his tribe' and 'shall be entitled to loyalty, respect and obedience of all the Blacks resident within his area' from then on.[34]

Local law, by contrast, is of a much more processual nature. Status and rights require persistent legitimisation, revalorisation, affirmation within the changing social and political context. As they are often not explicated, it is hard to draw them out of their context, to transform 'local law' into 'idealised customary norms'. 'It depends' should be the answer to questions concerning the rights of women, property owners, or traditional leaders. How difficult it is to disentangle rights from their context and freeze them on paper became visible in the process of drawing up municipal boundaries in 2000. Suddenly, vague borders between chieftaincies, plots of land loaned long ago, had to be delimited and put down on paper. This caused many clashes, with deaths all over the country.[35]

This persistent renegotiation of 'legal' status makes it hard to settle cases 'once

[34] Resp. S 1 Black Authorities Act 38/1927 and Parts of Ss 5 and 6 of the Regulations Prescribing the Duties, Powers, Privileges and Conditions of Service in Proclamation 110/1957 as amended up to Proclamation 110/1991.

[35] Jubie Matlou, 'Demarcation Upsets Chiefs'; 'Chiefs Face Mbeki over Traditional Land'; 'Traditional Leaders Reject Municipalities.'

and for all'. 'Cases here just go on and on, rotting away,' as one Hoepakranz *kgoši* said, while outlining a divorce case that had been heard by him three times, by a neighbouring *kgoši* and by the magistrate. This case was no exception: parties will often forum-shop, take their disputes to different courts in which they feel they have a distinctive advantage, or come back to the customary court which once resolved their case if they feel that a changed socio-political situation might result in a different outcome. Court cases, the places where 'life and logic meet', are reopened if life's circumstances have changed. 'The more disputes are settled,' as Strathern writes, 'the more they will erupt' (1985:123)

One classic example of the processual character of local law is the way in which customary marriages are sealed. As with the Tswana, the sealing of a marriage among the Bapedi is a process which can take many years and in which a web of relationships and obligations is slowly woven between the families concerned through an amalgam of concrete actions such as official visits and the exchange of gifts and money.

> The substance of a bond cannot be determined, in advance of interaction, by the mere passage of prestations or other formal procedures; rather, the content of such interaction, over time, gives form to the relationship and the reciprocal expectations and entitlements that it will involve. Hence, while a union endures, these expectations and entitlements will become manifest in the ordinary course of everyday life. Only when the union is threatened do the questions of jural status and liability arise. In other words, conjugality is seen by the Tswana more as a state of becoming than as a state of being (Comaroff and Roberts, 1981:166).

While there are idealised customary norms on the steps to take to seal a marriage, these are either drawn out over decades or not followed at all. As P. Nkosi, from Hoepakranz, explained:

> If people want to get married the man's family must first go *kokota (*to greet) the wife's family, by paying 50 or 100 rand. Then the negotiations can start. If, for instance, they agree that the *mmagadi (*bridewealth) will be three cattle and R1000, the man's family will pay a *lay-bye*. The lady will then be brought to the man's family *go ja letswai* (to eat salt): to see how he lives. The man's family will slaughter a goat, and prepare it without salt. That is the tradition. She goes back to her family, and after that comes back for a longer period. The man will then have to find two cows to make a *white wedding*, when the *kgoši* will approve of the marriage and they will sign the register.
>
> These things can take years, and many people don't do all the rituals any more or don't pay all that was agreed. Normally people only insist on marriage if a husband treats his wife badly because then he has paid for her and will treat her better. If all goes well it often takes longer to get married. My parents, who are very old, had a white wedding last year. This is the right way to do it, because then you know that the marriage has been a success.[36]

A customary marriage is not an event, but a process, in which what could be conceived as 'legal status' is intimately tied up with actual acts and accomplishments (Chanock, 1985:62; Griffiths, 1997:53).

Just as marriage is a 'state of becoming' rather than a 'state of being', so is *bogoši*, traditional leadership. Whether leadership has been successful and a traditional leader is entitled to 'respect, obedience and loyalty' will often be clear only after a long period of rule, and a newly elected traditional leader will

[36] Interview, 1 February 1999. This is a slightly abridged version of P. Nkosi's account of the official rituals.

constantly have to legitimise, reaffirm, and revalorise his position. As we saw in the previous chapter, Mamone residents found it hard to evaluate their traditional leader: 'He is still young, we still have to see his true colours.' But when he did not attend enough meetings and did not show the required respect for his councillors, rumours quickly spread about his brother possibly being the rightful heir instead of him. Of course, the *kgoši* did by then have a certificate of appointment and the full backing of the state system.

With this paradox, we return to our central concern: how, in the governance of Sekhukhune daily life, does this absolutist, binary system of state law with its emphasis on legal certainty interact with the local, processual and persistently renegotiated legal culture where it concerns the position of traditional leaders? The rest of this chapter will be devoted to this question, looking first at succession to the throne and then at the rights and duties of traditional leaders as understood locally. In debates on these issues, state law was invoked at times by both rulers and ruled, with different outcomes each time.

3. Stories of succession

> 'In the old days we would physically fight over the throne, but today civilised traditional leaders prefer to go to court' – *kgoši* Masha

When asked about the main problems in the area, a Sekhukhune citizen will be sure to refer to the depressing lack of development and employment, but also to another issue deemed equally important: the rampant succession disputes that tear apart not only the paramountcy but every tiny hamlet as well: 'If only our leaders could stop fighting.' Their concern is understandable, for the importance of these often bitter and protracted battles should not be underestimated: they lead to the failure of development projects, political polarisation, and sometimes even to bloodshed. President Nelson Mandela was well aware of this when he visited the area just before the 1999 elections. During a closed meeting with the traditional leaders he pleaded with the two protagonists in the battle over the Sekhukhune paramountcy: 'I wish my two leaders here, my chief Rhyne and my chief K.K., my chief K.K. and my chief Rhyne, would find the courage to come together and settle this issue.'[37] His intervention – which could be considered that of just another state leader in a long line of governors and Native Commissioners confronted with local politics – did not help: the two leaders even refused to have a joint picture taken with the President.

Even if the legitimacy of a traditional leader is of a processual nature and cannot be achieved by mere succession to the throne, debates on succession issues are essential to understanding the power and authority of traditional leaders. Here, many of the features of Sekhukhune living law as described above come to the fore: how law, in various guises, is an important resource in essentially political struggles, next to other resources such as force, contacts with the spiritual world and political alliances, and how the importance of 'tradition' and 'culture' is widely acknowledged but their contents vehemently debated.

[37] Meeting, 27 May 1999. 'If I could muster the courage to talk to P.W. Botha,' Mandela continued, 'couldn't you and your tribe sit down together, find a solution and come tell Thabo Mbeki and myself what it is?'

They also show the relation between the national and the local, how 'official law' and 'living law' interact and thus shape the position of traditional leaders. In the rest of this section, I shall first give an overview of the 'official customary law' concerning succession in Sekhukhune and then compare it with the 'living law'. Then I shall look at the spheres of interaction, how the state deals with succession disputes, and illustrate this with three examples.

Succession: the official version

Codified customary law on succession can be found in customary law text-books, which in turn refer to the classic ethnographic works on the Bapedi (Du Plessis and Balatseng, 1997:353; Olivier et al., 1989:497; 1995:162). One such work, *Inheemse Publiekreg in Lebowa* (Indigenous Public law in Lebowa) reveals some of the methodology of this type of research and its agenda: the author thanks the Sotho specialists of the 14 (out of 113) Northern Sotho tribes he interviewed, mostly the traditional leader and five of his closest advisers. He states that: 'In this work an attempt is made to distil general rules out of the rules the various tribes provided. This does not only lead to more certainty of the rules of public law concerned and consistency in their application, but also enables the development of a general system of indigenous law' (Prinsloo, 1983:3). Nevertheless, even if they are generalised, these norms largely correspond to the 'idealised customary norms' quoted to me by Sotho *magoši* and *bakgomana.* Concerning succession, they can be summarised as follows:[38]

> A chief is succeeded by the eldest son of the candle-wife (*mohumagadi, mmasetšaba, lebone, timamollo)*
>
> This candle-wife comes from another royal family, is selected by the *bakgoma* and *bakgomana* (closest relatives of the chief), and her bridewealth is paid by the whole community
>
> If the candle-wife cannot give birth to a son, a stand-in (*seantlo)* from her family is betrothed in her place (sororate)
>
> If the *kgoši* does not succeed in impregnating the candle-wife or the *seantlo,* or dies before he has done so, a member of the royal family is appointed by the *bakgomana* (royal advisers) to 'raise seed' with her (levirate). If the candle-wife had not even been betrothed at the time of death, she can still be married by the tribe in the name of the deceased
>
> Only a son who has been born of the candle-wife or her *seantlo,* can become the *kgoši*
>
> If the *kgoši* dies and an heir has not yet been born or is still too young to ascend to the throne, a regent is appointed in his place. This can be either a younger brother or a paternal uncle of the deceased, or the candle-wife.

The guiding principle is thus that *kgoši ke kgoši ka madi a bogoši,* a chief is a chief by blood, but if the *kgoši* does not succeed in begetting a biological child with the candle-wife or her stand-in, a sociological son can be a substitute. The candle-wife stands central in succession issues. Because the whole community pays her bridewealth she is considered to be the whole community's mother (*mmasetšaba)* and her child also belongs to them: it will be remembered how in Chapter 4 Billy Sekwati's protests against the pressure on him to marry a new candle-wife were

[38] Mönnig (1967:249–66); Prinsloo (1983:33–50); Vorster, L.P. (1999:9).

met with comments like: 'He doesn't want to marry, *we* think it's time to get a new wife.'[39]

Living law

If the rules are relatively clear-cut, the reality is a lot messier. Even the ethnographers who provide the above list of rules complain how 'conflicting and rival claims ... have occurred more often than not during the history of the Pedi' and how 'succession rules have often been neglected' (Mönnig, 1967:264; Prinsloo, 1983:39). In an incisive article on the relation between achievement and ascription in succession to chieftaincy among the Tswana, John Comaroff remarks (1978:2) that

> rules ... cannot be assumed to determine the outcome of the indigenous political process. If they are read literally ... 80 per cent of all cases of accession to the chiefship represent 'anomalies'. Under such circumstances, the jural determinist assumption simply cannot be entertained: stated prescriptions do *not*, in general, decide who is to succeed.

A similar estimate can be made for the Bapedi: Sekhukhune history as well as current politics abounds with examples of *magoši* who were not successors according to the above rules, but had been accepted as such, or who were the eldest sons of the candle-wives but whose accession was bitterly contested in terms of customary law.

Clearly, something else is at stake, and there is a different logic underlying succession disputes than the above rules. This logic, I would argue, is the following: The system of succession in Sekhukhune contains a built-in vagueness and uncertainty that allows the best candidate out of a limited pool not only to accede to the chieftaincy, but also to argue this claim in terms of customary law. It thus allows for meritocracy within an ascriptive ideology.[40]

This uncertainty lies in the various stages of marrying the candle-wife, begetting the heir and appointing him as such. In Sekhukhune, in contrast to what is common among the Tswana, a chief often marries his candle-wife last. By that time, he will have a score of grown-up sons by other wives, eager to at least take up the position of regent. If the chief manages to beget a son with the candle-wife, doubt can easily be cast on her position at a later stage: Did she belong to the correct royal family? Were all the rituals complied with? Was it really the whole community that paid her bridewealth? Did she not have an affair at the time? If the candle-wife is barren or dies, and is replaced by a *seantlo*, the latter's relationship with the candle-wife can be questioned: Was she close enough to replace her? If the chief dies before a son is born, and the *bakgomana* secretly pinpoint someone to *go tsena tlong* (enter the house) in his place, this opens the way for later questioning of that person's identity: Was it really the chief's brother? Had the candle-wife not refused him?

All this is reinforced by the secrecy that surrounds the negotiations with the candle-wife's family and the conception of the heir. These are affairs of the *bakgomana*, not shared with the wider community. Far from being hailed as the future *kgoši*, possible candidates are often raised a long distance away from the

[39] In a similar vein, there was a protracted discussion during the adoption of the Customary Marriages Act as to whether candle-wives can only be divorced by the community, or by the *kgoši* as an individual.

[40] This is also Comaroff's central argument: Comaroff (1975,1978); Comaroff and Roberts (1981).

community. Although the official reason cited is fear of bewitchment, it also enables the royal family to watch the candidate critically while he is growing up and, if he is not up to standard, to put forward an alternative candidate provided with a legitimation in terms of customary law as to why he is the only rightful heir (Gluckman, 1965:138-9; Delius, 1983:84-5).

An example from Pedi history that still reverberates today shows how all this is played out. The case, which 'will always be the subject of endless argument among the Bapedi' and led to an important split among them, concerned the succession to King Sekwati, who died in 1861 (Hunt, 1931:294). Two of his possible successors, Sekhukhune I and Mampuru, fought over the throne throughout their lives, and even today the descendants in each lineage, *kgoši* Sekhukhune and Billy Sekwati Mampuru, claim paramountcy of the Bapedi by reference to this period (Delius, 1983:84-94; Hunt 1931:284-94; Mönnig, 1967:25-6). Put simply, the positions were as follows, Sekwati was the youngest of six brothers, all of whom had been killed in the battle against the Matabele. Among the dead was his eldest brother, Malekutu, for whom a candle-wife named Kgomo-Makatane had already been selected. Sekwati, the story goes, had ordered someone to have intercourse with her in his dead brother's name, from which Mampuru was born. In the succession dispute that was to follow, however, it was argued that (i) the seed-raiser was a commoner and (ii) that Malekutu had never actually married the candle-wife because he had not sent the customary black bull. These arguments were raised by Sekhukhune I, the powerful eldest son of Sekwati's first wife, who had claimed the throne by burying his dead father, and as a man of 'energy, resource and cunning' managed to garner a lot of support (Hunt, 1931:303). Nevertheless, apart from his apparent political backing, he also needed legitimation in customary law to become regent instead of Mampuru. Today, his descendants are regarded by the majority of the Bapedi as the rightful paramounts, if not by genealogy, then because 'you can't just claim paramountcy by pointing at history; you also need a following'.[41]

This is but one, be it a famous, example of the resources on which *magoši* in Sekhukhune draw to claim the throne. These can, and must, include issues like political backing, force, strategic alliances, support of the *bakgomana* and the populace, and money to be successful. At the same time, a legitimation in terms of customary law, attainable through the manipulation of facts and rules, is a *sine qua non.*[42] The intimate relation between achievement and ascription has been well expressed by John Comaroff (1978:16):

> ...winning the chiefship is a matter of achievement, an achievement gained largely by controlling resources and capabilities which are extrinsic to formal institutional arrangements. Yet such outcomes are rationalised in entirely ascriptive terms: the successful competitor *becomes* the rightful heir, and his mother's status as his father's principal wife is affirmed *after* event...By invoking rules in this way, the Tshidi maintain a performance-oriented system within the context of an agnatically ordered small-scale society. Moreover, in so doing, they resolve the fundamental dualism in their political ideology – i.e. the emphasis upon good government and the delegation of legitimacy to able men on the one hand, and the theory of ascription on the other.

[41] Interview, *kgoši* Malekane, 6 September 1999.

[42] Cf. Richard P. Werbner, 'Constitutional Ambiguities and the British Administration of Royal Careers among the Bemba of Zambia,' in Nader, p. 245.

As has been discussed earlier, there is hardly any research dealing with the effects of the state's recognition of traditional leadership and customary law on local legal and political dynamics (cf. Griffiths, 1997:28). Nevertheless, it is clear that 'official customary law' and 'living law' depart from different rationalities. Their interactions form the subject of the next sub-sections.

Interactions

If succession disputes have been part and parcel of Sekhukhune politics since recorded history, the state's recognition of traditional leaders has added another potent resource to these local struggles. If the ethnographers quoted above conclude with satisfaction that 'in the present time, where the incumbent has to be recognised by the European administration, succession tends to automatically follow the normal pattern, since the administration adds its recognition to that of the rightful heir and thus damps any claims of his brothers'(1960s) and 'these days breaking of the rules is not possible any more as succession is controlled and affirmed by a higher authority' (1980s), the question arises as to how recognition of certain incumbents by means of the absolutist state law has affected the local balance of power.[43] Generally speaking, state recognition has become another resource in the local struggle, and an important one. Before discussing its implications, it should be noted at the outset that, far from being a homogeneous entity, the state also consists of different offices and entities which can and do give weight to countervailing claims. Let us look briefly at the three main institutions involved in recognition of traditional leadership during the time of this research: the National and Provincial Departments of Traditional Affairs, the courts and the Ralushai Commission.

From the Sekhukhune Traditional Affairs official to the state anthropologists of the provincial department, the people working at the Department of Traditional Affairs are incessantly pulled into local succession disputes and play an important role in them. Officially, the 'tribe' (normally by means of the royal family) recommends a chiefly successor who is then appointed by the provincial premier. In practice, the department's anthropologists check the candidates against the files of genealogies they possess – which are already computerised at national level – and against the relevant anthropological handbooks and customary law text-books. If the candidate put forward does not meet the requirements of the 'official customary law' contained in these texts, a candidacy will generally be refused. As the Director of Traditional Affairs stated: 'We decide cases on the basis of genealogies and culture. Sometimes we have to go three or four generations back to find out what the customs of the people are. And this is really our problem, that some people do not want to follow their culture.'[44] A colleague cited the example of several communities which had put forward a woman as a candidate for chieftaincy: 'You can see that there are political motives at play there, one of these women is even a member of parliament. But we really can't allow people to just leave their custom if some learned people tell them to do so...'[45]

Other state institutions often implicated in succession disputes are the courts. The South African Supreme Court has heard scores of cases brought forward by

[43] The quotes come from Mönnig (1967:264–5) and Prinsloo (1983:39).
[44] Interview, Rev. Kekana, 6 March 1998.
[45] Interview, 4 March 1998.

candidates who feel that their contenders have been wrongly appointed. The judge's approach in the *K.K. Sekhukhune v. N. Ramodike and R. Sekhukhune* case – which we shall discuss in more extensively later – is illustrative. The judge concluded that the legal issue, as deduced from a complicated and long-drawn-out argument, was whether a *kgoši* who had renounced the throne could reclaim it later. He ruled that:

> There is no basis in customary law or history or logic for a contention that a *kgoši* who, of sound mind and fully capable of fulfilling the functions of a *kgoši*, renounced or repudiated his chieftainship, can reclaim it later...To hold otherwise would wreak havoc with societal patterns established by the tribe.[46]

A legal scholar, reviewing this case for the *Journal of South African Law*, complimented the judge on having done a good job in ascertaining the relevant customary law by means of expert witnesses, and concluded that the 'important judgement...will form a precedent for Northern-Sotho law, and even indigenous law as a whole' (Prinsloo, 1992:519). Apart from the regular courts, the Commission on the Restitution of Land Rights complained about receiving land claims that were essentially attempts to restore or establish chiefly authority (D. Gilfinnan, pers. comm., 9 June 1999).

If the Traditional Affairs officials and the courts often came up with conflicting decisions concerning succession disputes, the establishment of the Ralushai Commission in the Northern Province only added to the insecurity. This Commission, chaired by a professor who had earlier published a report on witchcraft in the province, was set up in 1996 to investigate claims that the former homeland government had 'irregularly deposed legitimate traditional leaders and replaced them with illegitimate chiefs'.[47] It promptly became a forum to which to take all succession disputes, whether they resulted from homeland deposures or not. However, its report had not yet been released by 2004 in spite of frequent marches by traditional leaders and other forms of protest: provincial premier Ramathlodi feared that the Commission's decisions on the 244 cases heard would lead to bloodshed and rioting and announced that he would wait for similar investigations in South Africa's other five provinces with traditional leaders before publication. His decision was probably wise: a brief glance through the – secret – report in 1999 revealed recommendations such as abolishing the practice of allowing candle-wives to reign as regents that had become common during the homeland days and going back to the custom of male primogeniture. Individual cases swarmed with references to the Black Administration Act and recommendations hardly compatible with human rights discourse. For example: 'the royal family should appoint a seed-raiser to make a child with the candle-wife as soon as possible.'

Even if the various state institutions can support different candidates, and codified customary law is hardly a straitjacket but allows substantial official agency, there are many commonalities in their approach.[48] First, there is a recurrent emphasis on absolute, fixed rights and a reliance on laws, legal precedent and experts to determine the contents of customary law. Next, there is the almost paternalistic desire to protect, and sometimes even explicitly revive,

[46] *K.K. Sekhukhune v. N. Ramodike and R. Sekhukhune*, unreported, p.55.

[47] Sapa, 'Investigation into Appointment of Northern Province Chiefs Could Be Extended.'

[48] Costa (1997; cf. Werbner, 'Constitutional Ambiguities', p. 270.

'custom' and 'culture' in the face of the onslaught of modernity. Thus, state institutions essentially favour ascription over achievement and can be pulled in as a conservative force in disputes that are often meant to ensure better governance locally.

Illustrations

Three divergent succession disputes can illustrate the intimate relation between ascription and achievement in these matters, the importance of state law as a resource, and the local effects of the state's ambivalence in these matters: the high-profile fight over the Sekhukhune paramountcy between K.K. and Rhyne Sekhukhune; the Ga-Masha dispute, which is hampering the opening of a mine in the area; and the rift in the remote mountain village of Hoepakranz.

K. K. v. Rhyne Sekhukhune

This dispute is between two grandsons of Sekhukhune II.[49] By the time Sekhukhune II died, his eldest son, Thulare, had already died, as had the candle-wife married for him, Lekgolane. In her place a *seantlo*, Mankopodi, was married, with whom a younger son of Sekhukhune II, Morwamotše, raised seed. The child born from this union, Rhyne, was considered the sociological eldest son of Thulare and the candle-wife. This Morwamotše III also had other wives, and the oldest son of his first wife is K. K. Sekhukhune.

From the outset, it was clear that Rhyne was the designated heir. He was called Sekhukhune III and sent to a special school for chiefs' sons. In the meantime, his mother, Mankopodi, reigned. Problems started in 1974, when Rhyne was 28 years old, had matriculated and was working for the Lebowa government. A number of *bakgomana* went to visit him and told him that the time had come for him to ascend the throne. When his mother, the regent Mankopodi, heard about this, she was furious, stating that it was her prerogative to decide when to hand over. Rhyne backed his mother and refused to return home to sign pension forms, upon which the *bakgomana* sent Mankopodi back to her native village in the midst of reciprocal accusations of witchcraft. The community, the *bakgomana* stated, had divorced the candle-wife. Instead, they appointed K. K. Sekhukhune as a regent (passing over other sons of Thulare), to marry a candle-wife in Thulare's name, raise seed with her and thus produce a new heir for the house of Thulare. After some discussion, this was affirmed by the Lebowa chief minister Pathudi, who appointed K. K. in Rhyne's place in 1976. A later court decision would summarise positions at the time by stating that 'obviously, the *de facto* position at Mohlaletse where Rhyne had no longer any following among the *bakgomana*, was a material factor in this decision'. It also mentions that the Secretary of Bantu Administration and Development was worried that other sons of Thulare had been bypassed in choosing K. K., but that he was assured by the *bakgomana* that K. K. as the acting chief would raise seed for that house.

In 1982, the political atmosphere in the Lebowa homeland changed, and Ramodike replaced Pathudi as chief minister. He set up an advisory board to look into the matter,

[49] The main sources for its reconstruction are: *K.K. Sekhukhune v N. Ramodike and R Sekhukhune Thulare*, 2078/89 unreported (1989); 'Minutes of the Meeting between Premier Ramathlodi and the Sekhukhune Tribal Authorities,' Nylstroom – Shangri-La Lodge, 1998; *Acting King Kgagudi Kenneth Sekhukhune v Premier of the Northern Province A.O.*, 22378/98 (2000); Delius (1996); Van Kessel and Oomen (1999); Hangwani Mulaudzi, 'Two Brothers Battle for the Pedi Throne.' *City Press*, 18 April 1999, p. 5; Carol Paton, 'The Men Who Would Be King,' *Sunday Times*, 15 November 1998, p. 4; Prinsloo (1992) and various interviews with the Department of Traditional Affairs, Prof. Ralushai, K.K. Sekhukhune and councillors and Mohlaletse citizens. All the quotes in the piece come from the 1989 judgment (resp. pp. 13, 16, 31, 33, 35, 39, 54), except for those at the end which come from the minutes of the Shangri-La meeting and the 2000 judgment.

which concluded that 'Rhyne should ... be given all that belongs to him' and that 'all belonged to the born *kgoši* (heir) and not to the shepherd'. K. K. protested, saying that he had been appointed by the *bakgomana*; a candle-wife had already been married and had produced a lawful heir; his appointment was according to the practice, customs and usage of the Marota tribe; and, finally, that Rhyne had belittled and insulted the Bapedi and their chieftaincy by his denunciation, and as a result the tribe would not accept Rhyne with joy, respect and peace.

Nevertheless, the cabinet decided to depose K. K. in 1989, arguing that 'the cabinet determines the genealogy and it does not matter what the *bakgoma* and *bakgomana* say. The genealogy is the decisive factor.'

With this backing, Rhyne encamped, together with his mother Mankopodi, in a mobile home next to the Mohlaletse palace where K. K. lived. He was protected by the South African Defence Force, which at one point shot three men protesting against what they felt to be an imposed presence. Meanwhile, K. K. appealed the cabinet decision to the Supreme Court. The case was decided in his favour in 1991. In the 56-page judgment, judge Van Dijkhorst paid a great deal of attention to the argument presented by K. K. and the *bakgomana* that Mankopodi had never been a *seantlo* for candle-wife Lekgolane, but just a nurse for her child who happened to be impregnated by Morwamotše III, and that *lobola* for Lekgolane had not been paid by the tribe, but by the royal house. He based his review on a range of factors, including the fact that, according to the 'correct traditional approach', the *bakgomana* own *bogoši*; 'the blot on Rhyne's birth'; the lack of support at Mohlaletse for Rhyne – 'a weakling, greatly dominated by his strong-willed mother'; and the fact that K. K. might be blind but had a good memory and was 'knowledgeable on customs and traditions'. Still, the decisive issue, as already referred to above, was whether customary law allowed a man who had once repudiated *bogoši*, to reclaim it. This, the learned judge ruled, was not the case, and he ordered the reinstatement of K. K.

In the meantime, the political climate had changed and Rhyne found new supporters in the newly elected ANC government. President Nelson Mandela, a great supporter of the traditional leadership, gave Rhyne a Mercedes-Benz as a present (upon which K. K.'s supporters bought him a luxury car as well). News quickly leaked out that the Ralushai Commission, with its emphasis on correct genealogies, had decided that Rhyne was the rightful heir. Strengthened by this, Rhyne and his supporters buried his mother Mankopodi in Mohlaletse once she had died, another event which led to violent clashes. A *bosberaad* on the issue was held between the half-brothers in Kruger Park in 1998. The suggestion of the Minister of Constitutional Development to create a 'win-win situation' by appointing both as chiefs and giving them equal resources was rejected. Rhyne's delegation called for release of the Ralushai report and 'implementing the culture of the Bapedi'; while K. K. called for implementation of the court decision. He also did this in a High Court case, in which Judge Claassen urged the premier to issue a certificate 'certifying that the applicant has been appointed both as acting *Kgoshi* and acting Paramount Chief of Sekhukhuneland'.

This ongoing case, any definite decision on which is expected by many to result in war between the Bapedi factions, illustrates a number of the points made above. First, the role of achievement in appointing a *kgoši*, in this case a regent. While Thulare had a number of other sons who could have been sought out as regents, the royal family chose – contrary to 'official customary law' – to install the son of a younger brother, from the sixth house. Next, there are the resources the protagonists draw on: K. K. clearly had the support of a large part of the community and of the *bakgomana*; he had charisma, and could collect enough money for the expensive court cases which he won. Rhyne had the support of the army and the police force in the 1980s, joined the ANC later on, often

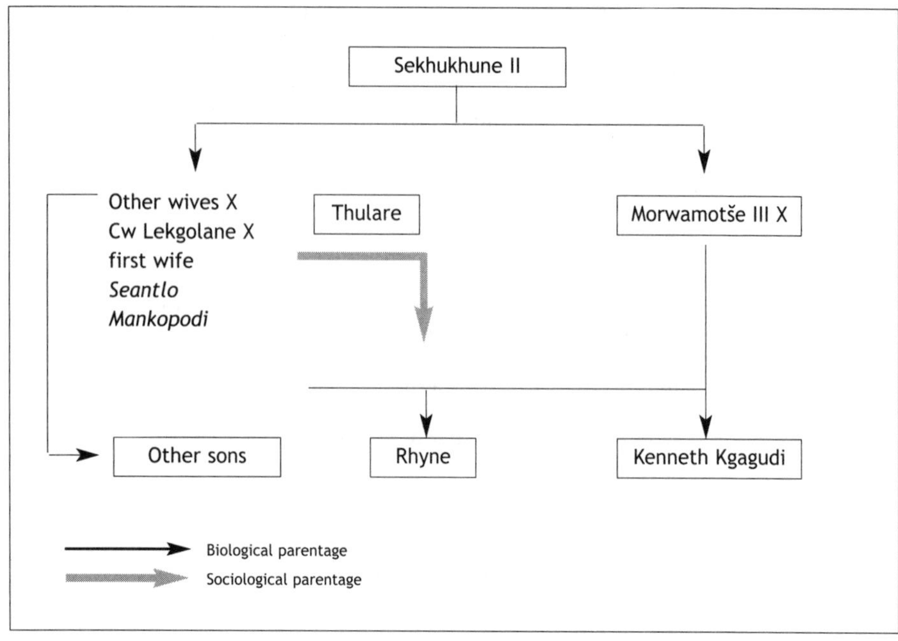

Figure 6.1 Skeleton genealogy of the Sekhukhune Royal House

received sympathetic press coverage and had his claim supported in the – unpublished but leaked – Ralushai Commission report. Nevertheless, both protagonists had to state their claims in terms of official customary law acceptable to the state. Rhyne's claim that he was the sociological son of Thulare was refuted by K.K.'s faction, who stated that Mankopodi had never been a candle-wife and that, thus, in the absence of a rightful heir, any of Sekhukhune's (grand)sons could act as a ruler. It is, of course, a matter of speculation what the course of action would have been if Rhyne had not obtained support from, first, the Lebowa and then the ANC government. But it is more than likely that the position of the popular K. K. Sekhukhune would have been much more secure, and the Mohlaletse citizens would not only have saved the High Court fees necessary to show their support but would also have been saved from the paralysing political deadlock of the past decades, a deadlock which largely ensued from the state's desire to 'implement custom' contrary to popular demand.

The next case is considerably less high-profile, but deals with an element of succession disputes already briefly referred to and still to be completely elaborated: their consequences for local development processes.

Johannes v. Manthe Masha

The succession dispute at Ga-Masha dates from 1980, with the death of *kgoši* Phathane Masha, who was only made a headman instead of a fully-fledged chief by the Lebowa government because of his anti-apartheid stance. He had ruled since 1919 and had gone to the magistrate's court in 1977 to have the tribe's genealogy drawn up (!) and to stipulate which of his sons should succeed him. By the time he died, however, this son had also already passed away. As a candle-wife, Manthe Masha had already been married to him, the *bakgomana* having ordered the former *kgoši's* third son, Johannes Masha, to raise seed with her. Manthe did not want this. As Johannes would testify in a later court case: 'applicant refused to come to me to have the child by me and chose to have nothing to do with me.'[50] Johannes' faction tried to chase Manthe back to her parents, and set fire to her house. She came back, stating that she would reign as a candle-wife, that the late *kgoši* had merely been an acting chief and that the son she had had with her husband Magomorule, was the rightful heir.[51] Johannes retorted that Pedi 'law, custom and tradition' had never allowed for chieftainesses and that he should be the *kgoši.*

The dispute simmered on. The quietly-spoken Manthe enjoyed a little more popular support (59 per cent during my 1999 survey),[52] but Johannes was a much more active 'ethnic broker' and sought permanent legitimation of his position in the magistrate's court and through the Land Claims Commission. The problems became acute again when, after the 1994 elections, the Masha community was able to reclaim a piece of land from which they had been forcibly removed in the 1940s. Both Johannes and Magomorule, as Manthe's husband, lodged a claim on behalf of the community and became caught up in a furious fight about who had the right to represent the Ba-Masha, critically slowing down the claim.

Things got worse when it transpired that the mineral vanadium had been detected under the land. The company that had obtained the exploitation rights visited the community, asked for the chief and was by chance taken to Manthe, with whom a 'tribal resolution' granting them the right to operate an open-pit mine was signed, on the promise of a car and an office. Furious, Johannes wrote to Vantech stating that they had by-passed 'the rightful owners' and accused them of blowing up the graves of his ancestors. One community member summed up the problem: 'In our situation we can't elect committees. Who should sign? And if there is money, who should get it?' As it stood, the dispute seriously threatened to deter the investor and thus deny the community the much-needed income and jobs, because, according to one Vantech manager, 'our stakeholders do not like these types of problems, we'd rather open up a mine in Australia instead'.[53]

By now, the way in which 'customary norms' are primarily drawn in to legitimate support for certain candidates will be familiar: while the appointment of a candle-wife as regent was never opposed in the Sekhukhune case, one of the central elements of Johannes' argument was that custom does not allow women to rule. Johannes himself is not the most logical heir, as Phathane's third son, but he can clearly muster more support than his brothers. Manthe Masha argues her case and that of her young son by going back to marriage politics in the early

[50] *Manthe Gauta Masha v Mamogudi Johannes Masha A.O.*, 10B/84 (1983).

[51] The argument for this was that Phathane's father, Sekgotho, had married a candle-wife, Ngwanamaepa, who remained childless but for whom a *seantlo* called Magatsela was married, who had a son, Nkotoane, of whom Magomorule, Manthe's customary husband, is a descendant. This, the argument goes, was the rightful customary line, while Phathane was only an acting chief. Johannes' faction vehemently opposed this version, by stating that Magatsela already had Nkotoane when she came to Ga-Masha and he could not therefore have been fathered by Sekgotho. Nevertheless, the fact that Phathane sought to have the genealogy recorded by the magistrate indicates that he in fact feared these types of allegations after his death: Ibid.

[52] Of the people who support traditional authority in Ga-Masha (N = 83), 41% were in favour of Johannes.

[53] Interview, 30 August 1999. See on this case, Tiny Mankge. 'Land Reform and Mineral Rights: Closing the Gap between Community Expectations and Government Policy on Mineral Rights and Land Rights.' http://www.mepc.org.za/mepb/landreform.htm: Minerals and Energy Policy Centre, 1999; Oomen, 'The Underlying Question'.

1900s, long before the memory of the present generation, so that it basically boils down to the political will to accept a certain version of facts and custom. But what the Masha case shows most of all is the disastrous effects succession disputes can have on the development process, and thus the importance of the state's attitude to them. As one Ga-Masha citizen says: 'We wish the government would solve this issue. They have all the right files and genealogies and know who is of royal blood.'[54]

While these two cases concerned traditional leaders explicitly recognised by the government, state recognition also plays a role in areas like Hoepakranz, where the *magoši* have received no explicit recognition.

Abel v. Joseph Nkosi

When we first visited Hoepakranz we were taken to *kgoši* Joseph Nkosi's, where, seated under the peach tree in his yard, we offered him a live chicken and Dutch teaspoons and asked for permission to undertake research. It was only during our third visit to the tiny mountain village that people started telling us that we had been horribly mistaken, and that Abel Nkosi was the real *kgoši*.

During our months in Hoepakranz, we discovered that Abel and Joseph shared the same grandfather, who had had four wives. Abel's father Johannes was the eldest son of the first wife, while Joseph's uncle Petrus was the eldest son of the fourth wife. During the Second World War, Petrus went to fight in Europe. On his return, he started to claim *bogoši*, in Joseph's version because he had previously been a chief and in Abel's version because of his new status. The notebooks of Abel's father are full of furious communications denouncing Petrus as an impostor who happened to have the support of Mankopodi Sekhukhune (Rhyne's mother), and asking the commissioner to remove him. At some point, Petrus was indeed removed from the village, but before his death he passed *bogoši* on to Joseph, a nephew. After his uncle's death in the early 1990s, Joseph took his corpse from the mortuary and, protected by armed assistants, buried it in Hoepakranz, thus reinstating Petrus and claiming to be his rightful heir.

Both contenders have access to different resources. Abel has the support of the magistrate, even if the Hoepakranz chieftaincy is not officially recognised, and his version of the genealogy is supported by various documents. As a Swazi chief, he is also in contact with the Swazi authorities. Soft-spoken and wise, he is the priest of the Dutch Reformed Church in the village, while his identical twin was the school principal for decades. In contrast, Joseph Nkosi is brash and outspoken, has the money to buy support and possesses the only tractor in the village. In addition to denouncing Abel's genealogy and calling him 'too soft, too poor and too Christian', he states that his chieftaincy is supported by both Sekhukhune contenders and calls for a vote on the subject.

'Waiting for the Ralushai Commission', therefore, also well captures the atmosphere in Hoepakranz, even if its citizens fear bloodshed when the results become known.

The Hoepakranz case demonstrates that succession disputes are part and parcel of local politics, even in areas where the state does not recognise chieftaincy. However, once such disputes have erupted, parties will draw in all possible resources to support their case. State support, whether through a letter with 'chief' in the letterhead, an appointment or a court verdict, is one such important resource. It is generally not decisive, as the fate of Rhyne Sekhukhune demonstrates: an unpopular contestant with state backing will still face denunciation

[54] Interview, 29 September 1999.

with reference to fact, functioning and custom in the local arena, and can be confronted with witchcraft and violence. But it can tip the scales. We have seen how succession disputes are generally about putting forward the most popular candidate and then legitimating his/her claim in terms of customary law. As the state, in contrast, often seeks to reinforce an absolutist, 'ossified' and conservative version of culture, this more often than not leads to a hampering of the local democratic process and search for good governance.

4. The Commission on the Tribal Constitution

> In the land of Bopedi, Mamone is a village that has been known for its peace, dignity, progress and law and order from the day it was founded. But the warmth and equality that once embraced this community vanished into thin air with the winds of life. Thulare's people must have been blinded by those winds, for their heads and ideas started to collide. It was only 19 years later that they woke up again, rubbing their eyes and trying to find each other.
>
> On 19 December 1998, the sun rose anew over Maroteng, the mountain Mahlole came alive again, and the community around it drew closer to find out if they were really seeing the great mountain of Mamone, or if they were still blinded. But when they looked at their village, it seemed wrapped in an old torn flea-ridden blanket, and in dire need of sleep. They found that the only needle with which to really repair the community was to write a tribal constitution, the law of the land, and this is why the community elected a committee to guide it in this story.
>
> To the community – the *kgôrôs*, the churches, sportsclubs and choirs, societies of shepherds and farmers, political and development organisations, traditional healers and (savings) societies, the youth, and any other citizen: this is the paper to fill in. Come together in droves to discuss and give your opinions as much as possible.
>
> The pride, peace, dignity and respect of the village are now on your back ... (Translated introduction to the questionnaire on the Tribal Constitution)

This is how Mamone citizens were introduced to the process of 'writing a tribal constitution', which started immediately after Billy Sekwati Mampuru's festive coronation on 19 December 1998. 'The time has come to go back to our roots,' as one villager said. With many others, he felt that the new national and local political order required a restatement of local rules with 'the national Constitution as a grandparent'. In contrast to what we have seen in the last section, the writing of the Mamone tribal constitution is an example of the way in which state law can also be drawn into the local social field: to stimulate local progress, to act on the side of the relatively powerless and to give them a distinct bargaining advantage. Instead of being drawn in to confirm the absolutist power of a traditional leader, common law assists in protecting his subjects against arbitrary rule. Let us take a brief look at the origins and development of the constitution-writing process, and then discuss its implications for a theory of negotiated law.

Forming the Commission

For the Mamone Bapedi, the coronation of Billy Sekwati Mampuru was probably just as important as the inauguration of Nelson Mandela as national President had been four years earlier. The community had been ripped apart by a succession dispute for 19 years, with the reigning candle-wife being attacked by

Box 6.1 Main Topics for Discussion – Mamone Tribal Constitution

1. Management
Structure – the royal palace – the Tribal Council – *botseta* (messengers) – traditional leadership – the *kgôrô's* – marrying the candle-wife – the initiation school – dispute resolution – managing the satellite villages

2. Land planning and nature conservation
Residential sites – cemeteries – fields – grazing land – business sites – immigrants

3. Culture and tradition
Totem – history – heritage- initiation school – clothing – working for the chief – wedding gifts to the chief – taboos – names – powers of women

4. Sports and art
Songs – dances – sports – clothing – art

5. Education

6. Health and sanitation
Sanitation – water – clinics

7. Religion
Traditional healers – spirit mediums – Christianity – clinics

8. Development
Development structures – disappointments – resources

an uncle against the backdrop of the apartheid struggles. Central to the preparation of the inaugural festivities was a special Coronation Commission, consisting of migrants, royals, schoolteachers and others, which organised the sponsoring of the limousine, the dancing groups, yellow T-shirts with Billy's picture on them, the sound system and the lush dinner for the VIPs who had shown up in large numbers. And after Billy had been inaugurated, it was from this Commission that the idea originated of writing a tribal constitution. 'The chief is our child, we must tell him how to rule us, so that his rule will be ours.'

Why a constitution? One reason could be that the process of negotiating the national Constitution had been well publicised over the Sotho radio station *Thobela FM*. Also, constitutions have long been part and parcel of local institutional life, as every self-respecting NGO, village development council or choir has its own, often elaborate, constitution. The rules drawn up, the Commission felt, would allow the community to return to 'traditional law and order' within the context of national changes. 'You know, our culture is still important. Traditional leaders are symbols of unity and custodians of our culture: without them we would be lost. But our new chief needs the support of the community, just as we need to be ruled fairly. It won't be easy for him to reign over all those literate people who know about the national Constitution. If we draw up these rules, we will be together.'

After receiving the blessing of Billy's mother, the Commission on the Tribal Constitution drew up an elaborate plan for consultation with all the Mamone Bapedi through their *magôrô*, wards, and other structures, on how they wanted to be ruled. The list of issues for discussion (see Box 6.1) is instructive of the local concerns: the government of the village is a central priority. 'This,' as the organisers would say during introductory meetings, 'is about who should be helping the *kgoši*. Are the *bakgomana* still important? Can they also be elected? Should there be women? We are living in a new world now.' Land and nature conservation was second on the list. 'Who should be responsible for giving out fields? Are people allowed to burn a plot of land because it's easier to get wood that way?' Tradition is also high on the list of local concerns: 'How can we generate income from tourists with our tradition? There was an old woman on television painting a car in Ndebele patterns the other day, can't we do something like that? What taboos do we have and why are they there? Should our children be allowed to go to initiation schools outside? Should we start allowing women at the *kgôrô* in these new times?' One recurrent question on education was whether it should be a local responsibility to ensure that children go to school. Development, the organisers felt, was also a central concern: 'What is the role of the *kgoši* in these things?' The deliberations, the Mamone people were warned, could take a long time: ' We will often come back to you to ask your opinions on certain matters, and only then draw up the draft constitution. The whole thing can easily take a year and a half...'

One meeting: dancing to different music

Of the ten meetings of the Commission I attended, I will recount one. It was a cold winter morning, and about 40 people had gathered in the tribal office, representing various *magôrô*, the ANC, the Ikageng (Let's Help Each Other) project, the Ararat Apostolic Church, the Mamone Farmers' Association, the Mamone Football Association, St Johns Faith Mission, Children for Peace, the RDP Committee, the Shepherds Against Stocktheft, funeral and other savings societies, and three different associations of traditional healers. Old men in ragged jackets, women wrapped in blankets with the traditional Pedi braids smelling of woodsmoke and mealiepap or in bright church clothing, diffident youngsters in jeans with floppy hats. For starters, one of the Commission members waved a little booklet containing the national Constitution: 'Who knows this document?' Most of those present shook their heads. 'You see, we must dance to a music whose tune we don't know. That is why we must write our own, and give the *kgoši* something with which he can rule us. We live a different life now, you don't build a house any more by drawing a line in the sand with your foot; you need a plan.'

After a lengthy discussion, the meeting divided into groups, each of which was to look into part of the national Constitution. As studiously as a Bible study group, our group read through the Bill of Rights and Chapter 12, on traditional leaders. Those who could not read pensively repeated what was read aloud, as they tried to understand the practical implications for life in Mamone. Could *mothubo*, for instance, the yearly hoeing for the chief, be considered forced labour in terms of section 13 of the Constitution? 'Of course not, we do this willingly,' said a young man. A woman of the same age disagreed: 'This comes from the days when chiefs did not get paid; now they can also hire some workers.' A blind man said: 'These words really hurt me. Doesn't the Bible also say that we should do these things with love? Our constitution should include this.' Similar divisions occurred over how people who refused to work for the chief should be treated; could they be punished?

This 'exit option' was also a recurrent theme once the plenary discussions resumed. What should be done with youngsters who refused to go to initiation school? Ostracise them, many agreed, because they might give away the secrets of the mountains. And what about migrants who refused to pay *seteke*, tribute to the chief? Or people who did not do anything for the *kgoši* at wedding ceremonies? But the most heated argument was on land ownership. Recently, the palace had reclaimed a number of agricultural plots in order to build a hospital on them. However, one woman said 'For black people a field is just like a bank. If we don't have that any more, we should at least get a job in the hospital.' 'To whom does the land actually belong?' asked someone else, 'To us or the *kgoši?*' Again, no consensus was reached but a clear dissatisfaction with the lack of communication by the royal house was apparent.

What was striking during this meeting and those before and after it was, on the one hand, the lack of clarity on customary rules and, on the other, the ease with which some rules were presented as being in need of revival while others were best forgotten. For instance, there was a long discussion on who could be a *bakgoma:* only the chief's younger brothers or an uncle as well? Opinions differed strongly. None of the people involved seemed to consider culture or tradition as fixed and immutable. Some issues, such as respect, needed revival. 'This is what the African Renaissance is all about, that people start thinking where they come from and what they'll go back to.' Many considered corporal punishment an anomaly, while others could not conceive of order without it, but would like to see it better regulated.

Royal reactions

Even if the turn-out at Commission meetings was generally high, not everybody was enthusiastic about the process. Some young people felt that '*Bogoši* and the constitution can never be married. These people here will never agree to things such as termination of pregnancy or equal treatment for women. You can talk about transformation until you are blue in the face, but the ones who should be transformed are the traditional leaders.'

Nevertheless, the process was essentially about transforming traditional leadership, and about using the national Constitution as a tool to negotiate a more secure local order, with less arbitrary power for traditional authority and more clarity about its duties, rules on land allocation and local development. This explains why the attitude of the royal house shifted from enthusiasm to watchfulness to irritation in the course of a few months. Even though the queen-mother had given her blessing to the process, and Billy's brothers had attended some early meetings, they refused actually to join in the discussions on what the rules should be. 'When you come to us with a draft, we will comment,' was the standard reaction.

This became even more hostile once the Commission started to hand out the questionnaires the introduction to which is quoted above. During one meeting, Billy's brother furiously waved the thick booklet. 'What are we supposed to think of questions like, "Do you like to be ruled by a *kgoši*"' "If you say no, what rule should we have instead?" and "Is tradition still important?"' The Commission tried to assure him that it was a way of obtaining people's opinions, to show how much support there was for traditional leadership, but it was in vain. 'How can you name the functions of a *kgoši*? They are obvious. We have just ended our divisions and now these questions can start them up again. Are they going to build or break us? This can really lead to war.'

From the perspective presented at the beginning of this chapter, the royal reaction is understandable. Instead of fixing rules and divorcing the legal from the political, the royal family prefers the uncertainty of local law, in which their powerful position gives them a distinct bargaining advantage. As one Commission member said: 'Of course the *mošate* is not happy with what we're doing. They benefit from all this confusion, like the lack of consultation over land.' The unclarity of norms is beneficial to those in power, who can draw from a whole pool of vague rules, notions, ideas, and state, biblical and other sources to support their position. To those who rule, there is a logic to the disorder. As Chabal and Daloz wrote: 'political actors in Africa seek to maximize their returns on the state of confusion, uncertainty, and sometimes even chaos, which characterizes most African polities.'

5. Conclusion

This chapter set out to answer two main questions: what is 'living law' in Sekhukhune and how does it interact with state law in determining the position of traditional leaders? I have argued that, far from consisting of a distinct and discernible system of customary rules, the main feature of 'living law' is its negotiated, relational and processual character and the way in which it is grafted into the social and political landscape, simultaneously oscillating with it and shaping it. In the negotiations that lead to the (re)production of local norms and thus of 'living law', actors rely on an infinite number of resources, ranging from political alliances and force to privileged knowledge and access to rules.

Rules thus have a double role: they are both a resource on which actors draw, and the vernacular in which cases are argued. To start with the latter: by framing their position in terms of rules, litigants legitimise it and tie it to the social order itself (Falk Moore, 1978:210). Thus, all that is deemed to be the basis of social order can also become a source of rules: traditional authority, culture, the Bible, the state, common sense. As we have seen repeatedly, the importance of these sources is widely acknowledged, but the contents of the rules they give rise to are open to discussion. Thus, while respect for tradition is highly valued, its contents can be vigorously debated. And while rules are deemed important and can influence outcomes, they cannot determine them. Instead, the availability of a wide pool of norms, rules and values, often contradictory and drawn from disparate sources, makes it possible for actors to draw on wider resources – position, force, alliances – to get their position accepted, and still legitimate it with reference to rules. While 'tradition', for instance, is generally deemed important, which version of tradition gets accepted depends on the powers to hand.

Two contrasting case studies illustrated the interaction between the absolutist state law and this negotiated living law in determining the position of traditional leaders. The Sekhukhune succession disputes demonstrated how people try to link ascription and achievement, and pursue good governance by first selecting – from within a limited pool – the best candidate and subsequently legitimising his claim in terms of customary law. For all its disruptive features, succession politics can be considered essential to the local democratic process. The existence of two rival chiefs forces both of them to gain the support of the populace through wise decisions and acceptable policies. If they do not, people can, and will, change sides. In these subtle processes, the state, for all its heterogeneity, generally supports the candidate whose reign is disputed by his 'subjects'. With its emphasis on genealogies, absolute rights and codified customary law, it can give less popular but more 'customary' candidates a distinctive advantage. 'Implementing custom', in the sense of absolutist, ossified positions, can thus thwart local, more democratic processes.

The Mamone Commission on the Tribal Constitution shows, on the other hand, how state law can also act on the side of progress. Here, Mamone citizens used the national Constitution as a resource in debates on local law, in order to create leverage in discussions over what the powers of the *kgoši* should be. In itself an illustration of the debated character of customary law, the process demonstrated how people hook on to human rights discourse in their search for a more just local order. Wide access to state law tipped the scales and gave the Commission a distinct bargaining advantage. Here, instead of acting in support of absolutist power for the traditional leader, state law assisted in providing a check on it.

Jointly, the cases teach us two vital lessons. The first concerns the importance of the locality in the appropriation, valorisation and renegotiation of state law (Falk Moore, 1973). While traditional authority areas are hardly bounded and distinct political entities, they do – in the eyes of most inhabitants – form separate spheres in which national law does not automatically apply but has to be reformulated in the context of local power relations. Naturally, those in power like the traditional leaders benefit most from shielding 'their areas' from the laws of the land, and leaving local law-making firmly tied to their power.

This brings us to the second lesson: the important role of information brokers. Within the communities discussed, there are often only a few people who have access to information on the contents of state law. These brokers are thus in a privileged position to translate, deconstruct or filter state law, bringing in those elements that are deemed useful and omitting others. The process in Mamone was relatively successful because of the wide dissemination of the Constitution, in a way that made it impossible for those in power to neglect its contents and thus equipped those seeking more legal certainty and less arbitrariness with an extra resource in their endeavours.

In combination, the lessons point to the best way to support local democratic processes that seek to create a more just local order within socio-political landscapes in which traditional authority and the moral landscape it embodies are highly valued. If one accepts that traditional authority areas are hardly homogeneous entities with accepted systems of customary norms, but rather sites where there is a constant debate over which rules to apply, and that both rules themselves and the knowledge of them are important resources in these negotiations, the dissemination of information, for instance on the Constitution, can critically help democratisation. Conversely, implementing 'codified custom', often drawn up decades before in a dialogue between local rulers and apartheid ethnologues, can lead to a stifling of these processes. Although state law will always have to be valorised and reappropriated locally, knowledge of its contents by as many local stakeholders as possible can aid this process. It is thus that we have made a first step in relinking the local and the national debates, the central concern of our final chapter.

7. *Conclusion*
Categories have Consequences
The Constitutive Effects of Cultural Rights Legislation

It is because law matters that we have bothered with this story at all.'
(Thompson, 1975:268)

1. Introduction

One day, as we sat on the porch, Patson Phala told me the story of his chief in Marulaneng. 'Did you know that that guy was originally a hobo? He fled to Johannesburg after the old chief had been killed and the royal palace burnt as a protest against the Bantustan system. A few years ago, the village decided that they needed a kgoši *again and some people went to look for him. They found him sleeping in the park, eating out of dustbins and speaking* tsotsi-taal, *slang. But they brought him back to Sekhukhune and now he's quite a well-liked chief because he speaks and listens directly to the people. Even if it is still not in deep Sepedi...'*

And so it was. Traditional leadership had been salvaged from the dustbin of history. All over South Africa, in parliament, during international conferences, in isolated hamlets, a call for the restoration of the dignity of the institution could be heard. Chiefs, politicians and ordinary people called for the dusting off of identities long dormant and revelled in the opportunities that democracy offered to cultural communities to 'explore, explain, reflect and rejoice in that which makes them unique'.[1] The previous chapters have guided us past some of these explorations: in heated public debates, behind closed doors in the presidential palace, in the Mamone *kgôrô*, in a ramshackle Hoepakranz school. Now, after this lengthy tour, the time has come to return to the three questions that instigated it. What was the relationship between the changing legal and socio-political position of traditional authority and customary law in post-apartheid South Africa? Why was this so? What does this teach us about the relation between law, power and culture in the post-modern world?

Post-apartheid South Africa provides an intriguing case study for looking at the changing position of chieftaincy, culture and custom. Not only is there the starkness of the contrast between the abhorrence of legislation based on cultural difference in the past and its enthusiastic embracement in the post-apartheid era. Also, the titillating excitement of the times, of the 'dawning of the dawn' of democracy, seemingly opened up all positions, and made them debatable. Whether they concerned the nature of power, the value of customary law or the importance of culture, arguments had to be stated explicitly and positioned against the myriad of other possibilities that South Africa's future seemed to encompass. All seemed in flux, and both politicians and Sekhukhune citizens had to argue why certain scenarios were preferable to others, why their version of

[1] Sapa. 'Address by Deputy President Jacob Zuma to the Opening Ceremony of the National Khoisan Consultative Conference.'

the future should be accepted. Thus, the few years after the landslide changes in 1994 provided insights that would have been impossible ten years previously. For even though much of the old order would fall into place again with surprising ease, as we have seen, for a specific moment in time it seemed as if everything was up in the air.

This was as much the case in Sekhukhune as it was in South Africa as a whole. Of all the polities I could have investigated – the international community, the provinces, NGOs – I chose to focus on the debates on traditional leadership and customary law. As it turned out, there were many commonalities: the way in which ideas about 'customary law' were embedded in the wider socio-political landscape and the importance of the 'power of definition': who, in a given setting, gets to define what 'custom', 'chieftaincy' and 'culture' are all about. But the purpose of this study was never to look at these polities in isolation. Instead, a central concern throughout has been to investigate the linkages between the local, the national and the global, the 'mutually constitutive character' of these orders. To what extent did national discourse reflect locally lived realities? And how were the debates and the political positions in Sekhukhune influenced by wider national and global events?

In order to knit together all the observations that have been made on these issues, I shall first briefly recapitulate, in sections 2 and 3, what has been said about the relationship between the changing legal and socio-political position of traditional authority and customary law in South Africa and in Sekhukhune, and on the reasons for it. Section 4 is then dedicated exclusively to one aspect of the linkage between the local and the national that, as stated in the Introduction, seems to have received so little academic attention while becoming increasingly important: What, in this case, were the constitutive effects of cultural rights legislation? What did the continued state support of traditional leadership and customary law *mean* locally, and how does it relate to the resurgence of traditional authority? Section 5 expands this argument and considers what the approach taken and the findings can add to the formulation of general theory on the relation between law, power and culture. In section 6 this leads to some tentative thoughts on alternative approaches to the legal recognition of cultural difference.

2. Definitions and Struggles

> Constitutional recognition may not be grounded in social or historical reality; it may simply be an imposition by the political elite, based on assumptions about rural realities. It should therefore have been preceded by a test of rural opinion to establish the saliency of this institution. (*Sowetan*, 17 July 2000)[2]

Despite the coming of democracy and the adoption of the new Constitution, traditional leaders managed to retain recognition of their institution, status and role' in the new Bill of Rights, bolstered by the retention of an estimated 10,000 pieces of apartheid legislation, continuing to make them 'decentralised despots' in their areas, with a wide array of functions pertaining to local government, land allocation and dispute settlement. The consequence was that South Africa remained a 'patchwork democracy', far from unified institutionally, in which the

[2] 'Traditional Leaders: Reinventing Their Roles.'

place where one lived determined the types of rights, the nature of local leadership and – in fact – whether one was a citizen or a subject. Addressing this old-order legacy thus proved to be difficult, and in practically all cases in which amendments were made to it, the traditional leaders seemed to emerge victorious.

Even if the struggle over the future of traditional leadership, at one level, was about chiefly sovereignty, all involved seemed to realise that what was really at stake was the definition of the institution. 'Never again', as Mandela said with foresight, 'shall anyone define the role of traditional leaders without their full participation.' Traditional leadership, like customary law, had proved to be potentially 'a weapon in the hands of traditionalists, revolutionaries and modernizing legalists', and the struggle was thus essentially about the soul of custom, the power to define the nature of chiefly authority, the contents of customary law, and the character of culture.

The prominence of traditional leaders in defining the future of the institution and the evolution of conditions favourable to its resurgence led not only to a reinforcement of the legal and socio-political position of traditional leaders in the national power landscape, but also to an acceptance of a certain understanding of the character and the value of traditional leadership. Versions of essentially negotiable and fluid concepts like 'culture', 'customary law', and 'chieftaincy' were enabled to enter policy and ultimately legislation. These versions appeared to rest on particular, and all too familiar, assumptions: of the irreconcilable difference, in terms of needs and aspirations, between 'rural' and 'urban'; of the 'community' nature of rural society; of the existence of coherent systems of customary law, and of the popularity of traditional leaders, as the sole representatives of these bounded communities.

How did these assumptions, which were at the root of not only the extent to which but also the way in which traditional leaders became recognised at the national level, compare with the locally lived reality of an area like Sekhukhune? One central reason for undertaking this study was the lack of empirical information on 'what goes on on the ground', people's perspectives on traditional leadership. Here, possibly surprisingly, the Sekhukhune data showed that – for all the variance between people and places – there was as much of a call for 'retraditionalisation' locally as there was nationally. After the *hlakahlaka* (mixed-up) years of apartheid, many Bapedi expressed the need to go back to the roots, to restore the old order. The freedoms of democracy, and the chances it offered to rethink and re-express identities, led to the revival of Pedi dancing, the zealous reinstallation of chiefs and calls for the reanimation of 'traditional' systems of dispute resolution. Not only did 80 per cent of the people interviewed say that they supported a traditional leader, but many of them also emphasised the changes that this support had undergone: 'During the struggle we'd fight like dogs with our chief, but now we're back together again.'

Viewed in this way, the *Sowetan* correspondent quoted above need not have worried, at least not about Sekhukhune: there was widespread support for traditional leadership. Nevertheless, his ponderings seem spot-on where they concern the gap between national assumptions of culture, custom, communities and chieftaincy and rural realities. While there was, *in abstracto*, support for institutions such as traditional leadership and customary law, the *character* of this support differed drastically from the ideas held, circulated and perpetuated in national discourse.

Let us start with the assumed popularity of traditional leadership. The national image here was of a single representative institution, with a fixed set of functions and responsibilities and an immutable support base, rooted firmly in tradition. However, even the briefest of visits to Sekhukhune would yield a quite different picture – of an institutionally plural landscape in which a colourful variety of actors compete, or sometimes cooperate, over local power. In each village, a different constellation of actors, like the widely influential *Mapogo*, the civic organisations, elected representatives, churches, business and migrants' organisations, worked with, or against, the traditional authorities in order to attain control over resources, boundaries, people and meaning. In many cases, the traditional authority formed a 'hegemonic bloc' together with, for instance, *Mapogo* and the churches, rallying round an ideology of restoring the old order and putting the young people back in their place. But not only were traditional leaders surrounded by a variety of other actors, the image of chiefs as sole representatives of their communities is also given the lie by their dependence on the support of others within the traditional authority itself, be it the royal family, the *bakgoma* or the Tribal Council. Traditional leaders could be seen to operate in three different spheres: of party politics, bureaucracy and palace politics. And while the first two isolated them from the complex webs of kinship and authority in which they were entangled locally, it was impossible to be successful in palace politics without support from a wider local network.

Also, we have seen how the functions and responsibilities of traditional leaders were far from fixed, and subject to persistent discussion. Even if most people theoretically approved of the notion of traditional leadership, there was a persistent struggle to make the institution more accountable, to ensure that it delivered, to open it up (or not) to women, to redefine its contents. Even if the way in which this was done differed from community to community – from the explicit writing of a tribal constitution in Mamone to citizens refusing to support a *kgoši* because of his unaccountable behaviour in Ga-Masha – this dynamic and debated character of traditional leadership was visible everywhere. Support for chieftaincy, it turned out, depended not only on individual and village characteristics but also on the governance of the chief concerned: wise, accountable, assertive, and 'obedient' traditional leaders who 'delivered' – projects, spoils – could count on additional support, making performance as much a source of legitimation as was tradition. Many Bapedi, for instance, related their support for traditional leadership to the failure of the elected local councils to deliver: 'As these boys have brought us nothing, for now let's keep the *magoši*.' Hence, while traditional leadership was generally 'popular', this popularity was far from fixed but instead marked by persistent debates on its contents, calls for change and threats to withdraw support.

A look at 'living law' revealed a similar discrepancy between the assumption held nationally – of a coherent and distinct system of customary law – and the dynamic and discursive local completion of the concept. While many Sekhukhune citizens acknowledged the importance of *melao*, law, this in no way meant that its contents were fixed. Rather, law as lived in day-to-day life and the values and norms it draws on are the outcome of an ongoing series of negotiations, firmly embedded in local power relations, in which actors can draw on a variety of resources. 'The loosely constructed repertoire' of custom is one, as are constitutional and developmental values, Biblical wisdom, force, common sense, and, for instance, information received over the radio. As Hellum (1999:62) defined it, local or living law is 'the outcome of the interplay between international law, state law and local norms that takes place through human interaction in different historical, social and legal contexts'. Far from 'customary law' and 'state law' being two distinct systems, state law is often drawn in as a resource, even if it always has to be validated and reaffirmed locally. And it was especially where there was widespread legal uncertainty, such as with the overlapping and contradictory official land legislation, that state law sided with the more powerful, those with privileged access to information, to the detriment of the marginalised in society. Nevertheless, even where norms were clear, as with the 'idealised customary law' on succession to the throne, those interested in predicting outcomes did better by looking at the power relations than the rules involved. Developments such as the writing of the tribal constitution in Mamone should thus be viewed in this light: as local attempts to codify rules and wrest them from the discretion of those in power.

Again with regard to the notion that rural society consists of communities coherent enough to be represented by a single institution such as traditional leadership, a superficial glance at Sekhukhune reality, a single visit to a village, would confirm this assumption. People identified strongly with their *setšaba* (which can mean community as well as nation) and related its identity to the presence of a chief: *setšaba ke setšaba ka kgoši* (a community is a community because it has a traditional leader). This, however, did *not* imply the supposed homogeneity, or even that people considered the chief to be the ideal spokesperson to represent the community in dealings with the wider world. Far from it. For one, communities were rife with gender and generational disputes. Also, practically every Sekhukhune community was torn apart by – often violent – succession disputes (which in themselves led to a kind of local two-party system, forcing traditional leaders to relinquish thoughts of autocratic governance, but that is another story). The Ga-Masha case demonstrated the difficulties in representing such a fractured village.

Turning now to the fourth assumption – rural-urban difference – the answer should again be multi-layered. Yes, many rural people appreciated traditional leadership and customary law. Yes, Sekhukhune residents (especially the migrants) felt that Bopedi is governed by other rules, a different pace, even a different normative order from *makgoweng* – the world of the whites. But this did not preclude most Bapedi from having the same democratic and materialist aspirations as, presumably, the rest of the population. Even though our respondents were keen to talk about chieftaincy and customary law, the last section of our questionnaire – 'further comments' – was invariably filled with remarks on the need for more jobs, more security, fixed land titles, roads, schools and electricity. 'We don't care too much who organises these things, as long as they are delivered.'

The stories from Sekhukhune thus showed a much more dynamic, negotiated and changeable order than that presented in the national debates. In that sense, the philosophising of the *Sowetan* correspondent quoted earlier, that 'constitutional recognition may not be grounded in social or historical reality; it may simply be an imposition by the political élite, based on assumptions about rural realities', was – for all the simplicity of the argument – more true than most observations heard in the national policy arena.

3. The constitutive effects of cultural rights legislation

> Law, whether enacted by bureaucrats, lawyers, or litigants, creates categories that become imposed on and practiced in the world. We should not be surprised that these categories have consequences: whether as basic as dictating causal logic, or as implicit as defining which kind of person can have an interest, or as inclusive as controlling how to convey value, the potential of legally mediated categories to mark difference, shape consciousness, and inform the actions of those who confront them is a crucial form of power (Espeland, 1994:1176)

So, we now have two sets of givens concerning the legal position of traditional authority and customary law. On the one hand, there are the codified versions of culture, custom and chieftaincy: the still applicable 1951 Black Authorities Act, which introduces Tribal and Regional Authorities and allocates chiefs functions ranging from tax collection to weed eradication; the 1957 Regulations prescribing the Duties, Powers, Privileges and Conditions of Service of Chiefs and Headmen, which entitle a chief to the 'loyalty, respect and obedience of all the Blacks resident in his area'; the myriad laws dealing with land allocation, which determine that 'tribal land' can be alienated only by 'tribal resolution'; the yellowing documents proclaiming Tribal Authorities and determining the number of 'tribal councillors' in each of them; the 1996 constitutional provisions forcing courts to apply customary law where 'this is applicable'; the 1998 Customary Marriage Act and Remuneration of Public Office Bearers Act – these are but a few examples from the enormous pile of official legislation dealing with the substance of chieftaincy and customary law. On the other hand, there are the ever-shifting dynamics of local law, the fluctuating and contested ideas on chiefly functions and authority, the ongoing debates on what local custom and culture are and should be. The question arises, of course, as to how these two sets are interlinked, what all these official laws mean and do locally or, to put it differently: What are the constitutive effects of cultural rights legislation?

Before I recapitulate what the scenes from Sekhukhune, the discussions held under the thorn-trees, in the *magôrô* and in the royal palaces, taught us on this issue, I need to put forward a few caveats. The first concerns the impossibility of neatly measuring the impact of 'the legal' on 'the local'. As set out in the Introduction, one can take an *instrumentalist* and a *constitutive* approach to the question of 'how law matters' (Garth and Sarat, 1998). An instrumentalist approach, which considers law as an independent variable whose local impact can be measured, not only poses general problems but would have been impossible in this case. For one thing, this particular linkage between the local and the national, the state recognition of certain forms and versions of culture, has been going on for decades, even centuries, making it impossible to distinguish between a 'before' and 'after' state recognition. Even though many official customary laws were revalorised in the post-apartheid era, their roots and the assumptions underlying them run much deeper. In addition, as has been a central argument throughout this work, it is impossible to isolate law from wider social forces. Thus, the legal reaffirmation of the position of traditional authority and customary law went hand in hand with political statements on the importance of chieftaincy, NGOs singling out traditional leaders as their main counterparts in development programmes, companies like Coca-Cola and Douglas

Colliery sponsoring royal coronations and the ANC executive telling local cadres that the time had come to make peace with the chiefs.

Pursuing an instrumentalist, isolationist approach would have made no sense against this background. Rather, I opted to look at the *constitutive* effects of cultural rights legislation. Such an approach sees law 'as the way of organizing the world into categories and concepts which, while providing spaces and opportunities, also constrains behaviour and serves to legitimate authority' (ibid.:4). The law categorises, demarcates subjects, defines powers, draws lines. And once they are singled out and defined in law, categories like 'a traditional leader', 'a tribal resolution', 'a customary marriage', 'a tribal authority' can have important local consequences, if not causatively then at least by structuring both 'thought and action' (ibid.: cf. Foucault, 1994). Of the many interlinked ways in which this occurs, I shall focus on three here: the construction of subjects, the local socio-political formations and the, often forgotten, material consequences of these categories, before returning to the relation between state recognition and chiefly resurgence.

Sekhukhune subjects

Legal categorisations impact, in a multitude of ways and in conjunction with a myriad of other forces, on the way people in Sekhukhune constitute themselves and their relations with others. They contribute to the creation of subjects which, as Foucault has underlined, is a fundamental, albeit sometimes nebulous, form of power (Foucault, 1994; Espeland, 1994; Ong, 1996). The process of 'subjectification', of self-making and being made at the same time, takes place within a multitude of force relations, a web of power, of which law is simultaneously a strand and an institutional crystallisation. As such, legal categories, although never in isolation, have consequences for how people understand the world and their own position in it.

Let us return to some of the examples of the way subjectification takes place in Sekhukhune. A prime illustration is the way the state classification and definition of 'chiefdom' impacts on the local order. Chiefly identity, as laid down in hundreds of laws and regulations, reinforced by magistrates and Traditional Affairs officials and – in the old days – by the army, is that of a bureaucrat, a local ruler singled out to represent the community and act as a portal to the state. The 1998 Municipal Structures Act and its amendments granting traditional leaders the right to make up *ex officio* 20 per cent of the membership of elected local councils is but one in a long line of laws individualising traditional leaders, isolating them from webs of kinship and turning them – in their individual capacity – into the spokespeople of communities.[3] This construction of chiefly identity had, of course, local repercussions on the way traditional leaders viewed themselves, and were considered by 'their subjects'. These subjects, by means of statements such as 'these chiefs guard us for the government' and 'he can give us all the stamps we need', depicted traditional leaders as gatekeepers to the outside world, as accountable to Pretoria as to them.

The remnants of old laws combined with their reinforcement in the new order also, in many ways, contributed to a, widely shared, understanding of Sekhukhune citizenship which revolved around being, first, a chiefly subject and only

[3] *Municipal Structures Act 117/1998, Municipal Structures Second Amendment Bill 2000.*

then a South African citizen. Without expressing allegiance to the traditional authority and respect for customary law and *setšo*, tradition, many things simply became much more difficult. A Mamone resident applying for a Permission to Occupy a plot of land had to fill in the names of his chief and headman on the form – a form providing solely for male occupancy. Similarly, the Mamone tribal authority demanded of people who wanted a business permit, or access to a plot of land on which to practise cultural dances, that they first underline their allegiance to the chief by contributing towards his coronation. Also, many traditional leaders refused to hand out land to someone without a *trekpas*. Even if all this was against South Africa's new Constitution, it did constitute Sekhukhune day-to-day reality, the law lived by people at the local level.

In a society where people were generally 'seen in their categories' (which, however, proved highly negotiable), legal categorisations underlined and reinforced all sorts of gender and generational cleavages. Take the fact, for instance, that magistrates still referred 'family and land matters' back to the customary courts, and would continue to do so if the policy proposals put forward by the traditional leaders were accepted. This meant that young people, or women, who had attempted to 'escape' the local normative order were put 'back in their place' with a vengeance. Another example out of many is the state recognition of initiation schools: the Northern Province Circumcision Act gave officially recognised traditional leaders the right to hold these schools, and stipulated that the 'premier may impose such conditions as he or she may deem desirable in regard to matters in connection with the conduct of the circumcision schools and the treatment of initiates.'[4] In this manner, important rituals in identity construction such as coming of age were, by means of legislation, tied to a bureaucratised form of chieftaincy.

Thus, subjectification in Sekhukhune could be said to take place in dialogue with the categories created by, among others, state law: even though people were no longer forced directly to identify as chiefly subjects, with their relations ruled by custom, the residues of these old categories proved difficult to escape from. Particular categorisations, in interaction with local beliefs and values, contributed to the creation of certain subjects: the process of 'self-making and being made' had as one point of reference the categories reflected in law, as they were communicated and reinforced through a wide variety of channels.

Political formations

Just as the categories imposed by law privilege certain trajectories of identity formation over others, and make certain images of the self more logical than alternatives, so they can also strengthen the position of certain actors in the local institutional landscape. As we have seen, a kaleidoscopic mix of local actors were involved – sometimes together, sometimes in competition – in the struggles for control over people, boundaries, resources and meaning. Some of these struggles were fought out in the language of (living) law: among them, the rights to a plot of land, a housing project, the holding of initiation schools or the question of whether female school teachers should be allowed to wear trousers. And state law and its categorisations added to all the things that actors in the local political arena could draw on in these struggles – reference to custom or culture, to

[4] *Northern Province Circumcision Act 6/1996*, s. 4.

religion, to one's position in society, to the threat of force. State law taking many guises, of course: a yellowing proclamation, something said during the programme 'rights talk' on *Thobela FM*, an earlier decision by the magistrate, the Constitution handed out to children at school, an ANC publication, the words of a visiting NGO official – whatever the form, it always potentially strengthened certain positions and weakened others.

This is not to say that state legal categories have a direct impact on local socio-political formations. Rather, they always have to be appropriated and validated within the local political arena, often undergoing quite drastic transformations in the process. Debates in the Madibong Tribal Council showed us such a display of the 'social life of norms'. Here, a rule introduced by a 1970s proclamation stating that 'tribal meetings' could only be held during the week – a clear attempt to exclude migrants from political decision-making – was presented as 'custom' in order to bar working women from the revamped Tribal Council. Also, laws not beneficial to the traditional authority were often ignored, while others – sometimes long repealed – would be implemented with a vengeance. Here, the fact that traditional leaders were often considered by the state to be community spokespeople and consequently became the only community representatives to be informed of legislative developments, strengthened their role as information brokers, applying those laws that suited them best. In addition, the post-apartheid patchwork legal situation in which nobody – from the president to the academic community – had a complete picture of which laws still applied where, worked to the advantage of the powerful, allowing them to choose from often contradictory laws those that reinforced their position.

Part of the validation and reinforcement of state law within local political relations was often the redefinition of central categories. In this vein, we have seen how the notion of '*ex officio* representation' as encompassing full voting rights for traditional leaders was quickly redefined to mean mere observer status. Similarly, the notion of a 'tribal resolution' to alienate community land proved malleable in the hands of potential beneficiaries. There are various official legal definitions of the concept, varying from 'a resolution passed by the tribe democratically and in accordance with the indigenous law or customs of the tribe' to 'a decision taken at a properly constituted meeting where a majority of the tribe is present or represented'.[5] In practice, 'tribal resolutions' whereby whole portions of land were lucratively signed away, came to be taken by the chief on his own or by someone representing him, the royal house, or the Tribal Council.

The above shows how far local appropriation of state legal categories was from a mechanical acceptance of national and provincial legislation, a passive living up to bureaucratic myths. Rather, categories were accepted, rejected or redefined in line with both local values and interests and as such did not determine the local power landscape, even if they did have an effect on it.

Material implications

The emphasis on the culturally productive capacity of law as well as its intimate connection with power relations should not obscure the material implications of

[5] *Upgrading of Land Tenure Rights Act 112/1991*, as amended by Department of Land Affairs. *Interim Procedures Governing Land Development Decisions Which Require the Consent of the Minister of Land Affairs as Nominal Owner of the Land*. Available from http://w3sli.wcape.gov.za/indexNet.htm, *Interim Protection of Informal Land Rights Act 31/1996*.

these categorisations. As Chanock wrote with insight on the emphasis on the cultural and the political in present-day socio-legal discourse (2000:35):

> We should ask what narratives are being replaced by the focus on 'culture'. Post-everythingism has not changed everything. In the post-communist world material explanations have dropped suddenly from social analysis. Yet one does not have to be clinging to the wreckage of Marxism, or conspiracy theory, to insist on the need for an adequate account of the material world in which concepts of rights are deployed.

Some of the most distressing examples of the material implications of the – overlapping and insecure – legal legacy of apartheid that we have seen concerned land tenure. The system, which did not allow freehold title except for communal property and firmly tied access to land to acceptance of chiefly authority, continued to exist all over Sekhukhune. As a result, women, young people, supporters of the wrong chief, strangers and the impoverished were denied access to land on a daily basis. Also, the insecurity of the tenure system, only worsened by the conflicting messages issued by the state on its future, made people, project developers and even the provincial government weary of investments in the 'traditional authority areas'. One never knew, after all, what would happen to a plot of land after a new chief had come to power.

As a result of this linkage between access to land and acceptance of chiefly authority, people will appropriate and invest in certain social identities because these form the key to access to a plot of land, a royal salary, a business permit. The woman parliamentarian who was 'considered to be like a man' and allowed to purchase a piece of land can serve as an example. Definition, both of people and of categories, makes a difference. For instance, the way in which a 'tribal resolution' is defined also helps to determine who, to quote a Mamone example, gets to share in the R500,000 that the developers of a shopping centre are prepared to pay for such a resolution. And whether one is considered a good wife, obedient to custom, can make the difference between winning a court case or losing – and paying a large fine. To lift briefly part of the Marxist wreckage out of the ocean of history, neither legal relations nor political forms can be understood without emphasising, the material conditions that underlie them (Marx, 1859:1).

Categories and chiefly resurgence

State law and its categorisations thus impacted on how Bapedi constituted themselves and their relations with the wider world, on local political formations and on who could claim access to resources. It strengthened political positions, rendered some scenarios more logical than others and thus functioned as a resource in the negotiations on the local order and the people's place in it. Not surprisingly, the state recognition of chieftaincy and the way in which this was implemented also turned out to have local repercussions: on chiefly identity, people's constitution of the self as chiefly subjects, on the relation between traditional authorities and other actors involved in the local power-play, and the division of spoils within the traditional authority areas. As such, the continued state support of traditional leadership in the post-apartheid era could well be an important factor contributing to its local resurgence. To quote Myers (1999:54): 'As long as the state supports and sustains the institution of traditional authority, the presumption of its legitimacy will fall naturally into place.'

It is important to proceed very carefully here, and to re-emphasise the dialectic, fluctuating character of the dynamics involved. I am not saying that the continued state recognition of traditional leadership and customary law created local support where there was none before – even though this was certainly the case at times. Allegiance to traditional leadership had long been central to the identity of many Bapedi: the revolt of the 1950s, for instance, can be understood as a local protest against the manipulation of the institution by the government of the day, and an underlining of its importance. The return to centre stage of many traditional leaders after the dawn of democracy was often experienced as locally driven, a way of asserting a place for Sekhukhune within the new order. Nevertheless, and this is what is often overlooked in debates on the resurgence of traditional leadership – the external support and the assumptions underlying it did help shape debates, strengthen positions and make certain outcomes simply more logical than others.

If the resurgence of traditional leadership in Sekhukhune occurred in dialogue with the wider world, law was, of course, only one of the languages in which messages, assumptions and aspirations were conveyed. There were a variety of other channels, some explicit, others more subtle. The magistrates and other officials who sent back people who turned to them without having first seen their chief reinforced chieftaincy outright. The same goes for the successful attempts of the ANC leadership to reconcile *kgoši* Kgoloko – accused of killing five comrades and subsequently forced to flee in the 1980s – with his community, in the end even by offering him a position as an ANC MP. There was also the ubiquitous presence of politicians and government officials at royal coronations and Contralesa get-togethers, and the fact that Mandela, when visiting Sekhukhune, spent so much more time with the chiefs than he did with the people. But the more implicit messages played a role as well. The undercapacity of elected local government and the neglect of civic organisations further contributed to the creation of a set of conditions that made increased support for traditional leadership, if not inevitable, at least a logical path to take.

The dynamic relation between the fluctuating local support for traditional leadership and events in the wider world became particularly clear when examining the discourses on the legitimation of adherence to the institution. People gave four equally important reasons for their (lack of) support for traditional leadership: tradition, performance, government support and the lack of alternatives. Of these, at least three were closely related to the backing that traditional leaders received 'from outside'. Obviously, this was most clearly so in those cases where people cited government support of traditional leadership as its main source of legitimacy: 'the chiefs work for the government in the villages'; 'they are the portals to government'. But performance, as a source of legitimacy, was also often explicitly linked to decisions made in the wider world: 'at least they are doing more for us than these young boys in the TLC'; 'he can organise projects for us'. Similarly, those people justifying their support for traditional leadership by pointing out that 'this is the only government we have' also commented on the failure of the state to establish a clear alternative to the institution. But even the fourth source of legitimation – tradition, culture, religion – can be said to have discursive relations with the wider world: a programme on the radio, Mbeki's emphasis on the African Renaissance, the sermon at the ZCC's Easter session.

What is clearly shown by the fluctuating and interrelated sources of legitimation of support for traditional leadership is the essential potential of the institution in the post-modern order. While traditional leaders can not only derive material *and* popular support from their inclusion within the wider state system, they can also tap other sources of legitimacy, and thus posit themselves as an alternative to it. During times when faith in the legal-rational state is said to be crumbling, and people disengaging from it, traditional authority is in the advantageous position of being able to draw on a variety of other sources of legitimation.

4. Law, power and culture

How can we now extend the lessons from Sekhukhune, for all their specificity, to the wider debate on the relation between law, power and culture? As set out in the Introduction, there is an urgent need to reconceptualise this relation now that, as part of the post-modern world order, more and more sub- and supranational polities are claiming legal recognition on the basis of their cultural difference. And are seeing these claims rewarded, as demonstrated by the Ethiopian Constitution which allows ethnic groups the right to secede, the far-reaching autonomy granted to *pueblos indigenes* in Colombia, the court victories of the aboriginal peoples of New Zealand and Canada and the general success of 'first nation' movements. Culture is back in politics, as an alternative source of legitimacy by which to challenge the legal-rational state, and it is interplaying in a myriad of ways with rights discourse. And even if, as we have seen in the Introduction, there is a host of recent literature on chieftaincy and customary law, this is either situated in the colonial era, or fails to posit the chiefly resurgence within the present global juncture.

Two of the central ideas to which lawyers and social scientists debating cultural rights cling with surprising doggedness, have been refuted – once again, one could say – by this study. One is 'the myth of the mirror': the notion that within a given nation there exists such a thing as an amalgam of coherent cultures, ready to receive state recognition. Rather, reality shows a murky picture of smudged lines and uncertain textures. Drawing certain features of 'culture' and 'custom' out of this blend for neat legal categorisation is in essence a political act, certain to privilege some voices, visions and versions while silencing others. When it comes to cultural rights legislation, for which the very rationale is the official acknowledgement of difference, it is often the most exotic, the most outlandish voices within the community concerned that get to speak loudest. Whether in New Zealand or South Africa, it is mostly the voices speaking for 'indigeneity', for 'difference', that get themselves heard by the law.

There is a second and similarly tenacious belief, that isolated, traditional communities have systems of socio-political and legal order which exist free from interaction with the outside world. Like Piot, I know of no 'bounded, culturally homogeneous African culture' and would rather describe even the most remote village encountered as a site – and also, in many ways, an effect – of the modern, one that is as privileged as any other, one that has shaped the modern as much as it has been shaped by it, and one that brings to the modern – that always uneven, often discordant, ever refracting, forever incomplete cultural/political project – its own vernacular modernity' (Piot, 1999:23,178). This dialectic, mutually constitutive dialogue between polities with their own political make-up and the wider world – the nation-state, the international community – is strengthened and given a particular twist when this wider world 'officially recognises' parts of local culture: its traditional leadership institutions, certain customary laws. This legal recognition, as has been set out in the previous section, is bound to have constitutive effects. It can influence the way people see themselves (take the former South African coloureds now coming out – and justifiably so – as Khoisan), the local power relations (Khoisan leadership is now debated in terms of genealogy rather than quality) and who gets access to which resources (from diamonds to tourist dollars) under which conditions. With the 'myth of the mirror' no longer holding and the image of traditional, isolated communities unaffected by state recognition having been shattered, what insights has this study offered to replace them?

To start with the idea that any understanding of law should be planted firmly in the power relations of the institutional landscape concerned: I have introduced the notion of 'negotiated law' to draw attention to the fact that the version of 'law' that makes it to the text-books, to court cases, to policy within a given setting is, on the one hand, a reflection of its power relations and, on the other, a crucial element in their constitution. This is as true for the debates on the definition of traditional leadership that rage nationally in South Africa as it is for living law in Sekhukhune, and comparable dialogues all over the world. Law cannot, and should not, be isolated from general socio-scientific understandings of the contemporary world. A constitutive approach to law reaffirms, to quote Garth and Sarat, 'both the importance of social science to law and the importance of law to social science' (1998:5). Nevertheless, even when law is pulled back into socio-scientific theory, this should be combined with an acknowledgement of its specific place in the socio-political landscape.

One aspect of this special place is the potentially double-sided character of law. Such is the nature of the 'paradoxical, polymorphous discourse of rights' that it can act as a weapon of both the mighty and the weak, as a tool of liberation and oppression (Comaroff and Comaroff, 1997:400). There is no better example of this than South Africa, where codified customary law was one of the main channels for the implementation of apartheid, but rights discourse simultaneously fuelled the struggle against it (Abel, 1995a). The scenes from Sekhukhune offered similar examples: of oppression in the name of *molao* but also of chiefly subjects seeking to curtail the more arbitrary powers of the traditional authority by drawing up a tribal constitution, and of women demanding more freedom with the national Constitution in hand. In short, of local politics being cast in rights discourse. Here, it also became clear that the greater the legal lack of clarity, the more contradictory and overlapping the rules, the more this benefits those in power rather than potentially acting as a shield against them. This was put succinctly by the Agricultural Affairs official in Sekhukhune, who said of the totally unclear local system of land administration: 'A lot of people benefit from this confusion.'

In looking at the relation between law, power and culture, I have repeatedly emphasised the importance of the 'power of definition'. Who, in a given situation, gets to categorise, to classify, to decide which elements in the mishmash of culture are worthy of official recognition? Which voices are heard and which are silenced? As Shipton and Goheen remarked about land law (1992:311).

> power and influence over land-holding mean power to define types of land, types of persons, and types of bonds between the two. Who has the power, for instance, to classify land as 'vacant and without owner', to approve a clan or corporation, or to designate a holding as being of 'uneconomic' size? Who, more basically still, gets to define what 'owner', 'corporation', and 'economic' mean?

When it comes to cultural rights legislation, those voices representing 'difference' – the *iwis*, traditional elders, tribal representatives – stand a much better chance of getting heard than other, more democratic, institutions. The problem here lies partly in the notion of representation: the persistent belief that 'traditional communities' are so homogeneous that they *can* be represented. Here, too, it is not too difficult to see how the Sekhukhune evidence, which contradicts this view, could easily be extended to other 'aboriginal communities'.

When considering which version of culture receives official recognition for what reasons, this issue of representation makes it worthwhile to make a distinction between the debates *within* certain polities, like the Sekhukhune traditional authority areas, and *between* them. While the open, overlapping, porous and persistently negotiated character of what constitutes a polity, who belongs to it and why cannot be emphasised enough, it is clear that there are certain social fields that are bound – in the eyes of both those inside and outside – by a specific political make-up. For one, we should look at which debates are wedged within the – porous – polity borders about who these authorities should be, what their right to govern is, and what rules they can issue and sanction. But the next step consists of considering, by means of notions such as representation, who gets to voice local debates to the outside world and which strands are sculpted into, for instance, state law. Such considerations should take into account the power relations within which these 'cross-boundary' negotiations take place. The 'imagined dialogue' between traditional leaders (as community representatives) and state officials, for instance, was not one between equals: the state – even though never as a monolithic entity – could draw the limits of recognition (the Constitution), held the purse-strings and had resort to other types of force. Similarly, the material implications of these debates should not be lost: which representations of culture make it to law determine who gets access to a state salary, to diamonds, to land and a variety of other spoils.

One of the most important lessons of this study, with a wider bearing than on Sekhukhune alone, concerns the constitutive effects of cultural rights legislation. When the legal recognition of culture is examined, Geertz's remark that 'legal thought is constitutive of social realities rather than reflective of them' takes on particular salience (1983:252). The images frozen in law, the categorisations chosen, these – always in conjunction with other forces – can have important local effects. The distorted picture perpetuated in legislation can potentially lead to 'retraditionalisation', the strengthening of patriarchical forms of rule, the exclusion by definition of the more marginalised in society from access to resources. For even if we have been sufficiently confronted with the partially self-regulating character of polities like Sekhukhune, with their ability to resist, deform and reinterpret national legislation, this legislation, as well as the images projected through it, *does* matter locally.

5. Alternatives

My argument has thus been that the South African state recognised chieftaincy and customary law on the basis of often faulty assumptions which, in the worst case, became self-fulfilling prophecies: chiefs as the only important local rulers, a given reluctance about elected local government, women and youth as marginalised, customary law as fixed and antithetical to human rights. Nevertheless, this book has also offered ample evidence of the local adherence to custom, chieftaincy and culture – albeit in ways often misread in policy fora – and their centrality to the identity of many South Africans. Their return to the roots and their appeal for local solutions to pressing problems form part of a worldwide movement, and seeking to counter it would seem to be as impossible as it would be inadvisable. What, then, should be the response to the need for formal recognition of cultural diversity without falling into the trap of freezing difference and thus strengthening local fissures and creating cleavages where there were none before? In passing, the tale of post-apartheid South Africa, both at national level and in Sekhukhune, has also shown some alternative ways in which it is possible meaningfully to do justice to cultural differences, which I shall reiterate by way of conclusion.

For one, the emphasis on the 'power of definition' has demonstrated the importance of listening to plural voices in debates – which are, after all, about the future not only of traditional leadership but also of rural society as a whole. By treating traditional leaders as the sole representatives of rural society, the government confirms a myth it has created itself. At all the conferences on 'Traditional Rule and Local Government' there is always a row of youngsters and rural women at the back, shaking their heads and clicking their tongues as 'their' chiefs rage on about how 'rural people don't want this democracy' and 'it is impossible to have two bulls in a kraal'. If the recognition of traditional leadership in the new South Africa is, as everyone seems to agree, essentially about its definition, the power to define should lie not with the government, not with parliament, not with traditional leaders, but with the people for whose benefit they are recognised. As Local Government Minister and tribal elder Sydney Mufamadi once told the traditional leaders, chieftaincy – also in the eyes of the government – should be an embodiment of the aspirations of the people: 'You will never go wrong if, in whatever you do, you regard the people as your main frame of reference.'[6]

Of course, allowing a variety of voices to speak on both what custom is and what it should be precludes the possibility of then neatly chiselling one version – of who owns land, what chiefly functions are, how inheritance takes place – into legislation. Rather, it argues in favour of procedurally recognising chieftaincy and customary law, but leaving its substantive completion to the people concerned, and thus allowing for local variance. Let us recall the three communities in the Northern Province which had proposed that their next chief be a woman. The state anthropologist, *Seymour's Customary Law* and Van Warmelo's *Bantu Tribes of South Africa* in hand and fiercely resolved to protect the culture part of his job description, reacted with horror, rejecting the application, stating that in these particular cultures it was always the eldest son of the

[6] Xolani Xundu, 'Rift Narrows on Traditional Leaders.' *Business Day*, 24 August 2000, p.2.

candle-wife who succeeded to the throne, and offering – on the basis of the genealogies in the departmental files – some suggestions as to who this should be. In such a case, would it not have been advisable to recognise traditional leadership but leave it to the people concerned to decide who the chief was and what he/she should do?

A more fortuitous example of how the government procedurally recognised customary law but left its substantive completion to the people was the Customary Marriages Act.[7] I recall a 1998 meeting in Pretoria when traditional leaders – again, as sole invitees for their communities – were asked to give their opinions on the contents of such an Act. The heated discussions in the conference room were mostly about the substantive requirements for the validity of such a marriage: when the future wife had planted a spear in the husband's courtyard, upon payment of a *lobola* of R20 or fewer cattle, when the marriage had been registered with the traditional leader and a fee paid to him. Fortunately, the South African Law Commission, after a private discussion, decided against writing any substantive requirements into the law, but left definitions open: 'the marriage must be negotiated and entered into or celebrated in accordance with customary law', this being 'the customs and usages traditionally observed among the indigenous people of South Africa and which form part of the culture of those peoples'.[8]

Inevitably, even if the law refrains from providing cut-and-dried definitions, a great deal can still go wrong in the implementation. Who gets to decide, in practice, what the customs and usages traditionally observed among the indigenous people of South Africa are? In the course of this study, we have seen how old-school government anthropologists and other officials trained in the structural-functionalist tradition would 'implement custom' with yellowing ethnographic text-books and apartheid proclamations to hand. Similarly, we have encountered magistrates relying on the same text-books for their understanding of custom, or – more frequently – sending all 'customary' land and family matters back to the customary courts, even if people are fearful of discrimination in them. Higher up the judicial hierarchy, we ran into judges like the one in the 1998 *Hlope v. Mahlalela a.o* case who criticised an expert because she could not differentiate between 'cultural practices and Swazi law', and ruled that 'it cannot be accepted that all cultural practices are indigenous law and vice versa'. If such people, the 'street-level bureaucrats' involved in the day-to-day encounters between the state and 'traditional communities', were to accept the negotiated, fluctuating, changeable nature of custom, culture and tradition and, for instance, its possible coexistence with human rights, a lot would be won. At the very least, it would allow the acceptance of 'new customs' that enjoy popular legitimacy and let alternative voices be heard in the state corridors.

A prerequisite here is abandoning the notion that customary law and human rights, tradition and modernity, chiefly rule and democracy, would somehow be antithetical. Stories like those from Sekhukhune, heard far too seldom, show how these dichotomies exist largely in policy documents and abstract scenarios presented at conferences, but disappear in the local courtyards, *magôrô* and schools, where people have long accepted these ideas. One example is the young

[7] *Customary Marriages Act 120/1998*, s 1(ii) jo 3(1) sub b.
[8] Ibid., H-I.

chief who was elected mayor (with 99 per cent of the votes), in rural Venda and, seated among the banana, mango, guava and papaw trees, described himself as a 'traditional leader and a politician at the same time'.[9] Another is Madibong, where *kgoši* Kgoloko revamped the Tribal Council to allow elected representatives and even invited two women to participate. Similarly, customary court cases were not argued in the language of customary law text-books, but in a discourse straddling reference to human rights, to the Bible, tradition, common sense and something read in the paper the other day.

If this is the heterogeneous, colourful local reality, then it would be a mistake merely to recognise *cultural difference* nationally: chiefly subjects should – as the Constitution allows them but practice often does not – have as much access to protection by the wider Bill of Rights as their urban peers. Their adherence to tradition should not rob them of the right to equality, to a fair trial, to secure property. It is of importance therefore that people are not 'locked up' in their culture because of where they live or, as still happens too often, the colour of their skin. This freedom to 'opt out' of chiefly rule was what the proposed s 32 of the interim Constitution was all about – allowing people choice over whether or not customary law should apply to their personal relationships. As we saw, this proposal was boycotted by the traditional leaders, just like the Land Rights Bill – another example of an attempt to give rural people a choice in matters of custom that failed for political reasons. The proposal to let citizens themselves choose what form of land tenure they preferred – through a traditional authority or a Communal Property Association – was eliminated by the traditional authorities, just like suggestions by the Law Commission to make the jurisdiction of traditional courts in criminal matters a matter of free choice: 'If people are allowed to choose where they go this will undermine the authority of the chief', as one traditional leader said (South African Law Commission, 1999).

Nevertheless, it is worthwhile to emphasise the limits of law once again. Even if state law allowed a plurality of voices, left the 'power of definition' to the people and offered them a clear choice to combine recognition of culture with protection of (other) human rights, all these could remain changes on paper which alter nothing in the world where magistrates' courts are remote, speak an unintelligible – both literally and metaphorically – language and necessitate the involvement of expensive lawyers.

It is clear that real change has to be forged locally, laboriously negotiated within local power relations. Here, returning the 'power of definition' to the people means empowering those marginal voices involved in the negotiation of local rule with additional resources. Even if such empowerment takes place largely through education and economic progress, knowledge of the official law can also be such a resource. We have seen how the Sepedi version of the Constitution handed out in Mamone schools elicited the idea of writing a tribal constitution, how discussions in the human rights programme of *Thobela FM* were brought into customary court sessions, how 'tribal councillors' demanded information on new laws and whether they 'were doing the right thing'. The lack of clarity on which official laws still apply is, as has been amply demonstrated, a powerful weapon in the hands of the privileged. Here, too, the relation between 'communities' and the wider state seems to be that of an hourglass, with the

[9] Xolani Xundu. 'This Is No Ordinary Chief Running for the Job of Mayor,' *Business Day*, 4 December 2000, p. 4.

traditional authority functioning as the neck privileged to pass on information on the community to the outside world, but also to determine what knowledge is filtered through to local people. After all 'perfect communication will leave the middle-man out of a job' (Collier, 1976; quoting Bailey, 1969).

Empowerment in the form of, *inter alia,* information about the formal legal framework is thus important. Nevertheless, the character of polities in Sekhukhune is such that people will still have to – slowly and incrementally – negotiate their own pace of change. That this is possible, and happens all over the place, is shown by the example of Rose Diphofa, with which I shall conclude:

At a certain point during my research in Sekhukhune a snippet of gossip suddenly surfaced in every conversation: with the watchmen, the ANC youngsters, the pre-school teachers, the tribal elders. Apparently an unmarried woman in Ga-Mphanama had had the audacity to ask her chief for a plot of tribal land, and, what is more, had received it. Curious, we drove on the dirt roads to the isolated village to be shown a brand-new shining corrugated iron hut, surrounded by freshly-swept red sand with cacti meticulously planted in it. The owner came rushing back from the river, a tub of washing on her head and fear in her eyes; white visitors are associated with the police, or tax collectors. But when we told her that we had come for a first-hand version of the small revolution in the village, her hands stopped trembling and a wide smile broke out.

For hours, Rose recounted every detail of her victory

> I am 40 years old, I have four children and a job as a petrol attendant, and no intention of ever getting married. In our culture, this means that you have to live with your parents, like a child. I have often wondered why this is. Especially now, with the new South Africa and the papers and the television at the bottle-shop telling us that women are also welcome to come in. So one day I decided that I would ask for my own piece of land. It was something that I wanted so badly that I would have been prepared to go to the police for it. But first I asked the *kgoši.* My uncle spoke up, on my behalf; women are not expected to speak in the customary court. But he put my case exactly as I wanted it, and after a very, very long discussion the court decided that times were indeed changing and that even an unmarried woman should be able to receive a plot of land. So this is how I got this house. The women from the savings club contributed to its decoration and helped me to build it. You know, it was like fighting a lion and it took both brains and courage. But it worked, and now there are many other women also asking for a plot of land.

As we left Rose, with the magnificent red and orange Sekhukhune sunset flaring up behind her, I recalled a line in one of the first publications of the Congress of Traditional Leaders in South Africa: 'Only the South African rural woman can say "when and where I enter, the whole of South African society enters with me"' (Ndou and Letsoalo, 1994:4). Clearly, South Africa's process of simultaneous 'formation and renewal', so sluggish at the national level, had long ago been picked up by those to whom it mattered most.

References

Abbink, Jon (1997) 'Ethnicity and Constitutionalism in Contemporary Ethiopia.' *Journal of African Law* 41: 159–74.

Abel, Richard (1995a) *Politics by Other Means: Law in the Struggle against Apartheid, 1980– 1994*. New York: Routledge.

——— (ed.) (1995b) *The Law and Society Reader*. New York: New York University Press, 1995.

Abrahams, Ray (1996) 'Vigilantism: Order and Disorder on the Frontiers of the State', in *Inside and Outside the Law: Anthropological Studies of Authority and Ambiguity*, ed. Olivia Harris, London: Routledge.

Abrahamsen, Rita (2000) *Disciplining Democracy: Development Discourse and Good Governance in Africa*. London: Zed Books.

Adams, Martin, Ben Cousins, and Siyabulela Manona (1999a) 'Land Tenure and Economic Development in Rural South Africa: Constraints and Opportunities.' Paper presented at the National Conference on Land and Agrarian Reform in South Africa, Johannesburg.

Adams, Martin, Sipho Sibando, and Stephen Turner (1999b) 'Land Tenure Reform and Rural Livelihoods in Southern Africa', *Natural Resource Perspectives* 39.

Albertyn, Catherine (1994) 'Women and the Transition to Democracy in South Africa', in *Gender and the New South African Legal Order*, ed. T.W. Bennett, G. Bradfield, A. Cockrell, R. Jooste, R. Keightly, C.M. Murray and D. Van Zyl Smit. Cape Town: Juta & Co.

Allott, Anthony (1980) *The Limits of Law*. London: Butterworths.

——— (ed.) (1970) *Judicial and Legal Systems in Africa* Vol. 28. London: Butterworth.

Anaya, S.J (1996) *Indigenous Peoples in International Law*. Oxford: Oxford University Press.

Anderson, Benedict (1983) *Imagined Communities: Reflections on the Origin and Spread of Nationalism*. London: Verso Editions.

Appadurai, A. (1996) *Modernity at Large: Cultural Dimensions of Globalization*. Minneapolis: University of Minnesota Press.

Appiah, K.A. (1991) 'Out of Africa: Topologies of Nativism', in *The Bounds of Race. Perspectives on Hegemony and Resistance*, ed. D. LaCapra, Ithaca, NY and London: Cornell University Press.

Ashforth, Adam (1997) 'Lineaments of the Political Geography of State Formation in Twentieth-Century South Africa.' *Journal of Historical Sociology* 10, no. 2: 101–26.

Assies, Willem (2000) 'Indigenous Peoples and Reform of the State in Latin America', in Willem Assies et al.: 3–21.

Assies, Willem, Gemma Van der Haar, and André Hoekema (eds) (2000) *The Challenge of Diversity: Indigenous Peoples and Reform of the State in Latin America*. Amsterdam: Thela Thesis.

Ayittey, G.B.N. (1991) *Indigenous African Institutions*. Ardsley-on-Hudson, NY: Transnational Publishers.

Bailey, F.G. (1969) *Strategems and Spoils: A Social Anthropology of Politics*. Oxford: Basil Blackwell.

Baker, Bruce (1997) 'Beyond the Long Arm of the Law: The Pattern and Consequences of Disengagement in Africa', *Journal of Commonwealth and Comparative Politics* XXXV, no. 3:53–74.

Bank, L. (1997) 'Of Livestock and Deadstock: Entrepreneurship and Tradition on the South African Highveld', in *Farewell to Farms: De-Agrarianisation and Employment in Africa*, eds D.F. Bryceson and V. Jamal. African Studies Centre Research Series. Aldershot: Ashgate.

Bank, L. and R. Southall (1996) 'Traditional Leaders in South Africa's New Democracy', *Journal of Legal Pluralism and Unofficial Law*, 37–8, Special double issue on The New Relevance of Traditional Authorities to Africa's Future: 407–30.

Barcham, Manuhuia (2000) '(De)Constructing the Politics of Indigeneity', in *Political Theory and the Rights of Indigenous Peoples* ed. Duncan Ivison, Paul Patton and Will Sanders, Cambridge: Cambridge University Press.

Barth, F. (1969) *Ethnic Groups and Boundaries: The Social Organization of Cultural Difference (Results of a Symposium Held at the University of Bergen, 23rd to 27th February 1967*. Bergen: Universiteitsforlaget.

Bayart, Jean-François (1989) *L'état en Afrique: la politique du ventre*. Paris: Fayard.

Beinart, William (1994) *Twentieth-Century South Africa*, Oxford and New York: Oxford University Press.

Beinart, William, and Saul Dubow (eds) (1995) *Segregation and Apartheid in Twentieth-Century South Africa: Rewriting Histories*. London: Routledge.

Bekker, J.C. (1989) *Seymour's Customary Law in Southern Africa*. 5th edn. Cape Town: Juta & Co.

Von Benda-Beckmann, Franz (1996) 'Citizens, Strangers and Indigenous Peoples: Conceptual Politics and Legal Pluralism', in *Law & Anthropology*, ed. Rene Kuppe and Richard Potz. The Hague: Martinus Nijhoff Publishers.

——— (1989) 'Scape-Goat and Magic Charm: Law in Development Theory and Practice', *Journal of Legal Pluralism and Unofficial Law* 28: 129–48.

——— (1984) 'Law out of Context: A Comment on the Creation of Traditional Law Discussion.' *Journal of African Law* 28, no. 1/2: 28–33.

Von Benda-Beckmann, Keebeth (1999) *Transnationale Dimensies Van Rechtspluralisme, Inaugurele Rede, Erasmus Universiteit Rotterdam*. Deventer: Gouda-Quint.

——— (1984) *The Broken Stairways to Consensus: Village Justice and State Courts in Minangkabau*. Dordrecht: ICG Printing.

Bennett, T.W. (1997) 'Proprietary Capacity of Children: A Study of Customary Law and the Bill of Rights in South Africa', *African Journal of International and Comparative Law* 83.

——— (1995) *Human Rights and African Customary Law*. Cape Town: Juta & Co.

——— (1991) *A Sourcebook of African Customary Law for Southern Africa*. Cape Town: Juta & Co.

Bern, John, and Susan Dodds (2000) 'On the Plurality of Interests: Aboriginal Self-Government and Land Rights', in *Political Theory and the Rights of Indigenous Peoples*, ed. Duncan Ivison, Paul Patton and Will Sanders. Cambridge: Cambridge University Press.

Berry, Sara (2000) *Chiefs Know Their Boundaries: Essays on Property, Power, and the Past in Asante, 1896–1996*. Oxford: James Currey: Portsmouth, NH: Heinemann.

——— (1989) 'Social Institutions and Access to Resources', *Africa* 59, no. 1: 41–55.

Bierbrauer, Gunter (1994) 'Toward an Understanding of Legal Culture: Variations in Individualism and Collectivism between Kurds, Lebanese, and Germans', *Law & Society Review* 28, no. 2: 243–64.

Bierschenk, Thomas, and Pierre-Yves Le Meur, eds (1999) *Negotiated Development : Brokers, Knowledge, Technologies, Bi-Annual Apad Bulletin*. Hamburg: Lit Verlag.

Bierschenk, Thomas and J.P. Olivier de Sardan (1998) *Les Pouvoirs au Village: Le Bénin Entre Démocratisation et Décentralisation*. Paris: Karthala.

——— (1997) 'Local Powers and a Distant State in Rural Central African Republic', *The Journal of Modern African Studies* 35, no. 3: 441–68.

Van Binsbergen, Wim (1999) *'Culturen Bestaan Niet': Het Onderzoek Van Interculturaliteit Als Een Openbreken Van Vanzelfsprekendheden*. Rotterdamse Filosofische Studies. Vol. XXIV. Rotterdam: Erasmus Universiteit.

Boonzaaier, Emile, and John Sharp (1988) *South African Keywords: The Uses & Abuses of Political Concepts*. Cape Town: David Philip.

Bothma, C.V (1976) 'The Political Structure of the Pedi of Sekhukhuneland', *African Studies* 35, no. 3–4: 177–206.

Bourdieu, Pierre (1993) '*Structures*, Habitus, *Practices*', in *Social Theory: The Multicultural & Classic Readings* ed. C. Lemert. Boulder, CO: Westview Press.

——— (1990) *The Logic of Practice*. Stanford, CA: Stanford University Press.

——— (1977) *Outline of a Theory of Practice*. Vol. 16, *Cambridge Studies in Social Anthropology*. Cambridge: Cambridge University Press.

Bronstein, Victoria (1998) 'Reconceptualizing the Customary Law Debate in South Africa', *South African Journal of Human Rights* 14, no. 3: 333–410.

Brown, M., J. Erasmus et al. (eds) (1998) *Land Restitution in South Africa: A long way home*. Cape Town: Idasa.

Bundy, Colin (1979) *The Rise and Fall of a South African Peasantry*. London: Heinemann.

Castells, Manuel (ed.) (1996) *The Rise of the Network Society*. 3 vols. Vol. 1, *The Information Age*. Cambridge: Blackwell Publishers.

Chabal, Patrick and Jean-Pascal Daloz (1999) *Africa Works: Disorder as Political Instrument*. Oxford: James Currey and Bloomington, IN: Indiana University Press.

Chambers, David. (2000) 'Civilizing the Natives: Marriage in Post-Apartheid South Africa.' *Daedalus: Special Issue 'The End of Tolerance: Engaging Cultural Differences'* 129, no. 4: 101–24.

Chanock, M. (2000) ' "Culture" and Human Rights: Orientalising, Occidentalising and Authenticity', in *Beyond Rights Talk and Culture Talk: Comparative Essays on the Politics of Rights and Culture*, ed. M. Mamdani. Claremont: David Philip Publishers.

——— (1991) 'Law, State and Culture: Thinking About 'Customary Law' after Apartheid,' *Acta Juridica* 10: 52–70.

——— (1985) *Law, Custom and Social Order: The Colonial Experience in Malawi and Zambia*. Cambridge: Cambridge University Press.

Chatterjee, P. (1993) *The Nation and Its Fragments:Colonial and Postcolonial Histories*. Princeton, NJ: Princeton University Press.

Chazan, Naomi (1988) *Politics and Society in Contemporary Africa*. Basingstoke: Macmillan Educational Books.

Cheater, Angela (ed.) (1999) *The Anthropology of Power: Empowerment and Disempowerment in Changing Structures*. London: Routledge.

Cliffe, Lionel (2000) 'Land Reform in South Africa,' *Review of African Political Economy* 84: 273–86.

Clifford, James (1988) *The Predicament of Culture*. Cambridge, MA: Harvard University Press.

Cloete, Fanie (1994)'Local Government Restructuring.' *Politikon* 21, no. 1: 42–65.

Coertze, R.D. (1990) *Bafokeng Family Law and Law of Succession*. Pretoria: Sabra.

Cohen, Anthony P. (2000) 'Introduction: Discriminating Relations: Identity, Boundary and Authenticity', in *Signifying Identities: Anthropological Perspectives on Boundaries and Contested Values*, ed. Anthony P. Cohen. London: Routledge.

Collier, Jane F. (1976) 'Political Leadership and Legal Change in Zinacatan,' *Law and Society* 11: 131–63.

Comaroff, Jean (1980) 'Healing and the Cultural Order: The Case of the Barolong Boo Ratshidi of Southern Africa,' *American Ethnologist* 7: 637–57.

Comaroff, Jean and John Comaroff (1997) *Of Revelation and Revolution: The Dialectics of Modernity on a South African Frontier*. Vol. II. Chicago: University of Chicago Press.

Comaroff, John (1997) 'The Discourse of Rights in Colonial South Africa: Subjectivity, Sovereignity, Modernity', in Sarat and Kearns: 193–238.

——— (1996) 'Ethnicity, Nationalism and the Politics of Difference in an Age of Revolution', in Wilmsen and McAllister, pp. 162–83.

——— (1978) 'Rules and Rulers: Political Processes in a Tswana Chiefdom,' *Man* 13, no. 1: 1–20.

Comaroff, John, and Simon Roberts (1981) *Rules and Processes: The Cultural Logic of Dispute in an African Context*. Chicago: Chicago University Press.

——— (1975) 'Talking Politics: Oratory and Authority in a Tswana Chiefdom', in *Political Langauge and Oratory in Traditional Society*, ed. Maurice Bloch. London: Academic Press.

——— (1974) 'Chiefship in a South African Homeland: A Case Study of the Tshidi Chiefdom of Boputhatswana', *Journal of Southern African Studies* 1: 36–51.

Connolly, William (ed.) (1984) *Legitimacy and the State*. Oxford: Basil Blackwell.

Corder, Hugh (1996) 'South Africa's Transitional Constitution: Its Design and Implementation', *Public Law* Summer: 291–308.

——— (1994) 'Towards a South African Constitution,' *The Modern Law Review* 57, no. 4: 491–533.

Costa, Anthony (1999a) 'Segregation, Customary Law and the Governance of Africans in South Africa.' PhD thesis, University of Cambridge.

——— (1999b) 'Chieftaincy and Civilisation: African Structures of Government and Colonial Administration in South Africa', *African Studies* 59, no. 1: 13–44.

——— (1998) 'The Myth of Customary Law.' *South African Journal on Human Rights* 14, no. 3: 525–38.

——— (1997) 'Custom and Common Sense: The Zulu Royal Succession Dispute of the 1940s', *African Studies* 56, no. 1: 19–42.

Cotterell, Roger (1992) *The Sociology of Law: An Introduction*. London: Butterworth.

——— (1983) 'Legality and Political Legitimacy in the Sociology of Max Weber', in *Legality, Ideology and the State*, ed. David Sugarman. London: Academic Press.

Cousins, Ben (2001) 'A Return to the Apartheid Era?' *Mail and Guardian* online.

——— (2000) *Land Reform at the Crossroads: Who Will Benefit?* Programme for Land and Agrarian Studies: University of the Western Cape, February.

Crehan, Kate (1997) *The Fractured Community: Landscapes of Power and Gender in Rural Zambia*. Berkeley & Los Angeles: University of California Press.

CSS (1995) 'October Household Survey 1995: Statistical Release P0317.' Pretoria: Central Statistical Service.

Currie, Iain (1998) 'Indigenous Law', in *Constitutional Law*, ed. Matthew et.al. Chaskalson, 36-

1–36–25. Kenwyn: Juta & Co.

——— (1994) 'The Future of Customary Law: Lessons from the Lobolo Debate', in *Gender and the New South African Legal Order*, ed. T.W. Bennett, G. Bradfield, A. Cockrell, R. Jooste, R. Keightly, C.M. Murray and D. Van Zyl Smit. Cape Town: Juta & Co.

Darian-Smith, Eve and P. Fitzpatrick (eds) (1999) *The Laws of the Postcolonial*. Vol. 5. Ann Arbor, MI: University of Michigan Press.

Davidson, Basil (1992) *The Black Man's Burden*. London: James Currey.

De Gaay Fortman, Bas and Paschal Mihyo (1993) 'A False Start – Law and Development in the Context of a Colonial Legacy', *Verfassung und Recht in Ubersee* 26, no. 2: 136–61.

De Haas, Mary and Paulus Zulu (1994) 'Ethnicity and Federalism: The Case of Kwazulu/Natal', *Journal of Southern African Studies* 20, no. 3: 433–46.

De Sousa Santos, B. (1992) 'State, Law and Community in the World System: An Introduction.' *Social & Legal Studies* 1: 131–42.

De Villiers, André and Will Critchley, eds (1997) *Rural Land Reform Issues in Southern Africa: Lessons for South Africa's Northern Province*. Pietersburg: Land Management and Rural Development Programme, University of the North.

De Villiers, Bertus (1998) 'Makuleke: Breakthrough in the Makuleke Land Claim Negotiations', *Custos* 8, May: 8–10.

——— (ed.) (1994) *Birth of a Constitution*. Kenwyn: Juta & Co.

De Villiers, Francois (1998a) *Traditional Leadership in Southern Africa*. Johannesburg: Konrad Adenauer Stiftung.

——— (ed.) (1998b) *Selected South African Legislation on Customary Law and Traditional Authorities*. Johannesburg: Konrad Adenauer Stiftung.

De Villiers, Francois, and J. Beukman (1995) *Wetbundel Vir Inheemse Reg*. Stellenbosch: UUB.

De Waal, Johan, Iain Currie and Gerhard Erasmus (1998) *Bill of Rights Handbook 1998*. Kenwyn: Juta & Co.

Delius, Peter (1996) *A Lion Amongst the Cattle: Reconstruction and Resistance in the Northern Transvaal*. Oxford: James Currey; Portsmouth, NH: Heinemann.

——— (1990) 'Migrants, Comrades and Rural Revolt: Sekhukhuneland 1950–1987', *Transformation* 13: 2–26.

——— (1983) *The Land Belongs to Us: The Pedi Polity, the Boers and the British in Nineteenth-Century Transvaal*. Johannesburg: Ravan Press.

D'Engelbronner-Kolff, Marina (2001) 'A Web of Legal Cultures: Dispute Resolution Processes Amongst the Sambyu of Northern Namibia.' PhD thesis, Vrije Universiteit.

Department of Constitutional Development (2000) 'A Discussion Document Towards a White Paper on Local Government in South Africa.' Pretoria: Department of Constitutional Development.

Department of Provincial and Local Government (2003) 'The White Paper on Traditional Leadership and Governance.' Pretoria: Department of Provincial and Local Government.

Depew, Robert C. (1994) 'First Nations Organizations: An Analytic Framework – a Report Prepared for Policy and Strategic Direction Department of Indian Affairs and Northern Development.' Ottawa, Ontario: Department of Indian Affairs and Northern Development.

Donders, Yvonne, Kristin Henrard, Anna Meijknecht and Sasja Tempelman (eds) (1999) *Law and Cultural Diversity*. Vol. SIM-special 25. Utrecht: SIM.

Doornbos, M. (2000) *Institutionalizing Development Policies and Resource Strategies in Eastern Africa and India: Developing Winners and Losers*. Basingstoke: Macmillan.

Douglas, Mary (1986) *How Institutions Think*. Syracuse, NY: Syracuse University Press.

Drummond, Susan G. (2000) 'The Process Geography of Law (as Approached through Andalucian Gitano Family Law)', *Journal of Legal Pluralism and Unofficial Law* 45: 49–70.

Du Plessis, Lourens (1994) 'A Background to Drafting the Chapter on Fundamental Rights', in Bertus De Villiers.

Du Plessis, Lourens, and Hugh Corder (1994) '1: The Background: Constitutional Transition in the Early 1990s', in *Understanding South Africa's Transitional Bill of Rights*, ed. Lourens Du Plessis and Hugh Corder, Kenwyn: Juta & Co.

Du Plessis, W. and D. Balatseng (1997) 'Succession of Chieftaincy: Hereditary, by Appointment or by Common Consent?' *Tydskrif vir hedendaagse Romeins-Hollandse reg* 59, no. 2: 349–55.

Du Toit, Andries (1998) 'The Fruits of Modernity: Law, Power and Paternalism in the Rural Western Cape', in *South Africa in Transition: New Theoretical Perspectives*, ed. David R. Howarth and Aletta J. Norval. Basingstoke: Macmillan.

Du Toit, Pierre (1995) *State Building and Democracy in Southern Africa: Botswana, Zimbabwe and South Africa*. Washington, DC: United States Institute of Peace.

Düsing, Sandra. (1996) 'Traditionelle Führungsstrukturen Im Demokratischen Konsolidierungsprozeß Südafrikas', in *Afrika: Stagnation Oder Neubeginn?: Studien Zum Politischen Wandel*, ed. Paul Kevenhörster and Dirk Van den Boom. Münster: Lit Verlag.

Ebrahim, Hassen (1998) *The Soul of a Nation: Constitution-Making in South Africa*. Cape Town: Oxford University Press.

Ehrlich, Eugen (1936) *Fundamental Principles of the Sociology of Law*. Trans. Walter L. Moll. Cambridge, MA: Harvard University Press.

Ellis, Stephen (2001) 'Gedachten over Afrika: Kanttekeningen Bij Het Begrip Ontwikkeling', *internationale Spectator* LV, no. 4: 180–84.

——— (ed.) (1996) *Africa Now: People, Policies, Institutions*. The Hague: DGIS in association with James Currey; Heinemann; David Philip.

Ellis, Stephen, and Tṣepo Sechaba (eds) (1992) *Comrades against Apartheid : The ANC & the South African Communist Party in Exile*. London & Bloomington, IN: James Currey & Indiana University Press.

Englebert, P. (2001) 'Back to the Future? Resurgent Indigenous Structures and the Reconfiguration of Power in Africa.' Paper presented at the Conference on Indigenous Political Structures and Governance in Africa, University of Ibadan, Nigeria 19–21 July.

——— (2000) *State Legitimacy and Development in Africa*. Boulder, CO: Lynne Rienner Publishers.

——— (1997) 'Feature Review: The Contemporary African State: Neither African nor State.' *Third World Quarterly* 18, no. 4: 767–75.

Eriksen, Thomas Hylland (2001) *Small Places, Large Issues: An Introduction to Social and Cultural Anthropology*. London: Pluto Press.

Espeland, Wendy (1994) 'Legally Mediated Identity: The National Environmental Policy Act and the Bureaucratic Construction of Interests', *Law & Society Review* 28, no. 5: 1149–79.

Evans, Ivan (1997) *Bureaucracy and Race: Native Administration in South Africa*. Berkeley, CA: University of California Press.

Falk Moore, Sally (1993) 'Changing Perspectives on a Changing Africa: The Work of Anthropology', in *Africa and the Disciplines*, ed. R.H. Bates, V.Y. Mudimbe and J. O'Barr. Chicago and London: University of Chicago Press.

——— (1986) *Social Facts and Fabrications: 'Customary' Law on Kilimanjaro 1880–1980*, Lewis Henry Morgan Lecture Series. Cambridge: Cambridge University Press.

——— (1978) 'Politics, Procedures and Norms in Changing Chagga Law', in *Law as Process: An Anthropological Approach*, ed. Falk Moore, London, Henley and Boston, MA: Routledge & Kegan Paul.

——— (1973) 'Law and Social Change: The Semi-Autonomous Social Field as an Appropriate Subject of Study', *Law and Society Review* 7: 719–46.

Faure, Murray and Jan-Erik Lane (eds) (1996) *South Africa: Designing New Political Institutions*. London: Sage Publications.

Feierman, Steven (1990) *Peasant Intellectuals: Anthropology and History in Tanzania*. Madison, WI: University of Wisconsin Press.

Ferguson, James (1994) *The Anti-Politics Machine: 'Development,' Depoliticization and Bureaucratic Power in Lesotho*. Minneapolis, MN: University of Minnesota Press.

Ferguson, James and Akhil Gupta (eds) (1997) *Culture, Power, Place: Explorations in Critical Anthropology*. Durham, NC and London: Duke University Press.

Fitzpatrick, P. (1983) 'Law, Plurality and Underdevelopment' in *Legality, Ideology and the State*, ed., D. Sugerman, London and New York: Academic Press.

Fleming, Sure (1996) 'Trading in Ambiguity: Law, Rights and Realities in the Distribution of Land in Northern Mozambique', in *Inside and Outside the Law: Anthropological Studies of Authority and Ambiguity*, ed. Olivia Harris. London: Routledge.

Friedman, Thomas (1999) *The Lexus and the Olive Tree: Understanding Globalization*. New York: Farrer Strauss and Giroux.

Foucault, Michel (1994) 'The Subject and Power', in *Power: Critical Concepts*, ed. John Scott, London: Routledge.

——— (1993) 'Power as Knowledge', in *Social Theory: The Multicultural & Classic Readings*, ed. Charles Lemert, Boulder, CO: Westview Press.

Fuller, Chris (1994) 'Legal Anthropology: Legal Pluralism and Legal Thought', *Anthropology Today* 10, no. 3: 9–12.

Gabor, Francis (1998) 'Quo Vadis Domine: Reflections on Individual and Ethnic Self-Determination under an Emerging International Legal Regime.' *The International Lawyer* 33, no. 3: 809–24.

Galenkamp, Marlies (1993) *Individualism Versus Collectivism: The Concept of Collective Rights*. Vol. 2,

Rotterdamse Filosofische Studies. ed. H.A.F. Oosterling and A.W. Prins. Rotterdam: Erasmus Universiteit.

Garth, B.G. and A. Sarat (1998) 'Studying How Law Matters: An Introduction', in *How Does Law Matter?*, ed. B. Garth and A. Sarat, 259. Evanston, IL: Northwestern University Press.

Geertz, Clifford (1983) *Local Knowledge: Further Essays in Interpretative Anthropology*. New York: Basic Books Inc.

——— (1973) *The Interpretation of Cultures: Selected Essays*. New York: Basic Books Inc.

Gellner, Ernest (1995) 'Culture, Constraint and Community', in *Anthropology and Politics: Revolutions in the Sacred Grove*, ed. Ernest Gellner, Oxford and Cambridge: Blackwell Publishers.

——— (1983) *Nations and Nationalism, New Perspectives on the Past*. Oxford: Blackwell.

Gérard, Philippe, François Ost, and Michel van de Kerchove (1996) *Droit Négocié, Droit Imposé?* Bruxelles: Publications des Facultés universitaires Saint-Louis.

Geschiere, Peter (1996) 'Chiefs and the Problem of Witchcraft: Varying Patterns in South and West Cameroon', *Journal of Legal Pluralism and Unofficial Law* 37–38, Special double issue on The New Relevance of Traditional Authorities to Africa's Future: 307–27.

——— (1993) 'Chiefs and Colonial Rule in Cameroon: Inventing Chieftaincy, French and British Style.' *Africa* 63, no. 2: 151–75.

——— (1989) *Moderne Mythen: Cultuur En Ontwikkeling in Afrika*. Leiden: Inaugural lecture.

Giddens, Anthony (1993) 'Post-Modernity or Radicalized Modernity?', in *Social Theory: The Multicultural & Classic Readings*, ed. Charles Lemert, Boulder, CO: Westview Press.

Glaser, B. and A. Strauss (1967) *The Discovery of Grounded Theory*. Chicago: Aldine.

Glendon, Mary Ann (1991) *Rights Talk: The Impoverishment of Political Discourse*. New York: The Free Press.

Gluckman, Max (1965) *Politics, Law and Ritual in Tribal Society*. Oxford: Basil Blackwell.

——— (1955) *The Judicial Process among the Barotse of Northern Rhodesia*. Manchester: Manchester University Press.

Goheen, Mitzi (1992) 'Chiefs, Sub-Chiefs and Local Control: Negotiations over Land, Struggles over Meaning', *Africa* 62, no. 3: 389–412.

Golan, D. (1994) *Inventing Shaka: Using History in the Construction of Zulu Nationalism*. Boulder, CO and London: Lynne Rienner Publishers.

Good, Kenneth (1997) 'Accountable to Themselves: Predominance in Southern Africa', *Journal of Modern African Studies* 35, no. 4: 547–73.

Gordon, Robert (1998) 'Apartheids Anthropologists: The Genealogy of Afrikaner Anthropology', *American Ethnologist* 15, no. 3: 535–53.

Gould, Jeremy (1997) *Localizing Modernity: Action, Interests and Association in Rural Zambia*. Vol. 40, *Transactions of the Finnish Anthropological Society*. Helsinki: Finnish Anthropological Society.

Gramsci, Antonio (1971) *Selections from the Prison Notebooks*. London: Lawrence and Wishart.

Griffiths, Anne M.O. (1997) *In the Shadow of Marriage: Gender and Justice in an African Community*. Chicago and London: University of Chicago Press.

Griffiths, J. (1996) *De Sociale Werking Van Het Recht: Een Kennismaking Met De Rechtssociologie En De Rechtsantropologie*. Nijmegen: Ars Aequi Libri.

——— (1986) 'What Is Legal Pluralism?' *Journal of Legal Pluralism and Unofficial Law* 24: 1–55.

Gulliver, P.H. (1979) *Disputes and Negotiations: A Cross-Cultural Perspective*. Edited by Donald Black, *Studies on Law and Social Control*. New York: Academic Press.

——— (1969) 'Case Studies of Law in Non-Western Societies', in Nader.

——— (1963) *Social Control in an African Society: A Study of the Arusha: Agricultural Masai of Northern Tanganyika, International Library of Sociology and Social Reconstruction*. ed. W.J.H. Sprott, London: Routledge & Kegan Paul.

Gurr, T.R. (1994) *Ethnic Conflict in World Politics*, Boulder, CO: Westview Press.

Habermas, Juergen (1984). 'What Does a Legitimation Crisis Mean Today? Legitimation Problems in Late Capitalism', in Connolly.

Hadland, Adrian and Jovial Rantao (1999) *The Life and Times of Thabo Mbeki*. Rivonia: Zebra Press.

Hammer, Michael (1998) ''Stool Rights' and Modern Land Law in Ghana: A Geographical Perspective on the Transformation of Tradition.' *Afrika Spectrum* 33, no. 1: 311–38.

Hammond-Tooke, W.D. (1997) *Imperfect Interpreters: South Africa's Anthropologists 1920–1990*. Johannesburg: Witwatersrand University Press.

——— (1975) *Command or Consensus: The Development of Transkeian Local Government*. Cape Town: David Philip.

——— (1974) *The Bantu-Speaking People of Southern Africa*. 2nd edn, London and Boston, MA: Routledge & Kegan Paul.

Hamnett, Ian (1975) *Chieftainship and Legitimacy: An Anthropological Study of Executive Law in Lesotho*, London and Boston, MA: Routledge & Kegan Paul.

Harding, Leonhard (1998) 'Einleitung: Tradition, Traditionelle Institutionen und Traditionelle Autoritäten in Afrika', *Afrika Spectrum* 33, no. 1: 5–17.

Harneit-Sievers, Axel (1998) 'Igbo "Traditional Rulers": Chieftaincy and the State in Southeastern Nigeria.' *Afrika Spektrum* 33, no. 1: 57–79.

Harries, C.L. (1929) *The Laws and Customs of the Bapedi and Cognate Tribes*. Johannesburg: Hortors Limited,

Hatt, D.G. (1996) 'Establishing Tradition: The Development of Chiefly Authority in the Western High Atlas Mountains of Morocco,' *Journal of Legal Pluralism and Unofficial Law* Vol. 37–38, Special double issue on The New Relevance of Traditional Authorities to Africa's Future: 123–53.

Hellum, Anne (1999) *Women's Human Rights and Legal Pluralism in Africa: Mixed Norms and Identities in Infertility Management in Zimbabwe, North-South Legal Perspectives*. Tano-Aschehoug: Mond Books.

Henrard, Kristin (2000) *Devising an Adequate System of Minority Protection: Human Rights, Minority Rights and the Right to Self-Determination*. The Hague: Kluwer.

Henrard, Kristin and Stefaan Smis (2000) 'Recent Experiences in South Africa and Ethiopia to Accommodate Cultural Diversity: A Regained Interest in the Right of Self-Determination', *Journal of African Law* 44:17–50.

Herbst, Jeffrey (2000) *States and Power in Africa: Comparative Lessons in Authority and Control*. Princeton, NJ: Princeton University Press.

Hinz, M.O. (1999) 'The Post-Independence Development of Traditional Government and Customary Law in Namibia'. Paper presented at the SASCA Conference 'Rural Governance in the new Millennium', Port Elizabeth, 23 June.

Hobsbawm, Eric and Terence Ranger (eds) (1983) *The Invention of Tradition*, Cambridge: Cambridge University Press.

Hofmeister, Wilhelm, and Ingo Scholz (eds) (1997) *Traditional and Contemporary Forms of Local Participation and Self-Government in Africa: International Conference – Nairobi, Kenya, 9–12 October 1996*. Johannesburg: Konrad Adenauer Stiftung.

Holleman, J.F. (1986) 'Trouble-Cases and Trouble-Less Cases in the Study of Customary Law and Legal Reform', in *Anthropology of Law in the Netherlands: Essays on Legal Pluralism*, ed. K. Von Benda-Beckmann and F. Strijbosch. Dordrecht: Foris Publications.

Holomisa, Pathekile (1996) 'Traditional Leaders', in *Aspects of the Debate on the Draft of the New South African Constitution Dated 22 April 1996*, ed. Konrad Adenauer Stiftung. Johannesburg: Konrad Adenauer Stiftung.

Hughes, David McDermott (1999) 'Frontier Dynamics: Struggles for Land and Clients on the Zimbabwe-Mozambique Border.' Ph.D dissertation, University of California.

Hunt, D.R. (1931) 'An Account of the Bapedi,' *Bantu Studies* V: 275–326.

Hunter, James Davison (1991) *Culture Wars: The Struggle to Define America*. New York: Basic Books.

Iliffe, John (1983) *The Emergence of African Capitalism*. London: Macmillan Press.

IMPD (1998) 'Good Governance at Local Level'. Paper presented at Good Governance at Local Level: Traditional Leaders and Rural Councillors Conference, East London.

Ismael, Nazeem (1999) 'Integrating Indigenous and Contemporary Local Governance: Issues Surrounding Traditional Leadership and Considerations for Post-Apartheid South Africa.' PhD thesis, University of the Western Cape.

Ivison, Duncan, Paul Patton and Will Sanders (2000) 'Introduction', in *Political Theory and the Rights of Indigenous Peoples*, ed. Duncan Ivison, Paul Patton and Will Sanders. Cambridge: Cambridge University Press.

James, D. (2000) '"After Years in the Wilderness": The Discourse of Land Claims in the New South Africa', *The Journal of Peasant Studies* 27, no. 3: 142–61.

——— (1999) 'Bagagesu (Those of My Home): Women Migrants, Ethnicity, and Performance in South Africa', *American Ethnologist* 26, no. 1: 69–89.

——— (1990)'A Question of Ethnicity: Ndzundza Ndebele in a Lebowa Village.' *Journal of Southern African Studies* 16, no. 1: 33–54.

——— (1985) 'Family and Household in a Lebowa Village.' *African Studies* 44, no. 2: 159–87.

Johnston, Darlene M. (1995) 'Native Rights as Collective Rights: A Question of Group Self-Preservation', in Kymlicka.

Jordan, Pallo (1997) 'The Evolution of So-called African Customary Law'. Paper presented at ANC 50th National Conference, Mafeking.

Just, P. (1992) 'History, Power, Ideology and Culture: Current Directions in the Anthropology of

Law.' *Law & Society Review* 26, no. 2: 373–411.
Kerr, A.J. (1997) 'The Bill of Rights in the New Constitution and Customary Law', *The South African Law Journal* 14: 346–50.
Van Kessel, Ineke (2000) *'Beyond Our Wildest Dreams': The United Democratic Front and the Transformation of South Africa*. Charlottesville, VA and London: University Press of Virginia.
Van Kessel, Ineke and Barbara Oomen (1999) 'One Chief; One Vote: The Revival of Traditional Authorities in Post-Apartheid South Africa', in *African Chieftaincy in a New Socio-Political Landscape*, ed. E.A.B. Van Rouveroy van Nieuwaal and Rijk Van Dijk. Leiden: African Studies Centre Leiden.
Van Kessel, I. and B. Oomen (1997) 'One Chief, One Vote: The Revival of Traditional Authorities in Post-Apartheid South Africa.' *African Affairs* 96: 561–85.
Klug, H. (1995) 'Defining the Property Rights of Others: Political Power, Indigenous Tenure and the Construction of Customary Law', *Journal of Legal Pluralism and Unofficial Law* 35: 119–48.
Konrad Adenauer Stiftung (1997) *Traditional Leadership in Southern Africa*. Johannesburg: Konrad Adenauer Stiftung.
——— (1996) 'Aspects of the Debate on the Draft of the New South African Constitution Dated 22 April 1996.' Paper presented at the the New South African Constitution conference, Umtata, 24–26 April.
——— (1994) 'The Role of Traditional Leaders in Local Government in South Africa.' Paper presented at the The Role of Traditional Leaders in Local Government, 27–28 October.
Kossler, Reinhart (1998) 'Traditional Communities and the State in Southern Africa', *Afrika Spectrum* 33, no. 1: 19–37.
Krige, E. Jensen, and J.D. Krige (1943) *The Realm of the Rain-Queen: A Study of the Pattern of Lovedu Society*. London: Oxford University Press.
Krige, Eileen Jensen (1974) 'Woman-Marriage, with Special Reference to the Lovedu – Its Significance for the Definition of Marriage.' *Africa* XLIV, no. 1: 11–37.
Kuper, Adam (1970) *Kalahari Village Politics, Cambridge Studies in Social Anthropology*. Cambridge: Cambridge University Press.
Kymlicka, Will (ed.) (1995) *The Rights of Minority Cultures*. Oxford: Oxford University Press.
Lahiff, Edward (1999) 'Land Tenure in South Africa's Communal Areas: A Case Study of the Arabie-Olifants Scheme.' *African Studies* 59, no. 1: 45–70.
La Prairie, Carol (1996) 'Introduction', *Journal of Legal Pluralism and Unofficial Law*. Special issue *Popular Justice: Conflict Resolution within Communities* 36:1–8.
Leftwich, Adrian (ed.) (1996) *Democracy and Development*. Cambridge: Polity Press.
Levett, Ann, Amanda Kottler, Erica Burman, and Ian Parker (eds) (1997) *Culture, Power & Difference: Discourse Analysis in South Africa*. London: Zed Books.
Levin, Richard (1994) 'Participatory Research and Democratic Agrarian Transformation: The Case of the Eastern Transvaal Central Lowveld', *Transformation* 25: 34–57.
Levy, Jacob T. (1997) 'Classifying Cultural Rights' in *Ethnicity and Group Rights*, ed. W. Kymlicka and I. Shapiro. New York: New York University Press.
Leys, Colin (1996) *The Rise and Fall of Development Theory*. London: James Currey.
Liebenberg, Ian (1998) 'The African Renaissance: Myth, Vital Lie, or Mobilising Tool?' *African Security Review* 7, no. 3: 42–50.
Lipsky, Michael (1980) *Street-Level Bureaucracy: Dilemma's of the Individual in Public Services*. New York: Russell Sage Foundation.
Lipton, Michael, Frank Ellis, and Merle Lipton (1996) *Land, Labour and Livelihoods in Rural South Africa*. III vols. Johannesburg: Indicator Press.
Lund, Christian (ed.) (1999) *Development and Rights: Negotiating Justice in Changing Societies*. London: Frank Cass Publishers.
Maine, H. (1861) *Ancient Law*. London: Dent.
Maloka, E. (1995) 'Traditional Leaders and the Current Transition.' *African communist*, no. 141: 35–43.
Maloka, Tshidiso (1996) 'Populism and the Politics of Chieftaincy and Nation-Building in the New South Africa', *Journal of Contemporary African Studies* 14, no. 2: 173–96.
Mamdani, Mahmood (2000) 'Introduction', in *Beyond Rights Talk and Culture Talk: Comparative Essays on the Politics of Rights and Culture*, ed. M. Mamdani. Claremont: David Philip Publishers.
——— (1999) 'Commentary. Mahmood. Mamdani, responds to Jean Copan's Review in *Transformation* 36', *Transformation* 39, no. 2: 173–96.
——— (1996) *Citizen and Subject: Contemporary Africa and the Legacy of Late Colonialism*, Princeton Studies in Culture/Power/History. Princeton, NJ: Princeton University Press.
Mandela, Nelson (1995) *Long Walk to Freedom: The Autobiography of Nelson Mandela*, Little Brown &

Co.
Mann, Kristin, and Richard Roberts (eds) (1991) *Law in Colonial Africa* in *Social History of Africa*. ed. Allen Isaacman and Luise White, Portsmouth, NH: Heinemann Educational Books; London: James Currey.
Mare, Gerhard (1993) *Ethnicity and Politics in South Africa*. London: Zed Books.
Marks, Shula and Stanley Trapido (eds) (1987) *The Politics of Race, Class and Nationalism in Twentieth Century South Africa*. London: Longman.
Marquardt, S. (1995) 'International Law and Indigenous Peoples', *International Journal on Group Rights* 3: 48–76.
Marx, Karl (1859) *A Contribution to the Critique of Political Economy*.
Mawhood, Philip (1982) 'The Place of Traditional Political Authority in African Pluralism', *Civilisations* XXXII – XXXIII: 209–37.
Maxwell, David (1999) *Christians and Chiefs in Zimbabwe: A Social History of the Hwesa People C. 1870s–1990s*. Edinburgh: Edinburgh University Press.
Mbaku, John Mukum (1999) 'The Relevance of the State in African Development', *Journal of Asian and African Studies* XXXIV, no. 3:298–320.
——— (1997) 'Africa in the Post-Cold War Era: Three Strategies for Survival', *Journal of Asian and African Studies* XXXII, no. 3–4: 223–44.
Mbeki, Govan (1964) *South Africa; the Peasant's Revolt*. Harmondsworth: Penguin Books.
Mbeki, Thabo (1998) *Africa: The Time Has Come. Selected Speeches of Thabo Mbeki*. Cape Town: Tafelberg Publishers.
Mbembe, Achille (2001) *On the Postcolony*. Berkeley: University of California Press.
McAllister, Pat A. (1997) 'Cultural Diversity and Public Policy in Australia and South Africa – the Implications of "Multiculturalism"' *African Sociological Review* 1, no. 2: 60–78.
McCann, Michael (1998) 'How Does Law Matter for Social Movements?', in *How Does Law Matter?*, ed. B. Garth and A. Sarat, Evanston, IL: Northwestern University Press.
McIntosh, Alastair, and Anne Vaughan (1994) 'Towards a Rural Local Government System for the Northern Transvaal.' Durban: Institute of Social and Economic Research, University of Durban Westville.
Meer, Shamin (ed.) (1997) *Women, Land and Authority: Perspectives from South Africa*. Cape Town: David Philip.
Merry, Sally Engle (2001) 'Crossing Boundaries: Ethnography in the Twenty-First Century', *Political and Legal Anthropology Review* 23, no. 2:127–33.
——— (1992) 'Anthropology, Law, and Transnational Processes', *Annual Review of Anthopology* 21: 357–79.
——— (1988) 'Legal Pluralism.' *Law and Society Review* 22, no. 5: 869–96.
Meyer, Birgit, and Peter Geschiere (1999) 'Introduction', in *Globalization and Identity: Dialectics of Flow and Closure*, eds Birgit Meyer and Peter Geschiere. Oxford: Blackwell.
Migdal, Joel (1988) *Strong Societies and Weak States: State-Society Relations and State Capabilities in the Third World*. Princeton, NJ: Princeton University Press.
Mönnig, H.O. (1967) *The Pedi*. 2nd edn Pretoria: J.L. van Schaik.
Mudimbe, V.Y. (1988) *The Invention of Africa: Gnosis, Philosophy, and the Order of Knowledge, African Systems of Thought*. Bloomington, IN; Indiana University Press and London: James Currey.
Munro, William, and Justin Barnes (1997). 'Dilemmas of Rural Local Government in Kwazulu-Natal', *Indicator SA* 14, no. 3: 75–80.
Murray, C. (1987) 'Displaced Urbanization: South Africa's Rural Slums', *African Affairs* (344): 311–329.
Musschenga, Albert (1998) 'Intrinsic Value as a Reason for the Preservation of Minority Cultures', *Ethical Theory and Practice* 1, no. 2: 201–25.
Myers, Jason C. (1999) 'The Spontaneous Ideology of Tradition in Post-Apartheid South Africa', *Politikon* 26, no. 1: 33–54.
Mzala (1988) *Gatsha Buthelezi: Chief with a Double Agenda*. Atlantic Heights, NJ: Zed Books.
Nader, Laura (ed.) (1969) *Law in Culture and Society*. Chicago: Aldine Publishing Company.
Nader, Laura, Klaus F. Foch, and Bruce Cox (1966) 'The Ethnography of Law: A Bibliographical Survey', *Current Anthropology* 7, no. 3: 267–94.
Naude, Piet (1995) *The Zionist Christian Church in South Africa: A Case-Study in Oral Theology*. Lewiston, NY: Edwin Mellen Press.
Ndou, R.S., and E. Letsoalo (eds) (1994) *The Future of the Institution of Hereditary Rule and Customary Law in South Africa*. Marshalltown: The Congress of Traditional Leaders of South Africa.
Nederveen Pieterse, Jan (1997) 'Deconstructing/Reconstructing Ethnicity.' *Nations and Nationalism* 3,

no. 3: 365–95.
——— (1994) 'Globalisation as Hybridisation', *International Sociology* 9, no. 2: 161–84.
Nicol, Mike (1997) *The Making of the Constitution: The Story of South Africa's Constitutional Assembly, May 1994 to December 1996*. Cape Town: Churchill Murray.
Nkadimeng, H.M. (1973) *Kgosi Sekwati Mampuru*. Pretoria: J.L. Van Schaik.
North, D.C. (1990) *Institutions, Institutional Change and Economic Performance*. Cambridge: Cambridge University Press.
Ntsebeza, Lungisile (2002) 'Structures and struggles of rural local government in South Africa: the case of the traditional authorities in the Eastern Cape'. PhD thesis, Grahamstown: Rhodes University.
——— (1999) 'Land Tenure Reform, Traditional Authorities and Rural Local Government in Post-Apartheid South Africa: Case Studies from the Eastern Cape.' Cape Town: School of Government, University of the Western Cape, Programme for Land and Agrarian Studies.
——— (1998) 'Rural Local Government in Post-Apartheid South Africa.' *African Sociological Review* 2, no. 1: 153–64.
Ntsebeza, Lungisile and Fred Hendriks (2000) 'The Chieftaincy System is Rooted in Apartheid', http://www.sn.a/wmail/issues/000218/NEWS143.html: Sangonet.
Olivier de Sardan, J.P., ed. (1995) *Anthropologie et Développement*. Paris: Karthala.
——— (1986) *Logiques, Détournements Et Dérives: Les Societés Paysannes Face Aux Projets De Développement*. Braga: European Congress Rural Sociology.
Olivier, N.J.J et al. (1989) *Privaatreg Van Die Suid-Afrikaanse Bantoetaalsprekendes*. 3rd edn Durban: Butterworth.
Olivier, N.J.J., J.C. Bekker, N.J.J Olivier (Jnr), and W.H. Olivier (1995) *Indigenous Law*. Vol. 32, *The Law of South Africa*. ed. Joubert, Durban: Butterworth.
Omer-Cooper, J.D. (1996) 'South Africa', in *Africa South of the Sahara*, London: Europa Publications Limited.
Ong, Aihwa (1996) 'Cultural Citizenship as Subject-Making', *Current Anthropology* 37, no. 5: 737–62.
Van Onselen, Charles (1996) *The Seed Is Mine: The Life of Kas Maine. A South African Sharecropper 1894–1985*. Cape Town: David Philip.
Oomen, Barbara (2000a) '"We Must Now Go Back to Our History": Retraditionalisation in a Northern Province Chieftaincy,' *African Studies* 59, no. 1: 71–95.
——— (2000b) *Tradition on the Move: Chiefs, Democracy and Change in Rural South Africa*. Edited by Madeleine Maurick and Marlene Cornelis. Vol. 6, *Niza-Cahiers*. Amsterdam: Netherlands Institute for Southern Africa.
——— (2000c) 'Traditional Woman-to-Woman Marriages and the Recognition of Customary Marriages Act.' *Tijdskrif vir Hedendaagse Rooms-Hollandse Reg* 63, no. 2: 274–82.
——— (1999a) 'Vigilante Justice in Perspective: The Case of Mapogo a Mathamaga', *Acta Criminologica: South African Journal of Criminology* 12, no. 3: 45–53.
——— (1999b) 'Group Rights in Post-Apartheid South Africa: The Case of the Traditional Leaders.' *Journal of Legal Pluralism and Unofficial Law* 44: 73–103.
——— (1999c) 'Women Challenging Society: Stories of Women's Empowerment in Southern Africa', in *Niza-Cahiers*, ed. Madeleine Maurick and Bram Posthumus. Amsterdam: Netherlands Institute for Southern Africa.
——— (1998a) 'The Recognition of Group Rights in Post-Apartheid South Africa'. Paper presented at the Commission on Folk Law and Legal Pluralism, Williamsburg, VA.
——— (1998b) 'Review Symposium: Mahmood Mamdani and the Analysis of African Society' *Journal of Legal Pluralism and Unofficial Law*, no. 40: 171–7.
——— (1996) 'Talking Tradition: The Position and Portayal of Traditional Leaders in Present-day South Africa', MA thesis, University of Amsterdam.
Otto, Jan-Michiel (2001) 'Goed Bestuur En Rechtzekerheid Als Doelen Van Ontwikking', in *Ontwikkelingsbeleid En Goed Bestuur*, ed. Wetenschappelijke Raad voor het Regeringsbeleid. Den Haag: Sdu Uitgevers.
——— (1997) '"Good Governance": Bestuur en Recht in De Nederlandse Ontwikkelingssamenwerking.' Leiden: Van Vollenhoven Institute.
——— (1987) *Aan De Voet Van De Piramide: Overheidsinstellingen En Plattelandsontwikkeling in Egypte: Een Onderzoek Aan De Basis*. Leiden: DSWO Press.
Peires, J.B. (1992) 'The Implosion of Transkei and Ciskei', *African Affairs* 91: 365–87.
Petersen, H. and H. Zahle (eds) (1995) *Legal Polycentry: Consequences of Pluralism in Law*. Aldershot: Dartmouth.
Pillay, N. and C. Prinsloo (1995) 'Tradition in Transition?: Exploring the Role of Traditional

Authorities', *Information update* 5, no. 3: 7–14.

Piot, Charles (1999) *Remotely Global: Village Modernity in West-Africa*. Chicago: University of Chicago Press.

Posel, Deborah (1995) 'State, Power and Gender: Conflict over the Registration of African Customary Marriage in South Africa C. 1910–1970', *Journal of Historical Sociology* 8, no. 3: 223–56.

——— (1991) *The Making of Apartheid, 1948–1961:Conflict and Compromise, Oxford Studies in African Affairs*. Oxford: Clarendon Press.

Preece, Jennifer Jackson (1997) 'National Minority Rights vs. State Sovereignty in Europe: Changing Norms in International Relations', *Nations and Nationalism* 3, no. 3: 345–64.

Prinsloo, M.W. (1992) 'Afsetting Van 'N Regent: Uitskakeling Van Die Opvolger Tot Stamhoofdskap by 'N Noord-Sothostam.' *Tydskrif vir Hedendaagse Romeins-Hollandse Reg*, no. 3: 515–19.

——— (1983) *Inheemse Publiekreg in Lebowa*. Pretoria: Van Schaik.

——— (1978) *Die Inheemse Strafreg Van Die Noord-Sotho, Publikasiereeks Van De Randse Afrikaanse Universiteit*. Johannesburg.

Quinlan, T. (1996) 'The State and National Identity in Lesotho.' *Journal of Legal Pluralism and Unofficial Law* 37–38, Special double issue on The New Relevance of Traditional Authorities to Africa's Future: 377–405.

Ranger, Terence (1993) 'The Invention of Tradition Revisited: The Case of Colonial Africa', in *Legitimacy and the State in Twentieth Century Africa: Essays in the Honour of A.H.M. Kirk-Greene*, ed. Terence Ranger and O. Vaughan. Basingstoke: Macmillan.

——— (1982) 'Tradition and Travesty: Chiefs and the Administration in Makoni District, Zimbabwe, 1960–1980.' *Africa* 53, no. 3: 20–41.

Rathbone, Richard (2000) *Nkrumah & the Chiefs: The Politics of Chieftaincy in Ghana 1951–60*, Western African Studies. Accra: F. Reimmer; Athens, OH: Ohio University Press; Oxford: James Currey.

Ray, D. I., and E.A.B. Van Rouveroy van Nieuwaal (1996) 'The New Relevance of Traditional Authorities in Africa. The Conference: Major Themes; Reflections on Chieftaincy in Africa; Future Directions', *Journal of Legal Pluralism and Unofficial Law*. Special double issue on The New Relevance of Traditional Authorities to Africa's Future: 1–38.

Reno, William (1998) *Warlord Politics and African States*. Boulder, CO: Lynne Rienner Publishers.

Ritchken, Edwin (1995) 'Leadership and Conflict in Bushbuckridge: Struggles to Define Moral Economies within the Context of Rapidly Transforming Political Economies (1978– 1990)' PhD thesis, University of Witwatersrand.

——— (1990a) 'Rural Politics: Introduction', *South Africa Contemporary Analysis* 5: 390–402.

——— (1990b) 'The Kwandebele Struggle against Independence.' *South Africa Contemporary Analysis* 5: 426–45.

Roberts, Simon (1984) 'Introduction: Some Notes on "African Customary Law"', *Journal of African Law* 28, no. 1.

——— (1979) *Order and Dispute: An Introduction to Legal Anthropology*. Harmondsworth, Middlesex: Penguin Books.

Robertson, Michael (ed.) (1990) *South African Human Rights and Labour Laws Yearbook*. Cape Town: Oxford University Press.

Robins, Steven (2001) 'Whose 'Culture', Whose 'Survival'? The Komani San Land Claim and the Cultural Politics of 'Community' and 'Development' in the Kalahari.' *Journal of Southern African Studies* 27, no. 4: 833–53.

——— (1997) 'Transgressing the Borderlands of Tradition and Modernity: Identity, Cultural Hybridity and Land Struggles in Namaqualand (1980–1994).' *Journal of Contemporary African Studies* 15, no. 1: 23–44.

Ross, Robert (1993) 'The Politics of Tradition in Africa.' *Groniek* 22, no. 122: 47–55.

Van Rouveroy van Nieuwaal, E.A.B. (1996) 'Status and Chiefs: Are Chiefs Mere Puppets?' *Journal of Legal Pluralism and Unofficial Law*, Vol. 37–8. Special double issue on The New Relevance of Traditional Authorities to Africa's Future: 39–78.

Van Rouveroy van Nieuwaal, E.A.B., and R. Van Dijk (eds) (1999) *African Chieftaincy in a New Socio-Political Landscape*. Hamburg: Lit Verlag.

Van Rouveroy van Nieuwaal, E.A.B. and D. I. Ray (1996) *The New Relevance of Traditional Authorities in Africa*. Vol. 37–38, *Journal of Legal Pluralism and Unofficial Law*.

Van Rouveroy van Nieuwaal, E.A.B. and W. Zips (1998) *Sovereignty, Legitimacy and Power in West African Societies: Perspectives from Legal Anthropology. African Studies* Vol. 10. Leiden: African Studies Centre.

Russel Bernard, H. (1995) *Research Methods in Anthropology: Qualitative and Quantitative Approaches*.

London: Sage Publications.
Sachs, Albie (1997) 'South Africa's Unconstitutional Constitution: The Transition from Power to Lawful Power.' *Saint Louis University Law Journal* 41, no. 4: 1249–58.
——— (1990) *Protecting Human Rights in a New South Africa*. Oxford: Oxford University Press.
Sachs, Wolfgang (1992) *The Development Dictionary: A Guide to Knowledge as Power*. Johannesburg; Witwatersrand University Press; London and Atlantic Heights, NJ: Zed Books.
Sahlins, Marshall (1999) 'What Is Anthropological Enlightment? Some Lessons of the Twentieth Century.' *Annual Review of Anthropology*: ii-xxiii.
Said, Edward W. (1978) *Orientalism*. New York: Pantheon.
Sansom, B. (1970) 'Leadership and Authority in a Pedi Chiefdom', PhD thesis, University of Manchester.
Sarat, Austin, and Thomas R. Kearns (eds) (1997) *Identities, Politics and Rights*, The Amherst Series in Law, Jurisprudence and Social Thought. Ann Arbor, MI: University of Michigan Press.
Schapera, Isaac (1969) 'Uniformity and Variation in Chief-Made Law: A Tswana Case Study', in Nader.
Scharf, Wilfried (1992) *Community Courts*. Vol. 6, *Developing Justice Series*. Cape Town: SJRP & LEAP Institute of Criminology, University of Cape Town.
Schipper, M. (1993) 'Culture, Identity and Interdiscursivity', *Research in African Literatures* 24, no. 4: 39–48.
Schirmer, Stefan (1996) 'Removals and Resistance: Rural Communities in Lydenburg, South Africa, 1940–1961', *Journal of Historical Sociology* 9, no. 2.
Schmidt-Jortzig, Edzard (1998) A. *Die Stellung der Traditional Leaders in der Neuen Sudafrikanischen Verfassung: Eine Untersuching unter Besonderer Berucksichtigung Deutscher Verfassungsdogmatik*. Vol. 1, *Recht Und Verfassung in Sudafrika* ed. Ulrich Karpen, Ingo Von Munch and Hans-Peter Schneider. Baden-Baden: Nomos Verlagsgesellschaft.
Scott, James (1998) *Seeing Like a State: How Certain Schemes to Improve the Human Condition Have Failed*, Yale Agrarian Studies. New Haven, CT & London: Yale University Press.
——— (1985) *Weapons of the Weak: Everyday Forms of Peasant Resistance*. New Haven, CT & London: Yale University Press.
Segasvary, Victor (1995) 'Group Rights: The Definition of Group Rights in the Contemporary Legal Debate Based on Socio-Cultural Analysis', *International Journal on Group Rights* 3: 89–107.
Seleoane, Mandla (1997) 'Recognition of Indigenous Peoples in International Law: Recent Developments', in *The Rights of Indigenous People: A Quest for Coexistence*, ed. Bertus De Villiers, Pretoria: HSRC.
Sewell, William H. (1999) 'The Concept(s) of Culture', in *Beyond the Cultural Turn: New Directions in the Study of Society and Culture*, ed. Victoria E. Bonnell and Lynn Hunt, 35–61. Berkeley and Los Angeles, CA: University of California Press.
Shipton, Parker, and Mitzi Goheen (1992). 'Understanding African Land-Holding: Power, Wealth and Meaning', *Africa* 62, no. 3: 307–25.
Silbey, Susan S. (1997) '"Let Them Eat Cake!": Globalization, Postmodern Colonialism, and the Possibilities of Justice.' *Law & Society Review* 31, no. 2: 207–35.
Singleton, Sara, and Michael Taylor (1992) 'Common Property, Collective Action and Community.' *Journal of Theoretical Politics* 4, no. 3: 343–51.
Sitas, Ari (1998). 'South Africa in the 1990s: The Logic of Fragmentation and Reconstruction.' *Transformation* 36: 37–50.
Skalnik, P. (1996) 'Authority Versus Power: Democracy in Africa Must Include Original African Institutions.' *Journal of Legal Pluralism and Unofficial Law* Vol. 37–8, Special double issue on The New Relevance of Traditional Authorities to Africa's Future: 109–22.
Skweyiya, Zola (1993) 'What future for chiefs?' *New Ground: The Journal of Development and Environment* 13, 2–4.
Snyder, Francis G. (1981) 'Anthropology, Dispute Processes and Law: A Critical Introduction.' *British Journal of Law & Society* 8, no. 2: 141–80.
South African Law Commission (2003) 'Project 90, Traditional Courts and the Judicial Function of Traditional Leaders', Pretoria.
——— (1999) 'Discussion Paper 82: The Harmonisation of the Common Law and Indigenous Law – Traditional Courts and the Judicial Function of Traditional Leaders.' Pretoria.
Spear, Thomas (2003) 'Neo-traditionalism and the limits of invention in British colonial Africa', *Journal of African History* 44: 3–27.
Stack, Louise (1997) *Custom and Justice: The Traditional Legal System: Problems and Possibilities*. Vol. 10–1, *Policy: Issues and Actors*. Johannesburg: Centre for Policy Studies.

Starr, June and Jane F. Collier (1989) 'Introduction', in *History and Power in the Study of Law*, ed. J. Starr and J.F. Collier. Ithaca, NY and London: Cornell University Press.

Strathern, Marilyn (1995) *Shifting Contexts: Transformations in Anthropological Knowledge*. London: Routledge.

——— (1985) 'Discovering 'Social Control'.' *Journal of Law and Society* 12, no. 2 : 111–34.

Strauss, A., and J. Corbin (1990) *Basics of Qualitative Research*. Newbury Park, CA: Sage.

Sugarman, David (ed.) (1983) *Legality, Ideology and the State*, Law, State and Society Series. London: Academic Press.

Switser, Les (1993) *Power & Resistance in an African Society: The Ciskei Xhosa and the Making of South Africa*. Madison, WI: University of Wisconsin Press.

Tamanaha, Brian (2000) 'A Non-Essentialist Version of Legal Pluralism.' *Journal of Law and Society* 27, no. 2: 296–321.

Tapscott, Chris (1995) 'Changing Discourses of Development in South Africa', in *Power of Development*, ed. Jonathan Crush. London and New York: Routledge.

Taylor, Charles (1992) *Multiculturalism and 'the Politics of Recognition'*. Princeton, NJ: Princeton University Press.

Tempelman, S. (1997) 'Cultural Identity and the Price of Recognition'. Unpublished research report.

Thompson, E.P. (1975) *Whigs and Hunters: The Origin of the Black Act*. New York: Pantheon Books.

Thornton, Robert (1996) 'The Potentials of Boundaries in South Africa: Steps Towards a Theory of the Social Edge', in *Postcolonial Identities in Africa*, ed. Richard Werbner and Terence Ranger, London: Zed Books.

Traditional Authorities Research Group (1996) 'The Administrative and Legal Position of Traditional Authorities in South Africa and Their Contribution to the Implementation of the Reconstruction and Development Programme.' Potchefstroom: University of the North, University of the North West, Potchefstroom University for CHE, University of Natal; Pietermaritzburg; University of Zululand; Leiden University.

Von Trotho, T. (1996) 'From Administrative to Civil Chieftaincy: Some Problems and Prospects of African Chieftancy', *Journal of Legal Pluralism and Unofficial Law*, Special double issue on The Relevance of Traditional Authorities to Africa's Future: 79–107.

Turner, Brian S. (ed.) (1996) *The Blackwell Companion to Social Theory*. London: Blackwell.

Vail, Leroy (ed.) (1989) *The Creation of Tribalism in Southern Africa*. Berkeley, CA: University of California Press.

Vale, Peter, and Sipho Maseko (1998) 'South Africa and the African Renaissance', *International Affairs* 74, no. 2: 271–87.

Vansina, Jan (1992) 'A Past for the Future?' *Dalhousie Review*: 8–23.

Various authors (1996) *Journal of Legal Pluralism and Unofficial Law* 37–38, Special double issue on The New Relevance of Traditional Authorities to Africa's Future.

Vaughan, Olufemi (2000) *Nigerian Chiefs: Traditional Power in Modern Politics, 1890s–1990s*. Rochester Studies in African History and the Diaspora. Rochester, NY: University of Rochester Press.

Vedeld, T. (1997) 'Village Politics: Heterogeneity, Leadership and Collective Action among the Fulani of Mali'. PhD thesis, Agricultural University, Norway.

Vermeulen, Hans, and Cora Govers (1994) *The Anthropology of Ethnicity: Beyond 'Ethnic Groups and Boundaries'*. Studies on Migration and Ethnicity. Amsterdam: Het Spinhuis.

Vilakazi, Herbert (1999) 'Africanization, the African Renaissance and the Role of the Intelligentsia.' Council for African Thought.

Vorster, L.P. (1999) 'Traditional leadership and the Recognition of Customary Marriages Act'. Paper presented at the SASCA Conference,' Rural Governance in the New Millennium', Port Elizabeth, 23 June.

Waldmeier, Patty (1997) *Anatomy of a Miracle: The End of Apartheid and the Birth of a New South Africa*. Harmondsworth: Penguin.

Van Warmelo, N.J. (1935) *A Preliminary Survey of the Bantu Tribes of South Africa*. Pretoria: Government Printer.

Weber, Max (1993) 'What Is Politics?', in *Social Theory: The Multicultural & Classic Readings*, ed. Charles Lemert, Boulder, CO: Westview Press.

——— (1978) 'Economy and Society', in *Economy and Society*, ed. Guenther Roth and Claus Wittich. Berkeley, CA: University of California Press.

Weinberg, Paul (2000) *Herovering Van Het Paradijs: Reizen Met Inheemse Volken Van Zuidelijk Afrika*. Amsterdam: Mets & Schilt.

Werbner, Richard (1996) 'Introduction: Multiple Identities, Plural Arenas', in *Postcolonial Identities in*

Africa, ed. Richard Werbner and Terence Ranger. London: Zed Books.
Van Wijk, David, Johan Dugard, Bertus De Villiers, and Dennis Davis (eds) (1995) *Rights and Constitutionalism: The New South African Legal Order*. Oxford: Clarendon Press.
Williams, J.M. (2001) 'Blurring the Boundaries of Tradition: the transformation and legitimacy of the chieftaincy in South Africa'. PhD thesis, University of Wisconsin.
Williams, J. M (2000) 'The Struggle for Social Control in South Africa: Traditional Leaders and the Establishment of the Local State in Kwazulu-Natal.' Paper presented at the 43rd Annual meeting of the African Studies Association, Nashville, TN.
Wilmer, Franke (1993) *The Indigenous Voice in World Politics: Since Time Immemorial, Violence, Cooperation, Peace*. Newbury Park, CA: Sage Publications.
Wilmsen, Edwin N. and Patrick McAllister (eds) (1996) *The Politics of Difference: Ethnic Premises in a World of Power*. Chicago and London: University of Chicago Press.
Wilson, Richard (2000) 'Reconciliation and Revenge in Post-Apartheid South Africa.' *Current Anthropology* 41, no. 1: 75–98.
——— (1997) 'Human Rights, Culture & Context: An Introduction', in *Human Rights, Culture & Context: Anthropological Perspectives*, ed. Richard A Wilson, Chicago: Pluto Press.
Worden, Nigel (1994) *The Making of Modern South Africa: Conquest, Segregation and Apartheid*, Oxford: Blackwell.
Young, Crawford (ed.) (1999) *The Accommodation of Cultural Diversity: Case Studies*. Basingstoke: Macmillan.
——— (1993a) 'The Dialectics of Cultural Pluralism: Concept and Reality', in *The Rising Tide of Cultural Pluralism: The Nation State at Bay?*, Madison, WI: University of Wisconsin Press.
——— (1993b) *The Rising Tide of Cultural Pluralism: The Nation State at Bay?* Madison, WI: University of Wisconsin Press.
Yusuf, Abdulqawi (1994) 'Reflections on the Fragility of State Institutions in Africa', *African Yearbook of International Law* 2:3–8.
Zuma, Thando (1990a) 'The Role of the Chiefs in the Struggle for Liberation', *The African Communist* 121: 65–76.
——— (1990b) 'Revolt in the Bantustans.' *African Communist*, 122.
Zungu, S. (1995) 'Inappropriate Modern Gadgets?', *Democracy in Action* 9, no. 3: 23.

Index